T0330323

Credit Risk Measurement In and Out of the Financial Crisis

Founded in 1807, John Wiley & Sons is the oldest independent publishing company in the United States. With offices in North America, Europe, Australia and Asia, Wiley is globally committed to developing and marketing print and electronic products and services for our customers' professional and personal knowledge and understanding.

The Wiley Finance series contains books written specifically for finance and investment professionals as well as sophisticated individual investors and their financial advisors. Book topics range from portfolio management to e-commerce, risk management, financial engineering, valuation and financial instrument analysis, as well as much more.

For a list of available titles, please visit our Web site at www.Wiley Finance.com.

Credit Risk Measurement In and Out of the Financial Crisis

New Approaches to Value at Risk and Other Paradigms

Third Edition

ANTHONY SAUNDERS
LINDA ALLEN

WILEY

John Wiley & Sons, Inc.

Published by John Wiley & Sons, Inc., Hoboken, New Jersey.
Published simultaneously in Canada.

For general information on our other products and services or for technical support, please contact our Customer Care Department within the United States at (800) 762-2974, outside the United States at (317) 572-3993 or fax (317) 572-4002.

Wiley also publishes its books in a variety of electronic formats. Some content that appears in print may not be available in electronic books. For more information about Wiley products, visit our web site at www.wiley.com.

Library of Congress Cataloging-in-Publication Data:
Saunders, Anthony, 1949-
  Credit risk management in and out of the financial crisis : new approaches to value at risk and other paradigms / Anthony Saunders, Linda Allen. — 3rd ed.
     p. cm. — (Wiley finance series)
  Rev. ed. of: Credit risk measurement. 2nd ed. c2002.
  Includes bibliographical references and index.
  ISBN 978-0-470-47834-9 (cloth)
  1. Bank loans. 2. Bank management. 3. Credit—Management. 4. Risk management. I. Allen, Linda, 1954- II. Saunders, Anthony, 1949- Credit risk measurement. III. Title.
  HG1641.S33 2010
  332.1'20684—dc22

                                                                    2009044765

Printed in the United States of America

10 9 8 7 6 5 4 3 2 1

Contents

List of Abbreviations

ABCP	asset-backed commercial paper
ABS	asset-backed security
AE	average exposure
AMA	advanced measurement approach
ARM	adjustable rate mortgage
ARS	adjusted relative spread
ABX	index of mortgage-backed security values
BHC	bank holding company
BIS	Bank for International Settlements
BISTRO	Broad Index Secured Trust Offering
BRW	benchmark risk weight
BSM	Black-Scholes-Merton Model
CAPM	capital asset pricing model
CBOE	Chicago Board Options Exchange
CDO	collateralized debt obligation
CDS	credit default swap
CFTC	Commodity Futures Trading Commission
CIO	collateralized insurance obligation
CLN	credit-linked note
CLO	collateralized loan obligation
CMO	collateralized mortgage obligation
CMR	cumulative mortality rate
CRE	commercial real estate
CS	credit spread
CSFP	Crédit Suisse Financial Products
CVR	contingent value rights
CWI	creditworthiness index

CYC	current yield curve
DD	distance to default
DM	default mode model
EAD	exposure at default
EBITDA	earnings before interest, taxes, depreciation, and amortization
EC	European Community
ECA	Export Credit Agency
EDF	expected default frequency
EDP	estimated default probability
EE	expected exposure
EL	expected losses
EVA	economic value added
EVT	extreme value theory
FA	foundation approach
FAS	Financial Accounting Standard
FASB	Financial Accounting Standards Board
FD	fair disclosure
FDIC	Federal Deposit Insurance Corporation
FNMA	Federal National Mortgage Association
FHFA	Federal Housing Finance Agency
FIs	financial institutions
FSHC	financial service holding company
FSA	Financial Services Authority
FSLIC	Federal Savings and Loan Insurance Corporation
FSO	financial statement only
FV	future value
FX	foreign exchange
FYC	forward yield curve
GEV	generalized extreme value
GDP	gross domestic product
GLB	Graham-Leach-Bliley (author discretion)
GPD	Generalized Pareto Distribution
GNMA	Government National Mortgage Association
GSE	government sponsored enterprise
GSF	granularity scaling factor
IDR	implied debenture rating

IIF	Institute of International Finance
IMF	International Monetary Fund
IRB	internal ratings-based model
ISDA	International Swaps and Derivatives Association
IQR	interquartile range
LAS	Loan Analysis System (KPMG)
LBO	leveraged buyout
LDC	less developed country
LDCs	less developed countries
LGD	loss given default
LPC	Loan Pricing Corporation
LTV	loan to value
M	maturity
LIBOR	London Inter-Bank Offered Rate
MBS	mortgage-backed security
MD	modified duration
MMR	marginal mortality rate
MPT	modern portfolio theory
MRC	marginal risk contribution
MTM	mark-to-market model
NAIC	National Association of Insurance Commissioners
NASD	National Association of Securities Dealers
NGR	net to gross (current exposure) ratio
NPV	net present value
NRSRO	nationally recognized statistical rating organization
OAEM	other assets especially mentioned
OBS	off-balance-sheet
OCC	Office of the Comptroller of the Currency
OECD	Organization for Economic Cooperation and Development
OFHEO	Office of Federal Housing Enterprise Oversight
OIS	overnight index swap
ONI	Office of National Insurance
OPM	option-pricing model
OTC	over-the-counter
OTS	Office of Thrift Supervision
PD	probability of default

QDF	quasi default frequency
QIS	Quantitative Impact Study
RAROC	risk-adjusted return on capital
RBC	risk-based capital
REIT	real estate investment trust
Repo	repurchase agreement
RN	risk-neutral
ROA	return on assets
ROC	receiver operating characteristic
ROE	return on equity
RORAC	return on risk-adjusted capital
RMBS	residential mortgage-backed security
RTC	resolution trust corporation
RW	risk weight
RWA	risk-weighted assets
SBC	Swiss Bank Corporation
SEC	Securities and Exchange Commission
SIV	structured investment vehicle
SM	standardized model
SME	small and medium enterprise
SPE	special-purpose entity
SPV	special-purpose vehicle
TBTF	too big to fail
TRACE	Trade Reporting and Compliance Engine
UL	unexpected losses
VAR	value at risk
VIX	volatility index
WACC	weighted-average cost of capital
WAL	weighted-average life
WARR	weighted-average risk ratio
ZYC	zero yield curve

Preface

It might seem the height of hubris to write a book on quantitative models measuring credit risk exposure while the wreckage of the credit crisis of 2007 is still all around us. However, in our view, it is just at this time that books like this one are needed. While credit risk measurement models are always in need of improvement, we cannot place all of the blame for the crisis on their failure to detect risk and accurately value credit instruments. Models are only as good as their assumptions, and assumptions are driven by market conditions and incentives. The first three chapters of this book are devoted to a detailed analysis of the before, during, and aftereffects of the global financial crisis of 2007–2009.

In this edition, we build on the first two editions' approach of explaining the economic underpinnings behind the mathematical modeling, so as to make the concepts accessible to bankers and finance professionals as well as students. We also compare the various models, explaining their strengths and their shortcomings, and describe and critique proprietary services available.

The first section (Chapters 1–3) describes bubbles and crises in order to understand the global financial crisis of 2007–2009. The second section presents several quantitative models used to estimate the probability of default (PD). The two major modeling approaches are the options-theoretic structural models (Chapter 4) and the reduced form models (Chapter 5). The options-theoretic approach explains default in structural terms related to the market value of the firm's assets as compared to the firm's liabilities. The reduced form approach statistically decomposes observed risky debt prices into default risk premiums that price credit risk events without necessarily examining their underlying causality. In Chapter 6, we compare and contrast these and other more traditional models (for example, Altman's Z score and mortality models) in order to assess their forecasting accuracy.

Estimation of the expected probability of default is only one, albeit important, parameter required to compute credit risk exposure. In Chapter 7, we discuss approaches used to estimate another critical parameter: the loss given default (LGD). We also describe how the credit risk of a portfolio is determined in Chapter 8. In the subsequent three chapters, we combine these parameters in order to demonstrate their use in credit risk assessment. Value at risk (VAR) models are discussed in Chapter 9; stress test (including a description of the U.S. government stress testing of 19 systemically important financial firms, released in March 2009) is discussed in Chapter 10; and Chapter 11 describes risk-adjusted return on capital (RAROC) models that are used to allocate capital and even compensation levels within the firm.

The final section deals with credit risk transfer mechanisms. In Chapter 12, we describe and analyze credit default swaps (CDS) and asset-backed securities (ABS). Chapter 13 discusses capital regulation, focusing on Basel II risk-based capital requirements and proposed reforms.

We have many people to thank, but in particular, we would like to thank Anjolein Schmeits for her insightful comments and careful reading of the manuscript.

PART

One

Bubbles and Crises: The Global Financial Crisis of 2007–2009

Setting the Stage for Financial Meltdown

INTRODUCTION

In this first chapter we outline in basic terms the underlying mechanics of the ongoing financial crisis facing the financial services industry, and the challenges this creates for future credit risk models and modelers.

Rather than one crisis, the current financial crisis actually comprises three separate but related phases. The first phase hit the national housing market in the United States in late 2006 through early 2007, resulting in an increase in delinquencies on residential mortgages. The second phase was a global liquidity crisis in which overnight interbank markets froze. The third phase has proved to be the most serious and difficult to remedy and was initiated by the failure of Lehman Brothers in September 2008. The lessons to be learned for credit risk models are different for each of these phases. Consequently, we describe first how we entered the initial phase of the current crisis. In the upcoming chapters, we discuss the different phases and implications of the global financial crisis that resulted from the features that characterized the run-up to the crisis.

THE CHANGING NATURE OF BANKING

The traditional view of a bank is that of an institution that issues short-term deposits (e.g., checking accounts and certificates of deposit) that are used to finance the bank's extension of longer-term loans (e.g., commercial loans to firms and mortgages to households). Since the traditional bank holds the loan until maturity, it is responsible for analyzing the riskiness of the borrower's activities, both before and after the loan is made. That is, depositors delegate the bank as its monitor to screen which borrowers should receive loans and to oversee whether risky borrowers invest loan proceeds in economically viable (although not risk-free) projects see Diamond [1984].

In this setting, the balance sheet of a bank fully reflects the bank's activities. The bank's deposits show up on its balance sheet as liabilities, whereas the bank's assets include loans that were originated by the bank and are held to maturity. Despite the simplicity of this structure, traditional banking is not free of risk. Indeed, the traditional model tended to expose the bank to considerable liquidity risk, interest rate risk, and credit risk. For example, suppose a number of depositors sought to withdraw their deposits simultaneously. In order to meet depositors' withdrawals the bank would be forced to raise cash, perhaps by liquidating some assets. This might entail the selling of illiquid, long-term loans at less than par value. Thus, the bank might experience a market value loss because of the liquidity risk associated with financing long-term, illiquid assets (loans) with short-term, readily withdrawable liabilities (deposits).

With respect to interest rate risk in the traditional banking model, a good example occurred in the early 1980s when interest rates increased dramatically. Banks and thrift institutions found that their long-term fixed-rate loans (such as 30 year fixed-rate mortgages) became unprofitable as deposit rates rose above mortgage rates and banks earned a negative return or spread on those loans.

The traditional banking model has always been vulnerable to credit risk exposure. Since traditional banks and thrifts tended to hold loans until maturity, they faced the risk that the credit quality of the borrower could deteriorate over the life of the loan.

In addition to the risk exposures inherent in traditional banking, regulatory requirements began to tighten in the late 1980s and early 1990s. For example, the Basel I capital regulations requirement (the so-called 8 percent rule) set risk-based capital standards that required banks to hold more capital against risky loans and other assets (both off and on the balance sheet). Capital is the most expensive source of funds available to banks, since equity holders are the most junior claimants and are viewed as the first line of defense against unexpected losses. When the risk of losses increases and additional capital is required, the cost of bank funds increases and bank profitability falls.

As a result, the traditional banking model offered an insufficient return (spread) to compensate the bank for assuming these substantial risk exposures. Consequently, banks increasingly innovated by creating new instruments and strategies in an attempt to reduce their risks and/or increase their returns. These strategies are of much relevance in understanding the first (credit crisis) phase of the 2007–2009 crisis. Most important among these strategies were: (1) securitization of nonstandard mortgage assets;

(2) syndication of loans; (3) proprietary trading and investment in non-traditional assets, such as through the creation of hedge funds; and (4) increased use of derivatives like credit default swaps to transfer risk from a bank to the market at large.

Securitization

Securitization involves a change in strategy from a traditional bank's policy of holding the loans it originates on its balance sheet until maturity. Instead, securitization consists of packaging loans or other assets into newly created securities and selling these asset-backed securities (ABSs) to investors. By packaging and selling loans to outside parties, the bank removes considerable liquidity, interest rate, and credit risk from its asset portfolio. Rather than holding loans on the balance sheet until maturity, the originate-to-distribute model entails the bank's sale of the loan and other asset-backed securities shortly after origination for cash, which can then be used to originate new loans/assets, thereby starting the securitization cycle over again. The Bank of England reported that in the credit bubble period, major UK banks securitized or syndicated 70 percent of their commercial loans within 120 days of origination.[1] The earliest ABSs involved the securitization of mortgages, creating collateralized mortgage obligations (CMOs).

The market for securitized assets is huge. Figure 1.1 shows the explosive growth in the issuance of residential mortgage-backed securities (RMBSs) from 1995 to 2006, in the period just prior to the 2007–2009 crisis. Indeed, Figure 1.2 shows that, as of the end of 2006, the size of the RMBS market exceeded the size of global money markets. While the markets for collateralized loan obligations (CLOs) and collateralized debt obligations (CDOs) were smaller than for RMBS, they had also been rapidly growing until the current crisis.[2] Figure 1.3 shows the volume of CDO issuance in Europe and the United States during the 2004 through September 2007 period. The three-year rate of growth in new issues from 2004 through 2006 was 656 percent in the U.S. market and more than 5,700 percent in the European market.

The basic mechanism of securitization is accomplished via the removal of assets (e.g., loans) from the balance sheets of the banks. This is done by creating off-balance-sheet subsidiaries, such as a bankruptcy-remote special-purpose vehicle (SPV, also known as special-purpose entity, or SPE) or a structured investment vehicle (SIV). Typically, the SPV is used in the more traditional form of securitization. In this form, a bank packages a pool of loans together and sells them to an off-balance-sheet SPV—a company that is specially created by the arranger for the purpose of issuing the new securities.[3] The SPV pools the loans together and creates new securities backed by

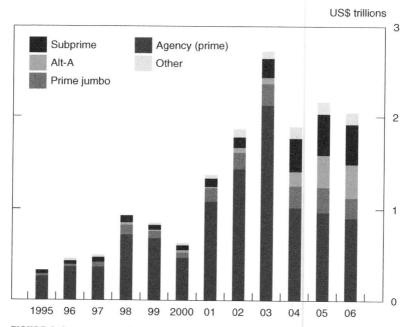

FIGURE 1.1   U.S. Residential Mortgage-Backed Securities Issuance
Note: Issuance is on a gross basis.
Source: Bank of England, *Financial Stability Report* no. 22, October 2007, page 6.

the cash flows from the underlying asset pool. These asset-backed securities can be based on mortgages, commercial loans, consumer receivables, credit card receivables, automobile loans, corporate bonds (CDOs), insurance and reinsurance contracts (Collateralized Insurance Obligations, CIOs), bank loans (CLOs), and real estate investment trust (REIT) assets such as commercial real estate (CRE CDOs).

Figure 1.4 illustrates this traditional form of securitization. The SPV purchases the assets (newly originated loans) from the originating bank for cash generated from the sale of ABSs. The SPV sells the newly created asset-backed securities to investors such as insurance companies and pension funds. The SPV also earns fees from the creation and servicing of the newly created asset-backed securities. However, the underlying loans in the asset pool belong to the ultimate investors in the asset-backed securities. All cash flows are passed through the SPV and allocated according to the terms of each tranche to the ultimate investors.[4] The SPV acts as a conduit to sell the securities to investors and passes the cash back to the originating bank. The ABS security investor has direct rights to the cash flows on the underlying

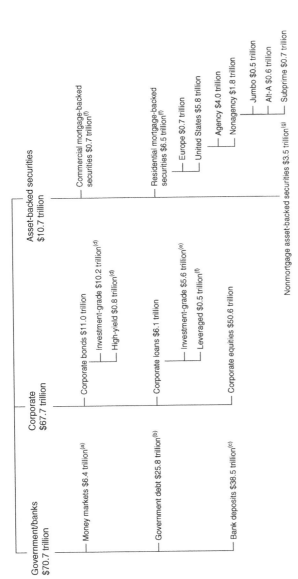

FIGURE 1.2 Size of Global Securities Markets

Note: All data are global at end of 2006 unless otherwise stated.

a Euro area, the United Kingdom, the United States, and international money market instruments outstanding.

b Excludes local government debt and government agency debt. In the United States, for example, agency and municipal debt totaled $4.6 trillion at 2007 end-Q1.

c End of 2005 except for the United Kingdom and the United States.

d Aggregate of Africa, Europe, the Middle East, and the United States.

e Aggregate of Euro area, the United Kingdom, and the United States.

f Aggregate of Europe and the United States.

g Aggregate of Europe and the United States. Includes securitized home equity loans, auto loans, consumer loans, credit card debt, student loans, and other sorts of nonmortgage loans.

Source: Bank of England, *Financial Stability Report* no. 22, October 2007, page 20.

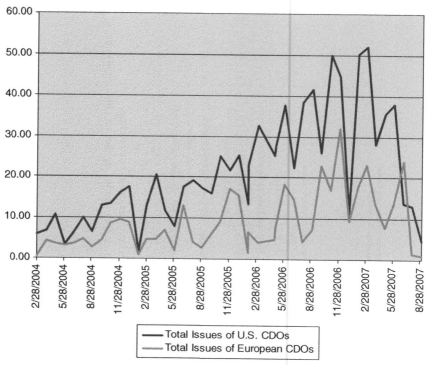

FIGURE 1.3 U.S. and European CDO Issuance 2004–2007
Source: Loan Pricing Corporation web site, www.loanpricing.com/.

assets. Moreover, the life of the SPV is limited to the maturity of the ABS. That is, when the last tranche of the ABS is paid off, the SPV ceases to exist.

While this method of securitization was lucrative, financial intermediaries soon discovered another method that was even more lucrative. For this form of securitization, an SIV is created. In this form, the SIV's lifespan is not tied to any particular security. Instead, the SIV is a structured operating company that invests in assets that are designed to generate higher returns than the SIV's cost of funds. Rather than selling the asset-backed securities directly to investors in order to raise cash (as do SPVs), the SIV sells bonds or commercial paper to investors in order to raise the cash to purchase the bank's assets. The SIV then holds the loans purchased from the banks on its own balance sheet until maturity. These loan assets held by the SIV back the debt instruments issued by the SIV to investors. Thus, in essence the SIV itself becomes an asset-backed security, and the SIV's commercial paper liabilities are considered asset-backed commercial paper (ABCP).

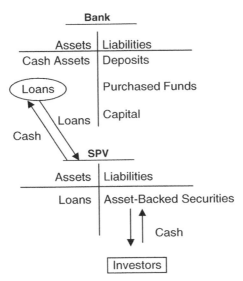

FIGURE 1.4 The Traditional Securitization Process

Figure 1.5 shows the structure of the SIV method of asset securitization. Investors buy the liabilities (most often, asset-backed commercial paper) of the SIV, providing the proceeds for the purchase of loans from originating banks. The SIV's debt (or ABCP) is backed by the loan or asset portfolio held by the SIV. However, the SIV does not simply pass through the payments on the loans in its portfolio to the ABCP investors. Indeed, investors have no direct rights to the cash flows on the underlying loans in the portfolio; rather, they are entitled to the payments specified on the SIV's debt instruments. That is, the SIV's ABCP obligations carry interest obligations that are independent of the cash flows from the underlying loan/asset portfolio. Thus, in the traditional form of securitization, the SPV only pays out what it receives from the underlying loans in the pool of assets backing the ABS.

In the newer form of securitization, the SIV is responsible for payments on its ABCP obligations whether the underlying pool of assets generates sufficient cash flow to cover those costs. Of course, if the cash flow from the asset pool exceeds the cost of ABCP liabilities, then the SIV keeps the spread and makes an additional profit. However, if the assets in the underlying pool do not generate sufficient cash flows, the SIV is still obligated to make interest and principal payments on its debt instruments. In such a situation the SIV usually has lines of credit or loan commitments from the sponsoring bank. Thus, ultimately, the loan risk would end up back on the sponsoring bank's balance sheet.[5]

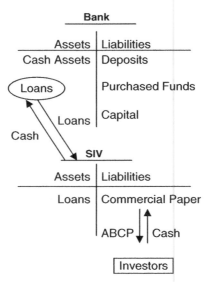

FIGURE 1.5   A New Securitization Process

Because of the greater expected return on this newer form of securitization, it became very popular in the years leading up to the financial crisis. Whereas an SPV only earns the fees for the creation of the asset-backed securities, the SIV also earns an expected spread between high-yielding assets (such as commercial loans) and low-cost commercial paper as long as the yield curve is upward-sloping and credit defaults on the asset portfolio are low. Indeed, because of these high potential spreads, hedge funds owned by Citicorp and Bear Stearns and others adopted this investment strategy. Until the 2007–2009 crisis, these instruments appeared to offer investors a favorable return/risk trade-off (i.e., a positive return) and an apparently small risk given the asset-backing of the security.

The balance sheet for an SIV in Figure 1.5 looks remarkably similar to the balance sheet of a traditional bank. The SIV acts similarly to a traditional bank—holding loans or other assets until maturity and issuing short-term debt instruments (such as ABCP) to fund its asset portfolio. The major difference between an SIV and a traditional bank is that the SIV cannot issue deposits to fund its asset base (i.e., it's not technically a *bank*).

However, to the extent that many SIVs used commercial paper and interbank loans (such as repurchase agreements or repos)[6] to finance their asset portfolios, they were subject to even more liquidity risk than were traditional banks. A first reason for this is that in the modern financial market, sophisticated lenders (so-called suppliers of *purchased funds*) are prone to *run* at the first sign of trouble, whereas small depositors are slower to react. That is, interbank lenders and commercial paper buyers will withdraw funds (or refuse to renew financing) more quickly than traditional core depositors, who may rely on their bank deposits for day-to-day business purposes.

Second, bank deposits are explicitly insured up to $250,000 and, for those in banks viewed as too big to fail, a full implicit 100 percent. Thus, the liquidity risk problems were exacerbated by the liquidity requirements of the SIVs that relied on short-term sources of funding, such as commercial paper, which had to be renewed within nine months, and repurchase agreements, which must be fully backed by collateral at all points in time in the absence of a deposit insurance umbrella. Consequently, if the value of its portfolio declined due to deterioration in credit conditions, the SIV might be forced to sell long-term, illiquid assets in order to meet its short-term liquid debt obligations. In the next chapter, we show that this was a key part of the contagion mechanism by which the subprime market credit crisis was transmitted to other markets and institutions during the crisis.

Loan Syndication

Whereas packaging and selling loans to off-balance-sheet vehicles is one mechanism banks have found to potentially reduce their risk exposures, a second mechanism has been the increased use of loan syndication. A loan is syndicated when a bank originates a commercial loan, but rather than holding the whole loan, the originating bank sells parts of the loan (or *syndicates* it) to outside investors. Thus, after a syndication is completed, a bank may retain only 20 percent of the loan (with its associated risk exposure) while transferring the remaining part of the loan, in this case 80 percent, to outside investors. Traditionally these outside investors were banks, but the range of buyers has increasingly included hedge funds, mutual funds, insurance companies, and other investors. Figure 1.6 shows that dating back to the early 2000s, nonbank institutional investors comprised more than 50 percent of the syndicated bank loan market.

The originating bank in a loan syndication is called the *lead arranger* (or *lead bank*). Typically, the lead arranger lines up the syndicate members before the loan is finalized so that the originating bank only *warehouses* the loan for a short time, often only a few days. In a loan syndication, the lead bank (also known as the *agent* or *arranger*) and the borrower agree on the terms of the loan, with regard to the coupon rate, the maturity date, the face value, collateral required, covenants, and so on.[7] Then the lead bank assembles the syndicate, together with other lenders, called *participants*. Figure 1.7 illustrates the syndication process.

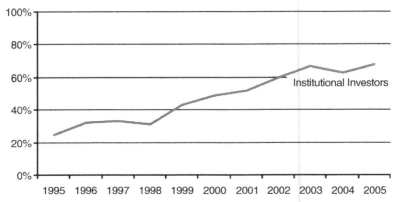

FIGURE 1.6 Composition of Loan Investors in the Syndicated Bank Loan Market
Source: V. Ivashina and A. Sun, "Institutional Stock Trading on Loan Market Information," Harvard Business School Working Paper, August 2007, Figure 1.1.

Syndicates can be assembled in one of three ways:

- *Firm commitment (underwritten) deals.* The lead bank commits to making the loan in its entirety, warehouses it, and then assembles participants to reduce its own loan exposure. Thus, the borrower is guaranteed the full face value of the loan.
- *Best efforts deals.* The size of the loan is determined by the commitments of banks that agree to participate in the syndication. The borrower is not guaranteed the full face value of the loan.
- *Club deals.* For small deals (usually $200 million or less), the loan is shared among banks, each of which has had a prior lending relationship with the borrower.

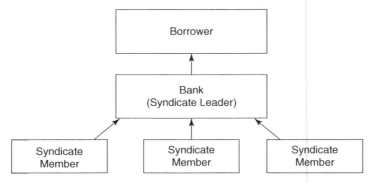

FIGURE 1.7 Syndicated Lending
Note: The arrows reflect the direction of the flow of funds.

The loan's risk determines the terms of the syndicated loan. Primary market pricing of the loan at the issuance stage typically consists of setting the loan's coupon rate. Most syndicated loans are floating rate loans tied to a market benchmark such as the London Interbank Offered Rate (LIBOR) or the U.S. prime rate. LIBOR is the cost of short-term borrowings on the overseas interbank U.S. dollar market for prime bank borrowers. The U.S. prime rate is the base interest rate set on loans for a bank's borrowers, although the bank can offer loans at rates below prime to its very best customers if it so chooses.

Investment-grade loan syndications are made to borrowers rated BBB–/Baa3 or higher.[8] Coupon rates for investment-grade loans are typically set at LIBOR plus 50 to 150 basis points.[9] Leveraged loans are non-investment-grade loans made to highly leveraged borrowers often with debt to EBIT ratios exceeding 4:1. Because of the greater risk of default, coupon rates on leveraged loans are generally set much higher than for investment-grade loans. Syndicated leveraged loans are often pooled together and securitized in the form of CLOs.

Once the terms of the loan syndication are set, they cannot be changed without the agreement of the members of the loan syndicate. Material changes (regarding interest rates, amortization requirements, maturity term, or collateral/security) generally require a unanimous vote on the part of all syndicate participants. Nonmaterial amendments may be approved either by a majority or super-majority, as specified in the contractual terms of the loan syndication. The assembling and setting of the terms of a loan syndication are primary market or *originating* transactions. After the loan syndication is closed, however, syndicate members can sell their loan syndication shares in the secondary market for syndicated bank loans.[10]

While syndicated lending has been around for a long time, the market entered into a rapid growth period in the late 1980s, as a result of the banks' activity in financing takeovers, mergers, and acquisitions. At that time, there was also a wave of leveraged buyouts (LBOs) in which managers and investors in a firm borrow money in order to buy out the public equity of the company, thereby taking it private. When a takeover, acquisition, or LBO is financed using a significant amount of bank loans, it is often a highly leveraged transaction. These deals fueled the first major growth wave in the syndicated bank loan market during the early 1990s. This growth stage was ended, however, by the credit crisis brought on by the July 1998 default on Russian sovereign debt and the near-default of the Long Term Capital Management hedge fund in August 1998. The annual growth in trading volume in the secondary syndicated bank loan market was 53.52 percent in 1996–1997, 27.9 percent in 1997–1998, and only 1.99 percent in 1998–1999, according to the Loan Pricing Corporation (LPC) web site. The

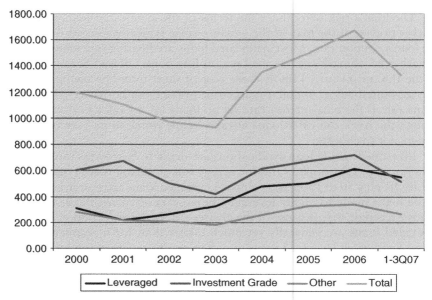

FIGURE 1.8   Syndicated Bank Loan Market Activity, 2000–2007
Source: Loan Pricing Corporation web site, www.loanpricing.com/.

bursting of the high-tech bubble in 2000–2001 and the subsequent recession caused even further declines in syndicated bank loan market activity.

After annual declines in syndicated bank loan issuance during 2000–2003 (see Figure 1.8), the syndicated market recovered in 2004–2006. Total syndicated loan volume increased by 44.93 percent in 2004. Figure 1.8 shows that the market continued to grow until the year 2006. This growth was fueled by the expansion of credit for business growth and private equity acquisitions. However, the impact of the credit crisis is shown in the 20.53 percent decline in syndicated bank loan volume during the first three quarters of 2007.

Proprietary Investing

As traditional on-balance-sheet investing in loans became less attractive, both in terms of return and risk, banks continued to seek out other profit opportunities. This has taken the form of an increased level of trading of securities within the bank's portfolio—that is, buying and selling securities such as government bonds. In addition, banks established specialized off-balance-sheet vehicles and subsidiaries to engage in investments and investment strategies that might be viewed as being too risky if conducted on their balance sheets. For example, banks established (through lending and/or equity participations) hedge funds, private equity funds, or venture funds.

Hedge funds, private equity funds, and venture funds are investment companies that have broad powers of investing and can often act outside the controls of regulators such as the Securities and Exchange Commission (SEC) that regulate most U.S.-based investment funds. Circumvention of regulatory oversight can be accomplished by establishing the fund in a favorable regulatory environment offshore (e.g., the Cayman Islands) and/or by restricting the number of investors in the fund. In general, a hedge fund with fewer than 100 investors, each of whom have been certified as having significant wealth and thus, by implication, investment sophistication, will be outside the regulatory oversight of the SEC or the Federal Reserve System.

It should be noted that the term *hedge fund* is often a misnomer. Many of these funds do not seek to hedge or reduce risk, but in fact do the reverse by seeking out new and potentially profitable investments or strategies to generate higher profits, often at considerable risk. The term *hedge fund* stems from the fact that these investment vehicles often are structured to benefit from mispricing opportunities in financial markets, and thus do not necessarily take a position on the overall direction of the market—in other words, they are neither long (buy) nor short (sell) assets, but are neutral (hedged), seeking to gain whether market prices move up or down. Many hedge funds invested in the asset-backed securitization vehicles originated by banks, discussed earlier: asset-backed commercial paper, CLOs, and CDOs. At the start of the 2007–2009 financial crisis, it was estimated that there were over 9,000 hedge funds in existence with over $1 trillion in assets.[11] Banks are exposed to hedge funds through the provision of prime brokerage services such as trading and execution, clearance and custody, security lending, financing, and repurchase agreements, as well as through proprietary investing.

Credit Default Swaps

In recent years, there has been an explosive growth in the use of credit derivatives. Estimates in June 2001 put the market at approximately $1 trillion in notional value worldwide. The Bank for International Settlements (BIS) reported the notional amount on outstanding over-the-counter (OTC) credit default swaps (CDS) to be $28.8 trillion in December 2006, up from $13.9 trillion as of December 2005 (an increase of 107 percent).[12] By 2008, estimates put the notional value over $60 trillion. It is clear that the market for credit derivatives has grown, and continues to grow, quite rapidly. While a majority of these OTC CDSs were single-name instruments, a large proportion were multiname CDSs involving baskets of credit instruments (see the discussion in Chapter 12).

The growth in trading of credit derivatives that are designed to transfer the credit risk on portfolios of bank loans or debt securities facilitated a net overall transfer of credit risk from banks to nonbanks, principally insurance and reinsurance companies. As will be shown in Chapter 12, banks, securities firms, and corporations tend to be net buyers of credit protection, whereas insurance companies, hedge funds, mutual funds, and pension funds tend to be net sellers. Insurance companies (and especially reinsurance companies) view credit derivatives as an insurance product, in which their relatively high credit ratings, often based on the profitability of their underlying casualty and life insurance business, can be used to insure the buyers of credit protection (e.g., banks) against risk exposure to their loan customers. Just as individuals may purchase home owners insurance or automobile insurance to protect themselves from losses from adverse events (such as fires or car accidents), CDS buyers purchase CDS contracts to protect themselves from losses resulting from adverse credit events (such as bankruptcy or default). The CDS seller insures the buyer against these losses.[13] Once the largest insurance company in the world, AIG was heavily involved in issuing CDS contracts during the pre-crisis period, ultimately leading to its bailout by the U.S. government in September 2008.

Credit derivatives such as CDSs allow banks and other financial institutions to alter the risk/return trade-off of a loan portfolio without having to sell or remove loans from the bank's balance sheet. Apart from avoiding an adverse customer relationship effect (compared to when a bank sells a loan of a relationship borrower), the use of credit derivatives (rather than loan sales or securitization) may allow a bank to avoid adverse timing of tax payments as well as liquidity problems related to buying back a similar loan at a later date if risk/return considerations so dictate. Thus, for customer relationship, tax, transaction cost, and liquidity reasons, a bank may prefer the credit derivative solution to loan portfolio optimization rather than the more direct (loan trading) portfolio management solution. Banks can essentially rent out their credit portfolios to financial intermediaries that have capital but do not have large loan-granting networks.

By selling CDSs, the insurance company or, for example, foreign bank can benefit from the return paid for credit risk exposure without having to actually commit current resources to purchasing a loan. Moreover, usually the insurance company or foreign bank has no banking relationship with the borrower and, therefore, would find it costly to develop the appropriate monitoring techniques needed to originate and hold loans on the balance sheet. This is not to imply that buying a credit derivative totally removes credit risk from a bank's balance sheet: As an example, the buyers of AIG's CDSs faced the counterparty risk that the seller, AIG, would default on its obligation to cover any credit losses incurred under the CDS contract, something that would probably have happened if AIG was not bailed out in September 2008.

The growing use of CDSs and other derivative instruments transfers risk across financial intermediaries. However, the use of derivatives engenders counterparty risk exposure, which may be controlled using margin and collateral requirements. Moreover, each institution sets a credit limit exposure for each counterparty. Not only may the collateral/margin protection mechanism break down if the seller of the insurance (CDS) cannot post sufficient collateral (as was the case for AIG in 2007–2008), Kambhu et al. (2007) note that these systems may also fail as a result of free-rider problems and negative externalities. For example, competition among CDS buyers may lead to inadequate monitoring of counterparty exposures as banks rely on each other to perform due diligence on the seller. Moral hazard concerns arise if banks undertake riskier positions under the assumption that they have hedged their exposure, and CDS protection may be fleeting if CDS market liquidity evaporates or asset correlations go to 1.0, as is typical during a financial crisis.

REENGINEERING FINANCIAL INSTITUTIONS AND MARKETS

The common feature uniting the four innovations previously discussed—securitization, loan syndication, proprietary investing, and growth of the credit default swap market—is that the balance sheet no longer reflects the bulk of a bank's activities or credit risk. Many of a bank's profit and risk centers lie off its balance sheet in SPVs or SIVs, hedge funds, and CDSs. Although bank regulators attempt to examine the off-balance-sheet activities of banks so as to ascertain their safety and soundness, there is far less scrutiny of off-balance-sheet activities than there is for their on-balance-sheet activities (i.e., traditional lending and deposit taking). To the extent that counterparty credit risk was not fully disclosed to or monitored by regulators, the increased use of these innovations transferred risk in ways that were not necessarily scrutinized or understood. It is in this context of increased risk and inadequate regulation that the credit crisis developed.

Before we turn, in the next chapter, to the incipient causes of the crisis, a discussion of how undetected risk could build up in the system is in order. Financial markets rely on regulators, credit rating agencies, and banks to oversee risk in the system. We now describe how each of these failed to perform their function in the years leading up to the crisis.

Regulators

In 1992, U.S. bank regulators implemented the first Basel Capital Accord (Basel I).[14] Basel I was revolutionary in that it sought to develop a single capital requirement for credit risk across the major banking countries of the world.[15] Basel I has been amended to incorporate market risk (in 1996), as well as updated to remedy flaws in the original risk measurement methodology stemming from the inaccuracies in credit risk measurement (see the discussion in Chapter 13).

Toward the end of the 1990s, regulators recognizing the unintended risk-inducing consequences of some of the features of Basel I sought to amend the capital requirements. In 1999, the Basel Committee began the process of formulating a new capital accord (denoted Basel II) that was intended to correct the risk mispricing of loans under Basel I. After much debate, the proposal for Basel II was finalized in 2006, and subsequently adopted throughout the world. The global financial crisis of 2007–2009, however, revealed flaws in Basel II, and in January 2009 the Basel Committee suggested further changes that would increase risk weighting and make the system more sensitive to the risk exposure inherent in ABSs, CDSs, and the off-balance-sheet activity described in this chapter (see the discussion in Chapter 13).

Another regulatory change in the United States during this period was the passage of the Graham-Leach-Bliley (GLB) Act of 1999, which enables bank holding companies to convert to financial service holding companies (FSHCs). These FSHCs could combine commercial banking, securities broker-dealer activities, investment banking, and insurance activities under one corporate holding company umbrella, thereby encouraging the growth of universal banking in the United States. However, it is not clear that this deregulation has contributed in any meaningful way to the buildup of credit and other risks. Securitization and loan syndication were permitted activities for U.S. banks even under the Glass-Steagall Act of 1933 that preceded the passage of the GLB. Moreover, banks could always engage in proprietary trading strategies. Thus, the passage of the GLB Act did not materially affect banks' abilities to shift risk off their balance sheets, although it did add to the risk complexity of these organizations.

Credit Rating Agencies

Credit rating agencies are paid by issuers of securities to analyze risk and provide the results of their analysis to the general market in the form of ratings. Indeed, credit rating agencies are exempt from fair disclosure laws (such as Regulation FD) that require all institutions to have the same access to material and forward-looking information.[16] Thus, they are entitled to receive private information about the firms that issue debt instruments so as to use this information in formulating their ratings.

Many institutional investors (e.g., insurance companies and pension funds) rely on credit ratings in order to determine whether they can invest in particular debt issues. Specifically, many institutions are precluded by regulation or charter from buying below-investment-grade debt issues, rated below BBB– for S&P or below Baa3 for Moody's. Also, debt issues may specify covenants based on credit ratings that may trigger a technical violation if a borrower's credit rating falls below a certain level. Credit derivatives and insurance products utilize credit rating downgrades as a possible trigger for a credit event. Thus, credit ratings have become central features of global credit markets.[17]

The Securities Exchange Act of 1934 gave the SEC the ability to confer the designation of "Nationally Recognized Statistical Rating Organization" (NRSRO). Historically, these firms have been Moody's, S&P, and Fitch.[18] This has created a virtual oligopoly that has reduced competitive pressures to improve rating accuracy and timeliness. For example, all three major rating agencies (Moody's, S&P, and Fitch) rated Enron investment-grade until just four days prior to its default on December 2, 2001. Perhaps in response to this type of failure, the SEC conferred the NRSRO certification on Dominion Bond Rating Service (of Toronto, Canada) in February 2003, and AM Best (focusing on the insurance and banking industries) received this designation in 2006. On December 21, 2007, Egan-Jones Ratings also received this designation.

As noted earlier, typically the rating agencies are paid by the debt issuer for their services. This has created a potential conflict of interest such that ratings agencies may be reluctant to act too aggressively to adjust their ratings downward for fear of offending issuing clients. The major ratings agencies have traditionally adopted a through-the-cycle methodology that smoothes ratings and prevents them from expeditiously adjusting their ratings to reflect new information, although more recently Moody's and Fitch have provided implied credit ratings as a new product based on CDS spreads, which are presumed to be more timely metrics of issuer credit risk.

By contrast, Egan-Jones Ratings (EJR) receives no fees from issuers, relying entirely on buyer or institutional investors such as hedge funds and pension funds to pay for their ratings. Thus, EJR ratings are more oriented toward providing timely information regarding valuation that is useful to the investment community. Beaver, Shakespeare, and Soliman (2006) have compared EJR ratings to Moody's ratings and find that EJR ratings lead

Moody's in both upgrades and downgrades. EJR ratings upgrades precede Moody's by an average of six months, and downgrades by between one and four months. Moreover, "EJR rating upgrades (downgrades) have a significantly larger positive (negative) contemporaneous [equity] abnormal return than does Moody's . . . consistent with EJR's investor orientation."[19] These results are supported by those of Johnson (2003), who finds that EJR's downgrades for the lowest investment-grade rated issuers lead S&P's and occur in smaller steps. Thus, EJR's role in providing services to the buy-side investor community are reflected in its expeditious (*point-in-time*) incorporation of new information into ratings on a real-time basis. In contrast, Moody's and S&P play a contractual role in debt covenants and permissible portfolio investments and are thus more conservative and focused on incorporating negative information. Offering empirical support for this, Kim and Nabar (2007) use equity prices to examine Moody's bond ratings, and find that downgrades are timelier than upgrades.

During the current crisis the reputations of the three major credit rating agencies have been additionally harmed by their misrating of ABS tranches and the fact that they engaged in a potential conflict of interest in both helping to design the structure of ABS issues for a fee and then charging a fee for the publication of those ratings.[20] Indeed, in the fall of 2008 more than 2,000 ABSs had to be drastically downgraded as the credit risk assumptions employed in the ABS tranching were shown to be extremely optimistic.

Market Value Accounting

One of the oft-cited causes of the 2007–2009 financial crisis has been market value accounting, specifically Financial Accounting Standard (FAS) 157 which calls for fair value accounting. Under FAS 157, banks have to write down the value of their assets to reflect their lower market valuations during the market decline. Critics claim that since financial markets essentially were shut down, any market values were either speculative (since prices were often completely unavailable) or fire sale prices reflecting the extreme lack of market liquidity. Requiring banks to drastically write down the value of assets that they had no intention of selling had the impact of generating capital charges, which required banks to raise capital at the worst possible time, thereby creating a feedback effect that caused banks to hoard their liquidity and capital, which in turn exacerbated the downturn. Because of this, pressure to defer mark-to-market accounting treatment was successful in getting the Financial Accounting Standards Board (FASB) to vote on April 2, 2009, to allow companies to use "significant judgment" in valuing assets, thereby reducing the amount of write-downs they must take on impaired investments, including mortgage-backed securities.

Ryan (2008) correctly refocuses attention on the excessive risk taking and bad decision making that is really behind the crisis, as follows (pages 4–5):

The subprime crisis was caused by firms, investors, households making bad operating, investing and financing decisions, managing risks poorly, and in some instances committing fraud, not by accounting. While the aforementioned accounting-related feedback effects may have contributed slightly to market illiquidity, the severity and persistence of market illiquidity during the crisis is primarily explained by financial institutions' considerable risk overhang and need to raise capital, as well as by the continuing high uncertainty and information asymmetry regarding subprime positions. . . . The best way to stem the credit crunch and damage caused by these actions is to speed the price adjustment process by providing market participants with the most accurate and complete information about subprime positions. Although imperfect, fair value accounting provides better information about these positions and is a far better platform for mandatory and voluntary disclosures than alternative measurement attributes, including any form of amortized cost accounting.

Providing banks with the discretion to choose their own so-called fair value (or fairy tale valuation) is the opposite of accountability and objective standards of disclosure and risk measurement could have mitigated the severity of the 2007–2009 crisis.

SUMMARY

The years preceding the financial crisis that began in 2007 were characterized by a dramatic increase in systemic risk of the financial system, caused in large part by a shift in the banking model from that of "originate and hold" to "originate and distribute." In the traditional model, the bank takes short-term deposits and other sources of funds and uses them to fund longer-term loans to businesses and consumers. The bank typically holds these loans to maturity, and thus has an incentive to screen and monitor borrower activities even after the loan is made. However, the traditional banking model exposes the institution to potential liquidity risk, interest rate risk, and credit risk.

In attempts to avoid these risk exposures and generate improved return/risk trade-offs, banks shifted to an underwriting model in which they originate or warehouse loans, and then quickly sell them (i.e., distribute them to the market). There are several forms that the originate-and-distribute model takes. One is securitization, in which a bank packages loans into asset-backed securities such as mortgage-backed securities, collateralized debt obligations, collateralized loan obligations, and so on. Another is loan syndication, in which the lending bank organizes a syndicate to jointly make the loan. Along with the increasing trend toward off-balance-sheet proprietary investing and growth of credit derivatives, these innovations have the impact of removing risk from the balance sheet of financial institutions and shifting risk off the balance sheet. That is, risk is shifted to other parties in the financial system.

Since the underwriters of ABSs were not exposed to the ongoing credit, liquidity, and interest rate risks of traditional banking, they had little incentive to screen and monitor the activities of borrowers for whom they originated loans. The result was a deterioration in credit quality, at the same time that there was a dramatic increase in consumer and corporate leverage, which were not detected by regulators. The combination of the two permitted the undetected buildup of risk in the financial system that created the preconditions for a credit bubble. In Chapter 2, we describe the credit bubble buildup and its bursting, as reflected in the post-2007 credit crisis.

APPENDIX 1.1: RATINGS COMPARISONS FOR THE THREE MAJOR RATING AGENCIES

Table 1.1 shows how Standard & Poor's ratings can be mapped onto comparable Moody's and Fitch IBCA ratings.

TABLE 1.1   Mapping of Standard & Poor's, Moody's, and Fitch IBCA Credit Ratings

Standard & Poor's Credit Rating	Moody's Credit Rating	Fitch IBCA Credit Rating
AAA	Aaa	AAA
AA+	Aa1	AA+
AA	Aa2	AA
AA−	Aa3	AA−
A+	A1	A+
A	A2	A
A−	A3	A−

Standard & Poor's Credit Rating	Moody's Credit Rating	Fitch IBCA Credit Rating
BBB+	Baa1	BBB+
BBB	Baa2	BBB
BBB−	Baa3	BBB−
BB+	Ba1	BB+
BB	Ba2	BB
BB−	Ba3	BB−
B+	B1	B+
B	B2	B
B−	B3	B−
CCC+	Caa1	CCC+
CCC	Caa2	CCC
CCC−	Caa3	CCC−
CC	Ca	CC
C	C	C
D		D

Source: Bank for International Settlements, "Long-Term Rating Scales Comparison," April 30, 2001, www.bis.org.

CHAPTER 2

The Three Phases of the Credit Crisis

INTRODUCTION

In Chapter 1, we described how credit risk built up in the financial system over the decade prior to 2007. Although this period was certainly not free of crises (e.g., the 1997 East Asian currency crisis; the summer 1998 Russian default and Long Term Capital Management insolvency; the March 2000 bursting of the tech bubble; and the September 11, 2001, World Trade Center attack), it was generally a period of historically low credit risk and defaults. Global equity markets grew over this period as credit markets expanded in size and complexity, and both consumers and corporations took leverage to historically high levels. In this chapter, we discuss the bursting of the credit bubble and the contagious transmission of the crisis from the subprime mortgage market to the financial system as a whole.

BURSTING OF THE CREDIT BUBBLE

While it is difficult to date the beginning of the post-2007 global financial crisis, the preconditions for such a crisis were building from 2001, and in particular after the terrorist attacks on 9/11. In fact, the immediate response to the terrorist attacks by regulators was to create stability in the financial markets by providing liquidity to banks and other financial institutions alike. For example, the Federal Reserve lowered the short-term money market rate that banks and other financial institutions pay in the federal funds market, the market for overnight borrowings among major banks, and even made lender-of-last-resort funds available to nonbank financial institutions such as investment banks. This had the immediate effect of lowering short-term borrowing rates for other market instruments, such as short-term borrowings of dollars abroad (the London Interbank Offered Rate, or LIBOR). In fact, very soon nominal short-term rates fell to close to the then historically low levels of 1 percent.

Perhaps not surprisingly, given low interest rates and the increased liquidity provided by central banks, such as the Federal Reserve, there ensued a rapid expansion in consumer, mortgage, and corporate debt financing. Thus, demand for residential mortgages and credit card debt rose dramatically. Moreover, commercial demand for loans increased, and it became increasingly less expensive for private equity firms to undertake takeovers financed via commercial loans (often in the form of highly leveraged syndicated bank loans).

However, what is important for understanding the credit risk exposures is that it was not just the increase in the *quantity* of consumer and commercial debt, but also the simultaneous decline in the *quality* of that debt. Specifically, as the demand for mortgage debt grew, especially among those who had previously been excluded from participating in the market because of their poor credit ratings, banks and other financial institutions began lowering their credit quality cut-off points. Moreover, to boost their earnings, in the market now popularly known as the *subprime* market, banks and other mortgage-supplying institutions often offered relatively low teaser rates on adjustable rate mortgages (ARMs); while the initial interest rates might be exceptionally low, a substantial step-up in rates could occur after the initial rate period expired two or three years later, and again if market rates rose in the future.

Under the traditional banking structure, banks might have been reluctant to so aggressively pursue low credit quality borrowers for fear that the loans would default. However, under the originate-and-distribute model of banking (see Chapter 1), asset securitization and loan syndication allowed banks to generate large loan origination fees while retaining little or no part of the loans, and hence avoid the default risk on loans that they originated. Thus, as long as the borrower did not default within the first months after a loan's issuance (a condition that was not met for some of the riskiest vintage of 2006–2007 originations) and the loans were sold or securitized without recourse back to the bank, the issuing bank could ignore longer-term credit risk concerns.

As the supply of subprime mortgages increased after 2001, housing prices began to rise in all parts of the United States. Figure 2.1 shows that as mortgage rates declined, housing prices increased during the 2000–2005 period. Indeed, as of the end of 2005, real residential construction represented more than 5 percent of U.S. GDP, and housing starts reached record highs. With hindsight, many now view this run-up in housing prices over the 2001–2005 period as a bubble that was unsustainable.

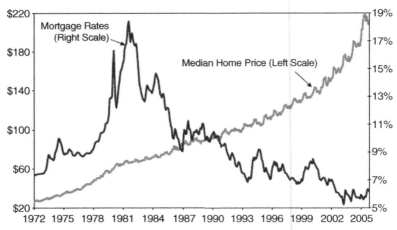

FIGURE 2.1   Median U.S. Home Prices in Thousands of Dollars
Notes: Median U.S. home prices in thousands of dollars, not seasonally adjusted.
Average conventional 30-year commitment rates on fixed rate mortgages.
Source: Standard & Poor's, "S&P/Case-Shiller® Metro Area Home Price Indices,"
May 2006, 27; National Association of Realtors, Federal Home Loan Mortgage
Corporation.

With growing originations of subprime mortgage debt, banks turned
to asset-backed securitization (ABSs), as discussed in Chapter 1. However, underlying mortgages that were often of relatively low quality
were not eligible for securitization by government-sponsored entities
such as FNMA, GNMA, or Freddie Mac. To gain investors' interest,
and obtain favorable credit ratings from credit rating agencies such as
Standard and Poor's and Moody's, these pools of subprime mortgages
were often regionally diversified and mixed with other assets. Thus, an
entire market for subprime mortgage-backed securities (MBSs) developed, backed by pools of mortgages granted to borrowers with poor
creditworthiness. Banks such as Countrywide specialized in issuing high-
risk Alt-A mortgage-backed securities.[1] These were based on pools of
mortgages issued to borrowers with inadequate documentation (e.g., no
income check) or to borrowers with uneven credit histories.

Moreover, the rising prices of houses pushed many of these high-risk
loans into the *jumbo* market, above the $417,000 GNMA limit (or
$625,500 in Alaska, Hawaii, Guam, and the U.S. Virgin Islands) for federal
government insurance. Many of these subprime mortgages were granted to
speculators and high-income individuals who wanted larger loans (with
higher loan-to-value ratios—that is, lower down payments or less equity
investment) for purchases of second homes, condominium investments,

speculative real estate investment, and refinancing. The expectation was that the loans would be refinanced (or the speculative investment sold) before a higher step-up rate on the teaser ARMs kicked in. That is, only to the extent that the loans could not be refinanced, they would be repriced after three years to higher market-based rates. In addition, lenders increasingly extended second-lien mortgages that piggybacked other loans used to cover the down payment. A *Wall Street Journal* study (Brooks and Ford [2007]) shows that the amount of second-lien mortgages increased to 22 percent of all mortgages in 2006, up from 12 percent in 2004.[2] Thus, there was little or no cushion between underlying property values and the amount of mortgage indebtedness.

Credit rating agencies often granted ABSs comprising these so-called Alt-A and subprime MBSs the highest ratings, usually in the AAA to AA range, because of the diversified nature of the mortgage pools and their assumptions about the future (upward) course of housing prices, as well as various credit enhancements. That is, if housing prices continued to rise, then even if the borrower experienced difficulties in repaying a mortgage, the lender would be able to repossess the house and sell it without incurring a loss on the mortgage. Moreover, if housing prices had continued to rise, the borrower would have been able to refinance the high-rate mortgage with lower-cost refinancing at a low introductory rate, thereby creating revolving, sequential refinancings to avoid the step-up in subprime mortgage rates. Thus, the market was betting that housing prices would increase fast enough to erase the impact of poor credit quality and rising default probabilities. Moreover, the implicit assumption driving the subprime mortgage market was that even if housing prices leveled off (or declined) in one geographic region, this would be offset by continuing increases in other regions, and therefore, the geographically diversified nature of mortgage pools would further alleviate any possible credit losses.

It was not only in the subprime mortgage market that the credit boom was evident. Consumer credit debt soared, as did the amount of syndicated lending and securitized commercial loans (CLOs), often providing the financing of takeovers. During the 2004–2005 period, the annual rate of growth of new CLO issues was around 30 percent and new issues were heavily oversubscribed.[3] By November 2006, the volume of new issues in the CLO market was $466 billion for the 11 months of 2006, an increase of 58 percent from a similar 11-month period in 2005.[4] Both the quantity of commercial lending increased and the quality deteriorated, just as in the mortgage market. The analogs to the low-quality Alt-A and subprime mortgages for the commercial credit market were the highly leveraged and *covenant-lite* loans that had little lender protection mechanisms and offered very generous promised terms to borrowers with little equity.[5]

Further building the bubble was the growth of structured investment vehicles (SIVs) (see the discussion in Chapter 1) composed of relatively longer-term subprime mortgage pools that were often used to back issues of short-term commercial paper—so-called asset-backed commercial paper conduits (ABCP)—and other short-term sources of financing (e.g., repurchase agreements). This meant that commercial paper, which matures within 270 days and therefore has to be continuously reissued, was used to finance the securitization of long-term, illiquid subprime mortgage assets. Fooled by the high ratings of the credit rating agencies (which were subject to conflicts of interest since the rating agencies owed much of their revenues to these securitizations; see Chapter 1), relatively favorable returns, and a housing price boom, investors such as pension funds, hedge funds, and mutual funds as well as foreign banks and other financial institutions became increasingly attracted to these instruments, with the ABCP market increasing to over $1 trillion in face value outstanding.[6] The growth of this market increased the supply of financing to the subprime market, thereby further encouraging the origination of more subprime and Alt-A mortgages.

High housing prices and easy credit fueled consumer spending financed with increased indebtedness. Thus, consumer demand propped up the economy, providing businesses with high profits and driving rising stock markets throughout the world. The effect of this, however, was the creation of a credit bubble which would throw the world into crisis when it burst.

The growth and decline in real estate prices throughout the United States is shown in Figure 2.2. Housing prices (as measured by the Office of Federal Housing Enterprise Oversight, or OFHEO, and Federal Housing Finance Agency, or FHFA, housing price index) fell precipitously from their peak at the beginning of 2006. This process occurred simultaneously throughout the country. As noted in the previously cited 2007 *Wall Street Journal* study:

> . . . *an analysis of more than 130 million home loans made over the past decade reveals that risky mortgages were made in nearly every corner of the nation, from small towns in the middle of nowhere to inner cities to affluent suburbs. . . . [Moreover,] the data contradict the conventional wisdom that subprime borrowers are overwhelmingly low-income residents of inner cities. Although the concentration of high-rate loans is higher in poorer communities, the numbers show that high-rate lending also rose sharply in middle-class and wealthier communities.*[7]

The geographic impact of falling house prices, inflated by the subprime mortgage crisis, spread across the United States, thereby undermining the geographic diversification assumptions used in constructing many subprime

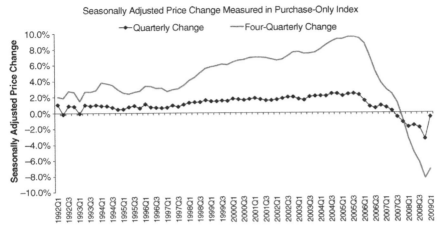

FIGURE 2.2 FHFA House Price Index History for United States
Source: Federal Housing Finance Agency news release, May 27, 2009, page 6.

asset-backed mortgage pools. Figure 2.3 shows how widespread the housing price declines were in the United States over the 2008–2009 period. However, as will be described shortly, the crisis exhibited three phases.

PHASE 1: CREDIT CRISIS IN THE MORTGAGE MARKET

As house prices started to fall during 2006, the Federal Reserve started to raise interest rates in the money market as it began to fear inflation. Since many of the subprime mortgages originated in the 2001–2005 period had floating rates (i.e., were ARMs) with high step-up rates, the cost of meeting mortgage commitments rose to unsustainable levels for many low-income households.

The confluence of falling house prices, rising interest rates, and rising mortgage costs led to a wave of mortgage defaults in the subprime market and foreclosures that only reinforced the downward trend in house prices shown in Figure 2.2. As this happened, the poor quality of the collateral and credit quality underlying subprime mortgage pools became apparent, with default rates far exceeding those apparently anticipated by the rating agencies in setting their initial ratings for various tranches of subprime mortgage securitizations ratings. These effects built throughout 2006 and through the middle of 2007. By February 2007, the percentage of subprime mortgage-backed securities delinquent by 90 days or more was 10.09 percent, which was substantially higher than the 5.37 percent rate in

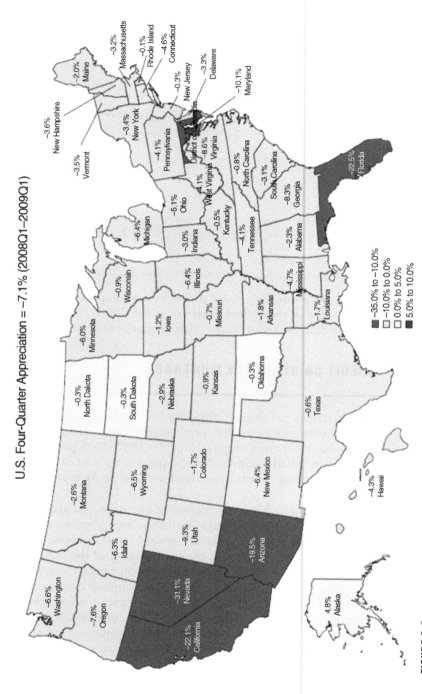

U.S. Four-Quarter Appreciation = –7.1% (2008Q1–2009Q1)

New Hampshire –3.6%
Vermont –3.5%
Maine –2.0%
Massachusetts –3.2%
Rhode Island –0.1%
Connecticut –4.6%
New Jersey –0.3%
Delaware –3.3%
Maryland –10.1%
New York –3.4%
Pennsylvania –4.1%
District of Columbia
West Virginia –8.6%
Virginia –4.1%
North Carolina –0.8%
South Carolina –3.1%
Florida –22.5%
Ohio –5.1%
Kentucky –0.5%
Tennessee –4.1%
Georgia –8.3%
Alabama –2.3%
Michigan –6.4%
Indiana –3.0%
Illinois –6.4%
Mississippi –4.7%
Louisiana –1.7%
Wisconsin –0.9%
Iowa –1.2%
Missouri –0.7%
Arkansas –1.8%
Minnesota –6.0%
North Dakota –0.3%
South Dakota –0.3%
Nebraska –2.9%
Kansas –0.9%
Oklahoma –0.3%
Texas –0.6%
Montana –2.6%
Wyoming –6.5%
Colorado –1.7%
New Mexico –6.4%
Idaho –6.3%
Utah –9.3%
Arizona –19.5%
Washington –6.6%
Oregon –7.6%
Nevada –31.1%
California –22.1%
Hawaii –4.3%
Alaska 4.8%

- ■ –35.0% to –10.0%
- □ –10.0% to 0.0%
- □ 0.0% to 5.0%
- ■ 5.0% to 10.0%

FIGURE 2.3 Four-Quarter Change by State: Purchase-Only Index (Seasonally Adjusted)
Source: Federal Housing Finance Agency news release, May 27, 2009, page 15.

May 2005.[8] The number of subprime mortgages that were more than 60 days behind on their payments was 17.1 percent in June 2007, 18.7 percent in July 2007, and over 20 percent in August 2007.[9] As borrowers had difficulty repaying their existing mortgages, they found it impossible to refinance their existing loans prior to the higher step-up interest rate kicking in. By autumn 2007, the National Association of Realtors was projecting a decline of 24 percent in new home sales and 8.6 percent in existing home sales.[10] Major assumptions underlying credit risk measurement models (i.e., that on default the *loss given default*, or LGD, of mortgages would be relatively low) proved faulty.

First, any model is only as good as its assumptions. The assumption that geographic diversification would protect mortgage portfolios from credit losses was consistent with past experience. The models failed to account for the nationwide (rather than geographically isolated) decline in housing prices. A nationwide housing price decline was an extreme tail event and therefore not considered a plausible scenario, even in value at risk (VAR) models that were supposed to measure unexpected losses at very low levels of probability. Thus, the credit risk measurement models performed badly, in part, because the input assumptions proved to be inaccurate. Exacerbating this effect was the failure of many models to incorporate correlations across assets and across risk exposures, such as correlations across real estate markets. However, Loeffler (2008) shows that if banks had used a simple autoregressive model of housing prices (using the OFHEO index, which dates back to 1975), they would have been able to forecast housing price declines that were even worse than those that actually occurred, suggesting that risk measurement tools, if applied correctly, would have alerted banks to the risk of falling housing prices.[11] Thus, he concludes that either "risk managers failed to apply their [risk measurement] tool boxes, or that bank managers overruled their risk managers' assessments."

That brings us to the second point. Even if the credit risk measurement models had performed better (or had been more widely applied), financial firms were pursuing an originate-to-distribute model in which risk was removed from the balance sheet, such that originating financial intermediaries no longer had the incentive to screen and monitor credit risk exposures. Thus, the most sophisticated players in the market paid no attention to early warning signs since they thought that they had transferred their risk to outside investors. Gorton (2008) notes that while securitization is not the cause of the 2007–2009 financial crisis, the necessary reliance of investors on underwriters' production of information (to avoid costly duplication) can generate panic when external signs (e.g., ABX prices) show that risk has increased, but investors cannot pinpoint the source of that risk. Investors then rationally run from all risky financial investments, generating a flight to quality and a general shutdown in financial markets.[12] As will be discussed later in this chapter, this underwriting failure contributed to the third and most devastating phase of the crisis.

Usually a crisis needs a particular event to trigger it. While in the case of the first phase of the crisis it is hard to point to one such event, some of the earliest credit losses took place during the spring of 2007. The second largest subprime lender, New Century Financial, was hit by a large number of mortgage defaults, and filed for bankruptcy on April 2, 2007, after it was unable to meet its lenders' calls for more collateral on its credit lines. Bear Stearns High-Grade Structured Credit Master Fund (the investment vehicle for four Bear Stearns hedge funds, heavily invested in subprime CMOs, CLOs and CDOs) and Dillon Read Capital Management (DRCM), a subsidiary of UBS, also experienced substantial losses during that spring. Figure 2.4 shows that these events led to the dramatic worldwide increase in spreads on residential mortgage-backed securities (RMBSs) during the summer of 2007, thereby causing the prices of RMBSs to fall throughout the world and global mortgage market activity to grind to a halt. Such a link across highly segmented international residential real estate markets was unanticipated by virtually all credit risk models.

On July 31, 2007, the $20 billion Bear Stearns hedge funds announced that their portfolios were worthless, despite Bear Stearns' provision of backup liquidity in the form of a $3.2 billion line of credit, and filed for bankruptcy. These funds mostly utilized repurchase agreements, rather than commercial paper, to fund their subprime and other ABS securities portfolio. This transmitted the crisis to yet another short-term credit market: the interbank market.

The follow-on effects were substantial. Investors began to lose further confidence in the quality of credit ratings and the rating agencies, especially regarding the quality of the investment-grade-rated tranches of ABS. On October 11, 2007, Moody's downgraded more than 2,000 subprime MBSs with an original value of $33.4 billion.[13] Thus, all other debt issues—from the interbank market to the corporate bond market, including the so-called investment-grade market—were negatively affected by a flight to quality to default-risk-free U.S. government securities. This resulted in falling prices (rising interest rates or *credit spreads*) on privately issued debt securities and rising prices and lower rates on government-issued securities. As noted by the Bank of England, "This fundamental uncertainty about the value of ABS began to cause problems in a wider set of markets. The near closure of primary issuance markets of collateralized loan obligations, and an increase in risk aversion among investors, left banks unable to distribute leveraged loans that they had originated earlier in the year."[14] As a result, credit

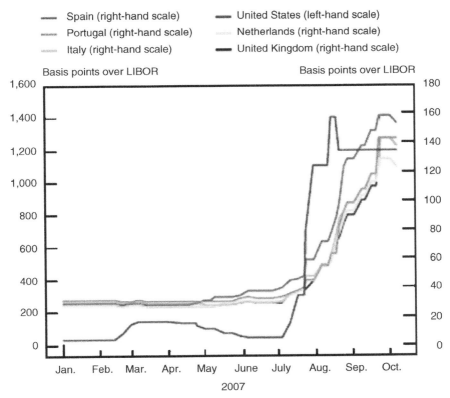

FIGURE 2.4 Residential Mortgage-Backed Securities Spreads
Note: (a) A-rated 5-year spreads over LIBOR except for Spain, which uses 10-year spreads over LIBOR. (b) All countries' data are prime residential mortgage-backed securities except for the United States, which uses home equity loans, which will tend to be of lower quality.
Source: Bank of England, *Financial Stability Report* no. 22, October 2007, page 7.

markets throughout the world suffered from high spreads and drastically curtailed liquidity.

PHASE 2: THE CRISIS SPREADS—LIQUIDITY RISK

Phase 2 of the financial meltdown began during the summer of 2007 when German savings bank IKB and British bank Northern Rock failed.[15] Although both were bailed out by their respective regulatory agencies, the extent of the problems caused by the decline in ABS values caught many investors by surprise and induced a second stage of the crisis—a liquidity crisis. Specifically, in early August 2007, IKB announced that it had exposure of €17.5 billion, or $24 billion, to the U.S. subprime market and stood to lose up to one-fifth of the value of those investments. Moreover, its affiliate, Rhine Funding, could not sell commercial paper to finance those assets. The IKB failure was soon followed by the announcement that Sachsen LB, a bank owned by the German state of Saxony, had received a bailout of €17.3 billion, or $23.3 billion, because of its exposure to the subprime market.

The major U.S. subprime mortgage lender, Countrywide, announced in August that it was drawing down on backup lines of credit because of its growing losses. Ultimately, a liquidity run on Countrywide was stemmed only after a $2 billion equity investment by Bank of America on August 23, 2007. However, a number of other ABCP issuers such as the SIVs also began having difficulty refinancing their short-term commercial paper issues because of investor concerns about the quality of the underlying collateral of subprime mortgages and other assets, despite the purported AA or AAA ratings these issues may have received from the rating agencies.

Investor concerns about credit quality in the subprime mortgage market spread like wildfire throughout the global financial system. Brunnermeier (2009) points out that this contagion was spread across markets by "network effects," since financial institutions are simultaneously borrowers and lenders. If there are concerns about counterparty credit risk, the long and short positions fail to cancel one another out, leading to financial gridlock and the lockdown in financial markets.

The impact of the phase 2 liquidity crisis can be seen in the spread between Aaa-rated corporate bonds and three-month U.S. Treasury bills, shown in Figure 2.5. From January 2007 through April 2007, the spread between Aaa corporates and three-month U.S. Treasury bills averaged 44 basis points. By contrast, this same spread, between May 2007 and October 2007, averaged 129 basis points. During the period from November 2007 to February 2008, the spread between Aaa corporates and three-month U.S. Treasury bills widened to an average of 242 basis points—more than five times the spread during the first quarter of 2007.

This flight to quality impacted other short-term rates as well, as all short-term rates diverged. The spread between three-month commercial paper issued by financial companies and three-month Treasury bills was 28 basis points during January through April 2007, 81 basis points during May through October 2007, and 139 basis points from November 2007 to February 2008. Thus, hedge funds and SIVs issuing ABCP to finance long-term risky asset portfolios, such as RMBSs including subprime mortgages, were caught in a liquidity squeeze on top of the underlying credit quality

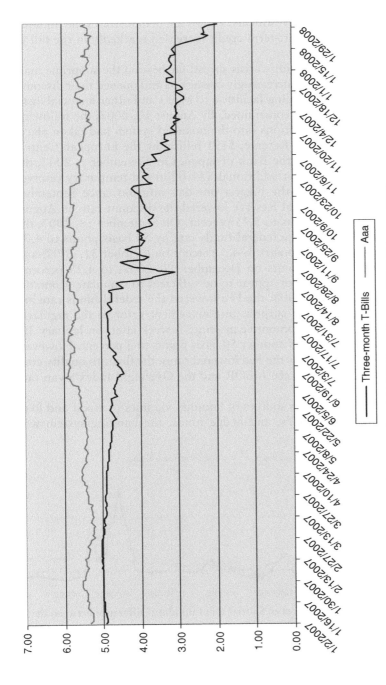

FIGURE 2.5 Aaa Bond Rates and Three-Month U.S. T-Bill Rates, January 2007–February 2008
Source: St. Louis Federal Reserve Bank database, Federal Reserve Economic Data (FRED) web site, http://research.stlouisfed.org/fred2/.

problems posed by those investments. Figure 2.6 demonstrates the liquidity squeeze, as the cost of short-term credit increased markedly in the fall of 2007.[16]

As the scale of the liquidity crisis spread far beyond the subprime market, central banks became increasingly concerned and opened their discount windows (central bank lending facilities) to banks and other financial institutions that were liquidity constrained. By August 10, 2007, the following central bank liquidity injections into the financial system had taken place: $43 billion by the Federal Reserve, $191 billion by the European Central Bank, and $8.4 billion by the Bank of Japan. On November 1, 2007, the Federal Reserve injected an additional $41 billion in temporary reserves into the banking system, the biggest one-day infusion since September 2001.[17] Further, the Federal Reserve lowered the discount rate on August 17, 2007, by 50 basis points to 5.75 percent. On September 18, 2007, the Federal Reserve lowered the federal funds rate by 50 basis points to 4.75 percent; another 25 basis points to 4.5 percent on October 31, 2007; and again another 25 basis points on December 11, 2007, to 4.25 percent. When these rate cuts did not appear to be sufficient to stimulate economic activity, on January 22, 2008, the Fed lowered the federal funds rate another 75 basis points in a surprise announcement prior to the regularly scheduled Open Market Committee meeting. A week later, on January 30, 2008, the Fed lowered rates another 50 basis points to 3 percent. However, as Figure 2.6 shows, even as the Fed lowered rates, the flight to quality continued and the spread between LIBOR and the Overnight Index Swap rate widened further.

As providers of backup sources of liquidity via lines of credit and loan commitments to SPVs, SIVs, and hedge funds, the banking system was

FIGURE 2.6   The Increasing Cost of Short-Term Liquidity: Difference between the LIBOR and the Overnight Index Swap Rate
Source: "Domestic Open Market Operations During 2008," Federal Reserve Bank of New York, Markets Group report, January 2009, Chart 1.

forced to absorb much of the impact of the absence of liquidity in global credit markets. As roll-overs of ABCP met with resistance, the SIVs began to draw down their committed lines of credit with major banks (often their parent banks) to meet their funding needs. Together with the inability of banks to securitize and syndicate their own newly originated lending, this created an unintended expansion of banks' balance sheets. Indeed, one could view this asset warehousing as a first-stage reversion to the traditional banking model, in which the bank holds loans on its books and must therefore obtain financing and capital to fund those investments—in other words, reintermediation.

The Bank of England issued a *Financial Stability Report* in which it estimated that British banks would be forced to absorb an additional £147.4 billion in risk-weighted assets, representing 12 percent of the banks' wholesale lending base. This would crowd out much new lending and stress the capacity constraints of the banking system, just at a time when liquidity risk exposures were climbing. Moreover, it would add to the amount of (expensive) regulatory capital that banks would have to raise as a buffer against the increased risk and size of their balance sheets. Thus, market participants hoarded capital and liquidity and global financial markets shut down during phase 2 of the crisis.[18]

PHASE 3: THE LEHMAN FAILURE—UNDERWRITING AND POLITICAL INTERVENTION RISK

It is usually at the stabilization stage of the financial crisis that the vulture funds, sovereign wealth funds, and workout specialists typically begin to hunt for bargains to purchase securities selling at depressed prices. That is, since financial markets often overshoot during crises and decline more than is warranted by fundamentals, vulture investors usually seek to buy assets at fire sale prices and then work out the problem assets and recoup their investment plus profits.[19] This form of distressed investing was instrumental in lifting financial markets out of previous crises (e.g., the crisis during the summer of 1998 precipitated by the Russian default and the Long Term Capital Management debacle).

This recovery process was halted by the unexpected events of the weekend of September 13–14, 2008—dubbed by the *Wall Street Journal* "the weekend that Wall Street died"—which culminated on September 15 in the bankruptcy of Lehman Brothers, the nationalization of AIG, and the acquisition of Merrill Lynch by the Bank of America (see Craig et al. [2008]). Until then, large financial institutions were thought to be too big to fail (TBTF) because of their importance to the operation of global financial markets. That is, it was widely thought that the government could not afford to let any of the largest banks fail because of the knock-on impact of losses that would ripple through the entire financial system.

Lehman Brothers was widely believed to have an implicit TBTF guarantee, particularly after the government bailout of Bear Stearns in March 2008. Therefore, it came as an enormous shock to financial markets that U.S. regulators did not offer a bailout package to Lehman. The systemic ripple effects were massive—extending to all financial markets. Concerns about haphazard governmental interventions, as evidenced by the apparently inconsistent application of TBTF principles, contributed to the ensuing downturn that we refer to as the third phase of the crisis. During this phase, credit risk and liquidity risk were again exacerbated, so that the third phase of the crisis includes a repeat of both phases 1 and 2. That is, the deterioration in financial and economic conditions triggered a lockdown in financial markets (increased liquidity risk exposure, as shown by widening LIBOR-OIS spreads in Figure 2.6) and an increase in delinquencies (increased credit risk exposure, as shown by increased loan CDS index spreads in Figure 2.7).[20]

On top of the governmental policy risk associated with haphazard and inconsistent application of intervention policies (e.g., the changing objectives of the Troubled Asset Relief Program, TARP, established on

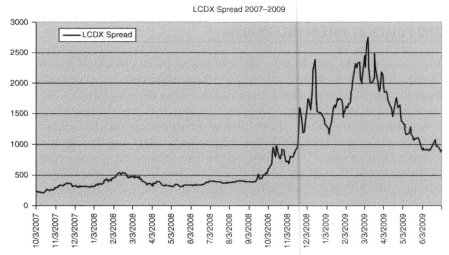

FIGURE 2.7 The Cost of Credit Risk and Loan Index Swap Spreads
The LCDX is a composite of three different indices that were offered consecutively over the time period.
Source: Reuters Loan Pricing Corporation web site, www.loanpricing.com/.

October 3, 2008—see the discussion in Chapter 3), it became apparent that there was something fundamentally unsound in the way that underwriters had implemented the securitizations during the bubble years. It was becoming increasingly clear that vulture capitalists were finding it difficult to recoup their investments in the so-called toxic asset-backed securities because of the complexity and difficulty in valuing many of the distressed assets. Specifically, fundamental structural problems in the underwriting of the MBSs and other toxic securities began to surface. For example, when distressed asset investors attempted to foreclose on the underlying loan collateral, they often found that the underwriters, in their hurry to do the deal and securitize the loans during the boom period, had failed to perfect the liens. They found that some securitizations did not have fundamental identification information about the underlying assets necessary to restructure the securitizations. They also found that in some deals the right to restructure the securities was limited by covenant. That is, in their rush to do the deals during the bubble period, underwriters failed to follow their own due diligence and operational procedures. As noted by Gretchen Morgenson of the *New York Times*:[21]

> [L]*awyers who represent candidates for modifications* [*of MBSs*] *say the programs are hobbled by the complexity of securitization pools that hold the loans, as well as uncertainty about who actually owns the notes underlying the mortgages.*
>
> *Problems often emerge because these notes—which are written promises to repay the full amount of a mortgage—weren't recorded properly when they were bundled by Wall Street into pools or were subsequently transferred to other holders.*
>
> *How can a loan be modified, these lawyers ask, if the lender cannot prove that it actually owns the note? More and more judges are asking the same thing about lenders trying to foreclose on borrowers.*
>
> *And here is another hurdle: Most loan servicers—the folks responsible for handling all the paperwork surrounding monthly mortgage payments—aren't set up to handle all of the details involved in a modification.*

The weekend of September 13–14, 2008, started the process of revelation of the fundamental underwriter risk and governmental policy risk hazards of the financial crisis (e.g., the unanticipated bankruptcy of the venerable investment house Lehman Brothers). This phase, together with the resurgence of liquidity and credit risk problems in the global financial system, was not foreseen. In this third, most intractable phase, fundamental structural, legal, and political features of the toxic assets and financial intermediaries have stressed global financial markets. For example, Gretchen Morgenson states in a March 2009 article:[22]

> [T]he impact of another lax practice is only beginning to be seen. That is the big banks' minimalist approach to meeting legal requirements—bookkeeping matters, really—when pooling thousands of loans into securitization trusts.
>
> Stated simply, the notes that underlie mortgages placed in securitization trusts must be assigned to those trusts soon after the firms create them. And any transfers of these notes must also be recorded.
>
> No one knows how many loans went into securitization trusts with defective documentation. But as messes go, this one has, ahem, potential. According to Inside Mortgage Finance, some eight million nonprime mortgages were put into securities pools in 2005 and 2006 and sold to investors. The value of these loans was $797 billion in 2005 and $815 billion in 2006.
>
> If notes underlying even some of these mortgages were improperly assigned or lost, that will surely complicate pending legislation intended to allow bankruptcy judges to modify mortgage terms for troubled borrowers. . . .
>
> Samuel L. Bufford, a federal bankruptcy judge in Los Angeles since 1985, has overseen some 100,000 bankruptcy cases. He said that in previous years, he rarely asked for documentation in a foreclosure case but that problems encountered in mortgage securitization have made him become more demanding. . . .
>
> "My guess is it's because in the secondary mortgage market they have been sloppy," Judge Bufford added. "The people who put the deals together get paid for the deal, but they don't get paid for the paperwork."

These fundamental operational problems made investors leery about purchasing ABSs even at fire sale prices for fear that underwriting lapses will prevent them from restructuring the securities and earning a return on their investment. The original investors in the ABSs had no way to determine whether underwriters of ABSs performed their jobs diligently. The nature of ABSs is their lack of transparency. Investors in ABSs rely on underwriters to follow well-established rules and procedures for the construction of the securities. However, a breakdown in incentives led banks to ignore their own standards. Improper documentation and legal follow-through resulted in a failure to clearly assign property rights in these toxic ABSs, which currently prevents the resurgence of the securitization market. As of the beginning of 2010, banks are still holding on to these operationally-flawed assets as lawsuits attempt to sort out the tangles. However, during this long, drawn-out process, the unavailability of the securitization outlet makes banks reluctant to originate new loans, thereby preventing a full economic recovery.

The third phase of the 2007–2009 crisis is unprecedented in the recent history of financial markets. The extent of this stage is demonstrated in dramatic increases in market volatility. Figure 2.8 shows that during the third phase of the crisis (after September 2008), the Chicago Board Options Exchange (CBOE) Volatility Index (VIX) rose to heights unseen since the index's introduction in January 1990. The VIX is known as the "investor fear gauge."[23] The higher the index, the more fear in the market, and the extraordinarily high current level of the VIX during the third phase of the crisis indicates unprecedented levels of fear and uncertainty. Figure 2.8 shows that the VIX did not reach current heights during earlier crises—for example, during either the 1998 Long Term Capital Management/Russian government default crisis, or the bursting of the high-tech bubble in March 2000, or in the aftermath of 9/11. The fear in the market during phase 3 of the crisis was almost double the level seen during the worst previous crisis since the introduction of the index in 1990, indicating that current financial conditions were far more precarious than in past crises.

The unprecedented nature of the 2007–2009 financial crisis in recent times is also illustrated by the Kansas City Financial Stress Index (KCFSI) shown in Figure 2.9.[24] The 11 component variables in the KCFSI are: the three-month LIBOR/three-month Treasury bill (TED) spread; the two-year (fixed for floating rate) swap spread; the off-the-run/on-the-run 10-year benchmark Treasury spread; the Aaa/10-year Treasury spread; the Baa/Aaa spread; the high-yield bond/BBB spread; the consumer ABS/5-year Treasury spread; the correlation between the S&P 500 stock index and 2-year Treasury bond returns; the CBOE VIX; the idiosyncratic volatility of bank stock prices (measured as the standard deviation of the deviation between daily bank stock index values and the S&P 500 Index over a monthly period); and a cross-section dispersion of bank stock returns (the interquartile range of unexpected returns, relative to the S&P 500, of the 100 largest commercial banks).[25] The KCFSI indicated substantially higher levels of financial stress during the 2007–2009 crisis, as compared with all earlier crises during the 1990–2006 period. Moreover, Figure 2.10 shows how each of the

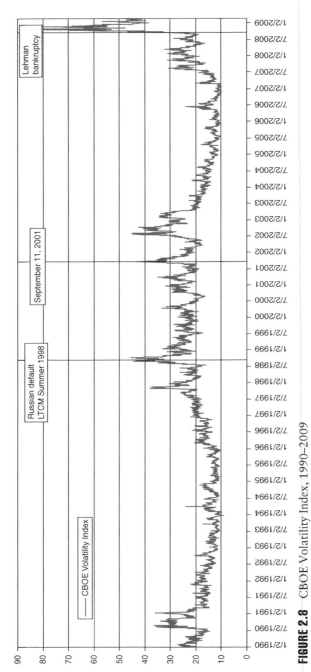

FIGURE 2.8 CBOE Volatility Index, 1990–2009

Source: Yahoo! Finance.

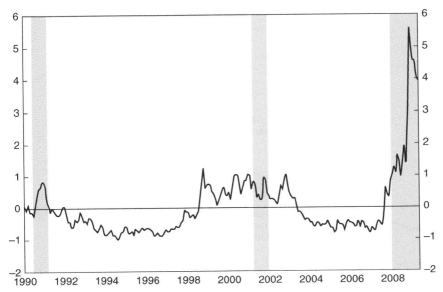

FIGURE 2.9 Kansas City Financial Stress Index (KCFSI)
Note: Index is calculated using data from February 1990 to March 2009. Shaded areas are recessions.
Source: C. S. Hakkio and W. R. Keeton, "Financial Stress: What Is It, How Can It Be Measured, and Why Does It Matter?" Federal Reserve Bank of Kansas City, *Economic Review*, Second Quarter 2009, Chart 1, page 21.

events in the unfolding of the crisis from 2007 to 2009 contributed to the level of financial stress in the economy.

SUMMARY

The economy relies on financial institutions to act as specialists in risk measurement and risk management. The importance of this was demonstrated in the aftermath of the banks' failure to perform this critical function during the global financial crisis, which resulted in the worldwide breakdown in credit markets, as well as an enhanced level of equity market volatility. When banks fail to perform their critical risk measurement and risk management functions, the result is a crisis of confidence that disrupts financial markets. Even interbank short-term credit markets may seize up, with banks unwilling to lend to each other because of uncertainty about their own and their competitors' precarious financial condition. This hoarding of

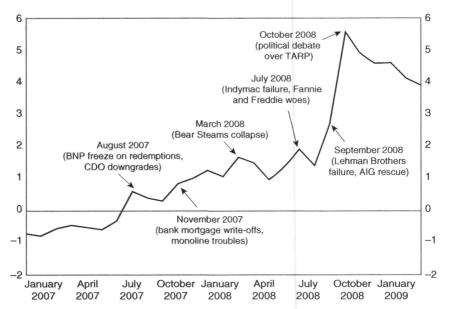

FIGURE 2.10 Kansas City Financial Stress Index 2007–2009
Note: Index is calculated using data from February 1990 to March 2009.
Source: C. S. Hakkio and W. R. Keeton, "Financial Stress: What Is It, How Can It Be Measured, and Why Does It Matter?" Federal Reserve Bank of Kansas City, *Economic Review*, Second Quarter 2009, Chart 3, page 26.

liquidity prevents banks from providing the fundamental credit required to keep the financial system working.

In this chapter, we identified three phases to the financial crisis. Phase 1 was a credit crisis, centered on delinquencies in mortgage-backed securities and related instruments. Phase 2 was a liquidity crisis in which even short-term money markets ceased to function because of the hoarding of liquidity by financial institutions unwilling to lend to one another even in the overnight interbank market. Phase 3 was induced by the failure of Lehman, demonstrating an inconsistent and haphazard application of government intervention policies, as well as evidence of shoddy underwriting and lack of due diligence that hampers the working out and restructuring of the toxic assets to this date.

In Chapter 3, we discuss policies undertaken to alleviate the crisis and restructure the global financial architecture so as to prevent recurrence.

CHAPTER 3

The Crisis and Regulatory Failure

INTRODUCTION

One fundamental lesson of the 2007–2009 crisis is that when financial institutions fail to perform their risk management functions, then financial markets and the real economy are adversely impacted. And when financial markets freeze, the government is left as the ultimate provider of liquidity and credit to the economy. In this chapter, we discuss the regulatory and governmental responses to ameliorate the crisis, as well as proposals for restructuring of the financial system so as to prevent the recurrence of similar crises in the future. International bank capital requirements, known as the Basel Accord, are described at length in Chapter 13.

CRISIS INTERVENTION

The U.S. Federal Reserve was extensively involved in seeking remedies for the economic crisis, augmenting its easy-money policy (put in place during the summer of 2007) with expansions in the safety net made available to nonbank financial institutions.[1] One of the key components of the Fed's safety net is the lender of last resort privilege. This enables banks to meet their short-term, nonpermanent liquidity needs by borrowing directly from the central bank—at the discount window.

Historically, primary credit at the discount window in the United States was available to healthy banks for short periods up to a few weeks to meet temporary liquidity needs. Secondary credit was available to troubled banks, but only for a short period of time until the institution returned to market sources of funds. Any bank that used the discount window, however, had to pledge "high-quality liquid assets" as collateral. Indeed, the

Fed specifies that "The Reserve Banks will consider accepting as discount window collateral any assets that meet regulatory standards for sound asset quality."[2] This includes government obligations and AAA-rated asset-backed securities. Depending on the security, the Federal Reserve assesses haircuts of between 2 and 40 percent, thereby reducing the collateral valuations to between 60 and 98 percent of market value.

However, in response to the financial crisis of 2007–2009, the Federal Reserve Bank, together with the U.S. Treasury, the Federal Deposit Insurance Corporation (FDIC), and other national banks throughout the world, announced a series of unprecedented programs, which are listed in Table 3.1.[3] For example, on December 12, 2007, the Federal Reserve announced a new Term Auction Facility (TAF) which provided term loans to depository institutions against a wide array of collateral previously deemed unacceptable as collateral against discount window borrowing. The initial auction injected $20 billion of 28-day funds into the U.S. banking system. The impact of these programs is shown in Figure 3.1 by the dramatic increase in liquidity injected into the system by the Federal Reserve.

TABLE 3.1 Unprecedented Crisis Intervention Programs from the Federal Reserve, U.S. Treasury, and the FDIC

Inception Date	Program Name	Description
8/17/2007	Term Discount Window	Banks get 90-day financing using broad collateral rather than overnight discount window loans.
12/12/2007	Term Auction Facility (TAF)	Banks bid on 28- or 84-day financing.
3/7/2008	Term Repo Operations	Offers 28-day repos to primary dealers using open market operations securities collateral.
3/11/2008	Term Securities Lending Facility (TSLF)	Offers 28-day lending of non-Treasury securities to finance investments.
3/17/2008	Primary Dealer Credit Facility (PDCF)	Discount window for primary dealers, but only overnight loans and investment-grade securities as collateral.
9/17/2008	Supplementary Financing Program (SFP)	Off-cycle T-bill program to issue T-bills and drain liquidity without selling securities.

TABLE 3.1 (Continued)

Inception Date	Program Name	Description
9/19/2008	Asset-Backed Commercial Paper Money Market Fund Liquidity Facility (AMLF)	Discount rate funding to buy asset-backed commercial paper from money market funds.
9/19/2008	Guarantee Program for Money Market Funds	FDIC-like insurance to certain money market funds for balance as of 9/19/08.
10/3/2008	Troubled Asset Relief Program (TARP)	Originally to purchase $700 billion of ABS contracts, then used for capital injection into large banks.
10/14/2008	Commercial Paper Funding Facility (CPFF)	Federally funded SIV to act as buyer of last resort for commercial paper issues.
10/14/2008	Temporary Liquidity Guarantee Program by the FDIC	Fully insures non-interest-bearing accounts and government guarantees newly issued bank debt; raised deposit insurance to $250,000.
11/25/2008	Term Asset-Backed Securities Loan Facility (TALF)	Fed will lend up to $200 billion on a nonrecourse basis to holders of certain AAA-rated ABSs backed by newly issued consumer and small business loans.
2/25/2009	Capital Assistance Program (CAP)	Government-provided capital as a bridge to private capital for banks that failed the stress test (see Chapter 10).
3/23/2009	Public-Private Investment Program (PPIP)	Government-financed private purchases of legacy loans and toxic assets.

Note: In addition to these crisis intervention programs, the Treasury, Fannie Mae, and Freddie Mac initiated several homeowner relief plans to assist responsible homeowners in avoiding foreclosure through loan modification.

These actions were coordinated with other central banks throughout the world. For example, on December 12, 2007, the Bank of England announced the expansion of its long-term (3-month through 12-month terms) open market repo operations, increasing the amount of funds available from £2.85 billion to £11.35 billion and widening the range of acceptable collateral. When the crisis intensified during the first months of 2008, on

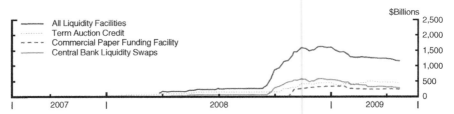

FIGURE 3.1   Credit Extended through Federal Reserve Bank Liquidity Faculties
Source: www.federalreserve.gov/monetarypolicy/bst.htm.

March 11, around the same time that it arranged the acquisition of Bear Stearns by JPMorgan Chase, the Federal Reserve established the Term Securities Lending Facility (TSLF), which extended $200 billion of credit to nondepository institutions (primary dealers) via access to the discount window for loans with terms of up to 28 days (rather than overnight). Moreover, on March 14, 2008, the Fed authorized JPMorgan Chase to borrow on behalf of Bear Stearns, a nonbanking firm that previously had no discount window privileges.

However, in September 2008, after the failure of Lehman Brothers and the bailout of AIG, together with the sale of Merrill Lynch to Bank of America (discussed in Chapter 2 as part of phase 3 of the crisis), it became clear to U.S. policy makers that a more comprehensive plan was required. On October 14, 2008, the FDIC temporarily (through December 31, 2013) increased deposit insurance coverage from $100,000 to $250,000 per depositor under the Temporary Liquidity Guarantee Program. In addition, the Emergency Economic Stabilization Act (EESA) was passed by Congress on October 3, 2008. Its major feature was the creation of a $700 billion Troubled Asset Relief Program (TARP). The initial objective was to repurchase illiquid securities from the banks in order to enable them to resume lending and other normal banking functions. However, the Treasury had not prepared a plan to identify the fair market price of these assets so as to determine which assets should be included in the plan, although there was some discussion about using a reverse auction in which the banks would specify reservation prices for their securities. Indeed, it was not until March 2009 (and the introduction of the Public-Private Investment Program (PPIP, discussed later in this chapter), that the government announced a two-pronged plan to purchase troubled mortgages and ABSs from bank balance sheets.[4]

Largely in response to the slow start of TARP in the United States, the Treasury announced on October 14, 2008, that instead of buying troubled assets, it would directly recapitalize banks by purchasing up to $250 billion in senior preferred shares in troubled banks; in other words, it switched from a plan of troubled asset repurchases to that of direct equity investment. The maximum subscription amount for each bank was the lesser of $25 billion or 3 percent of risk-weighted assets. The senior preferred shares qualified as Tier 1 capital and carried a cumulative dividend rate of 5 percent annually for the first five years and 9 percent after the fifth year. However, since the shares were nonvoting, the U.S. Treasury did not impose any governance changes on the banks, with the exception of the rules written into the Congressional EESA that restricted executive compensation by allowing clawbacks, prohibiting golden parachutes, and instituting a tax deduction limit for all compensation levels above $500,000.[5]

As the government safety net expanded and as additional firms became financially distressed, there was a structural shift that will impact the financial industry far into the future: principally the shift by the two main remaining independent investment banks, Goldman Sachs and Morgan Stanley, toward adopting a bank holding company (BHC) charter. In September 2008, as the stand-alone investment company model looked increasingly unstable, both switched to a BHC charter with the rapid approval of the Fed. In November 2008, American Express joined them. Even General Motors (via its financing arm, GMAC) adopted a BHC designation in order to obtain access to the financial support associated with bailout policies and the banking safety net provided by the government.

The Obama administration introduced two new crisis intervention plans, as well as a restructuring plan called the Obama-Geithner Plan, which is described in the next section. Table 3.1 shows that the two new crisis intervention plans were the Capital Assistance Plan (CAP) and the Public-Private Investment Program (PPIP). We will describe the CAP in Chapter 10 (where we discuss stress testing). The $1 trillion PPIP initially contained two components: (1) government-financed purchases of toxic bank loans, dubbed *legacy loans*; and (2) provision of low-cost government financing to private investors (e.g., hedge funds) to buy troubled asset-backed securities (*legacy securities*) from the banks. The legacy loan portion of the program required private investors to contribute $6 for every $100 face value of loans purchased. To value these loans, the FDIC would conduct an auction. Suppose that the price were $84. Out of this purchase price, the FDIC would guarantee $72 of financing, the Treasury would provide $6, and the private investor would provide $6. Thus, the effective private sector leverage was 14 to 1 (or 84/6). The legacy securities portion of the program entails the approval of up to five asset managers "with a demonstrated track record of purchasing legacy securities." The government would provide a dollar-for-dollar match for all capital invested in the program by the private asset managers. The

Treasury also planned to lend to the PPIP, such that for every $100 invested by the private sector, the government contribution could be as high as $300. Despite the 3:1 government to private investment ratio, the proceeds of the investment were to be shared equally between the public and private sector.

Despite these incredibly generous terms, the PPIP was viewed with suspicion by banks and other financial firms from its introduction. Asset managers were concerned about participating because of the furor about executive compensation plans that led President Obama to propose capping executive pay at all financial firms that participate in bailout plans. Moreover, the banks themselves were concerned about selling loans and securities at fire sale prices, thereby causing them to take additional write-downs and further impairing their capital. Indeed, some banks expressed interest in bidding on their own toxic loans using government financing under the PPIP legacy loans program, but the FDIC prohibited this.[6] Therefore, because of lack of participation on both the investor (buyer) and bank (seller) side, the FDIC shelved the legacy loan portion of the PPIP in June 2009. The legacy securities portion of the program, although still formally in place, has not been implemented as of this writing. Therefore, the toxic assets still remain on the banks' balance sheets.[7]

In contrast, the toxic assets held by U.S. savings and loan associations were efficiently resolved by the Resolution Trust Corporation (RTC), created in 1989 to address the thrift crisis of the 1980s, which at the time represented the greatest collapse of financial institutions in the United States since the 1930s. Ultimately, the RTC took possession of 747 thrifts with total assets of $394 billion.[8] The ultimate total cost of the thrift cleanup was $152.9 billion, with the U.S. taxpayer bearing 81 percent of the total resolution costs from 1986 to 1995, suggesting a recovery rate of over 70 percent (based on $519 billion in total thrift assets resolved; see Curry and Shibut [2000]). As will be discussed in Chapter 7, this represents an acceptable recovery rate on bank loans.

In addition to the programs listed in Table 3.1, the U.S. government introduced several programs designed to encourage lenders to modify the terms of mortgages so as to avoid foreclosure, including President Obama's Making Home Affordable program introduced in March 2009. The program offers incentives to change mortgage terms by providing $1,000 for each modified loan. The Office of the Comptroller of the Currency (OCC) and Office of Thrift Supervision (OTS) suggest that the program had little immediate impact on mortgage foreclosures, reporting that delinquencies and foreclosures continued to increase during the first quarter of 2009, although the number of loan modifications increased 55 percent from the previous quarter (OCC [2009]).

However, Professor Alan White (2008) examined data on 3.5 million subprime and Alt-A mortgages (see the discussion in Chapter 1) in Wells Fargo's securitization pools that were originated during 2005 through 2007, and found that

> . . . *while the number of modifications rose rapidly during the crisis, mortgage modifications in the aggregate are not reducing subprime mortgage debt. Mortgage modifications rarely, if ever, reduced principal debt and in many cases increased debt. Nor are modification agreements uniformly reducing payment burdens on households. About half of all loan modifications resulted in reduced monthly payments, while many modifications actually increased the monthly payment.*

Moreover, Figure 3.2 shows that the most important explanation for mortgage foreclosures is negative equity or loan principal in excess of the house market value. That is, the absence of proper incentives on the part of both borrowers and lenders explains the high delinquency and foreclosure rate during the crisis. Thus, it is unclear whether the number of loan modifications is the proper metric for judging the efficacy of programs to resolve the foreclosure crisis.

No Skin in the Game

Causes of mortgage foreclosures, second half of 2008

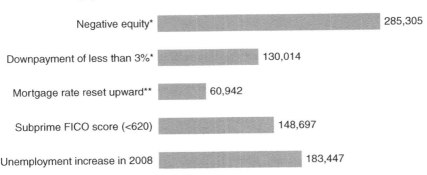

*Factors based on equity.

**Complex subprime products.

FIGURE 3.2 Causes of Mortgage Foreclosures, second half of 2008
Source: S. Liebowitz, "New Evidence on the Foreclosure Crisis," *Wall Street Journal,* July 3, 2009, A13.

LOOKING FORWARD: RESTRUCTURING PLANS

Every crisis spawns proposals for reform, and this one has been no exception. This section cannot comprehensively cover all of the proposals considered, but rather selectively surveys several prominent plans proposed during the crisis. The Paulson blueprint was publicized in March 2008, followed by the Senior Supervisors Group Plan. A year later, in March 2009, the Obama-Geithner Plan was proposed. This section outlines these proposals.

The Paulson 2008 Blueprint

As the crisis has unfolded, it has become increasingly clear that the financial system regulation needs to be restructured and that the 1999 Financial Services Modernization Act (also known as the GLB Act—see the discussion in Chapter 1) has failed to deliver a more efficient, profitable, and, most importantly, sound financial system. In March 2008, the Treasury published the first major proposal for the restructuring of the U.S. financial system (see Paulson et al. [2008], hereafter referred to as the Paulson blueprint) in order to propose a new system of regulation and supervision. The focus was to allow financial institutions to engage in a complex and comprehensive set of financial activities, but to eliminate the confusing net of regulatory oversight that was largely an artifact of historically separate chartering (banks, investment firms, insurance companies, and so on.). The Paulson plan considered three stages of reform: short-term, medium-term, and long-term, which are discussed next.

Short-Term Crisis-Related Recommendations   The Paulson blueprint provided three areas of response to the financial crisis: (1) Revamp the President's Working Group (PWG) on Financial Markets, (2) formulate a Mortgage Origination Commission (MOC); and (3) broaden access to liquidity and funding, by expanding discount window access to nondepository institutions. The PWG was established in the wake of the 1987 stock market crash, and consists of representatives from the Treasury Department, the Federal Reserve, the SEC, and the Commodity Futures Trading Commission (CFTC). The Paulson blueprint advocated expanding membership to include representatives of the FDIC, the OTS, and the OCC. The objective of the PWG should be to "facilitate better inter-agency coordination and communication in four distinct areas: mitigating systemic risk to the financial system, enhancing financial market integrity, promoting consumer and investor protection, and supporting capital markets efficiency and competitiveness" (Paulson, 2008, 6).

Directly related to the crisis were recommendations regarding the mortgage market and gaps in oversight of mortgage origination. The plan advocated the creation of an interagency committee composed of representatives of the Federal Reserve, the OCC, the OTS, the FDIC, the National Credit Union Administration, and the Conference of State Bank Supervisors, which would develop uniform licensing requirements for mortgage originators that focus on personal integrity, educational requirements, testing criteria, and license revocation procedures. The Paulson blueprint also called for clarification of oversight responsibility for all mortgage originators, whether they are affiliates of banks or stand-alone entities.

Medium-Term Regulatory Restructuring Recommendations The Paulson blueprint provided additional recommendations to improve the efficacy of financial regulation in the medium-term. One suggestion was to eliminate the thrift charter. Another was to transfer supervision of state-chartered banks to a federal regulator, such as the Federal Reserve or the FDIC, in order to eliminate the dual banking system of federal and state charters. According to the plan, a federal charter should be established for payment and settlement systems that settle transactions in both large value and retail claims, so as to minimize the systemic consequences of payment system failure.

The market for insurance has become national and indeed global since the passage in the 1940s of the McCarran-Ferguson Act, which specified that insurance companies be regulated at the state level. Consequently, the Paulson blueprint recommends the establishment of an optional federal charter for insurance companies to specify the lines of insurance each nationally regulated company could sell. The Office of National Insurance (ONI), situated within the Treasury Department, would oversee the industry to maintain safety and soundness, enhance competition in national and international markets, and increase market efficiency. To modernize the regulation of the insurance industry, the Paulson blueprint advocated the Congressional creation of an Office of Insurance Oversight (OIO).

The bifurcation between futures and securities regulation is no longer relevant in today's interrelated markets, especially given the gray area as to what is called a derivative and what is a security. The Paulson blueprint suggested the merging of the SEC and the CFTC. However, to preserve the CFTC's "principles-based regulatory philosophy," the plan stated that the SEC should be updated and streamlined in order to expedite the rule-making process to keep up with financial innovation and harmonize regulations across markets. Indeed, the Madoff $65 billion Ponzi scheme and other scandals and the failures of SEC oversight have propelled the need to reform securities regulation to the short term. The Paulson blueprint, furthermore, embraced self-regulatory organizations for the oversight of broker-dealers and investment advisers, and for setting trading rules particularly in over-the-counter markets.

Long-Term Suggestions for an Optimal Supervisory Framework   The Paulson blueprint views the functional system of regulation with separate charters and regulatory agencies for banking, insurance, securities, and futures to be outdated, duplicative, and inefficient. In its place, the Paulson blueprint advocates an "objectives-based" regulatory approach revolving around three regulatory objectives: (1) market stability regulation dealing with the overall systemic condition of financial markets and the impact on the econ-omy, to be performed by the Federal Reserve; (2) safety and soundness pru-dential regulation "to address issues of limited market discipline caused by government guarantees," performed by a newly created Prudential Finan-cial Regulatory Agency (PFRA); and (3) business conduct regulation to promote consumer protection and supervision of business practices, to be covered by the newly established Conduct of Business Regulatory Agency (CBRA) (Paulson [2008], 14).

Parallel to the three objectives-driven supervisory agencies would be three federal charters for financial institutions (FIs). Depository institutions with FDIC insurance would receive a federal insured depository institution (FIDI) charter. Insurers selling retail products with some form of a govern-ment guarantee would receive a federal insurance institution (FII) charter. All other types of FIs would receive a federal financial services provider (FFSP) charter. The FDIC would be reconstituted as the Federal Insurance Guarantee Corporation (FIGC), with responsibility for the Federal Insur-ance Guarantee Fund (FIGF). Finally, a new Corporate Finance Regulator would be formed to manage disclosure, corporate governance, accounting issues, and so on. Figure 3.3 shows the outline of the Paulson plan for objec-tive-based regulation. A glance at the interlocking responsibilities (shown by the arrows) across this array of regulatory agencies demonstrates that the Paulson plan is hardly less complicated than the existing regulatory structure.

Too Big and Too Many to Fail   An issue that was not fully addressed in the Paulson proposal was the moral hazard induced by *too big to fail* (TBTF) privileges in the system. As the crisis intensified, a two-class system devel-oped. Large institutions—regardless of charter—such as AIG, Fannie Mae, and Freddie Mac, were TBTF and received bailout funds from the govern-ment. In contrast, Lehman was allowed to fail, although the detrimental effects of that decision led to clear adverse systemic impact and, to a certain extent, initiated the third phase of the current crisis (see Chapter 2).

Treasury Proposals: Regulation by Objectives

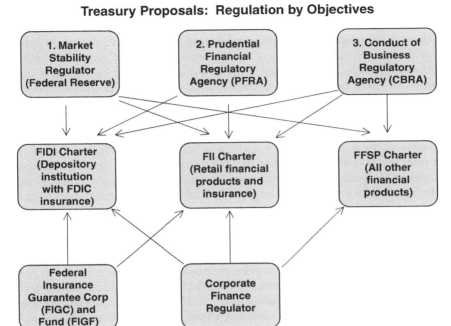

FIGURE 3.3 Paulson Plan

The problem with TBTF is that it creates perverse incentives that exacerbate systemic risk in the long term. It is no accident that the banking system in the United States has been consolidating at a rapid pace in the wake of the crisis. For example, Wells Fargo's purchase of Wachovia, JPMorgan Chase's purchases of Bear Stearns and Washington Mutual, and Bank of America's purchase of Merrill Lynch are likely to impose further systemic risk exposure on the financial system, as more institutions fall under the TBTF umbrella. Consolidation exacerbates the systemic consequences of future cyclical downturns, thereby making government bailouts more likely and incentivizing FIs to take on riskier positions. These perverse incentives result in a banking system with a "heads, I win; tails, you lose" contest. When risk shifting pays off, the bank's shareholders gain, but when they fail, the government bails the institution out.

The current system of bank regulation must be designed to limit bank risk taking in order to mitigate systemic risk as well as individual FI failure. The most important component of the regulatory restrictions designed to limit excessive risk taking are the capital requirements that limit the bank's leverage and relate the required capital cushion to the individual bank's risk exposure (see also the discussion of Basel capital requirements in Chapter 13). Acharya (2000) notes, however, that this emphasis on the individual bank in the formulation and implementation of capital requirements may have the unintended consequence of increasing systemic risk. Individual banks have the incentive to ignore the externality of their behavior on the payoffs of other banks in the system and to undertake correlated investments (*herding behavior*) that exacerbate systemic risk. In addition, Acharya and Yorulmazer (2005) and Brown and Dinc (2007) show that the *too many to fail* (TMTF) phenomenon also exists in many countries throughout the world. When the number of failed banks is large, the regulator may find it optimal ex post to bail out all of the banks, thereby creating incentives for banks to herd, increasing systemic risk exposure. Thus, while only large banks are impacted by the TBTF phenomenon, even small banks may respond to the TMTF incentives.

In order to mitigate these perverse incentives, Acharya (2000) advocates "collective" regulatory policies that are a function of the joint failure of banks, rather than individual banks' failure probabilities. In this vein, a systemic risk bank surcharge has been proposed that would be added to the deposit insurance premium and or be reflected in an additional capital charge for potential systemic risk causation. This surcharge would increase in good times and with the systemic risk exposure of each financial intermediary, thereby providing self-insurance for the banking industry in the event of a systemic crisis. The surcharge would be higher the larger the bank (more likely to be TBTF) and the more correlated its risks are to other banks in the system (TMTF). Priced properly, this surcharge could mitigate some of the systemic risk stemming from the unintended negative herding consequences engendered by capital regulation.[9] This type of ex ante systemic-risk-based pricing of insurance guarantees or bank capital requirements appears to be missing in the Paulson plan.

The Senior Supervisors Group (SSG) Plan

In March 2008, seven major financial regulators (the U.S. Federal Reserve Bank, the U.S. Securities and Exchange Commission, the U.S. Office of the Comptroller of the Currency, the U.K. Financial Services Authority, the Swiss Federal Banking Commission, the Banque de France Banking Commission, and the German Federal Financial Supervisory Authority) released a report describing their deliberations on a plan for reform. Their recommendations for improved risk modeling centered on implementation of the Basel II Accord, will be described in Chapter 13. However, they also called for liquidity risk management, enhanced prudential supervision, and greater disclosure and transparency.

This Senior Supervisors Group (SSG) identified four risk measurement and management shortcomings that hampered a bank's ability to withstand the current crisis: (1) lack of effective firmwide risk identification and analysis; (2) inconsistent application of rigorous and independent valuation models throughout the financial institution; (3) ineffective management of funding liquidity, capital, and the balance sheet; and (4) gaps in informative and responsive risk management practices and reporting. These four factors highlight the importance of communication within a financial institution to identify risk exposures and hedge effectively at the firm level. The SSG stressed the importance of independent assumptions built into rigorous models, rather than the bank's reliance on external credit ratings.

They concluded that financial firms should have control over balance sheet growth and liquidity needs, as well as potential off-balance-sheet risks. Moreover, the better-performing financial intermediaries had more flexible risk measurement models with "more adaptive (rather than static) risk measurement processes and systems that could rapidly alter underlying assumptions in risk measures to reflect . . . management's best sense of changing market conditions" (SSG [2008], 4). Poorly performing financial firms failed to incorporate correlations and potential basis risk between cash instruments and securitizations or derivatives into their analysis. The SSG concluded that the contingent liquidity risk associated with off-balance-sheet entities (such as SIVs) and securitization pipelines (such as leveraged syndicated bank loans and subprime mortgages) were underestimated during the buildup period leading to the crisis.

The SSG responded to these observations by calling for a program for stronger supervisory oversight covering four proposals:

1. Strengthen the "efficacy and robustness of the Basel II capital framework by . . . enhanc[ing] the incentives for firms to develop more forward-looking approaches to risk measures . . . and set[ting] sufficiently high standards for what constitutes risk transfer. . . . "
2. Manage liquidity risk.
3. "Review and strengthen, as appropriate, existing guidance on risk management practices, valuation practices, and the controls over both."
4. Facilitate interaction among regulators, market participants and "other key players (such as accountants)" to improve public disclosure.

The 2009 Obama-Geithner Plan

On March 26, 2009, Treasury Secretary Timothy Geithner announced an initial outline of a new regulatory plan to restructure the financial system to prevent future crises:

To address these failures will require comprehensive reform—not modest repairs at the margin, but new rules of the road. The new rules must be simpler and more effectively enforced and produce a more stable system, that protects consumers and investors, that rewards innovation and that is able to adapt and evolve with changes.[10]

And in the press release relating to the Obama administration's proposed reforms:

The President's comprehensive regulatory reform is aimed at reforming and modernizing our financial regulatory system for the 21st *century, providing stronger tools to prevent and manage future crises, and rebuilding confidence in the basic integrity of our financial system—for sophisticated investors and working families with 401(k)s alike.*[11]

The Plan involves four broad components:

1. Addressing Systemic Risk: *This crisis—and the cases of firms like Lehman Brothers and AIG—has made clear that certain large, interconnected firms and markets need to be under a more consistent and more conservative regulatory regime. It is not enough to address the potential insolvency of individual institutions— we must also ensure the stability of the system itself.*
2. Protecting Consumers and Investors: *It is crucial that when households make choices to invest their savings we have clear rules of the road that prevent manipulation and abuse. While outright fraud like that perpetrated by Bernie Madoff is already illegal, these cases highlight the need to strengthen enforcement and improve transparency for all investors. Lax regulation also left too many households exposed to deception and abuse when taking out home mortgage loans. [This would include oversight to prevent predatory lending practices.]*
3. Eliminating Gaps in Our Regulatory Structure: *Our regulatory structure must assign clear authority, resources, and accountability for each of its key functions. We must not let turf wars or concerns about the shape of organizational charts prevent us from establishing a substantive system of regulation that meets the needs of the American people.*
4. Fostering International Coordination: *To keep pace with increasingly global markets, we must ensure that international*

*rules for financial regulation are consistent with the high stan-
dards we will be implementing in the United States. Additionally, we will launch a new, three-pronged initiative to address
prudential supervision, tax havens, and money laundering
issues in weakly-regulated jurisdictions.*

Specific proposals were offered in five key areas:

1. Promote robust supervision and regulation of financial firms.
2. Establish comprehensive regulation of financial markets.
3. Protect consumers and investors from financial abuse.
4. Provide the government with the tools it needs to manage financial
   crises.
5. Raise international regulatory standards and improve regulatory
   cooperation.

In this section, we discuss the five key areas of the Obama-Geithner
Plan, as well as industry, political, and public reactions.

Promote Robust Supervision and Regulation of Financial Firms   To achieve this
objective the Obama-Geithner Plan proposes the creation of a new Financial Services Oversight Council. This agency would "facilitate information
sharing and coordination, identify emerging risks, advise the Federal Reserve on the identification of firms whose failure could pose a threat to
financial stability . . . and provide a forum for resolving jurisdictional dis-
putes between regulators."[12] Membership includes the Secretary of the
Treasury, the Chairman of the Board of Governors of the Fed, the Director
of the National Bank Supervisor, the Director of the Consumer Financial
Protection Agency (to be formulated under the Plan—see discussion in
the next section), the Chairman of the SEC, the Chairman of the CFTC, the
Chairman of the FDIC, and the Director of the Federal Housing Finance
Agency, supported by a permanent staff situated in the Department of
the Treasury. Public criticism has centered on fears of injecting political
considerations into what should be an apolitical process to conduct monetary policy and banking supervision. However, there is recognition that systemic risk must be better measured and controlled in the system.

Another part of this portion of the Obama-Geithner Plan would be to
empower the Federal Reserve to supervise on a consolidated basis systemically important (due to size, leverage, and/or interconnectedness) financial
holding companies (FHCs) that are considered to be too big to fail. This
would include nonbank financial firms and even unregulated or foreign subsidiaries of FHCs (see Chapter 1) with potential impact on the stability of

the financial system, and would replace the SEC's Consolidated Supervised Entity Program, which would be eliminated. This portion of the proposal has been quite controversial because of concerns of overconcentration of power within the Federal Reserve System.[13]

The Plan envisions the creation of a Treasury working group to study ways to strengthen capital requirements and address the poor incentives induced by executive compensation plans that reward short-term performance without consideration of long-term or risk-based consequences. Part of the capital reforms would be to change accounting standards so as to employ more forward-looking loan loss provisioning standards. Legislation was encouraged that would make compensation committees more independent of management.

To close the loopholes in banking supervision, a new federal agency, the National Bank Supervisor, would be created to conduct prudential oversight for all federally chartered depository institutions. The federal thrift charter would be eliminated. The separation of banking from commerce would be "re-affirmed and strengthened" (Obama-Geithner Plan [2009], 12). Market reaction has expressed concerns about the creation of yet another regulatory structure.

The regulatory umbrella would be extended to cover hedge funds, insurance companies, money market mutual funds, and government-sponsored enterprises (GSEs) such as Fannie Mae and Freddie Mac. The proposal calls for study to determine how these entities can be made more stable and less susceptible to runs and excessive risk taking. For example, the SEC is instructed to investigate methods (such as requiring liquidity buffers, requiring maximum weighted-average maturities of assets, tightening credit concentration limits, allowing redemption suspension, etc.) in order to stabilize the net asset value of money market mutual funds and control the risk of breaking-the-buck par valuation.

Establish Comprehensive Regulation of Financial Markets All over-the-counter (OTC) derivatives would be subject to regulation under the Plan. Securitization markets should be better regulated, with the objective of improved transparency and standardization of securitization products. For example, the electronic database reporting corporate bond transactions, the Trade Reporting and Compliance Engine (TRACE), would be expanded to include asset-backed securities (see the discussion of TRACE in Chapter 5). External credit ratings should be strengthened and subject to more effective international oversight. Other than requiring a different rating scale for securitization products than for debt instruments, there is not a lot of detail regarding these proposals, and it is somewhat disappointing that the Obama-Geithner Plan did not address the more fundamental conflicts inherent in the external credit rating system (see the discussion in Chapter 1).

The Plan advises the SEC and the CFTC to harmonize their regulations of futures and other securities. There have been calls to eliminate the CFTC (generally considered to be the more lenient of the two oversight agencies) and to transfer the CFTC's responsibilities to the SEC (see the Paulson blueprint discussion earlier in this chapter). However, the Plan did not advocate this change. This has fueled the public perception that the Plan is marginal in scope and does not break with current practice in a fundamental way, thereby missing the opportunity to rework the foundations of financial market structure and institutional regulation. For example, the overlap between the SEC and the CFTC, particularly in the area of derivatives, has led to proposals to merge the agencies so as to improve the effectiveness of government oversight.[14] However, the Plan does not call for this, but rather calls for authority to prevent "market manipulation, fraud and other market abuses," without any specifics.

The Plan also calls for the Federal Reserve to oversee the settlement systems and liquidity involving systemically important financial firms, with the objective of maintaining the integrity of the payment system. Part of this proposal involves the creation of a central clearing counterparty for credit derivatives such as credit default swaps (see Chapter 12). Currently, there are seven proposed and approved clearinghouses for credit default swaps: two in the United States (ICE and the Chicago Mercantile Exchange) and five in Europe (NYSE-Liffe-LCH, Clearnet, ICE Trust Europe, Eurex, LCH.Clearnet SA, and the CME Group).[15]

Protect Consumers and Investors from Financial Abuse The major proposal in this section of the Plan is to create a new Consumer Financial Protection Agency "to protect consumers of credit, savings, payment, and other consumer financial products and services, and to regulate providers of such products and services" (Obama-Geithner Plan [2009], 14). This independent agency "with stable, robust funding" would have sole rule-making authority for consumer financial protection laws, coordinate enforcement with the states and the Department of Justice, have supervisory and enforcement authority over all persons covered by its statutes (including depository institutions), and conduct periodic reviews of regulations. The Plan also calls for enhancement of the tools and resources available to the Federal Trade Commission for consumer protection.

Disclosure would be improved by an expanded SEC empowered to promote greater transparency of financial markets, standardization of information about simple plain-vanilla products, foster fairness, and improve access through enforcement of fair lending practices. A Financial Consumer

Coordinating Council would be established under the aegis of the Financial Services Oversight Council. Retirement security would be promoted through strengthened employer and private retirement plans that encourage savings.

Provide the Government with the Tools It Needs to Manage Financial Crises   This portion of the Plan has been controversial because there are those who have called for the breaking up of TBTF financial firms into smaller, more manageable pieces, each of which would not be able to threaten the stability of the financial system. Instead, the Plan envisions designating these systemically important TBTF FHCs as "Tier 1 FHCs" and creating "a resolution regime to avoid . . . a disorderly resolution [that] would have serious adverse effects on the financial system or the economy. The regime would supplement (rather than replace) and be modeled on to the existing resolution regime for insured depository institutions under the Federal Deposit Insurance Act" (Obama-Geithner Plan [2009], 16). Moreover, the Federal Reserve would have to obtain the approval of the Treasury to lend under "'unusual and exigent circumstances.'"

Concerns about the "Tier 1" designation have been expressed by commentators such as Peter Wallison of the American Enterprise Institute, who argues that this would create more "Fannies and Freddies," with detrimental moral hazard impacts on the financial system. Holman Jenkins Jr. writes: "A new 'resolution regime' might be useful but not if it places more AIGs in government hands. Better would be a rule that automatically imposes stiff debt-for-equity haircuts on bondholders if a firm needs long-term government financing to survive."[16]

Raise International Regulatory Standards and Improve Regulatory Cooperation The Plan calls for revision of the Basel II international bank capital requirements in order to improve risk measurement and counteract procyclical effects (see Chapter 13). A newly enhanced and restructured Financial Stability Board together with national regulatory authorities are encouraged to "enhance supervision of internationally active financial firms" (Obama-Geithner Plan 2009, 16), improve oversight of global financial markets, develop better coordination of cross-border crisis prevention and resolution programs. By the end of 2009, the Obama-Geithner Plan calls upon national authorities to implement the G-20 commitment to register hedge funds in order to disclose their systemic risk exposures.[17] International accounting standards should be developed to "set a single set of high quality" accounting rules, including a forward-looking loan provisioning procedure (Obama-Geithner Plan [2009], 18).

Further Commentary on the Obama-Geithner Plan   The Plan is heavy on regulatory structure such as creating several new agencies, but light on substance. For example, the Plan does not eliminate financial market dependence on external credit ratings that are provided by agencies with no accountability and subject to severe conflicts of interest. Rather than requiring better disclosure from credit rating agencies, the dismal performance of these firms (during this as well as previous crises) could be used as motivation to remove the government imprimatur from their activities and open the market to competition among financial market analysts in risk and value assessment—similar to the system of independent analysts in equity markets. This would require the removal of external credit ratings triggers in capital requirements, asset eligibility, concentration limitations, and so on. Instead, financial firms would be responsible for designing their own risk measurement models and conducting their own due diligence of financial products so as to determine and disclose their risk exposures.

Although the Plan creates an entire new prudential oversight procedure focusing on systemic risk, it is unclear what new information will be available to the newly established agencies that is not currently available to bank regulators and supervisory authorities. Rather than focusing solely on oversight, which is only completely accurate in 20/20 hindsight, the Plan largely ignores the importance of ex ante incentives (with the possible exceptions of consideration of the governance implications of executive compensation packages and forward-looking loan provisioning procedures). For example, large, systemically important financial intermediaries currently hold a TBTF option issued by the government at zero cost. That is, they are not charged for the systemic risk exposure that they impose on the entire economy. An incentive-based plan would instead levy a TBTF option premium charge on these financial firms that would be collected in good times (perhaps as a surcharge to the bank's deposit insurance premium).[18] This would build up a fund that could be used to self-insure the banking system against some crises.

Moral hazard considerations are alleviated somewhat when the risk taker must bear the consequences of excessive risk taking. Use of the TBTF banks' own funds to bail out systemically important firms, along the lines of a deductible on an insurance product, could remove some incentives to roll the dice (and take on excessive risk) using the taxpayer's money. Moreover, individualized TBTF premiums could remove some of the herding incentives that cause all financial firms to overindulge together, thereby reinstating the diversification benefits that could mitigate the frequency and severity of financial crises.

SUMMARY

Financial institutions are the most heavily regulated of all firms in the economy. As financial markets and intermediation evolve, regulation must be updated in order to remain effective. This process is expedited during times of financial turbulence. During crises, such as the global financial crisis of 2007–2009, there are calls for government and regulatory authorities to intervene in order to provide short-term remedies. Moreover, crises reveal shortcomings in regulation, leading to proposals for longer-term reforms. In this chapter, we have covered an array of regulatory proposals ranging from short-term responses to the financial crisis to long-term revisions in financial market regulation that seek to restructure the global financial infrastructure. The major lesson that appears to have been learned is that the regulatory system will have to be redesigned to better control for and price the systemic risk posed by individual financial institutions. Thus, going forward, the integration of systemic risk buffers into Basel capital requirements as well as into deposit insurance premiums, without inducing unsustainable impacts on bank profitability, should become the number one priority regulatory concern.

Probability of
Default Estimation

Loans as Options: The Moody's KMV Model

INTRODUCTION

The idea of applying option pricing theory to the valuation of risky loans and bonds has been in the literature at least as far back as a 1974 article by R. C. Merton. In recent years, Merton's ideas have been extended in many directions. One example is the generation of structural default prediction models (e.g., Moody's KMV model) that produce and update default predictions for all major companies and banks that have their equity publicly traded.[1] In this chapter, we first look at the link between loans and options and subsequently investigate how this link can be used to derive a default prediction model.

THE LINK BETWEEN LOANS AND OPTIONS

Figure 4.1 shows the payoff function to a bank lender of a simple loan. Assume that this is a one-year loan and the amount, B, is borrowed on a discount basis. Technically, option formulas (discussed later) model loans as zero-coupon bonds with fixed maturities. Over the year, a borrowing firm will invest the funds in various projects or assets. Assume that at the end of the year the market value of the borrowing firm's assets is A_2. The owners of the firm then have an incentive to repay the loan (B) and keep the residual ($A_2 - B$) as profit or return on investment. Indeed, for any value of the firm's assets exceeding B, the owners of the firm will have an incentive to repay the loan. However, if the market value of the firm's assets is less than B (e.g., A_1 in Figure 4.1), the owners have an incentive (or option) to default and to turn over the remaining assets of the firm to the lender (the bank).

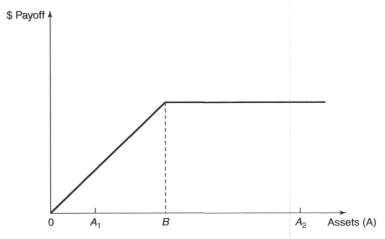

FIGURE 4.1 The Payoff to a Bank Lender

For market values of assets exceeding B, the bank will earn a fixed upside return on the loan; essentially, interest and principal will be repaid in full. For asset values less than B, the bank suffers increasingly large losses. In the extreme case, the bank's payoff is zero: principal and interest are totally lost.[2]

The loan payoff function shown in Figure 4.1—a fixed payoff on the upside, and long-tailed downside risk—might be immediately familiar to an option theorist. Compare it with the payoff to a writer of a put option on a stock, shown in Figure 4.2. If the price of the stock (S) exceeds the exercise price (X), the writer of the option will keep the put premium. If the price of the stock falls below X, the writer will lose successively large amounts.

Merton (1974) noted this formal payoff equivalence; that is, when a bank makes a risky loan, its payoff is isomorphic to writing a put option on the assets of the borrowing firm. Moreover, just as five variables enter the classic Black-Scholes-Merton (BSM) model of put option valuation for stocks, the value of the default option (or, more generally, the value of a risky loan) will also depend on the value of five similar variables.

In general form:

$$\text{Value of a put option on a stock} = f(\bar{S}, \bar{X}, \bar{r}, \bar{\sigma}, \bar{\tau}) \tag{4.1}$$

$$\text{Value of a default option on a risky loan} = f(A, \bar{B}, \bar{r}, \sigma_A, \bar{\tau}) \tag{4.2}$$

where S, X, A, and B are as defined earlier (a bar above a variable denotes that it is directly observable); r is the risk-free interest rate; σ and σ_A are,

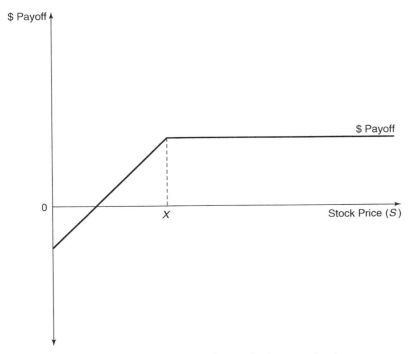

FIGURE 4.2 The Payoff to the Writer of a Put Option on a Stock

respectively, the volatilities of the firm's equity value and the market value of its assets; and τ is the maturity of the put option or, in the case of loans, the time horizon (default horizon) for the loan.

In general, for options on stocks, all five variables on the right-hand side (RHS) of equation (4.1) are directly observable; however, this is true for only three variables on the RHS of equation (4.2). The market value of a firm's assets (A) and the volatility of the market value of a firm's assets (σ_A) are *not* directly observable. If A and σ_A could be directly measured, the value of a risky loan, the value of the default option, and the equilibrium spread on a risky loan over the risk-free rate could all be calculated directly (see Merton [1974] and Appendix 4.1).

Some analysts have substituted the observed market value of risky debt on the left-hand side (LHS) of equation (4.2) (or, where appropriate, the observed interest spread between a firm's risky bonds and a matched risk-free Treasury rate) and have assumed that the book value of assets equals the market value of assets. This allows the implied volatility of assets (σ_A) to be backed out from equation (4.2), (for example, see Gorton and

Santomero [1990] and Flannery and Sorescu [1996]). However, without additional assumptions, it is impossible to impute two unobservable values (A and σ_A), based solely on one equation (4.2).[3]

THE MOODY'S KMV MODEL

The innovation of the Moody's KMV Model is that it turns the bank's lending problem around and considers the loan repayment incentive problem from the viewpoint of the borrowing firm's equity holders.[4] To solve for the two unknowns, A and σ_A, the model uses (1) the structural relationship between the market value of a firm's equity and the market value of its assets, and (2) the relationship between the volatility of a firm's assets and the volatility of a firm's equity. After values of these variables are derived, an expected default frequency (EDF^{TM}) or probability of default measure for the borrower can be calculated.

Figure 4.3 shows the loan repayment problem from the side of the borrower (the equity holder or owner of the firm). Suppose the firm borrows B and the end-of-period market value of the firm's assets is A_2 (where $A_2 > B$). The firm will then repay the loan, and the equity holders will keep the residual value of the firm's assets ($A_2 - B$). The larger the market value of the

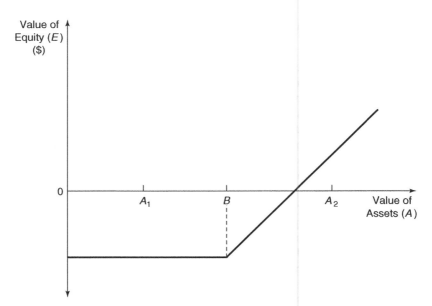

FIGURE 4.3 Equity as a Call Option on a Firm

firm's assets at the end of the loan period, the greater the residual value of the firm's assets to the equity holders. However, if the firm's assets fall below B (e.g., are equal to A_1), the equity holders of the firm will not be able to repay the loan.[5] They will be economically insolvent and will turn the firm's assets over to the bank.[6] Note that the downside risk of the equity holders is truncated no matter how low asset values fall, compared to the amount borrowed. Specifically, *limited liability* protects the equity holders against losing more than L their original stake in the firm. As shown in Figure 4.3, the payoff to the equity holder in a leveraged firm has a limited downside and a long-tailed upside. Those familiar with options will immediately recognize the similarity between the payoff function for an equity holder in a leveraged firm and buying a call option on a stock. Thus, we can view the market-value position of equity holders in a borrowing firm (E) as isomorphic to holding a call option on the assets of the firm (A).

In general terms, equity can be valued as:

$$\bar{E} = h(A, \sigma_A, \bar{B}, \bar{r}, \bar{\tau}) \tag{4.3}$$

In equation (4.3), the observed market value of a borrowing firm's equity (which equals the price of shares times the number of shares outstanding) depends on the same five variables as in equation (4.2), as per the BSM model for valuing a call option on the assets of a firm. However, a problem still remains: how to solve for two unknowns (A and σ_A) from one equation (where E, r, B, and τ and are all observable, as denoted by the bar above them).

Moody's KMV and others in the literature have resolved this problem by noting that a second relationship can be exploited: the theoretical relationship between the observable volatility of a firm's equity value (σ) and the unobservable volatility of a firm's asset value (σ_A).[7] In general terms:

$$\bar{\sigma} = g(\sigma_A) \tag{4.4}$$

With two equations and two unknowns, equations (4.3) and (4.4) can be used to solve for A and σ_A by successive iteration.[8] Explicit functional forms for the option-pricing model (OPM) in equation (4.3) and for the stock price/asset volatility linkage in equation (4.4) have to be specified. (A good discussion of these issues can be found in Jarrow and Turnbull [2000] and Delianedis and Geske [1998]). Moody's KMV uses an option-pricing BSM-type model that allows for dividends. The default exercise point, B, is taken as the value of all short-term liabilities (one year and under) plus half the book value of long-term debt outstanding.[9] (The precise strike price or *default point* has varied under different generations of the model, and there is a question as to whether net short-term liabilities should be used instead of total short-term liabilities.)[10] The maturity variable (τ) also can be altered according to the default horizon of the analyst; most commonly, it is set equal to one year. A slightly different OPM was used by Ronn and Verma (1986) to solve a very similar problem estimating the default risk of U.S. banks.[11]

After they have been calculated, the A and σ_A values can be employed, along with assumptions about the values of B, r, and τ, to generate a theoretically based EDF[TM] score for any given borrower. The idea is illustrated in Figure 4.4. Suppose that the values backed out of equations (4.3) and (4.4) for any given borrower are, respectively, A equal to $100 million and σ_A equal to $10 million.[12] The value of B is $80 million. In practice, the user can set the default point or *exercise price* (B) equal to any proportion of total debt outstanding that is of interest.

Suppose we want to calculate the EDF[TM] for a one-year horizon. Given the values of A, σ_A, B, and r, and with τ equal to one year, what is the (theoretical) probability of a borrowing firm's failure at the one-year horizon? As can be seen in Figure 4.4, the EDF[TM] is the shaded area of the distribution of asset values below B. This area represents the probability that the current value of the firm's assets, $100 million, will drop below $80 million at the one-year time horizon. The size of the shaded area, and therefore the EDF[TM], increases as the asset volatility, σ_A, increases; as the value of debt, B, increases; and as the initial market value of assets, A, decreases.

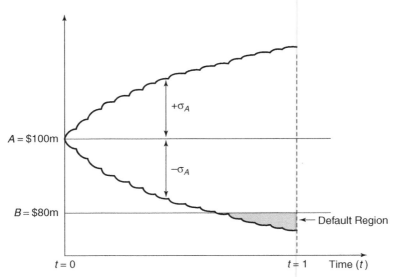

FIGURE 4.4   Calculating the Theoretical EDF[TM]

If it is assumed that future asset values are normally distributed around the firm's current asset value, we can measure the $t = 0$ (or today's) distance to default at the one-year horizon as:

$$\text{Distance to default (DD)} = \frac{A - B}{\sigma_A} = \frac{\$100 \text{ million} - \$80 \text{ million}}{\$10 \text{ million}} \quad (4.5)$$

$$= 2 \text{ standard deviations}$$

For the firm to enter the default region (the shaded area), asset values would have to drop by \$20 million, or 2 standard deviations, during the next year. If asset values are normally distributed, we know that there is a 95 percent probability that asset values will vary between plus and minus 2σ from their mean value. Thus, there is a 2.5 percent probability that asset values will increase by more than 2σ over the next year, and a 2.5 percent probability that they will fall by more than 2σ. In other words, there is an expected default frequency or EDF^{TM} of 2.5 percent.

We have included no growth in expected or mean asset values over the one-year period in Figure 4.4, but this can easily be incorporated. For example, if we project that the value of the firm's assets will grow 10 percent over the next year, then the relevant EDF^{TM} would be lower because asset values would have to drop by 3σ below the firm's expected asset growth path, for the firm to default at year-end.[13]

The idea of asset values being normally distributed around some mean level plays a crucial role in calculating joint default transition probabilities in CreditMetrics (see Chapter 9), yet there is an important issue as to whether it is (theoretically or empirically) reasonable to make this assumption.[14] With this in mind, rather than producing theoretical EDF^{TM}s, the Moody's KMV approach generates an empirical EDF^{TM} along the following lines.[15] Suppose that we have a large historical database of firm defaults and loan repayments, and we calculate that the firm we are analyzing has a theoretical distance to default of 2σ. We then ask the empirical question: What percentage of firms in the database actually defaulted within the one-year time horizon when their asset values placed them a distance of 2σ away from default at the beginning of the year, and how does that compare to the total population of firms that were 2σ away from default at the beginning of the year? This produces an empirical (nonparametric) EDF^{TM}:

$$\text{Empirical EDF}^{TM} = \frac{\substack{\text{Number of firms that defaulted within a year with asset} \\ \text{values of } 2\sigma \text{ from } B \text{ at the beginning of the year}}}{\substack{\text{Total population of firms with asset values} \\ \text{of } 2\sigma \text{ from } B \text{ at the beginning of the year}}}$$

Suppose, based on a worldwide database, it was estimated that 50 of 1,000 possible firms defaulted. The equation would be:

$$5 \text{ percent} = 50 \text{ defaults/Firm population of } 1,000$$

In this example, the empirical EDF^{TM} is 5 percent. This empirically based EDF^{TM} can differ quite significantly from the theoretically based EDF^{TM}. From a proprietary perspective, Moody's KMV advantage comes from accessing Moody's large worldwide database of firms that can produce such empirically based EDF^{TM} scores—Moody's KMV EDF^{TM} scores are estimated daily for more than 30,500 firms in 58 countries (see Dvorak [2008]).[16] Moody's KMV empirical EDF^{TM} is an overall statistic that can be calculated for every possible distance to default (DD) using data either aggregated or segmented by industry or region. To find the EDF^{TM} for any particular firm at any point in time, one must simply look up the firm's EDF^{TM} implied by its calculated DD.[17] The EDF^{TM} estimate ranges from 0.01 percent to 35 percent.[18] Firm-specific empirical EDF^{TM}s fluctuate over time as the firm's DD fluctuates (caused by changes in A, B, and σ_A) and as the overall empirical EDF^{TM} value changes for each DD measure (caused by changes in the historical distribution of defaults across all firms in the database).[19]

TESTING THE ACCURACY OF EDF^{TM} SCORES

Credit rating models map predicted default probabilities into a rating scale. External ratings provided by the major credit rating agencies (such as Moody's, S&P, and Fitch) utilize a scale that ranges from AAA to D.[20] Internal ratings are used at most large financial institutions to incorporate the banker's own assessment of default risk. Table 4.1 shows a mapping of external credit ratings to internal ratings and risk levels, whereas Table 4.2 maps the external credit ratings to EDF^{TM} scores (for non-financial companies in North America) as of January 2009. The cut-off EDF^{TM} score between investment-grade and below-investment-grade issues was 0.74 percent in January 2009, reflecting the deterioration in economic conditions. In contrast, this cut-off EDF^{TM} score was less than 0.10 percent at the end of 2006 before the onset of the global financial crisis.

Moody's maps EDF^{TM} scores to Moody's credit ratings using both a spot approach (based on current month data) and a long-term approach (based on five years of data). Since default probabilities vary greatly with the business cycle, increasing in downturns and decreasing in upturns (see Vassalou and Xing [2004], for example), EDF^{TM} scores should take

TABLE 4.1 An Example of a Loan Rating System and Bond Rating Mapping

Bond Rating	Score	Risk Level	Description
AAA	1	Minimal	Excellent business credit: superior asset quality, excellent debt capacity and coverage; excellent management with depth. Company is a market leader and has access to capital markets.
AA	2	Modest	Good business credit: very good asset quality and liquidity, strong debt capacity and coverage, very good management in all positions. Company is highly regarded in industry and has a very strong market share.
A	3	Average	Average business credit, within normal credit standards: satisfactory asset quality and liquidity, good debt capacity and coverage; good management in all critical positions. Company is of average size and position within the industry.
BBB	4	Acceptable	Acceptable business credit, but with more than average risk: acceptable asset quality, little excess liquidity, modest debt capacity. May be highly or fully leveraged. Requires above-average levels of supervision and attention from lender. Company is not strong enough to sustain major setbacks. Loans are highly leveraged transactions due to regulatory constraints.
BB	5	Acceptable with care	Acceptable business credit, but with considerable risk: acceptable asset quality, smaller and/or less diverse asset base, very little liquidity, limited debt capacity. Covenants structured to ensure adequate protection. May be highly or fully leveraged. May be of below-average size or a lower-tier competitor. Requires significant supervision and attention from lender. Company is not strong enough to sustain major setbacks. Loans are highly leveraged transactions due to the obligor's financial status.
B	6	Management attention	Watch list credit: generally acceptable asset quality, somewhat strained liquidity, fully leveraged. Some management weakness. Requires continual supervision and attention from lender.

(Continued)

TABLE 4.1 *(Continued)*

Bond Rating	Score	Risk Level	Description
CCC	7	Special mention (OAEM)	Marginally acceptable business credit; some weakness. Generally undesirable business constituting an undue and unwarranted credit risk but not to the point of justifying a substandard classification. Although the asset is currently protected, it is potentially weak. No loss of principal or interest is envisioned. Potential weaknesses might include a weakening financial condition; an unrealistic repayment program; inadequate sources of funds; or lack of adequate collateral, credit information, or documentation. Company is undistinguished and mediocre.
CC	8	Substandard	Unacceptable business credit; normal repayment in jeopardy. Although no loss of principal or interest is envisioned, a positive and well-defined weakness jeopardizes collection of debt. The asset is inadequately protected by the current sound net worth and paying capacity of the obligor or pledged collateral. There may already have been a partial loss of interest.
C	9	Doubtful	Full repayment questionable. Serious problems exist to the point where a partial loss of principal is likely. Weaknesses are so pronounced that, on the basis of current information, conditions, and values, collection in full is highly improbable.
D	10	Loss	Expected total loss. An uncollectible asset or one of such little value that it does not warrant classification as an active asset. Such an asset may, however, have recovery or salvage value, but not to the point where a write-off should be deferred, even though a partial recovery may occur in the future.

macroeconomic conditions into account. Figure 4.5 shows that EDF™ scores tend to increase during recessions and market downturns. This was certainly the case during the global financial meltdown of 2007–2009, with EDF™ scores reaching historically high levels throughout the world.

Accurate default risk estimates should offer timely forecasts of default. Korablev and Dwyer (2007) compare the timeliness of Moody's KMV

TABLE 4.2 Mapping of EDF^{TM} Scores to Credit Ratings

	Investment Grade		
Rating	Median	Lower Bound	Upper Bound
Aaa	0.042%	0.010%	0.046%
Aa1	0.049%	0.046%	0.051%
Aa2	0.052%	0.051%	0.063%
Aa3	0.076%	0.063%	0.091%
A1	0.109%	0.091%	0.131%
A2	0.157%	0.131%	0.181%
A3	0.209%	0.181%	0.241%
Baa1	0.278%	0.241%	0.321%
Baa2	0.370%	0.321%	0.466%
Baa3	0.586%	0.466%	0.737%
	Sub-Investment Grade		
Ba1	0.926%	0.737%	1.165%
Ba2	1.465%	1.165%	1.884%
Ba3	2.423%	1.884%	3.116%
B1	4.006%	3.116%	5.151%
B2	6.624%	5.151%	8.498%
B3	10.902%	8.498%	13.986%
Caa1	17.942%	13.986%	23.018%
Caa2	29.530%	23.018%	29.952%
Caa3	30.379%	29.952%	31.251%
Ca	32.149%	31.251%	35.000%
C	35.000%	35.000%	35.000%

Source: © Moody's Analytics, Inc. and/or its affiliates. Reprinted with permission. All Rights Reserved.

EDF^{TM} scores to long-term mappings of Moody's credit ratings for U.S. firms over the period 1996–2006. Panel A of Figure 4.6 shows that EDF^{TM} scores show a steep increase (signaling increased default risk) about 24 months prior to default, as compared to the approximately 13-month average lead time provided by Moody's credit ratings, suggesting that EDF^{TM} scores lead ratings by 11 months for public, non-financial firms in

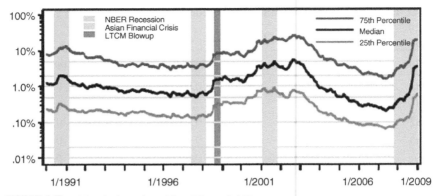

FIGURE 4.5a   North American Non-Financial Firms
Source: © Moody's Analytics, Inc. and/or its affiliates. Reprinted with permission.
All Rights Reserved.

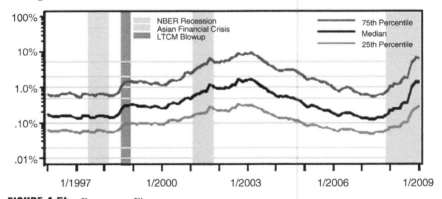

FIGURE 4.5b   European Firms
Source: © Moody's Analytics, Inc. and/or its affiliates. Reprinted with permission.
All Rights Reserved.

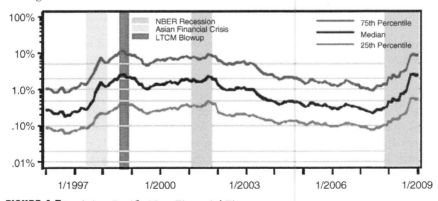

FIGURE 4.5c   Asian-Pacific Non-Financial Firms
Source: © Moody's Analytics, Inc. and/or its affiliates. Reprinted with permission.
All Rights Reserved.

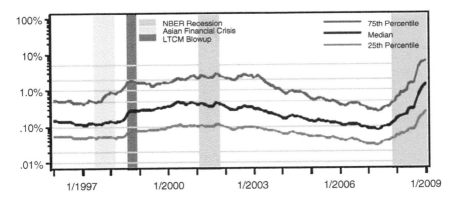

FIGURE 4.5d Financial Firms

Note: Figure 4.5 shows one-year EDF™ scores.

Source: © Moody's Analytics, Inc. and/or its affiliates. Reprinted with permission. All Rights Reserved.

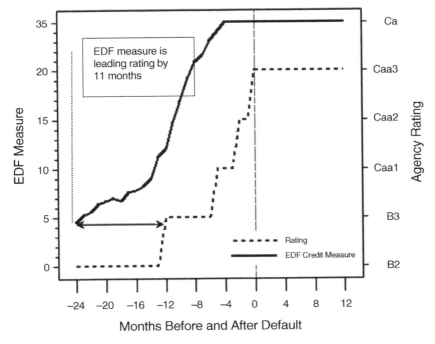

FIGURE 4.6a Panel A

Source: © Moody's Analytics, Inc. and/or its affiliates. Reprinted with permission. All Rights Reserved.

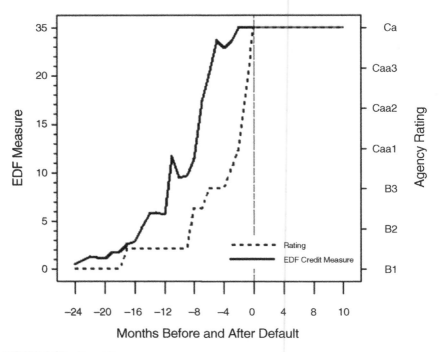

FIGURE 4.6b Panel B

Source: © Moody's Analytics, Inc. and/or its affiliates. Reprinted with permission. All Rights Reserved.

North America with sales exceeding $30 million. Panel B of Figure 4.6 presents the results for 6,789 European non-financial firms with sales exceeding $30 million.[21] In this sample, EDF^{TM} scores provide a lead time of only about 2 months, increasing dramatically around 11 months prior to default, in contrast to ratings which increased 9 months prior to default. Finally, Panel C of Figure 4.6 shows that the median EDF^{TM} scores for 11,509 non-financial Asian companies lead agency ratings by approximately 10 months in forecasting bankruptcy.

Another way to compare the timeliness of credit rating default predictions to EDF^{TM} scores is to examine specific cases. Figure 4.7 shows the KMV-produced EDF^{TM} scores for Comdisco Inc. over a five-year period (using a log-scale) compared to S&P ratings. The significant increase in Comdisco's EDF^{TM} in June 1998, followed by further deteriorations during 1999–2000, provided early warning signs of credit problems. Comdisco filed for Chapter 11 bankruptcy protection on July 16, 2001. The company's S&P rating was unchanged at BBB until it was first slightly

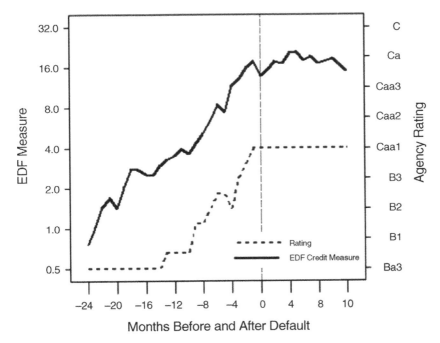

FIGURE 4.6c Panel C

Source: © Moody's Analytics, Inc. and/or its affiliates. Reprinted with permission. All Rights Reserved.

downgraded in July 2000 and not again until March 2001. If rating agencies are reluctant to precipitously downgrade their customers, it may not be surprising that credit ratings lag EDF^{TM} scores when credit quality is deteriorating.

However, Figure 4.8 shows that agency ratings lag EDF^{TM} scores in forecasting credit quality improvements as well as deteriorations. USG Corporation's credit rating was upgraded twice during the period from September 1996 to June 1999. During that entire period of credit quality improvement, KMV EDF^{TM} scores were below the implied agency ratings, suggesting that S&P ratings lagged EDF^{TM} scores even for credit upgrades. Moreover, when USG Corporation's credit began to deteriorate in June 1999, S&P ratings lagged behind EDF^{TM} scores in forecasting the turnaround in USG's credit quality (not reflected in ratings until October 2000) as well as its ultimate descent into bankruptcy; USG Corporation filed for Chapter 11 on June 25, 2001.

On December 2, 2001, Enron Corporation filed for Chapter 11 bankruptcy protection. At an asset value of $49.53 billion, this was the largest

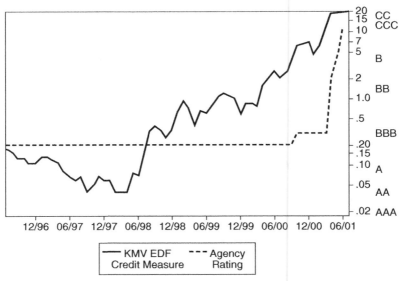

FIGURE 4.7   KMV Expected Default Frequency™ and Agency Rating for USG Corporation
Source: © Moody's Analytics, Inc. and/or its affiliates. Reprinted with permission. All Rights Reserved.

bankruptcy filing in U.S. history (at least until Lehman's bankruptcy declaration on September 15, 2008, with $613 billion in debt). For months prior to Enron's bankruptcy filing, a steadily declining stock price reflected negative information about the firm's financial condition, potential undisclosed conflicts of interest, and dwindling prospects for a merger with Dynegy Inc. However, as Figure 4.9 shows, the S&P rating stayed constant throughout the period from the end of 1996 until November 28, 2001, when Enron's debt was downgraded to junk status just days before the bankruptcy filing.[22] In contrast, Moody's KMV EDF™ scores provided early warning of the start of a deterioration in credit quality as early as January 2000, with a marked increase in EDF™ after January 2001, 11 months prior to the bankruptcy filing.

There are those who have stated that the global financial meltdown of 2007–2009 was largely the result of a failure of credit risk measurement. However, Figure 4.10 shows that credit signals of impending insolvency were available in real time. Panel A (B) of Figure 4.10 shows the Moody's KMV EDF™ scores for Fannie Mae (Freddie Mac) from October 2007 until the government bailout on September 7, 2008. EDF™ scores show the increasing risk of default for both companies throughout 2008, in contrast to credit ratings that were unresponsive to the growing risk exposure. The

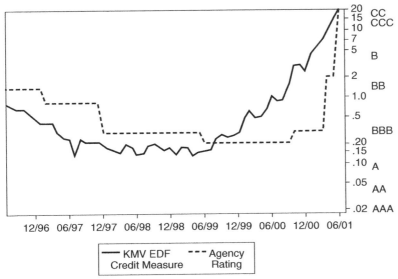

FIGURE 4.8 KMV Expected Default Frequency™ and Agency Rating for
USG Corporation
Source: © Moody's Analytics, Inc. and/or its affiliates. Reprinted with permission.
All Rights Reserved.

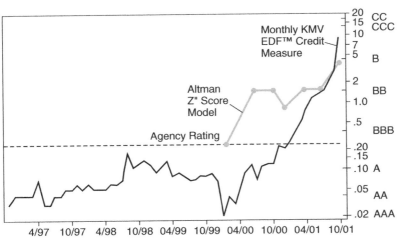

FIGURE 4.9 KMV Expected Default Frequency™ and Agency Rating for
Enron Corporation
Source: © Moody's Analytics, Inc. and/or its affiliates. Reprinted with permission.
All Rights Reserved.

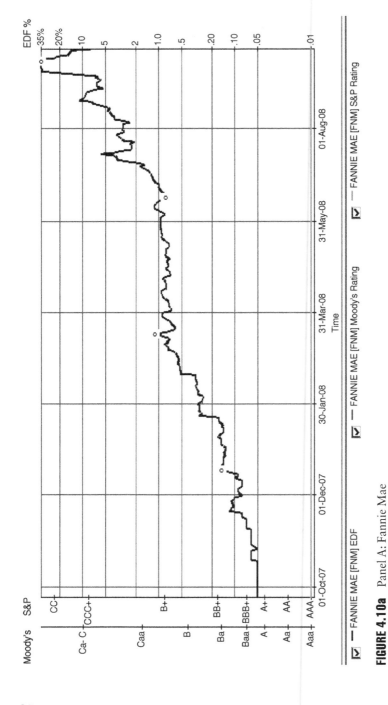

FIGURE 4.10a Panel A: Fannie Mae

Source: © Moody's Analytics, Inc. and/or its affiliates. Reprinted with permission. All Rights Reserved.

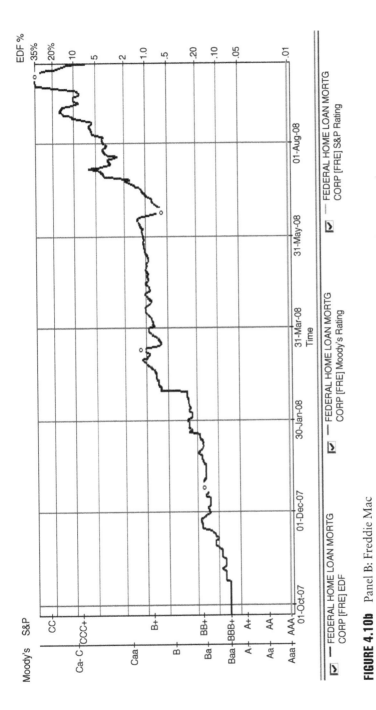

FIGURE 4.10b Panel B: Freddie Mac

Source: © Moody's Analytics, Inc. and/or its affiliates. Reprinted with permission. All Rights Reserved.

bailout was a watershed incident in the spreading of the crisis since it involved government-sponsored entities (GSEs) believed to be under the implicit protection of the U.S. government (see the discussion in Chapter 2).

Accurate credit rating measures must minimize both Type 1 and Type 2 errors. That is, an accurate measure must keep defaulters from being mislabeled as good borrowers (Type 1 error) and, the other way around, not mislabel good-quality borrowers as possible defaulters (Type 2 error). One way to measure this predictive ability is to use a power curve, as shown in Figure 4.11, which analyzes U.S. non-financial firms with publicly traded equity and more than $30 million in sales.[23]

Figure 4.11compares EDF^{TM} scores to long-term Moody's credit ratings, and shows that if the bottom 20 percent of the rankings (i.e., Type 2 errors classifying good loans as bad) are held to a maximum of 20 percent, then the KMV EDF^{TM}s eliminate approximately 88 percent of the defaults, whereas the Moody's ratings only exclude 75 percent of the defaults. Thus, the Type 1 error (i.e., classifying bad loans as good) for the EDF^{TM} score is 12 percent (i.e., the EDF^{TM} cannot exclude 12 percent of the defaults), whereas the credit ratings' Type 1 error is 25 percent. Estimating the overall power of the two methodologies, the EDF^{TM} score accuracy ratio is 0.88 (out of 1), as compared to the Moody's rating accuracy ratio of only 0.75, suggesting that EDF^{TM} scores outperform credit ratings in their ability to predict default. Sellers and Arora (2004) find an accuracy ratio of 0.83 on rated financial firms and 0.73 on all financial firms over 1996–2003.[24] In comparison, Vassalou and Xing (2004) find that the traditional Merton model has an accuracy ratio of 0.592 for non-financial companies over the period from 1971 to 1999.

CRITIQUES OF MOODY'S KMV EDF^{TM} SCORES

The greater sensitivity of EDF^{TM} scores discussed previously, compared to rating-based systems, comes from the direct link between EDF^{TM} scores and stock market prices. As new information about a borrower is generated, its stock price and stock price volatility will react, as will its implied asset value (A) and standard deviation of asset value (σ_A).[25]

KMV EDF^{TM} scores have been criticized on the basis that they are not true probabilities of default. This is reflected in the poor results obtained when using KMV empirical EDF^{TM}s in order to replicate risky bond prices; see Kao (2000) and Eom et al. (2004). These results may obtain because the Merton model solves for risk-neutral probabilities of default (EDF^{TM}s) that represent the probability that the asset value will fall below the value of debt, assuming that the underlying asset return (change in asset value) process has a mean return equal to the risk-free rate. In contrast, the KMV

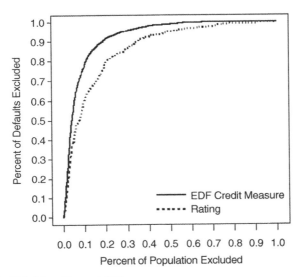

FIGURE 4.11 U.S. Non-Financial Firms
Source: © Moody's Analytics, Inc. and/or its affiliates. Reprinted with permission.
All Rights Reserved.

empirical EDF^{TM} uses the assets' expected return in place of the risk-free rate. Thus, if the assets' expected return exceeds the risk-free rate (as would be the case in the presence of systematic risk exposure), then the risk-neutral EDF^{TM} exceeds the KMV empirical EDF^{TM} and the KMV measure under-estimates the true probability of default.[26]

The KMV measure can be adjusted to overcome this problem by esti-mating the systematic risk premium over the risk-free rate. Intuitively, the empirical EDF^{TM} is adjusted upward to reflect the additional compensation necessary to compensate risk-averse investors for the sensitivity of asset val-ues to unexpected market fluctuations. Thus, there is an additional term in the equity valuation equation (4.3) as follows:

$$\bar{E} = h(A, \sigma_A, \bar{B}, \bar{r}, \bar{\tau}, \pi) \qquad (4.6)$$

where π is the (instantaneous) expected excess return on risky assets.

This adds an additional unknown, thereby requiring an additional equation for estimation. Kealhofer (2000) estimates π using the continuous-time capital asset pricing model (CAPM), which estimates the required re-turn as a function of the risk-free rate and the asset's correlation (ρ_{AM}) with the return on a market index such as the S&P 500. The KMV empirical EDF^{TM} can be transformed into the risk-neutral EDF^{TM} by applying the asset correlation (ρ_{AM}) and a scaling parameter equal to the Sharpe ratio (i.e., the risk premium on systematic risk divided by the standard deviation of the market index). Using 24,465 bond prices over 1992–1999, Bohn (2000a) was able to fit bond spreads using KMV empirical EDF^{TM}s adjusted by market Sharpe ratios.[27] Credit risk management requires both risk-neutral and empirical EDF^{TM}s. The risk-neutral EDF^{TM} is used to value the instruments in the portfolio, whereas the empirical EDF^{TM} is used to calculate value at risk (VAR); see Chapter 9.

Another potential problem in structural model estimation derives from the assumed relationship between observable equity volatility and unobservable asset volatility described in equation (4.4). As noted earlier, the application of the traditional Merton model uses two equations in order to solve for two unknown variables—asset values A and asset volatility σ_A. The second equation (4.4) specifies a nonstochastic relationship between observed equity volatility σ and unobservable asset volatility σ_A. However, Duan and Simonato (1998) has shown that this amounts to assuming that equity volatility is a constant. This is inconsistent with the stochastic asset volatility implied by the Merton model.

Duan and Simonato (1998) proposes instead the use of a statistical methodology to solve for the two unknowns in equation (4.3), replacing equation (4.4) with a maximum likelihood function that maps the unobserved firm asset value to the observed equity value, assuming that asset values are lognormally distributed. The methodology maximizes the likelihood that any pair of asset values and volatilities will be consistent with observed equity values at each point in time.[28] Ericsson and Reneby (2005) estimate this model and find that Duan and Simonato's maximum likelihood approach yields superior estimates of credit spreads. That is, three structural model specifications overestimate credit spreads by an average of 23 percent, whereas the maximum likelihood approach has negligible errors in estimating bond spreads.[29] Moody's KMV utilizes the maximum likelihood approach to estimate the empirical volatility used in the distance-to-default calculation, except if there has been a large corporate event such as a merger or acquisition (see Dwyer and Qu [2007]).

A fundamental problem with KMV-type models, and the BSM structural model approach on which it is based, is the implication for the probability of default and credit spreads as the time to default, or the maturity of debt, shrinks. Under normal BSM continuous-time diffusion processes for asset values, the probability that a firm's asset value (A) will fall below its debt boundary (B) (see Figure 4.4) declines dramatically as the default horizon (τ) goes to zero. Indeed, the implication of structural models is that the credit spread at the very short end of the risky debt market should be zero. (See Uhrig-Homburg [2002] for an illustrative example.)

In general, however, observable short-term credit spreads over the risk-free rate (say, in the short-term commercial paper and federal funds markets) are nonzero. It could be argued that this is due to liquidity and transaction cost effects, but there is a conflicting opinion that the structural models of the BSM (and KMV) type—and especially the underlying assumptions of these models, regarding the diffusion of asset values over time—underestimate the probability of default over short horizons.[30] Not surprisingly, considerable recent research has focused on resolving this issue by modifying the basic assumptions of the BSM model.

The work by Zhou (1997) attempts to address underestimation of short-horizon risk by allowing for jumps in the asset value (A) of the firm. Duffie and Lando (2001) propose that asset values, in the context of the structural model, are noisy in that they cannot be perfectly observed by outsiders. In this context, accounting information releases may partially resolve this information gap and lead to jumps in asset values as investors revise their expectations. Thus, imperfect information and fuzziness in observed asset values may potentially be integrated into the structural framework and may resolve the underestimation of default risk at the short horizon. These stochastic fluctuations in asset values cause default to occur suddenly whenever assets unpredictably fall below the debt boundary, thereby increasing default risk estimates above those obtained using the traditional Merton approach, in which default is triggered by a steady deterioration in asset values until the firm becomes insolvent.

The Merton model and Moody's KMV exogenously specify the default boundary to be equal to some representation of the face value of the firm's debt. Black and Cox (1976) considers the possibility that firms may issue equity in order to pay off their debt obligations and thereby avoid default. This endogenizes the default boundary, since the firm's shareholders will determine whether to refinance the debt. That is, the default boundary may not be equal to the face value of debt. The firm may refuse to make the required debt payments even though it is technically solvent, or alternatively, an insolvent firm may choose to service its debt; thus, the default boundary will be endogenously determined by value-maximizing equity holders. Leland (1994) finds that the endogenous default boundary is a function of bankruptcy costs and the debt tax shield.[31] Uhrig-Homburg (2002) incorporates the costs of issuing equity. Anderson, Sundaresan, and Tychon (1996) and Mella-Barral and Perraudin (1997) allow for debt renegotiations and strategic behavior, thereby building in agency costs as a friction to the traditional BSM model, and thereby obtaining more accurate default probability estimates.

Because an EDF^{TM} score reflects information signals transmitted from equity markets, it might be argued that the model is likely to work best in highly efficient equity markets and might not work well in many emerging markets. This argument ignores the fact that many thinly traded stocks are those of relatively closely held companies. Thus, major trades by insiders, such as sales of large blocks of shares (and thus, major movements in a firm's stock price), may carry powerful information signals about the future prospects of a borrowing firm.[32]

Various researchers have tested the accuracy of structural model default risk forecasts by comparing the different models' default probability estimates to observed bond spreads. Eom et al. (2004) compare the results of four structural models (plus the traditional Merton model) to observed credit spreads on 182 non-callable bonds. These four structural models relax some of the restrictive assumptions of the basic Merton model. For instance, whereas the Merton model assumes that the borrower's debt is a zero-coupon bond (or a portfolio of zero coupons with maturities corresponding to each coupon payment date), the Geske (1977) model permits borrowers to issue additional equity upon coupon payment dates in order to delay default. In contrast, Leland and Toft (1996) model continuous coupons, and incorporate bankruptcy costs and taxes. The Longstaff and Schwartz (1995) model incorporates a positive recovery rate in that default occurs prior to insolvency. The Collin-Dufresne and Goldstein (2001) model specifies a target leverage ratio that borrowing firms cannot deviate from except for short time periods. Eom et al. (2004) find that the Merton and Geske models tend to underestimate observed bond spreads, but that the remaining three models tend to overestimate spreads, particularly for bonds with high leverage or high volatility, whereas they substantially underestimate spreads for low risk. These problems are not limited to short-maturity debt instruments. Indeed, the more sophisticated models (e.g., those with stochastic interest rates) tend to have the most extreme errors.

Huang and Huang (2003) also compare structural model estimates to yield spreads for portfolios of bonds with the same credit rating. They calibrate each model's parameters to actual default experience, incorporating both the frequency and severity of default. This is particularly important since defaults tend to be highly correlated with macroeconomic conditions—that is, the stage of the credit cycle (see Dwyer [2007]). After carefully calibrating a wide variety of structural models, Huang and Huang (2003) find that credit risk accounts for less than 20 percent of the yield spread on investment-grade bonds of all maturities. For Baa-rated bonds, credit risk makes up approximately 30 percent of the yield spread, with even higher proportions for below-investment-grade bonds. They hypothesize that liquidity risk may be an important component of yield spreads.

Leland (2004) compares the default probability predictions of structural models that specify exogenous default boundaries (such as Longstaff and Schwartz [1995]) to those specifying endogenous default boundaries (such as Leland [1994], Leland and Toft [1996], and Acharya and

Carpenter [2002]). This approach contrasts with that of Eom et al. (2004) and Huang and Huang (2003), which compare structural model estimates to observed credit spreads. Credit spreads are estimates of expected losses, which can be calculated as PD × LGD, where PD is the probability of default and LGD is the loss given default. Leland (2004) focuses on structural models' ability to accurately predict PD, without considering their ability to estimate LGD.[33] Thus, problems associated with liquidity, recovery rates, and tax considerations should not undermine the tests of structural models' ability to accurately forecast default probabilities (as in Eom et al. [2004] and Huang and Huang [2003]).[34] Leland (2004) finds that structural models perform quite well for both investment-grade and junk bonds over the period 1970–2000, except at short maturities, for which default probabilities are underestimated (due to the standard options features built into the models). Moreover, Moody's KMV EDF[TM] scores are quite consistent with the PD estimates of more sophisticated models, with the exception of maturities longer than 10 years. However, EDF[TM] scores are not generally provided for maturities longer than five years.[35]

Another way to test the validity of structural models is to compare their estimates to data from the credit default swap (CDS) market. Longstaff et al. (2005), Ericsson et al. (2007), and Huang and Zhou (2008) claim that CDS spreads are less likely to be contaminated with a liquidity risk premium, and thus can provide a better test of default risk model accuracy than earlier studies estimating bond yield spreads.[36] Huang and Zhou (2008) compare the accuracy of various structural models of default risk using high-frequency intraday CDS spreads. Their results reject the traditional Merton model, the Black and Cox (1976) model, and the Longstaff and Schwartz (1995) model. The Collin-Dufresne and Goldstein (2001) model is the only one that they cannot reject in more than half of their sample firms. Huang and Zhou (2008) conclude that inclusion of a more flexible term structure model (i.e., more than one factor) of stochastic interest rates and an endogenous, time-varying leverage policy both improve the pricing accuracy of the structural credit risk model. However, they conclude that structural models do not estimate credit spreads accurately even when CDS spreads are used.

In contrast, Ericsson et al. (2007) use CDS spreads to test the following three structural models: Leland (1994), Leland and Toft (1996), and Fan and Sundaresan (2000), which endogenizes the firm's default boundary and reorganization in a game-theoretic setting involving debt holders and equity holders. Although they find the same underestimation of bond spreads as noted earlier (e.g., in Eom et al. [2004]), they find no systematic underestimation of CDS premia. They conclude that the difference between bond and CDS premium (consistently around 60 points over the 1997–2003 period) measures omitted factors such as liquidity, tax effects, duration, and so on. Thus, they conclude that structural models (particularly Leland and Toft [1996]) can be used to accurately price CDSs.

Bharath and Shumway (2008) note that the structure of the traditional Merton model makes it difficult to use standard econometric measures of forecast errors. In particular, they note that the traditional Merton model "... actually involves very little estimation. Instead, it replaces estimation with something more like calibration—solving for implied parameter values." They formulate a "naïve" version of the traditional Merton structural model and find that, while the model does not accurately quantify the probability of default, the structural model form nevertheless improves the predictive power of other default risk models.[37] Although Bharath and Shumway (2008) do not directly test the predictive power of KMV Moody's EDF[TM] scores, they note that, for a subset of 80 firms, the correlation between their measure of the traditional Merton model default probability and EDF[TM]s is 79 percent, thereby suggesting that their measure (which utilizes normal probability distributions) captures much of KMV Moody's default information. These results are consistent with those of Vassalou and Xing (2004) and Campbell et al. (2008) that find that the traditional Merton model itself has little predictive power to forecast default, although it can be useful in estimating equity returns, such that firms with high failure risk have higher equity risk measures (e.g., standard deviations and market betas) than firms with low failure risk. It is the option-theoretic approach that gives structural models their forecasting ability, despite somewhat restrictive assumptions.

In sum, the option pricing approach to bankruptcy prediction has a number of strengths. First, it can be applied to any public company. Second, by being based on stock market data rather than historic book value accounting data, it is forward-looking. Third, it has strong theoretical underpinnings because it is a structural model based on the modern theory of corporate finance, where equity is viewed as a call option on the assets of a firm and loans are viewed as incorporating put options written on the value of a firm's assets.

Against these strengths are four weaknesses: (1) It is difficult to construct theoretical EDF[TM]s without the assumption of normality of asset returns; (2) private firms' EDF[TM]s can be calculated only by using some comparability analysis based on accounting data and other observable characteristics of the borrower; (3) it does not distinguish among different types of debt according to their seniority, collateral, covenants, or convertibility;[38] and (4) it is *static* in that the Merton model assumes that once management puts a debt structure in place, it leaves it unchanged—even if the value of a firm's assets has doubled. As a result, the Merton model cannot capture the behavior of those firms that seek to maintain a constant or target leverage ratio across time (see Jarrow and van Deventer [1999]). In contrast, Mueller (2000) models leverage as a function of sensitivity to macroeconomic factors (e.g., GDP growth and risk-free interest rates). Thus, the long-run leverage ratio changes stochastically over time, thereby fitting the model to observed term structures of default.[39]

SUMMARY

The economic cause of default (or insolvency), as modeled by structural models of default probability, is the decline in the market value of the firm's assets below the value of the firm's debt obligations at a given horizon. Only if the assets' value exceeds the debt value will it be rational for equity holders, as residual claim holders, to exercise their "call option" on the firm's assets and repay the firm's debt. Thus, debt can be viewed as a short put option on the firm's assets; the shareholders will "sell" the firm's assets to the lenders (i.e., exercise the put option and default on the debt) if the market value of the assets is less than the put's exercise price, which is the repayment value of the debt, thereby determining the probability of default. The probability of default (the risk-neutral expected default frequency, EDF^{TM}) is the area under the asset value probability distribution below the default point. The distance to default (DD) is the number of standard deviations of the asset probability distribution between current asset value and the default point.

Moody's KMV applies structural models of default to their substantial credit history database in order to determine an empirical EDF^{TM} by examining the historical likelihood of default for any given DD level. Empirical EDF^{TM}s outperform ratings and statistical models in terms of their accuracy at predicting defaults. The primary advantage of structural models is that they input stock price data into an options-theoretic framework which is predictive and highly responsive to changes in the firm's financial condition. The primary disadvantage of structural models is their reliance on distributional assumptions (i.e., normality) that imply default probabilities that are not reflected in observed bond spreads.

APPENDIX 4.1: MERTON'S VALUATION MODEL

The equation for the market value of risky debt, $F(\tau)$, takes the form:

$$F(\tau) = Be^{-r\tau}\left[\left(\frac{1}{d}\right)N(h_1) + N(h_2)\right] \qquad (4.7)$$

where τ = the length of time remaining to loan maturity; that is,
$\tau = T - t$, where T is the maturity date, and t is current time (today)
d = the firm's (the borrower's) leverage ratio measured as $\frac{Be^{-r\tau}}{A}$, where the market value of debt is valued at the rate r, the risk-free rate of interest
$N(h)$ = a value computed from the standardized normal distribution tables. This value reflects the probability that a deviation exceeding the calculated value of h will occur:

$$h_1 = \frac{\left[\frac{1}{2}\sigma_A^2\tau - ln(d)\right]}{\sigma_A\sqrt{\tau}}$$

$$h_2 = \frac{\left[\frac{1}{2}\sigma_A^2\tau + ln(d)\right]}{\sigma_A\sqrt{\tau}}$$

where σ_A^2 measures the asset risk of the borrower—technically, the variance of the rate of change in the value of the underlying assets of the borrower.

This equation also can be written in terms of a yield spread that reflects an equilibrium default risk premium that the borrower should be charged:

$$k(\tau) - r = \left(\frac{-1}{\tau}\right)ln\left[N(h_2) + \left(\frac{1}{d}\right)N(h_1)\right]$$

where $k(\tau)$ = the required yield on risky debt
ln = natural logarithm
r = the risk-free rate on debt of equivalent maturity (here, one period)

An example:

$$B = \$100,000$$
$$\tau = 1 \text{ year}$$
$$r = 5 \text{ percent}$$
$$d = 90 \text{ percent or } .9$$
$$\sigma_A = 12 \text{ percent}$$

Substituting these values into the equations for h_1 and h_2, and solving for the areas under the standardized normal distribution, we find:

$$N(h_1) = .174120$$
$$N(h_2) = .793323$$

where

$$b_1 = \frac{-\left[\frac{1}{2}(.12)^2 - ln(.9)\right]}{.12} = -0.938$$

and

$$b_2 = \frac{-\left[\frac{1}{2}(.12)^2 + ln(.9)\right]}{.12} = +0.818$$

Thus, the current market value of the risky \$100,000 loan (L) is:

$$L(t) = Be^{-r\tau}\left[N(b_2) + \left(\frac{1}{d}\right)N(b_1)\right]$$

$$= \frac{\$100,000}{1.05127}[.793323 + (1.1111)(.17412)]$$

$$= \frac{\$100,000}{1.05127}[.986788]$$

$$= \$93,866.18$$

and the required risk spread or premium is:

$$k(\tau) - r = \left(\frac{-1}{\tau}\right)ln\left[N(b_2) + \left(\frac{1}{d}\right)N(b_1)\right]$$

$$= (-1)ln[.986788]$$

$$= 1.33 \text{ percent}$$

APPENDIX 4.2: MOODY'S KMV RISKCALC™

A critical input into the Moody's KMV EDF™ estimates of default risk is the stock price series. Therefore, the model, as described in this chapter, can only be estimated for publicly traded firms. However, Moody's KMV offers RiskCalc™ as a private firm default risk estimation model.[40] The basic (financial statement only, or FSO) model is built on a discriminant analysis approach similar to the Altman Z score model (see the discussion in Chapter 6). As noted in Dwyer et al. (2004), the model identifies key financial ratios that can be used as explanatory variables in estimating default risk. These variables involve firm-specific financial measures of leverage, profitability, liquidity, growth, debt coverage, size, and activity. The financial data used to measure each of these variables are transformed (using a nonlinear, nonparametric transformation) to reflect the relationship between the variable and default risk. For example, the relationship between net income (as a percent of total assets) and default risk is a downward sloping nonlinear function, such that the sensitivity of default risk to the income ratio declines as the ratio increases. Moreover, the relationship between default risk and growth rate is U-shaped, so that either very

TABLE 4.3 Financial Statement Ratios Used in Moody's KMV Private Firm Model

	United States	Canada	United Kingdom	Japan
Profitability	ROA Change in ROA	ROA Change in ROA	Net P&L to turnover Change in ROA	Gross profit to total assets Previous year's net income to previous year's net sales
Leverage	LTD to (LTD plus net worth) Retained earnings to current liabilities	LTD to (LTD plus net worth) Retained earnings to current liabilities	Liabilities to assets	Total liabilities less cash to total assets Retained earnings to total liabilities
Debt Coverage	Cash flow to interest expense	Cash flow to current liabilities	Cash flow to interest charges	EBITDA to interest expense
Liquidity	Cash and marketable securities to assets	Cash and marketable securities to assets	Current assets to current liabilities	Cash to total assets Trade receivables to net sales
Activity	Inventory to sales Change in AR turnover Current liabilities to sales	Inventory to sales Change in AR turnover Current liabilities to sales	Trade creditors to turnover (accounts payable to sales) Change in trade debtors to turnover (change in accounts receivable to sales)	Inventory to net sales
Growth	Sales growth	Sales growth	Turnover (sales) growth	Sales growth
Size	Total assets	Total assets	Total assets	Real net sales

Source: © Moody's Analytics, Inc. and/or its affiliates. Reprinted with permission. All Rights Reserved.

high or very low growth rates are consistent with higher risk of default. Table 4.3 shows the variables used in the model for private firms in the United States, Canada, the United Kingdom, and Japan.

In addition to the firm-specific variables in the FSO model, Moody's KMV RiskCalc[TM] offers a more comprehensive version that uses the public firm model in order to introduce industry- and economy-wide adjustments into default risk estimates. For example, default risk generally increases during industry retrenchment or general economic downturns. RiskCalc[TM] inputs an adjustment factor that is a function of the average distance-to-default measure from the public firm model in order to incorporate industry- or economy-wide trends. Dwyer et al. (2004) state that the accuracy ratio of the model without (with) industry controls over the one-year horizon is 54.4 percent (55.1 percent), which represents a statistically significant increase in the model's explanatory power. The model could also be used to generate a term structure of estimated default rates, and to conduct stress testing by providing a distribution of possible default rates.

CHAPTER 5

Reduced Form Models: Kamakura's Risk Manager

INTRODUCTION

The structural models described in Chapter 4 use the information embedded in equity prices in order to solve for default probabilities. Reduced form models use debt and other security prices to accomplish the same goal.[1] However, whereas structural models posit an economic process driving default (i.e., the point at which asset values fall below the repayment value of debt), reduced form models offer no economic model of default causality. In reduced form models, the default process itself is exogenous and observable in a default risk premium included in debt prices and yields. In a world free of arbitrage opportunities, expected returns on a risky asset must equal the return on a risk-free asset (the risk-free rate). More specifically, the observed yield on risky debt can be decomposed into a risk-free rate plus a risk premium. Reduced form models utilize this decomposition in order to solve for default probabilities, recovery rates, and risky debt prices.

The use of risk-neutral probabilities to value risky assets has been in the finance literature at least as far back as Arrow (1953) and has been subsequently developed by Harrison and Kreps (1979), Harrison and Pliska (1981), and Kreps (1982). In finance, it has been traditional to value risky assets by discounting cash flows on an asset by a risk-adjusted discount rate. To do this, one needs to know a probability distribution for cash flows and the risk-return preferences of investors. The latter are especially difficult to obtain. Suppose, however, it is assumed that assets trade in a market where *all* investors are willing to accept, from any risky asset, the same *expected* return as that promised by the risk-free asset.[2] Such a market can be described as behaving in a *risk-neutral* fashion.

In a financial market where investors behave in a risk-neutral fashion, the prices of all assets can be determined by simply discounting the expected future cash flows on the asset by the risk-free rate. The equilibrium relationship—where the expected return on a risky asset equals the risk-free rate—can be utilized to back out an implied risk-neutral probability of default (also called the *equivalent martingale measure*). In this chapter, we derive the risk-neutral default probability from observed bond spreads. A proprietary reduced form model is then examined: Kamakura's Risk Manager.

The major shortcoming of all reduced form models is their reliance on noisy bond price data. That is, the difference between risky bond yields (prices) and the equivalent maturity risk-free rate (price) may be the result of credit risk, but it can also be due to a liquidity premium, carrying costs, taxes, or simply data/pricing errors.[3] Therefore, we also discuss the determinants of bond spreads in this chapter.

DERIVING RISK-NEUTRAL PROBABILITIES OF DEFAULT

In this section, we first consider a discrete version of reduced form models in order to demonstrate the intuition behind the continuous-time versions often used in practice. We proceed from very simple assumptions and gradually add complexity.

Consider a B-rated $100 face value, zero-coupon debt security with one year until maturity and a fixed recovery rate (which is the same as 1 minus the loss given default, LGD). For simplicity, assume that the LGD is 100 percent—that is, the recovery rate is zero, so the entire loan is lost in the event of default. The current price of this debt instrument can be evaluated in two equivalent ways. First, the expected cash flows may be discounted at the risk-free rate, assumed to be an annual rate of 8 percent in our example. Since the security is worthless upon default, the expected cash flows are $100 \times (1 - PD)$, where PD equals the annual probability of default. If the security's price is observed to be $87.96, then we can solve for PD as follows:

$$\frac{100 \times (1 - PD)}{1 + .08} = 87.96 \qquad (5.1)$$

thereby obtaining a PD of 5 percent that satisfies the equality in equation (5.1). Equivalently, the security could be discounted at a risk-adjusted rate of return, denoted y, such that:[4]

$$\frac{100}{1 + y} = 87.96 \qquad (5.2)$$

thereby obtaining a value of $y = 13.69$ percent that satisfies equation (5.2).

Under our simplifying assumptions, the relationship between the risk-adjusted return, y, and the risk-free rate, denoted r, is:

$$1 + r = (1 - \text{PD})(1 + y) \tag{5.3}$$

or

$$1.08 = (1 - .05)(1.1369)$$

Since r and y are observable for traded debt securities (see, for example, the yield curves shown in Figure 5.1), equation (5.3) can be used to solve directly for the probability of default (PD) for B-rated corporate bonds, by simply rearranging the terms in equation (5.3):

$$\text{PD} = \frac{y - r}{1 + y} = \frac{0.1369 - 0.08}{1.1369} = 0.05 = 5\%$$

In general, the PD is not constant, but instead varies over time; therefore, we can express the probability of default as PD_t. If we convert equation (5.3) to its continuous-time equivalent, still assuming a zero recovery rate, we have:

$$y = r + PD_t \tag{5.4}$$

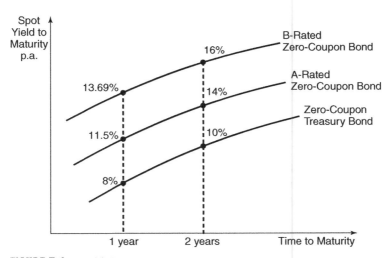

FIGURE 5.1   Yield Curves

That is, the yield on risky debt is composed of a risk-free rate plus a credit spread equal to the probability of default at any point in time t where PD_t is the stochastic default rate intensity.

Considering there are two points on the B-rated yield curve shown in Figure 5.1, let us decompose the credit spread included in the two-year zero-coupon B-rated corporate bond, which earns a yield to maturity of 16 percent per annum. In order to decompose this rate into its component parts, we must first solve for the one-year forward rate; that is, the rate on a B-rated one-year zero-coupon corporate bond to be received one year from now, denoted $_1y_1$.[5] Assuming that the expectations hypothesis holds, we can solve for the one-year forward rate on the corporate bond as follows:

$$(1 + _0y_2)^2 = (1 + _0y_1)(1 + _1y_1)$$

or, substituting the values from Figure 5.1:

$$(1 + .16)^2 = (1 + .1369)(1 + _1y_1)$$

Solving for $_1y_1$ yields a one-year forward rate on the one-year B-rated corporate bond of 18.36 percent. A similar exercise can be performed to determine the one-year forward rate on the one-year Treasury (risk-free) bond as follows:

$$(1 + _0r_2)^2 = (1 + _0r_1)(1 + _1r_1) \tag{5.5}$$

or, substituting the values from Figure 5.1:

$$(1 + .10)^2 = (1 + .08)(1 + _1r_1)$$

Solving for $_1r_1$ yields a one-year forward Treasury rate of 12.04 percent. We can now use these one-year forward rates in order to decompose the risky yield into its risk-free and credit risk spread components. Replicating the analysis in equation (5.3) for one-year maturities, but using one-year forward rates instead, we have:

$$1 + _1r_1 = (1 - PD_2)(1 + _1y_1) \tag{5.6}$$

$$1 + .1204 = (1 - PD_2)(1 + .1836)$$

obtaining the probability of default during the second year (conditional on no default occurring in the first year), $PD_2 = 5.34$ percent. That is, the probability of default for the B-rated corporate bond is 5 percent in the first year and 5.34 percent in the second year. Assuming independence across time, this result in a two-year cumulative PD of:

$$Cumulative\ PD = 1 - (1 - PD_1)(1 - PD_2)$$
$$= 1 - (1 - .05)(1 - .0534)$$
$$= 10.07\%$$

That is, the B-rated corporate bond has a 10.07 percent probability of defaulting some time over the next two years.

GENERALIZING THE DISCRETE MODEL OF RISKY DEBT PRICING

The risk-neutral default risk model described above assumes only two possible states: default or no default (with a given LGD in the default state; loss given default will be discussed further in Chapter 7). However, risky debt issues can experience declines in creditworthiness without defaulting. That is, the borrower's creditworthiness can migrate so that the PD goes up (or down) without actually triggering a default event. Changes in the PD will be reflected in changes in risky debt prices, such that as PD increases (decreases), all else being equal, credit spreads increase (decrease) and debt prices decline (rise).

The simple model presented in the previous section can be expanded to incorporate credit migration as well as default using a lattice or *tree* analysis. Risky debt values are computed for all possible transitions through various states, ranging from credit upgrades and prepayments, to restructurings and default. Often these migrations are analyzed in terms of credit rating transitions. Thus, a downgrade from a B rating to a C rating would be interpreted as an increase in PD. The historical yield data for publicly traded bonds in migrating from one credit rating to another can then be used as an input to estimate transition probabilities.

Figure 5.2 shows, in a simplified fashion, the potential transitions of the credit rating of a B-rated borrower over a four-year loan period using a tree diagram.[6] Given transition probabilities, the original grade B borrower can migrate up or down over the loan's life to different nodes (ratings), and may even migrate to D, or default (an absorbing state). Along with these migrations, one can build in a pricing grid that reflects the lender's current policy on spread repricing for borrowers of different quality (or, alternatively, a grid that reflects the spreads that the market charges on loans of different quality). Potentially, at least, this methodology can tell the lender

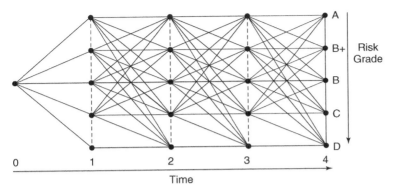

FIGURE 5.2 The Multiperiod Loan Migrates over Time

(e.g., the bank) whether it has a good or bad repricing grid in an expected net present value (NPV) sense (basically, whether the expected return on the loan equals the risk-free rate as in equation (5.3)).

When valuing a loan in this framework, valuation takes place recursively (from right to left in Figure 5.2), as it does when valuing bonds under binomial or multinomial models. For example, if the expected NPV of the loan in its final year is too high, and given some prepayment fee, the model can allow prepayment of the loan to take place at the end of period 3. Working backwards through the tree from right to left, the total expected NPV of the four-year loan can be determined. Moreover, the analyst can make different assumptions about spreads (the pricing grid) at different ratings and prepayment fees to determine the loan's value. In addition, other aspects of a loan's structure, such as embedded options, caps, amortization schedules, and so on, can be incorporated into a multinomial tree of possible outcomes.

Inputs to the model include the credit spreads for one-year option-free zero-coupon bonds for each of the 18 S&P or Moody's ratings classifications. Each node (reflecting annual revaluations) incorporates the risk-neutral probability of transition from one risk rating to another, typically averaging Moody's and S&P transition probabilities.[7] The loan value at each node is then recalculated using the market-based credit spread for each rating classification.

Using the hypothetical market data on bond yields from Figure 5.1, we can illustrate this approach to price a $100 two-year zero-coupon loan. Using an internal rating system, the loan is given a B rating upon its origination. Assuming a LGD is 100 percent (that is, the loan has a zero recovery rate), we have shown earlier in this chapter that the PD for B-rated corporate debt in the first year is 5 percent and, assuming there was no default in the first year, the PD in the second year is 5.34 percent.

However, default is not the only event that will affect the loan's value. For simplicity, we consider only two other possibilities: Either the loan's rating will remain at its current B rating or it will be upgraded one full letter grade to an A rating.[8] In our example, a hypothetical ratings transition matrix shows that the probability of an upgrade from B to A (in any period) is 1 percent and the PD is 5 percent (assuming that the beginning period rating was B). Moreover, the probability of a downgrade from A to B is 5.66 percent and the probability of migrating from A to default is 0.34 percent.[9] Finally, the probability of no change in credit rating is assumed to be 94 percent for all ratings classifications.

Figure 5.3 shows the backwards recursion process used to price the loan. Starting from period 2, the value of the loan is $100 as long as there is no default and $0 in the event of default. Moving back one year to period 1, let us first examine the B-rated node. If the loan is B-rated in period 1, then there is a 94 percent chance that it will retain that rating until period 2, a 1 percent chance that it will be upgraded to an A rating, and a 5 percent chance that it will default at the beginning of period 2. The D-rated node (default) is an absorbing state with a value of zero. Using equation (5.2) and the forward rates for each of the ratings obtained from the yield curve in Figure 5.1, the risk-neutral valuation of B-rated node in period 1 is as follows:[10]

$$0.94(100/1.1204) + 0.01(100/1.1204) + 0.05(0/1.1204) = \$84.79$$

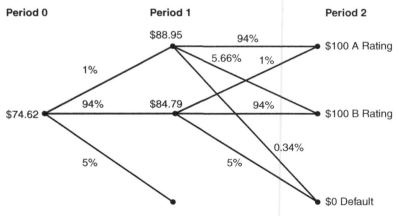

FIGURE 5.3 Risky Debt Pricing

Similarly, the risk-neutral valuation at the A-rated node in period 1 is

$$0.94(100/1.1204) + 0.0566(100/1.1204) + 0.0034(0/1.1204) = \$88.95$$

Moving back one more year to period 0, using the one-year risk-free spot rate of 8 percent per annum, the loan can be valued as

$$0.94(84.79/1.08) + 0.01(88.95/1.08) + 0.05(0/1.08) = \$74.62$$

Using a generalized version of equation (5.4) substituted into equation (5.2), we can also solve for the loan's credit spread, denoted CS (calculated as $y - r$ measured over the full maturity of the loan), which is defined to be a constant risk premium added to the risk-free rate to reflect the loan's risk exposure.[11]

$$74.62 = \frac{100}{(1 + .08 + CS)(1 + .1204 + CS)}$$

Using the one-year risk-free rate of 8 percent and the one-year forward risk-free rate of 12.04 percent, we obtain a credit spread of CS = 5.8 percent per annum.[12] This credit spread evaluates unexpected losses/gains from rating migration over the life of the loan as well as the probability of default. The credit spread can be further decomposed into expected and unexpected losses. Expected losses are derived using actual or historical default rates observed in ratings transition matrices. Unexpected losses are derived as the remaining portion of the total credit spread that compensates the lender for the (higher) risk-neutral default probability.[13]

THE LOSS INTENSITY PROCESS

The binomial tree model expands the range of possibilities and considers changes in PD without triggering default. However, the model still retains the simplifying assumption that the LGD (and thus the recovery rate) is fixed during the maturity of the loan or bond, and independent of PD.[14] If we remove this simplifying assumption, then the expected loss on default, EL, equals the probability of default (PD) times the severity or loss given default (LGD). That is, EL = PD × LGD. We can therefore rewrite equation (5.3) as:

$$1 + r = (1 - EL)(1 + y) = (1 - PD \times LGD)(1 + y) \qquad (5.3')$$

or in continuous time form, we can rewrite equation (5.4) as:[15]

$$y = r + [PD_t \times LGD_t]   \qquad\qquad (5.4')$$

Equation (5.4′) allows LGD to vary over time and expresses the yield on risky debt as the sum of the risk-free rate and the credit spread, comprised of PD times LGD. Using the rates from the yield curve in Figure 5.1, $r = 8$ percent and $y = 13.69$ percent, we can solve for PD × LGD = 5 percent, but there is an identification problem that requires an additional equation in order to disentangle PD from LGD.[16]

Reduced form models resolve the identification problem by specifying a functional form for the statistical distribution of PD_t, called the *intensity process*; hence their pseudonym of "intensity-based" models. In contrast to structural models, in which default is always triggered by an understood and expected economic event (e.g., asset value falling below debt payments), default occurs at random intervals in reduced form models.[17] Jarrow and Turnbull (1995) introduce one of the first reduced form default risk models, assuming a constant LGD and an exponentially distributed exogenous default process. In their approach, default follows a Poisson distribution and arises contingent on the arrival of some "hazard," meant in the insurance context as an unexpected loss event.[18] The intensity of the hazard arrival process is estimated empirically from bond price data, thereby eliminating the need to model the economic explanation for default. Because these types of models do not posit a causal relationship between firm value and default, they are more dependent on the quality of the bond pricing data than are structural models. Moreover, the parameters of the default intensity function may shift over time. The results, therefore, are very specific to the particular database used and the time period over which the parameters are estimated. For an explanation of the Poisson intensity process and a simulation of credit spreads using different parameter estimates, see Appendix 5.1.

Jarrow and Turnbull (1995) decompose credit spreads into a constant LGD and an independent default intensity process with a Poisson distribution that determines the time of default. In their model, the risk-neutral PD is the probability that the unpredictable default event precedes the maturity date of the debt, given the assumption of a Poisson hazard process. However, this makes the counterfactual assumption that default intensities are constant across firm types (e.g., as measured by firm credit rating) and over time (e.g., across business cycles).[19] Jarrow, Lando, and Turnbull (1997) incorporate historical transition probability matrices to estimate default as a Markov process contingent on firm credit ratings and assume a constant fractional LGD. Duffie and Singleton (1998) improve on the model fit by assuming a stochastic risk-free interest rate process and an empirically derived LGD. Longstaff and Schwartz (1995a) utilize a two-factor model that specifies a negative relationship between the stochastic processes determining credit spreads and default-free interest rates. Madan and Unal (2000) and Unal et al. (2001) compare senior and subordinated bond spreads (for firms with both securities outstanding) in order to isolate the LGD. Zhou (2001) examines default correlations across firms.

Many of the earlier reduced form models focused on modeling the default intensity, PD, and made simplifying assumptions about LGD in order to disentangle the two components of the credit spread, PD × LGD. Often this involved assuming that the LGD was either constant or proportional to bond values. However, these simplifying assumptions are counterfactual. For instance, observed recovery rates are volatile and show a cyclical component that is often correlated with PD. Moreover, the default intensity also fluctuates with the business cycle and systemic risk conditions. Das and Tufano (1996) allow a proportional LGD which can vary over time, but maintain the assumption of independence between LGD and PD. Duffie and Singleton (1999) allow for (economic) state-dependence of both LGD and PD, as well as interdependence between LGD and PD; however, they assume independence between firm asset value and the LGD and PD processes, an assumption that does not hold if, for example, the debt obligation is a large part of the issuer's capital structure. Bharath and Shumway (2008) use credit default swap (CDS) spreads to estimate the hazard function. They note that since the same recovery rate is used to estimate the PD and value the CDS, the LGD drops out of the valuation equation (in approximate terms) and thus they do not make any assumptions about LGD.

Chava and Jarrow (2004) improve on the estimation of the hazard function in Shumway (2001) by incorporating monthly data, rather than annual data. They also find that introducing industry effects significantly improved forecasting ability. Industry factors impact both PD and LGD, and therefore, Chava and Jarrow (2004) find that simply estimating the hazard function separately for each industry improves the model's explanatory power.[20] They also control for firm-specific characteristics, using financial ratios such as as: (1) net income to total assets; (2) total liabilities to total assets; (3) excess returns, defined as the firm's equity return minus the value-weighted CRSP market return; (4) firm size (log of equity market value) relative to the total equity market capitalization on NYSE; and (5) stock return volatility. Both Chava and Jarrow (2004) and Campbell, Hilscher, and Szilagyi (2008) find that the forecast accuracy improves when using market values for the firm-specific characteristics.[21] Campbell, Hilscher, and Szilagyi (2008) and Bharath and Shumway (2008) add the

KMV EDF^{TM} (see Chapter 4) into the estimation of the hazard functions in their reduced form models, and find relatively little additional explanatory power. However, Bharath and Shumway (2008) incorporate the Merton model options-theoretic measure of PD (plotting the distance to default assuming normal distributions) and find a marginal contribution as a predictor in hazard models. Thus, both Campbell, Hilscher, and Szilagyi (2008) and Bharath and Shumway (2008) conclude that the reduced form modeling is the state of the art in default risk estimation.[22] A commercial service that provides reduced form estimates of PD is Kamakura's Risk Information Services.[23]

KAMAKURA'S RISK INFORMATION SERVICES (KRIS)

Kamakura's Public Firm Model (part of KRIS) estimates PD for maturities ranging from one month to five years by incorporating firm-specific information, industry information, economic environment, and macroeconomic factors into a reduced form model. The model is based on Chava and Jarrow (2004), but there is also a version that adds the Merton options-theoretic estimate of PD as an additional explanatory variable (see Bharath and Shumway [2008]).

In Kamakura's reduced form model credit spreads are decomposed into PD and LGD by the use of both debt and equity prices in order to better separate the default intensity process from the loss recovery process.[24] The default hazard rate is modeled as a function of stochastic default-free interest rates, liquidity factors, and lognormal risk factors, such as a stochastic process for the market index. KRIS is benchmarked using credit spreads or bond prices, equity prices, and accounting data over a period of 1962 to 1990, with out-of-sample forecasting over 1991 to 1999. The five explanatory variables, used to parameterize the system are:

1. Return on assets (net income/total assets).
2. Leverage (total liabilities/total assets).
3. Relative size (firm equity value/total market value of the NYSE and AMEX).
4. Excess return (monthly) over the CRSP NYSE/AMEX index return.
5. Monthly equity volatility.

In March 2009, Kamakura upgraded the KRIS model to incorporate 40 key macroeconomic risk factors into the estimation of default probabilities for more than 20,000 public firms in 30 countries. This upgrade shows that home price-related risk factors represented the five most significant risk factors of the 40 factors in the study, whereas real growth in GDP and the U.S. unemployment rate had less explanatory power. Using the power curve (also known as Receiver Operating Characteristic, or ROC curve) to assess accuracy (e.g., see Figures 4.11 and 10.2), the Moody's KMV model correctly ranks 90.50 percent of the observations, as compared to 95.54 percent using KRIS for all public firms in the United States and Canada from 1990 to 2004. Chava and Jarrow (2004) find that the public firm model including firm-specific accounting variables has a 91.98 percent accuracy rate, based on the 20 percent PD exclusion (bottom two deciles). Moreover, the area under the ROC curve is 94.49 percent for the public firm model.[25]

Kamakura maintains a troubled company index, which comprises all firms with annualized monthly default probabilities in excess of 1 percent out of 20,000 firms in 29 countries. As of September 2008, the highest (lowest) value of the index was 28 percent in September 2001 (April and May 2006), with the long-run average of 13.4 percent. Figure 5.4 shows that 24.3 percent of public firms were troubled according to the index as of

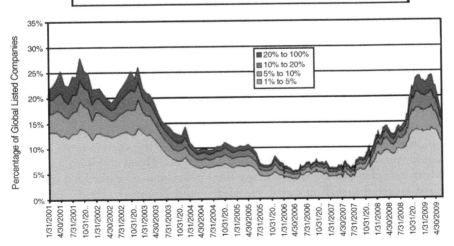

FIGURE 5.4 Kamakura's Troubled Company Index
Source: www.kamakuraco.com.

March 2009, representing a slight worsening from the 24 percent index level in December 2008.[26]

To illustrate, we describe a proprietary reduced form model—the Kamakura Corporation's Risk Manager (KRIS) uses bond prices, CDS spreads, equity prices, and accounting data in order to solve a reduced form model with stochastic default-free interest rates, a liquidity premium, and an endogenously determined LGD. This model decomposes observed yields on risky debt into a riskless rate and a credit spread, using either swap spreads or corporate bond yields in order to solve for the credit spread.[27] However, estimates of PD and LGD will be biased if corporate bond yields are affected by factors other than just the risk-free rate and the credit spread. Huang and Huang (2000) suggest that only a very small portion (only 24 percent for a 10-year Baa-Treasury yield spread) of the yields on investment-grade corporate bonds is determined by credit risk exposure.[28] Thus, a potential shortcoming to the reduced form model estimation of default risk is noise in bond and CDS prices. We therefore consider what factors, other than credit risk, determine actual bond spreads and prices.

DETERMINANTS OF BOND SPREADS

Figure 5.5 shows the size and distribution of global financial markets that comprised almost $150 trillion of securities as of December 2006. Nongovernmental debt obligations comprised $27.8 trillion, or almost 19 percent of the total. Despite the size of debt instruments outstanding, markets tend to be illiquid and less transparent than equity markets. One reason is that only a small fraction of the volume of corporate bond trading occurs on organized exchanges.[29] The rest of the trades is conducted over the counter by bond dealers. Saunders, Srinivasan, and Walter (2002) show that this interdealer market is not very competitive. It is characterized by large spreads and infrequent trades, which increase transaction costs and reduce market liquidity.

Bond features also impact transaction costs, and therefore market liquidity. Larger and more recent issues have lower transaction costs (higher liquidity); see Chakravarty and Sarkar (2003) and Hong and Warga (2000). More complex bonds, with sinking fund provisions or embedded options, have larger transaction costs; see Harris and Piwowar (2006). Edwards et al. (2007) find that larger transactions have lower costs. Some studies (e.g., Harris and Piwowar [2006], Chakravarty and Sarkar [2003], and Hong and Warga [2000]) find that bonds with more credit risk have higher transaction costs, but Schultz (2001) finds no relationship.

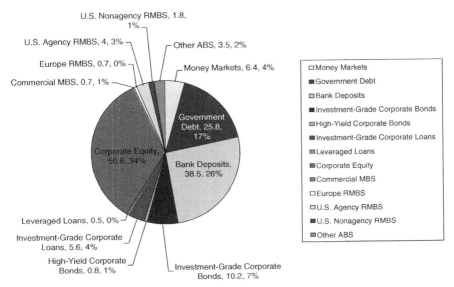

FIGURE 5.5 Global Financial Markets as of December 2006 ($ Trillions)
Source: Bank of England, *Financial Stability Report*, October 2007, Issue 22.

In July 2002, NASD introduced TRACE (Trade Reporting and Compliance Engine) in an attempt to increase price transparency in the U.S. corporate debt market. The system captures and disseminates consolidated information on secondary market transactions in publicly traded TRACE-eligible securities (investment-grade, high-yield, and convertible corporate debt).[30] Despite the introduction of this system to improve transparency in the corporate bond market, Goldstein and Hotchkiss (2007) find evidence of a price dispersion in the market such that there is a "difference in price paid across customer buys from the *same* dealer for the *same* bond on the *same* day" over the 2002–2006 period, with prices frequently differing by more than $2 per $100 face value. As TRACE expanded, this price dispersion was reduced but not eliminated. Goldstein, Hotchkiss, and Sirri (2006) find that increased transparency improves liquidity, but not for infrequently traded bonds. Hotchkiss and Jostova (2007), using the NAIC database of corporate bond trading by U.S. insurance companies, find that 79.4 percent (84.1 percent) of investment-grade (below-investment-grade) bonds never traded over the five-year period from 1995 to 1999. Thus, most corporate bonds trade infrequently in illiquid markets that are not transparent.

The implication of this lack of liquidity is that bond yields include a risk premium for illiquidity: Amihud and Mendelson (1991) find that bond illiquidity (i.e., trading transaction costs) influences yield to maturity. That is, liquidity measures the cost of rapidly converting an asset into cash (e.g., selling a corporate bond). In a market that is not transparent, investors bear these costs since they do not know whether they are transacting at accurate prices. Moreover, the over-the-counter, dealer-driven nature of the market requires a costly search for a trading partner. These costs are built into bond spreads, representing a liquidity risk premium on top of the default risk premium. However, Edwards et al. (2007) find that the introduction of TRACE increased transparency, suggesting a reduction in bond trading costs of $1 billion per year. Moreover, Longstaff, Mithal, and Neis (2005) show that bond spreads contain more of an illiquidity premium than CDS spreads.

The importance of liquidity to investors becomes apparent in its absence. During the economic crisis of 2007–2009, financial markets throughout the world shut down. Liquidity became an ever more important consideration for investors and the price of liquidity (the liquidity risk premium) soared, as shown in Figure 5.6. During the last months of 2008 (the third phase of the crisis—see the discussion in Chapter 2), the spread between LIBOR and the overnight index swap (OIS) rate soared from its historical level of about 10 basis points to more than 300 basis points, as investors demanded a high-risk premium for even the slightest amounts of illiquidity.[31] These spreads are built into bond yields, thereby complicating the decomposition of spreads into a measure of credit risk. That is, the considerable noise in bond prices, as well as investors' preferences for liquidity, suggest that there is a liquidity premium built into bond spreads. Thus, if risky bond yields are decomposed into the riskless rate plus the credit spread only, the estimate of credit risk exposure will be biased upward.

Risky corporate bonds also contain embedded options, such as call and conversion features, as well as covenants and sinking funds. These features have value that must be incorporated into analysis of bond spreads. A common practice is to avoid this complex valuation process and only consider option-free corporate bonds in empirical studies. However, this biases the sample since the subset of option-free bonds tends to have lower credit risk exposure than the general population. Thus, observed bond yields must be adjusted to reflect the value of increasingly complicated embedded options.

In the application of the models, furthermore, even the specification of the risk-free rate can be troublesome. Duffee (1998) finds that changes in credit spreads are negatively related to changes in risk-free interest rates for lower-credit-quality bonds.[32] Although Treasury yields are typically used to measure the risk-free rate, it may be more appropriate to use the highest-

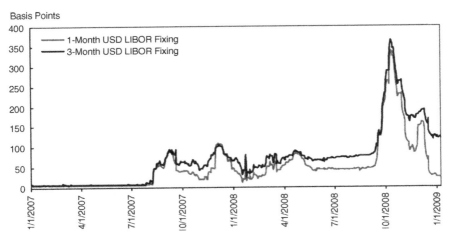

Basis Points

FIGURE 5.6 Spread of LIBOR to Overnight Index Swap Rate
Note: The LIBOR/OIS spread represents the difference between market rates and one measure of the expected path of the overnight effective rate for specific tenors. Historically, the spread has been narrow and relatively constant.
Source: Federal Reserve Bank of New York, Markets Group, *Domestic Open Market Operations During 2008*, Chart 1.

quality corporate bond yield as the benchmark default-free rate. Part of this stems from the asymmetric tax treatments of corporate and Treasury bonds. Bohn (2000b) claims that use of a default-free rate is more appropriate unless all other sources of risk are explicitly modeled.

There are also administrative costs of holding a portfolio of risky debt. This cost of carry was measured by Aguais et al. (1997) at about 15 to 16 basis points for high-credit-quality (rated A and AA) short-term loans.

Incorporating all of these considerations into our representation of risky bond yields requires the following restatement of equation (5.4′) as follows:

$$y = r_t + [PD_t \times LGD] + L_t + O_t + C + \varepsilon_t \qquad (5.4'')$$

where
r_t = stochastic risk-free rate
$PD_t \times LGD$ = credit spread
L_t = liquidity risk factor
O_t = value of embedded options
C = carrying costs, including tax considerations
ε_t = bond pricing error term

Reduced form models only focus on the problem of identifying the credit spread portion of observed bond yields and separating it into its two component parts: PD and LGD.

SUMMARY

Reduced form models decompose risky bond yields into the risk-free rate plus a credit risk premium. The credit spread consists of the risk-neutral probability of default (PD) multiplied by the loss given default (LGD). Reduced form models utilize data on bond spreads, credit default swap (CDS) spreads, equity prices, and firm accounting variables in order to estimate a hazard function to forecast default risk. Kamakura's Risk Information Systems (KRIS) estimates incorporate macroeconomic factors into the estimation of reduced form models for both publicly traded and private firms. The primary advantages of reduced form models over structural models like KMV Moody's are (1) their relative ease of computation, and (2) their better fit to observed credit spread data.

APPENDIX 5.1: UNDERSTANDING A BASIC INTENSITY PROCESS

Default probabilities can be modeled as a Poisson process with intensity h such that the probability of default over the next short time period, Δ, is approximately Δh and the expected time to default is $1/h$. Therefore, in continuous time, the probability of survival without default for t years is:[33]

$$1 - \text{PD} = e^{-ht} \tag{5.7}$$

Thus, if an A-rated firm has an h of .001, it is expected to default once in 1,000 years. Using equation (5.7) to compute the probability of survival over the next year, we obtain .999. Thus, the firm's PD over a one-year horizon is .001. Alternatively, if a B-rated firm has an h equal to .05, it is expected to default once in 20 years. Substituting into equation (5.7), we find that the probability of survival over the next year is .95 and the PD is .05.[34] If a portfolio consists of 1,000 loans to A-rated firms and 100 loans to B-rated firms, then there are 6 defaults expected per year.[35] A hazard rate can be defined as the arrival time of default—that is, $-p'_t/p_t$ where p_t is the probability of survival and p'_t is the first derivative of the survival probability function (assumed to be differentiable with respect to t). Since the probability of survival depends on the intensity h, the terms *hazard rate* and *intensity* are often used interchangeably.[36]

Default intensities may be affected by external macroeconomic events. Thus, default intensities may change over time. The probability of survival for t years can be expressed in discrete terms as

$$\mathrm{E}\left[e^{-(h_0 + h_1 + h_2 + \cdots + h_{t-1})}\right]$$

where $h_0 \ldots h_{t-1}$ are the time-varying default intensities in years $0, \ldots, t-1$.[37] If there is a joint macroeconomic or systemic factor J that impacts the default intensity of each firm i, then the total default intensity of firm i at time t can be expressed as:

$$h_{it} = p_{it} J_t + H_{it} \tag{5.8}$$

where $J_t =$ is the intensity of arrival of systemic events
            $p_{it} =$ is the probability that firm i defaults given a systemic event
            $H_{it} =$ is the firm-specific intensity of default arrival

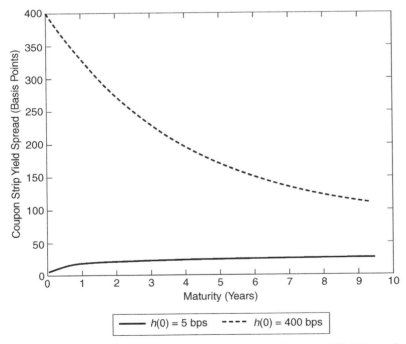

FIGURE 5.7   Term Structure of Coupon-Strip (Zero-Recovery) Yield Spreads
Source: Duffie and Singleton (1998), page 20.

Thus, the intensity of arrival of any kind of event is:

$$H_t = J_t + H_{1t} + \cdots + H_{nt}$$

Substituting the parameters of our earlier example into equation (5.7), if the A-rated firm defaults with probability .02 in the event of a systemic breakdown that occurs with a 1 percent probability, then the firm's default intensity increases to .0012 and it is expected to default once within the next 833 (as opposed to 1,000) years. Moreover, if the B-rated firm defaults with a probability of 50 percent if the systemic event occurs, then the firm's default intensity increases to .055 for one expected default within the next 18 (rather than 20) years. The introduction of time-varying default intensities causes the portfolio to have an expected 6.7 (rather than 6) defaults per year.

Duffie and Singleton (1998) formulate the firm-specific intensity process h as a mean-reverting process with independently distributed jumps that arrive at some constant intensity λ; otherwise h reverts at rate k to a constant θ. Figure 5.7 plots the credit spreads for two obligations with the same parameters ($\theta = 10$ basis points, $\lambda = 10$ basis points, $k = .5$, and $J = 5$), but with different initial default intensities.[38] The credit obligation with high credit risk has an initial default intensity of 400 basis points, whereas the low-risk obligation has an initial default intensity of 5 basis points.[39] Figure 5.7 shows that credit spreads are clearly sensitive to parameter estimates.

CHAPTER 6

Other Credit Risk Models

INTRODUCTION

In Chapters 4 and 5, we describe the two developing branches of academic work in credit risk modeling: structural models and reduced form models. In this chapter, we describe other, more established models, whose inceptions date back several decades. These models have proven their usefulness over the long run and continue to be used and improved as new modeling developments are incorporated into the fundamental models. We describe:

- Credit scoring systems, such as the Altman Z score model.
- Mortality rate systems, following the insurance industry's approach.
- Neural network systems.

Upon completing our survey of default probability estimation models, we undertake a broad comparison of their accuracy.

CREDIT SCORING SYSTEMS

Credit scoring systems can be found in virtually all types of credit analysis, from consumer credit to commercial loans. The idea is to identify certain key factors that determine the probability of default (as opposed to repayment), and combine or weight them into a quantitative score. In some cases, the score can be literally interpreted as a probability of default; in others, the score can be used as a classification system. That is, it places a potential borrower into either a good or a bad group, based on a score and a cutoff point. Full reviews of the traditional approach to credit scoring, and the various methodologies, can be found in Caouette, Altman, and Narayanan (1998). A good review of the worldwide application of credit-scoring models can be found in Altman and Narayanan (1997). Mester

(1997) documents the widespread use of credit scoring models, finding that 97 percent of banks use credit scoring to approve credit card applications, whereas 70 percent of the banks use credit scoring in their small business lending.[1]

There are four methodological forms of multivariate credit scoring models: (1) the linear probability model, (2) the logit model, (3) the probit model, and (4) the discriminant analysis model. One of the first credit scoring models was the Altman (1968) Z-score model, which is a classification model for corporate borrowers (but can also be used to get a default probability prediction).[2] Based on a matched sample (by year, size, and industry) of failed and solvent firms, and using linear discriminant analysis, the best-fitting scoring model for commercial loans took the form:

$$Z = 1.2X_1 + 1.4X_2 + 3.3X_3 + 0.6X_4 + 1.0X_5$$

where X_1 = working capital/total assets ratio
        X_2 = retained earnings/total assets ratio
        X_3 = earnings before interest and taxes/total assets ratio
        X_4 = market value of equity/book value of total liabilities ratio
        X_5 = sales/total assets ratio

As used by the credit officer, if a corporate borrower's financial accounting ratios (the X_i's), when weighted by the estimated coefficients in the Z function, result in a Z score below a critical value (in Altman's initial study this critical cutoff point was 1.81), the borrower would be classified as a "bad" credit risk, and the loan would be refused. The choice of the optimal cutoff credit score can incorporate changes in economic conditions. That is, if the economy is expected to decline, the cutoff point could be raised in order to decrease the probability of granting bad loans. This reduces the model's Type 1 error (lending to bad customers), but increases the model's Type 2 error (the likelihood that good customers will be denied credit).[3]

Over time, Altman has developed a number of variants of his basic model including a Z' (or Z-prime) and Z" (or Z-double-prime) credit scoring model. All of the Z score models use discriminant analysis on samples of failing and matched surviving firms to identify the variables and their weights so as to assign a score that best identifies the financial health of a firm. The resulting Z score derived from the model is an indication of financial health, such that the higher the Z score, the healthier the firm and the less likely it is to default on its obligations. The three Z-score models, discussed in more detail in Altman and Hotchkiss (2006), estimate different weighting schemes and explanatory variables that best estimate the Z score for the appropriate borrower type. For example, the Z'' model is designed to assess the health of nonmanufacturing firms and also has been used to assess the health of non-U.S. firms.

The Z'' score model takes the form:

$$Z'' = 3.25 + 6.56X_1 + 3.26X_2 + 6.72X_3 + 1.05X_4$$

where $X_1 = \dfrac{\text{Current assets} - \text{Current liabilities}}{\text{Total assets}}$

$X_2 = \dfrac{\text{Retained earnings}}{\text{Total assets}}$

$X_3 = \dfrac{\text{Earnings before interest and taxes}}{\text{Total assets}}$

$X_4 = \dfrac{\text{Book value of equity}}{\text{Total liabilities}}$

Once a company's accounting variables have been used to calculate the ratios X_1, X_2, X_3, and X_4 and these variables have been multiplied by the appropriate weights, a Z'' score can be calculated for the company.[4] Once calculated, the score can be mapped into an equivalent S&P (Moody's) rating based on historical links between the Z'' scores of companies and the implied agency rating. Table 6.1 shows Altman's mapping of the resulting

TABLE 6.1 Altman and Hotchkiss Mappings of Ratings to Different Z Scores

	Panel A: Average Z Scores by S&P Bond Ratings		
	Average Annual Number of Firms	Average Z Score	Standard Deviation of Z Score
AAA	66	6.20	2.06
AA	194	4.73	2.36
A	519	3.74	2.29
BBB	530	2.81	1.48
BB	538	2.38	1.85
B	390	1.80	1.91
CCC	10	0.33	1.16
D	244	−0.20	NA

(Continued)

TABLE 6.1 (*Continued*)

Panel B: Average Z″ Scores by S&P Bond Ratings	
Credit Rating	Average Z″ Scores
AAA	8.15
AA+	7.60
AA	7.30
AA−	7.00
A+	6.85
A	6.65
A−	6.40
BBB+	6.25
BBB	5.85
BBB−	5.65
BB+	5.25
BB	4.95
BB−	4.75
B+	4.50
B	4.15
B−	3.75
CCC+	3.20
CCC	2.50
CCC−	1.75
D	0.0

Source: E. Altman and E. Hotchkiss, *Corporate Financial Distress and Bankruptcy*, 3rd edition (New York: Wiley Finance, 2006), pages 247–248.

Z″ score to a credit rating, based on a sample of 750 U.S. companies (see pages 247–249 of Altman and Hotchkiss [2006]). Thus, on average, AAA firms have Z″ credit scores of 8.15 while those firms with a Z″ score of 3.75 have a rating of B−.

A number of issues need to be raised here. First, the model is linear whereas the path to bankruptcy may be highly nonlinear (the relationship between the X_i's is likely to be nonlinear as well). Second, with the exception of the market value of equity term in the leverage ratio, the Z score model is essentially based on accounting ratios. In most countries, accounting data appear only at discrete intervals (e.g., quarterly) and are generally based on historic or book value accounting principles. It is also questionable whether such models can pick up a firm whose condition is rapidly deteriorating (such as during the 2007–2009 financial crisis).

Indeed, as the world becomes more complex and competitive, the predictability of static Z-score models may worsen. A good example is Brazil. When fitted in the mid-1970s, the Z-score model did quite a good job of predicting default even two or three years prior to bankruptcy (see Altman, Baidya and Dias [1979]). However, more recently, even with low inflation and greater economic stability, this type of model has performed less well as the Brazilian economy has become more open (see Sanvicente and Bader [1998]). Moreover, Mester (1997) reports that 56 percent of the 33 banks that used credit scoring in order to approve credit card applications failed to predict loan quality problems. If credit scoring models are inaccurate for relatively homogenous credit card applications, how are they to evaluate complex large business loans?[5]

However, more recently, the discriminant model fit has been improved by considering a nonparametric approach (see Barniv and Raveh [1989]); the selection of explanatory variables with a multivariate normal distribution, (see Karels and Prakash [1987]); and a neural network, (see Coates and Fant [1993]). Interestingly, both J.P. Morgan and Nomura Securities undertook an equity trading strategy based on Altman Z scores during the market turmoil in the fall of 2008, noting that market collapses in August 2007, January 2008, March 2008, August 2008, and October 2008 were preceded by weak performance of the equity issued by less creditworthy firms, and similarly, recoveries were led by stronger credit companies. Thus, they advocated buying stock in companies with high Altman Z scores and selling companies with low Z scores. They claimed that this strategy was profitable on a cross-country basis. Finally, in March 2010, Altman, in association with Risk Metrics, has produced a revised Z-score methodology based on logistic regression that appears to perform better than the traditional Z-score models.

MORTALITY RATE SYSTEMS

Mortality models utilize techniques that are commonly used in the insurance industry. Based on a portfolio of loans or bonds and their historic default experience, a mortality rate system develops a table that can be used in a predictive sense for one-year, or *marginal*, mortality rates (MMR) and for multiyear, or *cumulative*, mortality rates (CMR). Combining such calculations with LGDs can produce estimates of expected losses.[6]

For example, to calculate the MMRs of B-rated bonds (loans) in each year of their life, the analyst will pick a sample of issue years—say, 1971 through 2000—and, for *each year t*, will look at the total value of grade B bonds defaulting in year *i* after issue. For example, for year 1 and year 2 default after issue we have:

$$\text{MMR}_{1t} = \frac{\text{Total value of grade B bonds defaulting in year 1 after issue in year } t}{\text{Total value of grade B bonds outstanding in year 1 after issue in year } t} \tag{6.1}$$

$$\text{MMR}_{2t} = \frac{\substack{\text{Total value of} \\ \text{grade B bonds defaulting in year 2 after issue in year } t}}{\substack{\text{Total value of grade B bonds outstanding in year 2} \\ \text{after issue in year } t \text{ (adjusted for defaults, calls, sinking} \\ \text{fund redemptions, and maturities in the prior year)}}} \tag{6.2}$$

And so on for $\text{MMR}_{3t}, \ldots, \text{MMR}_{nt}$.

The MMRs for each individual year can be combined to create a term structure of MMRs. Using each individual year's MMR_{it} in the term structure, the analyst calculates a weighted average over the entire sample period, which becomes the figure entered into the mortality table. The weights used should reflect the relative issue sizes w_t in different years, thus biasing the results toward the larger-issue years. The weighted average MMR in year 1 for a particular grade (MMR) would be calculated as:

$$\text{MMR}_1 = \sum_{t=1971}^{2000} \text{MMR}_{1t} \times w_t \tag{6.3}$$

To calculate a cumulative mortality rate (CMR)—the probability that a loan or bond will default over a period longer than a year after issue—it is first necessary to specify the relationship between MMRs and survival rates (SRs):

$$\text{MMR}_i = 1 - \text{SR}_t$$

or $\tag{6.4}$

$$\text{SR}_i = 1 - \text{MMR}_t$$

Consequently,

$$\text{CMR}_T = 1 - \prod_{t=1}^{T} \text{SR}_t \tag{6.5}$$

where $\prod$ = the geometric sum or product $\text{SR}_1 \times \text{SR}_2 \times \ldots \text{SR}_N$
         T = number of years over which the cumulative mortality rate is calculated

Mortality tables are generated from the calculations of the MMR and CMR. Table 6.2 shows marginal and cumulative mortality rates for syndicated loans and bonds over a 10-year horizon, as computed by Altman and Hotchkiss (2006). The table has an interesting feature: marginal mortality rates fluctuate non-monotonically over the life of the corporate bond.

Although not shown, each of the MMR estimates has an implied standard error and confidence interval. Moreover, it can be shown that as the number of loans or bonds in the sample increases (i.e., as N gets bigger), the standard error on a mortality rate will fall (i.e., the degree of confidence we have in using the MMR estimate to predict expected losses out-of-sample increases). This is because, in any period a loan or bond either dies or survives, the standard error (σ) of an MMR is:[7]

$$\sigma = \sqrt{\frac{MMR_t(1 - MMR_t)}{N}} \qquad (6.6)$$

which translates into:

$$N = \sqrt{\frac{MMR_i(1 - MMR_t)}{\sigma^2}} \qquad (6.7)$$

As can be seen from the preceding two equations, there is an inverse relationship between N (sample size) and the σ (standard error) of a mortality rate estimate. Suppose that $MMR_1 = .01$ is a mortality rate estimate, and we want to apply extreme actuarial principles of confidence in the stability of the estimate for pricing and prediction out-of-sample. Extreme actuarial principles might require σ to be one-tenth the size of the mortality rate estimate (or $\sigma = .001$). Plugging the values into equation (6.7), we have:

$$N = \frac{(.01)(.99)}{(.001)^2} = 9,900$$

This suggests that we would need almost 10,000 loan observations per rating class to get this type of confidence in the estimate. With 10 rating classes (as under most bank rating systems), we would need to analyze a portfolio of some 100,000 loans. With respect to commercial loans, very few banks have built information systems of this type. To get to the requisite large size, a cooperative effort among the banks themselves may be required. The end result of such a cooperative effort might be a national loan mortality table that could be as useful in establishing banks' loan loss reserves (based on expected losses) as the national life mortality tables are in pricing life insurance.[8]

TABLE 6.2 Mortality Rates by Original Rating—All Rated Corporate Bonds, 1971–2004[a]

		Years after Issuance[a]									
		1	2	3	4	5	6	7	8	9	10
AAA	Marginal	0.00%	0.00%	0.00%	0.00%	0.03%	0.00%	0.00%	0.00%	0.00%	0.00%
	Cumulative	0.00	0.00	0.00	0.00	0.03	0.03	0.03	0.03	0.03	0.03
AA	Marginal	0.00	0.00	0.32	0.16	0.03	0.03	0.00	0.00	0.03	0.02
	Cumulative	0.00	0.00	0.32	0.48	0.51	0.54	0.54	0.59	0.57	0.59
A	Marginal	0.01	0.10	0.02	0.09	0.06	0.11	0.06	0.21	0.11	0.06
	Cumulative	0.01	0.11	0.13	0.22	0.28	0.39	0.45	0.65	0.76	0.82
BBB	Marginal	0.36	3.22	1.43	1.28	0.77	0.45	0.20	0.20	0.14	0.40
	Cumulative	0.36	3.56	4.49	6.16	6.89	7.31	7.50	7.68	7.87	8.18
BB	Marginal	1.19	2.48	4.40	2.01	2.51	1.16	1.60	0.88	1.70	3.60
	Cumulative	1.19	3.64	7.88	9.74	12.00	12.93	14.36	15.07	16.52	19.60
B	Marginal	2.85	6.85	7.40	8.55	6.00	4.16	3.72	2.28	1.96	0.86
	Cumulative	2.85	9.51	16.20	23.37	27.94	30.96	33.46	34.97	36.25	36.80
CCC	Marginal	7.98	15.57	19.55	12.10	4.26	9.45	5.60	3.15	0.00	4.28
	Cumulative	7.98	22.31	37.50	45.06	47.37	52.35	55.01	56.43	56.43	58.30

[a]Rated by S&P at issuance based on 1,719 issues.
Source: Altman and Hotchkiss (2006), Table 7.12, page 171.

ARTIFICIAL NEURAL NETWORKS

The development of a computerized expert system to forecast the probability of default requires acquisition of the human expert's knowledge. Since this is often a time-consuming and error-prone task, many systems use induction to infer the human experts' decision processes by studying their decisions. Elmer and Borowski (1988) compare the bankruptcy predictions of an expert system to several credit scoring models and find that the expert system correctly anticipate over 60 percent of the failures 7 to 18 months before bankruptcy, whereas the credit scoring models have prediction rates of only 48 percent and 33 percent. Similarly, Messier and Hansen (1988) show that their expert system outperform credit scoring models and the human experts themselves in forecasting business failures.

The disadvantages of induction-based expert systems include:

■ The time and effort required to translate the human experts' decision processes into a system of rules.
■ The difficulty and costs associated with programming the decision algorithm and maintaining the system.
■ The inability or inflexibility of the expert system to adapt to changing conditions.

Artificial neural networks have been proposed as solutions to these problems. An artificial neural system simulates the human learning process such that the system learns the nature of the relationship between inputs and outputs by repeatedly sampling input/output information sets. Neural networks have a particular advantage over expert systems when data are noisy or incomplete, since the neural net system can make an educated guess much as would a human expert. Hawley, Johnson, and Raina (1990) describe how neural networks can incorporate subjective, nonquantifiable information into credit approval decisions. Kim and Scott (1991) use a supervised artificial neural network to predict bankruptcy in a sample of 190 Compustat firms. While the system performs well (87 percent prediction rate) during the year of bankruptcy, its accuracy declines markedly over time, showing only a 75 percent, 59 percent, and 47 percent prediction accuracy one year prior, two years prior, and three years prior to bankruptcy, respectively. Altman, Marco, and Varetto (1994) examine 1,000 Italian industrial firms from 1982 to 1992 and find that neural networks have about the same level of accuracy as do credit scoring models. Poddig (1995), using data on 300 French firms collected over three years, claims that neural networks outperform credit scoring models in bankruptcy prediction. However, he finds that not all artificial neural systems are equal, noting that the multilayer perception (or back-propagation) network is best suited for bankruptcy prediction. Yang et al. (1999) use a sample of oil and gas company debt to show that the back-propagation neural network obtained the highest classification accuracy overall, when compared to the probabilistic neural network and to discriminant analysis. However, discriminant analysis outperforms all models of neural networks in minimizing Type 2 classification errors.[9]

Neural networks are characterized by three architectural features: inputs, weights, and hidden units. Figure 6.1 shows a two-layer system with two hidden units and n inputs. The n inputs, $x_1, x_2, \ldots, x_n$, represent the data received by the system (for example, company financial ratios for the bankruptcy prediction neural networks). Each piece of information is assigned a weight $(w_{11}, w_{21}, \ldots, w_{n1})$ designating its relative importance to each hidden unit (y_1). These weights are learned by the network over the course of training. For example, by observing the financial characteristics of many bankrupt firms (the training process), the network learns the weights.

Each hidden unit computes the weighted sum of all inputs and transmits the result to other hidden units. In parallel, the other hidden units are weighting their inputs so as to transmit their signal to all other connected

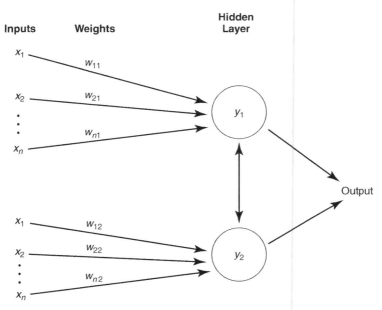

FIGURE 6.1 A Neural Network

hidden units. Receipt of the signal from other hidden units further transforms the output from each node, with the system continuing to iterate until all information is incorporated. This model incorporates complex correlations among the hidden units to improve model fit and reduce Type 1 and Type 2 errors. But care should be taken not to overfit the model. Overfitting results in a model that explains well in-sample, but may perform quite poorly in predicting out-of-sample.

Because of the large number of possible connections, the neural network can grow prohibitively large rather quickly. For a set of networks with 10 inputs and 12 hidden units, the maximum possible number of network configurations is 4.46×10^{43}.[10] Thus, various pruning methods exist to economize on the number of connections in the system. Weights and hidden units are pruned during the training stage so as to incorporate only those inputs that are relevant in obtaining the desired output.

A major disadvantage of neural networks is their lack of transparency. The internal structure of the network is hidden and may not be easy to duplicate, even using the same data inputs. This leads to a lack of accountability since the system's intermediate steps cannot be checked. Moreover, although the neural network is useful as a tool of classification or prediction, it does nothing to illuminate the process or the relative importance of the variables. That is, the neural net does not reveal anything about the intermediate steps that lead to the final output.

Since independent rating agencies, such as Moody's and Standard & Poor's, use human expert systems to incorporate subjective factors and non-quantifiable influences (such as changes in management or business cycle effects), neural networks can be used to forecast the corporate bond ratings issued by independent rating agencies. Moody and Utans (1994) find that neural networks outperform linear regressions in accurately classifying corporate bond ratings. Moreover, Singleton and Surkan (1994) show a 73 percent accuracy rate in predicting bond rating changes, as compared to a 57 percent accuracy rate using a credit scoring discriminant model. These results suggest that there is more to bond credit ratings than simply a weighted average of financial ratios.

COMPARISON OF DEFAULT PROBABILITY ESTIMATION MODELS

We have surveyed numerous quantitative models that can be used to forecast the probability of default for companies and individuals. Although we have discussed each model's advantages and disadvantages from a conceptual standpoint, this section provides a brief survey of some of the literature that performs a comparative analysis from a quantitative standpoint. That is, which of the models yields more accurate estimates of the likelihood of default? As always, there is no simple answer to this question, particularly since different models may be appropriate to solve different problems. Therefore, we provide the empirical results in this section and leave the conclusion to the reader's determination

Shumway (2001) compares reduced form hazard models with static credit scoring models.[11] He enters the accounting ratios used in credit scoring models into a reduced form model and finds that half of the ratios are statistically insignificant, suggesting that the credit scoring models may be misspecified. In addition to the accounting variables used in the static credit scoring models, Shumway (2001) adds market-based variables, such as the firm's equity market capitalization and the idiosyncratic (nonsystematic) portion of each company's stock return volatility (standard deviation). Table 6.3 shows that the accuracy of Shumway's model is 75 percent in out-of-sample tests, such that the model accurately predicts bankruptcies for 75 percent of the top 10 percent highest-risk companies. Consistent with this result, Bharath and Shumway (2008) compare structural models (e.g., the Merton options-theoretic model and the Moody's KMV model) to reduced form hazard models, and find that hazard models outperform structural models.[12]

TABLE 6.3   Forecast Accuracy with Market-Driven Variables (Probability Rankings versus Actual Bankruptcies)

Decile	Market	Accounting and Market
1	69.0	75.0
2	10.6	12.5
3	7.8	6.3
4	5.0	1.8
5	2.8	0.9
6–10	4.8	3.5
Possible	142	112

Note: This table presents a comparison of the out-of-sample accuracy of the bankruptcy models that contain market-driven variables. All of the models are estimated with data available between 1962 and 1983. Parameter estimates calculated with 1983 data are combined with annual data between 1984 and 1992 to forecast bankruptcies occurring between 1984 and 1992.

Source: Shumway (2001), page 122.

Hillegeist et al. (2002) compare credit scoring models (the Z score and the O score) to a structural model using a sample consisting of 65,960 firm-year observations including 516 bankruptcies during the 1979–1997 period.[13] They find that the structural model outperforms both credit scoring models. Table 6.4 examines the explanatory power of the two credit scoring models (Z score and O score) in the same

TABLE 6.4 Incremental Information Tests

Variable	Column 1	Column 2	Column 3
Constant	−6.40*	−6.30*	−5.76*
Bank rate	125.1*	126.4*	105.9*
Z score	0.09*		
Z score(n)		−0.37	
O score	0.00		
O score(n)		3.11*	
BSM-PB	3.62*	3.46*	2.87*
ExRet			−0.61*
Rsize			−9.63*
−2 Log likelihood	5,291	5,291	5,089
Wald X^2	1,306	1,215	1,157
Pseudo-R^2	0.12	0.12	0.16
Observations	65,960	65,960	65,960

"Bank rate" refers to the economywide rate of corporate bankruptcies among publicly-traded firms over the past 12 months. BSM-PB assumes dividend rate = 0 and asset growth rate = Adjusted ROA_{t-1}.
Z score is derived using the variables and parameter estimates of Altman (1968).
Z score(n) is derived from the variables used by Altman (1968) estimated using a discrete hazard model.
O score is derived using the variables and parameter estimates of Ohlson (1980).
O score(n) is the fitted probability of bankruptcy based on Ohlson (1980) estimates using a discrete hazard model.
ExRet is the firm's total return in year $t - 1$ minus the value-weighted return of the NYSE/AMEX/NASDAQ index in year $t - 1$.
Rsize is the logarithm of each firm's market capitalization measured at the beginning of the observation year, relative to the total capitalization of the firms in our sample.
*Significant at 1 percent or lower (two-sided test).

Source: © Moody's Analytics, Inc. and/or its affiliates. Reprinted with permission. All Rights Reserved.

regression with the Merton options-theoretic structural model (denoted BSM-PB) in order to assess each model's explanatory power in predicting bankruptcy. Whereas the explanatory power of the structural model estimate of default risk is statistically significant, the static credit scoring models' estimates are not. However, when estimating the Z score and the O score using a discrete hazard model, the explanatory power becomes statistically significant. Table 6.4 is based on a discrete hazard model with Huber-White standard errors to control for firm dependence. The dependent variable is bankruptcy in the 4 to 16 months following the fiscal year-end.

Similarly, Bohn et al. (2005) find that the KMV Moody's structural model estimate of default outperforms Altman's Z score model. As shown in Figure 6.2, the power (cumulative accuracy performance) curve of the KMV Moody's EDF™ score is higher than that of the Z score tested over the 1996–2004 period.[14] They find that the accuracy ratio of the KMV Moody's EDF™ is 77 percent using a subsample of firms over $30 million in asset size over the 2000–2004 subperiod. In contrast, using the same subsample of firms, the accuracy ratio of the Z score is only 58 percent. Credit ratings have an accuracy rate of 72 percent and the Merton options-theoretic model has a 60 percent accuracy rate over the 2000–2004 subperiod.

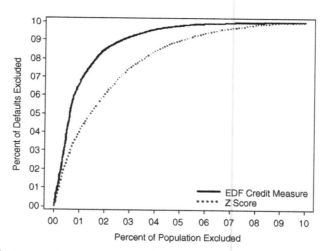

FIGURE 6.2 Comparing the Accuracy of EDF and Z Scores
Source: © Moody's Analytics, Inc. and/or its affiliates. Reprinted with permission. All Rights Reserved.

SUMMARY

In this chapter, we have surveyed several venerable models of default risk that continue to be utilized. Given the differing data requirements, these models are sometimes the only practical models that can be implemented, particularly when the data requirements (e.g., credit spread data) of reduced form models cannot be met. Thus, it is instructive to compare the accuracy of these models. Even though the credit scoring model underperforms the structural and reduced form models, it still has a relatively high degree of accuracy. Moreover, recent advances in modeling have improved the accuracy of these well-established models designed to forecast the probability of default.

Estimation of Other Model Parameters

CHAPTER 7

A Critical Parameter: Loss Given Default

INTRODUCTION

As discussed in Chapter 5, the loss given default (LGD) is a critical parameter used together with the probability of default (PD) to estimate expected credit losses, calculated as PD times LGD. The LGD can be defined as one minus the recovery rate (RR) on defaulted debt instruments. Despite its importance in credit risk measurement, LGD estimation is less developed than PD modeling. In this chapter, we describe how some of the credit risk models described in earlier chapters estimate LGD.

ACADEMIC MODELS OF LGD

Even if PD is relatively high, expected credit losses may be low if recovery rates are high. Thus, for example, if a loan is fully secured with marketable securities which can be sold at full value upon default, there may be no loss at all. Table 7.1 shows that even low-grade debt issues may experience low expected loss rates because LGD is substantially lower than 100 percent. That is, even if there is a default, some value is recovered (the RR is greater than zero, and LGD = 1 – RR).

Different types of debt instruments have different recovery rates. For example, more senior securities tend to have higher recovery rates than subordinated securities, all else equal. Figure 7.1 uses the recovery history included in the Moody's KMV database to show that the highest (lowest) LGD is for preferred stock and junior subordinated bonds (industrial revenue bonds, senior secured bonds, and senior secured loans).

Early models of credit risk tended to assume a fixed or nonstochastic LGD. The Basel Committee assessed a fixed 45 percent LGD on secured

TABLE 7.1 Mortality Loss Given Default by Original Rating—All Rated Corporate Bonds: 1971–2004

		Years after Issuance[a]									
		1	2	3	4	5	6	7	8	9	10
AAA	Marginal	0.00%	0.00%	0.00%	0.00%	0.00%	0.00%	0.00%	0.00%	0.00%	0.00%
	Cumulative	0.00	0.00	0.00	0.00	0.00	0.00	0.00	0.00	0.00	0.00
AA	Marginal	0.00	0.00	0.05	0.05	0.01	0.01	0.00	0.00	0.03	0.02
	Cumulative	0.00	0.00	0.05	0.10	0.11	0.12	0.12	0.12	0.15	0.17
A	Marginal	0.00	0.03	0.01	0.04	0.03	0.06	0.02	0.04	0.08	0.00
	Cumulative	0.00	0.03	0.04	0.08	0.11	0.17	0.19	0.23	0.31	0.31
BBB	Marginal	0.25	2.25	1.10	0.77	0.46	0.27	0.10	0.11	0.07	0.24
	Cumulative	0.25	2.49	3.57	4.31	4.75	5.00	5.10	5.21	5.27	5.50
BB	Marginal	0.69	1.44	2.55	1.16	1.46	0.60	0.90	0.38	0.84	1.28
	Cumulative	0.69	2.13	4.62	5.72	7.10	7.66	8.48	9.83	9.60	10.76
B	Marginal	1.83	4.75	5.18	5.72	4.06	2.41	2.54	1.34	1.02	0.64
	Cumulative	1.83	6.50	11.34	14.41	19.80	21.73	23.72	24.75	25.51	25.99
CCC	Marginal	5.33	11.68	14.67	9.32	3.10	7.28	4.31	2.52	0.00	3.22
	Cumulative	5.33	16.39	28.65	35.31	37.31	41.88	44.38	45.78	45.78	47.53

[a] Rated by S&P at issuance based on 1,604 issues.

Source: Altman and Hotchkiss (2006), Table 7.13, page 172.

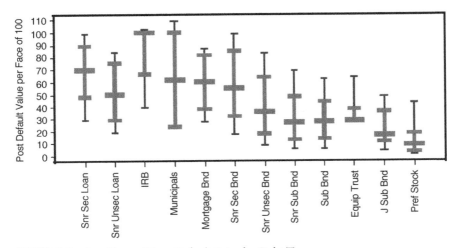

FIGURE 7.1 Box Plots of Post Default Price by Debt Type

Notes: The solid center line represents the median, the inner whiskers represent the interquartile range, and the outer whiskers represent the 10th to 90th percentile range of the distribution.

Source: © Moody's Analytics, Inc. and/or its affiliates. Reprinted with permission. All Rights Reserved.

loans if fully secured by physical, non-real-estate collateral, and 40 percent if fully secured by receivables (for the Basel II Internal Ratings-Based Foundation model, see Chapter 13). However, there is evidence suggesting that these fixed LGD rates may be too high for bank loans. A Citibank study of 831 defaulted corporate loans and 89 asset-based loans for 1970–1993 found recovery rates of 79 percent (or equivalently LGD equal to 21 percent). Similarly, high recovery rates were found in a Fitch Investor Service report in October 1997 (82 percent) and a Moody's Investor Service Report of June 1998 (87 percent), see Asarnow (1999). Carey and Gordy (2004) find an average LGD on bank debt of 23 percent.

However, Table 7.2 shows that using a large sample of Italian loans, Caselli et al. (2008) find an average (median) LGD of 54 percent (56 percent) and a standard deviation of 43 percent for the sample of 11,649 loans. The LGD for small and medium enterprises (SMEs) averaged 52 percent, but households had an average (median) LGD of 55 percent (68 percent) and a standard deviation of 45 percent This suggests that there is a wide dispersion in recovery rates across loans made to different industries and between different countries. Caselli et al. (2008) document one element of this dispersion by breaking down the loans by sector and find that the

TABLE 7.2 Relationship between Distance to Default and Recovery for U.S. Senior Unsecured Bonds

Loan Type	Number of Loans	Percent of Total	Mean LGD	Median LGD	Standard Deviation LGD
Small/Medium Businesses	6.034	51.80	0.52	0.52	0.41
Households	5,615	48.20	0.55	0.68	0.45
Entire Sample	11,649	100	0.54	0.56	0.43

Source: Caselli et al. (2008), page 8.

average (median) LGD for loans to SMEs range from 23 percent (4 percent) to 68 percent (98 percent). Similarly, the average (median) LGD for loans to households ranges from 15 percent (2 percent) to 79 percent (100 percent). Helwege et al. (2009) state that recovery rates on senior secured bonds between 1982 and 2007 ranged between 38 percent and 80 percent, with an average of 52 percent. In contrast, the credit default swap auction process yielded average recoveries of only 30 percent on senior bond auctions (see Chapter 12). Similarly, loan auctions during 2009 yielded low recovery rates (averaging 31 percent), perhaps demonstrating the distressed nature of the market during the time period.

An important distinction that may account for the disparity in estimates across studies is how the LGD is measured. Many studies use bond prices around the time of default as a measure of the recovery rate. For example, Moody's measures recoveries using the bid prices on defaulted bonds 30 days after the default occurs. Acharya et al. (2007) use trading prices of defaulted debt instruments just prior to the bankruptcy petition, or earliest available trading prices of the instruments received in a settlement or liquidation (e.g., acquisition, refinancing, distressed exchange, etc.). Debt prices around the default date are considered to be a measure of the recovery value of the debt if there is a market for the instrument. However, if there is no demand for these securities, or if the market is thin, the prices may be inaccurate or nonexistent.

In contrast, therefore, Caselli et al. (2008) use actual recovery data from bank loan workouts for their sample in order to measure the loss experienced by the lender upon default. Here the issues become quite practical. Specifically, what are the estimated recovery cash flows? Over what period of time are they to be collected? What is the estimated termination date for recoveries? And what is the discount rate to be applied to those cash flows? Each of these issues becomes relevant if the workout cost measure for recovery estimation is used by banks in the context of the Basel II IRB Advanced Model.

More fundamentally, academic research has shown that there is a stochastic component to LGD. That is, LGD is not fixed and may indeed fluctuate with both company-specific and economywide factors. Allen and Saunders (2004) survey the academic literature and note two areas of consensus. First, there is a positive correlation between asset and collateral values, thereby causing LGD (RR) to increase (decrease) as collateral values decrease. Altman (1989) finds significant positive correlations between recovery rates and external credit ratings just prior to default. Schuermann (2004) surveys evidence that recovery rates fluctuate over time and are negatively correlated with short-term default-risk-free interest rates because increases in interest rates (usually consistent with economic downturns) generally depress asset prices, thereby reducing recovery rates and increasing LGD. Calem and LaCour-Little (2004) estimate loss probability distributions for portfolios of mortgage loans and find that loan-specific characteristics (such as original loan to value ratios, measuring collateral, and borrower FICO scores) are important determinants of portfolio loss rates. Thus, LGD is a function of the underlying collateral value, which fluctuates over time.

The second area of consensus in the academic literature is that time-varying LGD has a systematic risk component—in other words, there is a cyclical component to LGD. Both historical evidence and the academic literature support this and suggest that systematic market factors affect both LGD and PD. Altman and Kishore (1996) find that recovery rates are time-varying. Maclachlan (1999) finds that credit spreads are highest and therefore bond prices are lowest during low points in the business cycle. This suggests a negative correlation between LGD and macroeconomic conditions because bond prices for distressed debt can be viewed as a lower bound on recovery amounts. Bangia, Diebold, and Schuermann (2002) use National Bureau of Economic Research (NBER) designations of contractions and expansions to find that economic capital is 30 percent higher in a contraction year than in an expansion year, suggesting that expected loss rates (that is, PD × LGD) are procyclical.

In addition to economywide factors impacting LGD, researchers have found that LGD depends on industry conditions. Acharya et al. (2007) find that RR in a distressed industry (i.e., an industry for which the median annual stock return for the three-digit SIC code is less than −30 percent) is reduced by $0.10 to $0.15 on the dollar as compared to the LGD of defaulted debt in nondistressed industries. Moreover, they find that this effect is exacerbated when industry assets are more specific (less generally usable by other firms in other industries) and the industry is more concentrated (reducing the demand for defaulted firm assets). These factors contribute to the fire sale price reductions required to dispose of defaulted firm assets, thereby reducing the recovery rate realized by creditors.

Many of the previously cited papers examining the systematic components in LGD do not generally consider whether LGD is correlated with PD. However, if LGD and PD are both impacted by the same factors, then the systematic component in LGD could be either exacerbated or mitigated. That is, if PD and LGD both increase in economic downturns and decrease in economic upturns, then the cyclical effect (as measured by both default correlations and LGD correlations) will be more pronounced. If, however, PD and LGD are negatively correlated (move in the opposite directions), then the cyclical effect in LGD may be reduced.

The question of the correlation between PD and LGD is an empirical one. Houweling and Vorst (2005) use a reduced form model to show that default swap prices are insensitive to the assumption of recovery values, although they do find a positive correlation between recovery rates and PD. Jokivuolle and Peura (2000) also model the recovery rate as a function of the PD and show that the expected LGD is a decreasing function of the growth rate in the value of collateral, an increasing function of the volatility of the collateral value, and an increasing function of the correlation between the collateral value and the value of the borrower firm's total assets. Moreover, the expected LGD is a decreasing function of the default probability of the borrower, given that the correlation between the collateral and the firm values is positive. This counterintuitive result obtains because of the use of an options-theoretic structural model to depict default. That is, low-PD firms must experience abnormally large negative shocks to asset values to enter the default region and therefore the value of their collateral is quite impaired. In contrast, high-PD firms (with a low distance to default) are thrown into default by only slight declines in asset values. Thus, the recovery rates of low-credit-quality firms tend to be higher than recovery rates in high-credit-quality firms in the Jokivuolle and Peura (2000) simulations.

Altman, Resti, and Sironi (2002) and Altman et al. (2005) exhaustively investigate the correlation between both ex post realized and simulated default rates and recovery rates. They find strong evidence of an inverse relationship such that recovery rates fall (rise) when PD increases (decreases). The explanation for this result stems from supply and demand considerations in the market for distressed debt. When default rates increase, for instance in cyclical downturns, there are likely to be more defaulted bonds available for sale on the distressed debt market. The demand for such below-investment-grade instruments is relatively inelastic since buyers are restricted to *vulture* funds and the relatively few financial intermediaries (e.g., hedge funds and sovereign wealth funds) that are permitted to invest in this paper.

Altman (1993) attempts to measure the size of demand in this market for "alternative investments" and estimates that the vulture funds had at least $7 billion under management in the 1991 recessionary period. In contrast, the supply of distressed and defaulted public and private bonds (selling at a credit spread at least 1,000 basis points over 10-year Treasury bond rates) was approximately $300 billion during the 1990–1991 period. Given the 10-to-1 disparity in size between the supply and demand sides of the market, Altman, Resti, and Sironi (2002) contend that even dramatic increases in demand would not be sufficient to absorb the increased supply during cyclical downturns. Thus, since supply increases during cyclical downturns whereas demand is relatively stable, the price of distressed debt declines, thereby reducing recovery values when defaults increase. However, explicitly controlling for macroeconomic effects (using variables like GDP and changes in GDP) yields insignificant and inconsistent results in the Altman, Resti, and Sironi (2002) model.

Supporting the previously cited findings, Frye (2000, 2003, and 2005) examines 859 bonds and loans that defaulted from 1983 to 2001 and finds a significant inverse (direct) relationship between PD and recovery rates (LGD). However, the empirical findings in Acharya et al. (2007) refute the hypothesis of a direct relationship between PD and LGD. They find that the PD is a significant factor explaining LGD only when industry factors are left out. However, when they incorporate a measure of industry distress, the impact of PD becomes statistically insignificant. Therefore, the correlation between PD and LGD that has been found in some empirical models may be an artifact of omitted variables. Thus, the relationship between PD and LGD is still an open question in the academic literature.

However, what seems to be clear from the literature is that LGD is a function of macroeconomic conditions. For example, Unal, Madan, and Guntay (2003) decompose the difference between the prices of senior versus junior debt in order to estimate the risk-neutral mean recovery rates on senior debt relative to junior debt that are independent of default probabilities. Thus, their model is an alternative to the use of either defaulted debt prices or post-default expected cash flows to measure LGD. The recovery rate in their risk-neutral valuation model is conditioned on the business cycle (measured using macroeconomic factors) and firm-specific information. Furthermore, Caselli et al. (2008) use a sample of 11,649 bank loans to pinpoint the macroeconomic explanatory variables for LGD on loans to both households and businesses (small and medium enterprises, or SMEs). They find that for households, the LGD is sensitive to the unemployment rate and household consumption patterns. For SMEs, LGD is sensitive to the total number of employed people and the GDP growth rate. They interpret their results as support for the Basel Committee's insistence that the LGD assumptions input into the Basel II capital model be estimated for downturns separately, so as to incorporate these cyclical patterns (see the discussion in Chapter 13). Levy and Hu (2007) develop a theoretical framework to account for LGD procyclical dynamics that incorporates increases in LGD during economic downturns.

The sensitivity of LGD to industry and macroeconomic factors is impacted by the debt structure. That is, senior secured debt may have a lower LGD than subordinated unsecured debt. However, Acharya et al. (2007) find that it is senior unsecured debt (as opposed to bank debt and subordinated debt) that is most exposed to the impact of fire sale increases in LGD when the borrower's industry is in distress. Thus, bank debt and collateralized debt have high recovery rates even during an industrywide crisis, except when the collateral consists of industry-specific assets. Chatterjee and Yan (2008) document the existence of contingent value rights (CVRs), which are put options that pay additional cash or securities when the issuer's share price falls below a prespecified trigger level. These instruments can be used in reorganizations and restructurings to increase RR if the firm experiences financial distress.[1] Thus, the structure of the firm's debt may be an important determinant of LGD.

DISENTANGLING LGD AND PD

It is standard practice in both the academic literature and in commercial risk management products to jointly estimate LGD and PD. That is, since the default risk premium is composed of the product of PD and LGD (i.e., expected loss EL = PD × LGD), one input must be fixed in order to economically identify the other. Typically, it is the LGD that is assumed fixed so as to estimate PD. As noted in Pan and Singleton (2008), this identification problem occurs when contracts are priced under the "fractional recovery of market value convention (RMV)" (see, e.g., Duffie and Singleton [1999]). Under this scenario, the LGD and the PD are inseparable, since the recoverable market value is itself a function of PD. Alternatively, however, pricing may take place under the "fractional recovery of face value (RFV)" method, in which case the LGD and the PD in the default risk premium are separable. Pan and Singleton (2008) use sovereign credit default swap (CDS) spreads for Mexico, Korea, and Turkey in order to separately identify PD and LGD, assuming RFV.[2]

Pan and Singleton (2008) use different maturities (1, 2, 3, 5, and 10 years) of sovereign CDSs in order to estimate the LGD over the period from

March 19, 2001, through August 10, 2006. They find sufficient sample sizes to reliably estimate LGD separately from PD. They estimate the hazard functions of PD and LGD for each of the four credit events specified in the ISDA standardized sovereign CDS contract: (1) obligation acceleration, (2) failure to pay, (3) restructuring, and (4) repudiation/moratorium.[3] They find that CDS spreads are sensitive to the LGD estimate for the 5-year and 10-year maturities, but not for the one-year contract. They view this as the result of "a liquidity or supply/demand premium . . . [in which] large institutional money management firms often use the short-dated CDS contract as a primary trading vehicle for expressing views on sovereign bonds." Thus, the presence of a liquidity risk premium may inject noise into the reduced form estimation of credit risk components.

Practitioners in the sovereign CDS market typically assume an LGD equal to 75 percent. Pan and Singleton's (2008) model supports this assumption for Korea, but not for Mexico and Turkey, for which they find LGD estimates in the region of 25 percent. They find that when their model is estimated for the less turbulent 2003–2006 period (i.e., with lower bid-ask spreads, implying more liquid CDS markets), the estimated LGD was close to 75 percent for Mexico, but still less than 50 percent for Turkey. They point to other credit-sensitive derivative products that could be used to solve for LGD in the presence of illiquidity problems that distort the pricing of credit spreads. Independently, Levy and Hu (2007) incorporate systematic risk into the recovery process, as well as the correlation between PD and LGD, and find that estimated spreads increase by 14 percent for a typical bond, and by 30 percent in some cases. Thus, there is still quite a bit of analytical work remaining in understanding and modeling the loss process.

MOODY'S KMV'S APPROACH TO LGD ESTIMATION

Moody's KMV LGD estimator, called LossCalc^{TM}, is a forward-looking estimator of recovery rates (i.e., postdefault debt prices) that incorporates an inverse relationship (negative correlation) between PD and RR, consistent with the work of Altman et al. (2005) and Frye (2005). Figure 7.2 shows that the RR for high-risk firms (with distance to default, DD, greater than 0.28) is lower than for low-risk firms.

The Moody's KMV LossCalc^{TM} model consists of a linear regression involving more than 4,000 recovery observations that occurred over more than 20 years.[4] Regression variables include PD (or Moody's KMV EDF^{TM}—see Chapter 4), collateral, debt type, seniority class, borrower location, and industry. The model can solve for a spot one-year LGD or a

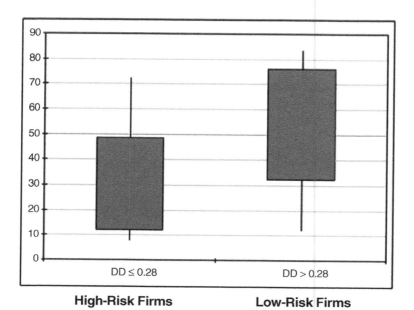

High-Risk Firms   **Low-Risk Firms**

FIGURE 7.2 Relationship between Distance to Default and Recovery for U.S. Senior Unsecured Bonds
Source: © Moody's Analytics, Inc. and/or its affiliates. Reprinted with permission. All Rights Reserved.

five-year term structure of LGDs. Incorporating macroeconomic conditions, Moody's KMV estimates a stressed LGD, as if the economy was at either a 10-year or 25-year low. Industry distress is also incorporated (see the earlier discussion of Acharya and Bharath [2007]) using the median distance to default by region, industry sector, and date (see Chapter 4).

The most important determinant of LGD in the Moody's KMV LossCalc^{TM} model is debt seniority, in both absolute and relative terms.[5] However, the model's R^2 measure of explanatory power ranges between 30 and 35 percent for the one-year and longer-term models. Thus, more than two-thirds of the variation in LGD is idiosyncratic and unexplained by the model. Because of this, it is necessary to include a measure of uncertainty about LGD into any credit risk analysis. That is, since there is a dispersion of possible values around the expected LGD, the error term of the basic regression should be considered. In the Moody's KMV LossCalc^{TM} model the variance of the error term is higher for low-LGD securities than for high-LGD securities. To incorporate this and other factors, the model uses the beta distribution to represent the variance in the LGD estimate. A similar type of beta distribution assumption has been employed in J.P. Morgan's CreditMetrics model.

The Moody's KMV LossCalc™ model is based on post-default debt prices. However, the model is validated using a sample of 1,323 observations of actual recovery rates. The correlation coefficient between recovery rates and post-default debt prices was 95 percent in this subsample, suggesting that the database proxies accurately for recovery rates. However, the test of any model is to determine how it performs out-of-sample. Moody's KMV performs a test of the model as compared to lookup tables of LGD (RR) historically used by bankers. Lookup tables specify the RR for each type of debt, industry or collateral, using average historical RR for each specification. Table 7.3 shows that the Moody's KMV LossCalc™ models

TABLE 7.3 Walk-Forward Analysis: Instantaneous Model

	LossCalc™ v3.0 In-Sample	LossCalc™ v3.0 Out-of-Sample	Best Lookup Table	Out-of-Sample Lookup Table
Correlation with actual recovery	0.602	0.545	0.521	0.462
Average error	−$0.13	$0.01	$1.70	$3.64

Walk-Forward Analysis: One-Year Model

	LossCalc™ v3.0 In-Sample	LossCalc™ v3.0 Out-of-Sample	Best Lookup Table	Out-of-Sample Lookup Table
Correlation with actual recovery	0.569	0.513	0.521	0.462
Average error	$0.55	$0.85	$1.70	$3.64

Walk-Forward Analysis: Long-Run Model

	LossCalc™ v3.0 In-Sample	LossCalc™ v3.0 Out-of-Sample	Best Lookup Table	Out-of-Sample Lookup Table
Correlation with actual recovery	0.550	0.497	0.521	0.462
Average error	$1.10	$2.75	$1.70	$3.64

Source: © Moody's Analytics, Inc. and/or its affiliates. Reprinted with permission. All Rights Reserved.

TABLE 7.4 Comparison of the Recovery of Face Value Estimates for the Economic and Recorded Default Dates

N = 73	Economic Default	Recorded Default
Mean	0.4879	0.5283
Median	0.45	0.5782
Standard deviation	0.3044	0.3151
First quartile	0.2	0.2225
Third quartile	0.76	0.8425

Source: X. Guo, R. A. Jarrow, H. Lin, "Distressed Debt Prices and Recovery Rate Estimation," January 26, 2009, Kamakura Research Paper, 17.

(focused on different time frames) each outperform the out-of-sample lookup table estimates over the period from 1996 to 2008. However, the long-run model underperforms the best lookup table, which is tabulated using a regression analysis.[6]

KAMAKURA'S APPROACH TO LGD ESTIMATION

Reduced form models (such as Kamakura's Risk Manager) model default as a sudden drop in debt value (a negative jump) at default. In contrast, structural models (such as Moody's KMV) model default as a gradual reduction (or negative diffusion) in a firm's values until the default point is reached. Guo et al. (2009) examine risky debt prices and find that the actual date of default does not always correspond to the date that the market first prices *impending* default. They define an *economic default date*, which more accurately models recovery rates. This date is the first date that the market prices the bond at the present value of its price on the *official* default date. Out of 96 debt issues in their sample, 73 experience economic default prior to actual default. Table 7.4 illustrates that the measure of the recovery rate is significantly different if the economic default date is used rather than the actual default date. Thus, Kamakura recommends modeling the recovery process from the economic default date, rather than the actual default date.

SUMMARY

In this chapter, we consider the other half of the expected loss calculation, the loss given default (LGD), or one minus the recovery rate (RR). Expected losses (EL) are calculated by multiplying the probability of default (PD) by LGD. LGD is usually measured using observed debt prices around the default date. However, another measure of LGD is to consider actual recoveries from defaulted debt workouts or from an options-theoretic model. In this chapter, we have shown that LGD is sensitive to macroeconomic conditions, industry factors, debt priority structure, and the treatment of the default date. Since this area has been less studied than the estimation of PD, many open questions remain, such as the relationship between PD and LGD and the best model specification of LGD forecasts.

CHAPTER 8

The Credit Risk of Portfolios and Correlations

INTRODUCTION

So far, we have considered default risk and credit risk exposure on a single-borrower basis. Indeed, much of the banking theory literature views the personnel at banks and similar financial institutions (FIs) as credit specialists who, through monitoring and the development of long-term relationships with customers, gain a comparative advantage in lending to a specific borrower or group of borrowers.[1]

However, investment principles dictate that diversification reduces risk. For example, investing in a single stock will expose the investor to both market (systematic) and company-specific (unsystematic) risk, but adding other stocks into a portfolio will tend to diversify away the unsystematic component of risk, thereby reducing the investor's risk exposure. Because of this fundamental principle of modern portfolio theory (MPT), required returns do not include a premium for unsystematic risk.

The same principle arises when investing in debt instruments that are exposed to credit risk. If one borrower's risk of default is inversely related to another borrower's default probability, then combining loans to both borrowers may reduce the investor's (lender's) overall credit risk exposure. That is, if there is negative correlation across borrower default probabilities, then a portfolio of loans may have lower risk than an individual loan, all else equal. In this chapter, we discuss the issue of portfolio diversification in the general context of MPT and then examine the estimation of correlations used in assessing a portfolio's credit risk exposure.[2]

MODERN PORTFOLIO THEORY (MPT): AN OVERVIEW

Modern portfolio theory is used to derive optimal portfolios in a mean-variance framework. That is, investors attempt to maximize expected returns (mean) and minimize risk (variance). The (mean) return and risk of a portfolio of assets, under the assumption that returns on individual assets are normally distributed (or that asset managers have a quadratic utility function), are given in equations (8.1), (8.2), and (8.3). The assumption that individual asset returns are normally distributed and/or that managers of a financial intermediary exhibit a particular set of preferences (quadratic utility) toward returns implies that only two moments of the distribution of assets returns are necessary in order to analyze portfolio decisions: (1) the mean return of a portfolio and (2) its variance (or the standard deviation of the returns on that portfolio). Since MPT is forward-looking, the expected return and risk measures are by definition unobservable. As a result, portfolio returns and risks are usually estimated from historical time series of the returns and risks on individual assets.

Given these assumptions, the mean return ($\bar{R}_p$) and the variance of returns (σ_p^2) on a portfolio of n assets can be computed as:

$$\bar{R}_p = \sum_{i=1}^{n} X_i \bar{R}_i \tag{8.1}$$

$$\sigma_p^2 = \sum_{i=1}^{n} X_i^2 \sigma_i^2 + \sum_{i=1}^{n} \sum_{\substack{j=1 \\ i \neq j}}^{n} X_i X_j \sigma_{ij} \tag{8.2}$$

or

$$\sigma_p^2 = \sum_{i=1}^{n} X_i^2 \sigma_i^2 + \sum_{i=1}^{n} \sum_{\substack{j=1 \\ i \neq j}}^{n} X_i X_j \rho_{ij} \sigma_i \sigma_j \tag{8.3}$$

where $\bar{R}_p$ = the mean return on the asset portfolio
           $\bar{R}_i$ = the mean return on the ith asset in the portfolio
           X_i = the proportion (weight) of the asset portfolio invested in the ith asset with $i = 1, \ldots, n$
           σ_i^2 = the variance of the returns on the ith asset
           σ_{ij} = the covariance of the returns between the ith and jth assets, with $j = 1, 2, \ldots, n$
           ρ_{ij} = the correlation between the returns on the ith and jth assets, where $-1 \leq \rho_{ij} \leq +1$

From equation (8.1), it can be seen that the mean return on a portfolio of assets ($\bar{R}_p$) is simply a weighted average (with weights X_i) of the mean returns on the individual assets in that portfolio ($\bar{R}_i$). By comparison, the variance of returns on a portfolio of assets (σ_p^2) is decomposable into two terms. The first term reflects the weighted sum of the variances of returns on the individual assets (σ_i^2), and the second term reflects the weighted sums of the covariances among the assets (σ_{ij}). Because a covariance is unbounded, it is common in MPT-type models to substitute the correlation among asset returns for the covariance term, using the statistical definition:

$$\sigma_{ij} = \rho_{ij}\sigma_i\sigma_j \qquad (8.4)$$

Because a correlation is constrained to lie between plus and minus one, we can evaluate the effect of varying ρ_{ij} on asset portfolio risk. For example, in the two-asset case, if ρ_{ij} is negative, the second term in equation (8.3) will also be negative and will offset the first term, which will always be positive.[3] By appropriately exploiting correlation relationships among assets, a portfolio manager can significantly reduce risk and improve a portfolio's risk-return trade-off.[4] Computationally, the efficient frontier, or the portfolio of assets with the lowest risk for any given level of return, can be determine by solving for the asset proportions (X_i) that minimize σ_p for each given level of returns ($\bar{R}_p$). In Figure 8.1, both B and C are efficient asset portfolios in this sense.

The best of all the risky asset portfolios on the efficient frontier is the one that exhibits the highest excess return over the risk-free rate (r_f) relative to the level of portfolio risk, or the highest risk-adjusted excess return:[5]

$$(\bar{R}_p - r_f)/\sigma_p \qquad (8.5)$$

This risk-return ratio is usually called the *Sharpe ratio*. Graphically, the optimal risky asset portfolio is the one in which a line drawn from the return axis, with an origin at r_f, is just tangential to the efficient frontier (this is shown as portfolio D in Figure 8.1). Because the slope of this line reflects the $(\bar{R}_p - r_f)/\sigma_p$ ratio for that portfolio, it is also the portfolio with the highest Sharpe ratio.[6]

APPLYING MPT TO NONTRADED BONDS AND LOANS

MPT has been around for over 40 years and is now a portfolio management tool commonly used by most mutual fund and pension fund managers. It has also been applied with some success to publicly traded junk bonds

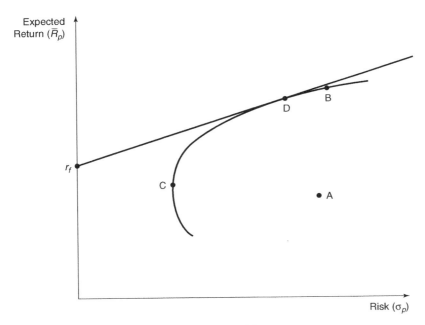

FIGURE 8.1   The Optimum Risky Loan Portfolio

when their returns have tended to be more equity-like than bond-like and when historical returns are available (see Altman and Saunders [1997]). With respect to most loans and bonds, however, there are problems with non-normal returns, unobservable returns, and unobservable correlations.[7]

Non-Normal Returns

Loans and bonds tend to have relatively fixed upside returns and long-tailed downside risks. Thus, returns on these assets tend to exhibit a strong negative skew and, in some cases, kurtosis (fat-tailedness) as well. MPT is built around a model in which only two moments—the mean and variance—are required to describe the whole distribution of returns. To the extent that the third (skewness) and fourth (kurtosis) moments of returns are important in fully describing the distribution of asset returns, the use of simple, two-moment MPT models becomes difficult to justify.[8]

Unobservable Returns and Correlations

An additional problem in the application of portfolio theory to credit risk measurement relates to the fact that most loans and corporate bonds are nontraded or are traded over-the-counter at very uneven intervals with little historical price or volume data. This makes it difficult to compute mean returns $(\bar{R}_i)$, the variance of returns (σ_i^2), and the covariance (σ_{ij}) or return correlations (ρ_{ij}) using historical time series. It is to this issue that we now turn.

ESTIMATING CORRELATIONS ACROSS NONTRADED ASSETS

Implementing the MPT was impractical when it was first introduced because of the large data requirements associated with estimating all possible pair-wise correlation coefficients in real time. For example, in 2008, Kamakura provided estimates of 4.85 million pairs of correlation coefficients covering all possible pairs of 21,000 public firms across 30 countries. This database management problem was exacerbated for nontraded assets, such as loans, that are of critical importance in credit risk assessment. In addition to the database management problem associated with large numbers of pair-wise correlations, the use of historical correlations is not reliable because of the instability associated with changing debt positions and credit quality of borrowing firms.

Partly as a response to the information costs associated with the data requirements of the MPT, the capital asset pricing model (CAPM) was introduced by William Sharpe, John Lintner, and Jan Mossin.[9] Together with the work of Harry Markowitz and Merton Miller, Sharpe's work on the CAPM won the Nobel Prize in economics in 1990. Among other contributions, the CAPM transferred the correlation analysis from a data-intensive pair-wise computation to a single regression analysis in which the correlation can be computed from the regression coefficient on an overall market risk index. That is, if all assets are correlated to the systematic market risk factor, then the correlation coefficient can be expressed in terms of the asset's beta, which is obtained from the following regression analysis:

$$R_i = r_f + \beta_i R_M \qquad (8.6)$$

where R_i is asset i's expected return, r_f is the risk-free rate, β_i is the estimated value of asset i's beta coefficient that measures systematic risk exposure, and R_M is the return on a market index (such as the S&P 500). Since unsystematic (company-specific) risk is diversifiable, the only risk that is priced according to the CAPM is systematic market risk. Each asset's market beta can then be used to calculate the correlation coefficient of the return on the asset ρ_{iM} as follows:

$$\rho_{iM} = \beta_i \sigma_M / \sigma_i \qquad (8.7)$$

Thus, for example, if asset A has a beta of 0.5 and asset B has a beta of -0.5, and both assets have the same standard deviation of returns, then assets A and B are perfectly negatively correlated from the standpoint of their systematic risk exposures. That is, when asset A has a positive return, asset B is expected to have a negative return of equal absolute value. If asset C has a beta of 0.5 and the same standard deviation of returns, then assets A (B) and C are perfectly positively (negatively) correlated. Thus, rather than calculating correlation coefficients for every possible pair of assets, the CAPM permits the computation of correlations using a single beta for each asset.

The commercial credit risk estimation products (e.g., Moody's KMV and the Kamakura Risk Manager) calculate correlation coefficients using a process based on an asset pricing model, as expressed in simple form in equation (8.7).[10] Of course, rather than using only a single market index (such as the S&P 500), the methodologies used by the commercial products incorporate more complex asset pricing models. For example, Chen et al. (2008) outline a reduced form model that estimates a two-factor model for interest rate risk and a one-factor model for default risk. They then use the estimated functional forms to solve for the correlation across the factors.[11] As an illustration of how commercial models utilize this methodology, we now describe the portfolio models of Moody's KMV and Kamakura.[12]

MOODY'S KMV'S PORTFOLIO MANAGER

KMV's Portfolio Manager can be viewed as a full-fledged MPT optimization approach because all three key variables—returns, risks, and correlations—are calculated. However, it can also be used to analyze risk effects alone, as will be discussed below. This section explains how the three key variables that enter into any MPT model can be calculated.

Returns

In the absence of historical returns on traded loans, the (expected) excess return over the risk-free rate on the ith loan ($R_i - r_f$) over any given horizon can be set equal to:

$$R_i - r_f = [\text{Spread}_i + \text{Fees}_i] - [\text{Expected loss}_i] - r_f \qquad (8.8)$$

or

$$R_i - r_f = [\text{Spread}_i + \text{Fees}_i] - [\text{EDF}_i \times \text{LGD}_i] - r_f \qquad (8.8')$$

The first component of returns is the spread of the loan rate over a benchmark rate such as the London Inter-Bank Offered Rate (LIBOR), plus any fees directly earned from the loan and expected over a given period (say, a year). Expected losses on the loan are then deducted because they can be viewed as part of the normal cost of doing banking business. In the context of a KMV-type model, where the expected default frequency (EDF) is calculated from stock returns (as in the Credit Monitor model), then, for any given borrower, expected losses will equal EDF_i times LGD_i, where LGD_i is the loss given default for the ith borrower (usually estimated from the bank's internal database). KMV deducts the risk-free rate, r_f, to present loan returns in an "excess return" format. Of course, if the bank desires, it can calculate the portfolio model using gross returns instead (i.e., not deducting r_f).[13]

Loan Risks

Again assume that the loan matures on or before the chosen credit risk horizon date. In the absence of return data on loans, a loan's risk (σ_i) can be approximated by the unexpected loss rate on the loan (UL_i)—essentially, the variability of the loss rate around its expected loss value ($EDF_i \times LGD_i$). There are a number of ways in which UL_i might be calculated, depending on the assumptions made about the maturity of the loan relative to the credit horizon, the variability of LGD, and the correlation of loan LGDs with EDFs. For example, in the simplest form, when a loan matures before the horizon, a default-only model (DM) can be employed where the borrower either defaults or doesn't default (i.e., there are no credit migrations as in a mark-to-market (MTM) model—see the discussion in Chapter 9), so that defaults are binomially distributed with a fixed LGD across all borrowers. Under these conditions, UL_i can be estimated as:

$$\sigma_i = UL_i = LGD \times \sqrt{(EDF_i)(1 - EDF_i)} \qquad (8.9)$$

where $\sqrt{(EDF_i)(1 - EDF_i)}$ reflects the variability of a default rate frequency that is binomially distributed.[14]

A slightly more sophisticated DM version would allow LGD to be variable, but factors affecting EDFs are assumed to be different from those affecting LGDs, and LGDs are assumed to be independent across borrowers.[15] In this case (see Kealhofer [1995]):

$$\sigma_i = \sqrt{EDF_i(1 - EDF_i)\overline{LGD}_i^2 + EDF_i VOL_i^2} \qquad (8.10)$$

where $\overline{\text{LGD}}_i$ is the expected value of borrower i's LGD, and VOL_i is the standard deviation (volatility) of borrower i's LGD.

Equation (8.10) can be generalized to solve for σ_i under a full mark-to-market (MTM) model with credit upgrades and downgrades as well as default. That is, for the case where the maturity of the loan exceeds the loan's credit horizon, the loan's risk is measured as:

$$\sigma_i = \sqrt{\text{EDF}_i(1 - \text{EDF}_i)\overline{\text{LGD}}_i^2 + \text{EDF}_i(\text{VVOL}_i)^2 + (1 - \text{EDF}_i)\text{VVOL}_i^2}$$
$$(8.10')$$

where VVOL_i (or valuation volatility) is the standard deviation of borrower i's MTM loan value in the nondefault state.

VVOL_i can be viewed as the standard deviation of asset values and can be calculated using the methodology outlined in Chapter 4. However, in Chapter 4 we focused on the area under the valuation distribution that fell below the default point (i.e., the region in which the value of assets fell below the debt repayment). Here we examine only the distribution of asset values above the default point in order to estimate the VVOL.[16]

Another difference between Moody's KMV's Portfolio Manager (PM) and the discussion of Moody's KMV in Chapter 4 is that PM does not assume normally distributed asset portfolios. Both an analytical approximation and the Monte Carlo method are used in the MTM version of PM so as to allow for the possibility of fat tails in the distribution of portfolio returns. The analytical approximation adjusts tail probabilities based on returns, the weighted average of individual loan ULs, and minimum and maximum possible portfolio values. The analytical approximation is most accurate for the 10 basis point level of tail risk (i.e., the worst one-thousandth of all possible outcomes). Monte Carlo simulation draws states of the world to estimate whether each borrower in the portfolio defaults and, if so, what the LGD would be, conditional on the random draw of overall business factors.[17] This process is repeated 50,000 to 200,000 times to determine a frequency distribution that approximates the distribution of the portfolio's value.[18]

Correlations

One important intuition from the structural form approach is that default correlations are generally likely to be low. To see why, consider the context of the two-state DM version of a KMV-type model. A default correlation would reflect the joint probability of two firms, G and F—say, for example,

General Electric and Ford—having their asset values fall below their debt values over the same horizon (say one year). In the context of Figure 8.2, the General Electric asset value would have to fall below its debt value (B_G in the figure), and the Ford asset value would have to fall below its debt value (B_F). The joint area of default is shaded, and the joint probability distribution of asset values is represented by the concentric circles. The circles are similar to those used in geography maps to describe the topographical characteristics (e.g., height) of hills. The inner circle is the top of the hill (high probability), and the outer circles are the bottom of the hill (low probability). The joint probability that asset values will fall in the shaded region is low (as shown) and will depend, in part, on the asset correlations between the two borrowers.[19] The two graphs below and to the left of the graph of the concentric circles represent the payoff on each firm's debt as a function of the market value of the firm's assets. Applying equation (8.4) to the

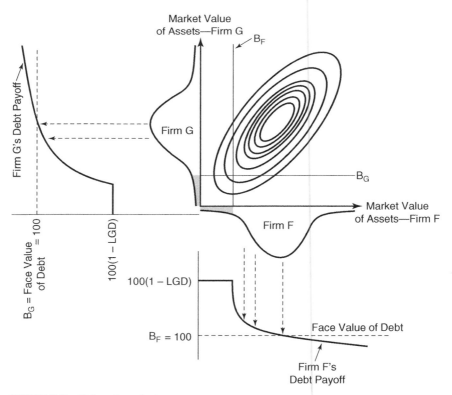

FIGURE 8.2 Value Correlation

simple binomial DM model for Ford (F) and General Electric (G) yields:

$$\rho_{GF} = \frac{\sigma_{GF}}{\sigma_F \times \sigma_G} \tag{8.4'}$$

or

$$\rho_{GF} = \frac{JDF_{GF} - (EDF_G \times EDF_F)}{\sqrt{(EDF_G)(1 - EDF_G)}\sqrt{(EDF_F)(1 - EDF_F)}} \tag{8.11}$$

The numerator of equation (8.11) is the covariance (σ_{GF}) between the asset values of the two firms, G and F. It reflects the difference between the cases where the two asset values are jointly distributed (JDF_{GF}) and where they are independent ($EDF_G \times EDF_F$).[20] The denominator reflects the standard deviation (σ) of default rates under the binomial distribution for each firm.

Although correlations may generally be low, Figure 8.2 can be used to understand the dynamics of how correlations may increase over time. For example, KMV correlations among U.S. firms have recently been rising. To see why, note that the leverage ratios of U.S. corporations have more than doubled over the past decade (i.e., in the context of Figure 8.2, B_F and B_G have both shifted up along their respective axes) and thus the cross-hatched area of joint default has expanded.[21]

Rather than seeking to directly estimate correlations using equation (8.11), Moody's KMV uses a multifactor stock-return model from which correlations are derived. The model reflects the correlation among the systematic risk factors affecting each firm and their appropriate weights. Moody's KMV's multifactor approach to calculating correlations is somewhat similar to the CreditMetrics stock-return factor approach to correlation calculation discussed more fully later in this chapter, except that KMV uses asset correlations rather than equity correlations.[22] Moody's KMV typically finds that correlations lie in the range .002 to .15. Gupton (1997) employs Moody's data over 1970–1995 to obtain implied default correlations between .0013 to .033 using CreditMetrics.[23] The low correlations obtained using all of these models are consistent with evidence showing a significant reduction in credit risk for diversified debt portfolios. Moody's KMV shows that 54 percent of the risk can be diversified away by simply choosing a portfolio composed of the debt issued by five different BBB-rated firms.[24] Barnhill and Maxwell (2001) show that diversification can reduce a bond portfolio's standard deviation from $23,433 to $8,102 ($9,518) if the portfolio consists of 100 bonds from 24 industry sectors (a single sector). Carey (1998) also finds significant diversification benefits across size, obligor concentration, and rating classification for a portfolio consisting of private placements.[25] However, some correlations can be quite high. In November 2008, Kamakura reported a 70 percent default correlation between Citigroup and Ford, as well as an 88 percent correlation coefficient between Ford and GM.

Calculating Correlations Using Moody's KMV's Portfolio Manager   To estimate correlations, Moody's KMV's Portfolio Manager decomposes asset returns into systematic and unsystematic risk using a three-level structural model. Asset returns are extracted from equity returns using the Moody's KMV Credit Manager approach outlined in Chapter 4 for imputing firm asset values. Using a time series of such asset values, asset returns can be calculated. Once asset returns are estimated, the first-level decomposition into risk factors is a single index model that regresses asset returns on a composite market factor that is constructed individually for each firm. The composite market factor used in the first-level analysis comprises a weighted sum of country and industry factors. These factors are estimated at the second level of analysis and may be correlated with each other.[26]

The second level separates out the systematic component of industry and country risk, each of which is further decomposed into three sets of independent factors at the third level. These third-level factors are: (1) two global economic factors—a market-weighted index of returns for all firms and the return index weighted by the log of market values; (2) five regional factors—Europe, North America, Japan, Southeast Asia, and Australia/New Zealand; (3) seven sector factors—interest sensitive (banks, real estate, and utilities), extraction (oil and gas, mining), consumer nondurables, consumer durables, technology, medical services, and other (materials processing, chemicals, paper, steel production).[27]

For any firm i, the multifactor model can be written as:

$$R_k = \sum_{G=1,2} \beta_{kG} R_G + \sum_{R=1,\dots,5} \beta_{kR} R_R + \sum_{S=1,\dots,7} \beta_{kS} R_S + \sum_I \beta_{kI} \varepsilon_I + \sum_C \beta_{kC} \varepsilon_C + \varepsilon_k$$

$$(8.12)$$

where $\beta_{kG}, \beta_{kR}, \beta_{kS}$ = firm k's beta coefficients on global, regional, and sector factors (from the third regression level)

R_G = the return on the two independent global economic factors

R_R = the return on the five independent regional economic factors

R_S = the return on the seven independent industrial sector effects

β_{kI}, β_{kC} = firm k's beta coefficients on the country- and industry-specific systematic risk components (from the second level)

ε_I = the industry-specific effect for industry I

ε_C = the country-specific effect for country C

ε_k = firm k's company-specific risk (from the first level)

We can express the asset variance for firm k as follows:

$$\sigma_k^2 = \sum_{G=1,2} \beta_{kG}^2 \sigma_G^2 + \sum_{R=1,\dots,5} \beta_{kR}^2 \sigma_R^2 + \sum_{S=1,\dots,7} \beta_{kS}^2 \sigma_S^2 + \sum_I \beta_{kI}^2 \sigma_I^2 + \sum_C \beta_{kC}^2 \sigma_C + \varepsilon_k^2$$

(8.13)

Equation (8.13) can be used to calculate correlations between firms j and k as follows:

$$\begin{aligned}\sigma_{jk} &= \sum_{G=1,2} \beta_{jG} \beta_{kG} \sigma_G^2 + \sum_{R=1,\dots,5} \beta_{jR} \beta_{kR} \sigma_R^2 + \sum_{S=1,\dots,7} \beta_{jS} \beta_{kS} \sigma_S^2 \\ &+ \sum_I \beta_{jI} \beta_{kI} \sigma_I^2 + \sum_C \beta_{jC} \beta_{kC} \sigma_C^2 \end{aligned}$$

(8.14)

Thus, the correlation coefficient between firms j and k is:

$$\rho_{jk} = \sigma_{jk} / \sigma_j \sigma_k$$

After they are calculated, the three inputs (returns, risks, and correlations) can be employed in a number of directions. One potential use would be to calculate a risk/return efficient frontier for the loan portfolio, as shown in Figure 8.1. Reportedly, one large Canadian bank manages its U.S. loan portfolio using a Moody's KMV-type model.[28]

A second use would be to measure the risk contribution of expanding lending to any given borrower. As discussed earlier in this chapter, the risk (in a portfolio sense) of any one loan will depend not only on the risk of the individual loan on a stand-alone basis, but also on its correlation with the risks of other loans. For example, a loan, when viewed individually, might be thought to be risky, but because its returns are negatively correlated with other loans, it may be quite valuable in a portfolio context in lowering portfolio risk. The measurement of the marginal contribution to the risk of a portfolio of any particular loan is called _loan transfer pricing_.

The effects of making additional loans to a particular borrower also depend crucially on assumptions made about the balance sheet constraint. For example, if investable or loanable funds are viewed as fixed, then expanding the proportion of assets lent to any borrower i (i.e., increasing the asset i's portfolio weight, X_i) means reducing the proportion invested in all other loans (assets). However, if the funds constraint is viewed as being nonbinding, then the amount lent to borrower i can be expanded without affecting the amount lent to other borrowers. In the KMV-type marginal risk contribution calculation, the funding constraint is assumed to be binding if:

$$X_i + X_j + \cdots + X_n = 1$$

By comparison, under CreditMetrics (see Chapter 9), marginal risk contributions are calculated assuming no such funding constraint; for example, a bank can make a loan to a twentieth borrower without reducing the loans outstanding to the 19 other borrowers.

Assuming a binding funding constraint, the marginal risk contribution for the ith loan (MRC$_i$) can be calculated as:[29]

$$\mathrm{MRC}_i = X_i \frac{\mathrm{dUL}_p}{\mathrm{dX}_i} \tag{8.15}$$

where UL$_p$ is the risk (standard deviation) of the total loan portfolio and X_i is the proportion of loan portfolio lent to the ith borrower:[30]

$$\mathrm{UL}_p = \sqrt{\sum_{i=1}^{N} X_i^2 \mathrm{UL}_i^2 + \sum_{i=1}^{N} \sum_{\substack{j=1 \\ i \neq j}}^{N} X_i X_j \mathrm{UL}_i \mathrm{UL}_j \rho_{ij}} \tag{8.16}$$

and

$$\sum_{i=1}^{N} X_i = 1$$

The marginal risk contribution can be viewed as a measure of the economic capital needed by the bank in order to make a new loan to the ith borrower because it reflects the sensitivity of portfolio risk (specifically, portfolio standard deviation) to a small percentage change in the weight of the asset (dX$_i$). Note that the sum of MRCs is equal to UL$_p$; consequently, the required capital for each loan is just its MRC scaled by the capital multiple (the ratio of capital to UL$_p$).[31]

KAMAKURA AND OTHER REDUCED FORM MODELS

It is also important to discuss default correlations derived from intensity-based models, such as the Kamakura Risk Manager (see Chapter 5). In these models, default correlations reflect the effect of events inducing *simultaneous* jumps in the default intensities of obligors. The causes of defaults themselves are not modeled explicitly; instead, the focus is on modeling various approaches to default-arrival intensity based on correlated *times to default*. This allows the model to answer questions such as what was the worst week, month, year, and so on, out of the past N years, in terms of loan portfolio risk? That worst period will be when correlated default intensities were the highest (defaults arrived at the same time). With joint credit events, some of the default intensity of each obligor is tied to such a marketwide event with some probability. For example, the intensity-based model of Duffie and Singleton (1998) allows for default intensities to be correlated through changes in default intensities themselves as well as joint credit events. In the Duffie and Singleton model, obligors have default intensities that mean-revert with correlated Poisson arrivals of randomly sized jumps. They then formulate individual obligor default intensity times as multivariate exponentials, which allows them to develop a model for simulating correlated defaults.

Duffie and Singleton (1998) consider a hazard function in which each asset's conditional default probability is a function of four parameters: λ, θ, k, and J.[32] That is, the intensity h of a loan's default process has independently distributed jumps in default probability that arrive at some constant intensity λ; otherwise, if no default event occurs, h returns at mean-reversion rate k to a constant default intensity θ. The jumps in intensity follow an exponential distribution with mean size of jump equal to J. Therefore, the form of the individual firm's probability of survival (conditional upon survival to date t) from time t to time s is:

$$p(t,s) = e^{\alpha(s-t)+\beta(s-t)h(t)}$$

where $\beta(t) = -(1 - e^{-kt})/k$
$\alpha(t) = -\theta[t + \beta(t)] - [\lambda/(J + k)][Jt - \ln(1 - \beta(t)J)]$

As a numerical illustration, suppose that $\lambda = .001$, $k = .5$, $\theta = .001$, $J = 5$, and $h(0) = .001$.[33] Then the arrival of a jump in default risk reduces the expected remaining life of the loan to less than three months. Thus, as a stand-alone asset, this loan is very risky. However, we must consider the credit risk of the loan in a portfolio, allowing for imperfectly correlated default arrival times. That is, the timing of sudden jumps of default arrival intensities may be imperfectly correlated across loans. For simplicity, assume that other parameters (i.e., the sizes of the jumps in default intensities) are equal and independent across loans and across time, thereby fixing the parameter values θ, k, and J.

Correlations across loan default probabilities occur because common factors affect the timing of jumps in default probabilities across assets (loans). Specifically, the intensity jump time, λ, can be separated into a common factor with intensity V_c and an idiosyncratic factor, V. Thus,

$$\lambda = vV_c + V \qquad (8.17)$$

where v is the sensitivity of the timing of jumps in default intensities to common factors.[34]

These common factors, V_c, can be viewed as macroeconomic factors, similar to those used in the multifactor models discussed earlier in this chapter. The correlation coefficient between the times to the next credit event for any pair of loans can be expressed as a simple function of v, V_c, and V. Pan and Singleton (2008) use sovereign credit default swap (CDS) spreads for Mexico, South Korea, and Turkey in order to estimate a similar jump process, assuming a single factor model. Although their model performs well at the longer maturities, they find pricing errors at the short-maturity, one-year contract, consistent with the existence of a liquidity premium in bond yields (see Chapters 5 and 7). Consistent with this view expressed by market practitioners, Pan and Singleton (2008) find larger bid-ask spreads for the one-year contract.

To illustrate this using a numerical example, Figure 8.3 shows a portion of a typical sample path for the total arrival intensity h of defaults for the following parameter values: $\lambda = .002$, $\theta = .001$, $k = .5$, $J = 5$, v $= .02$, and $V_c = .05$. Using equation (8.17), we can compute

$$V = .002 - (.02)(.05) = .001$$

We can also compute the probability that loan i's default intensity jumps at time t, given that loan j's intensity has experienced a jump, as:

$$vV_c/(V_c + V) = (.02)(.05)/(.05 + .001) = 2 \text{ percent}$$

Figure 8.3 shows a marketwide credit event occurring just prior to year 2.8 on the calendar time axis. This event instigates jumps in default intensity for several firms. These defaults are represented by the small x's along the bottom of the figure. Correlations across default intensities cause a rapid

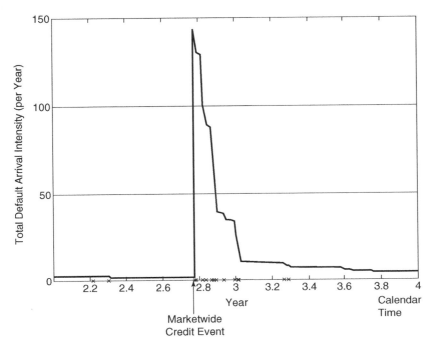

FIGURE 8.3 Correlated Default Intensity
Note: The figure shows a portion of a simulated sample path of total default arrival intensity (initially 1,000 firms). An x along the calendar time axis denotes a default event.
Source: Duffie and Singleton (1998).

increase in default risk in the period immediately surrounding the market-wide credit event. However, the mean reversion built into the intensity process (k is assumed to equal .5) causes the total arrival intensity for defaults to drop back almost to pre-event levels within one year.

Taking the scenario illustrated in Figure 8.3 as the base case, Duffie and Singleton (1998) also examine alternative correlation values: zero correlation ($v = V_c = 0$) and high correlations ($v = .02$ and $V_c = .1$). Figure 8.4 plots the probabilities of experiencing four or more defaults in any time window (of m days) for the three different assumptions about correlations: zero (low) correlation, medium correlation (the base case), and high correlation. Figure 8.4 shows the substantial impact that correlation has on the portfolio's credit risk exposure. This implies that the correlations in default risk shocks (i.e., the correlated jumps in default intensities) may make it

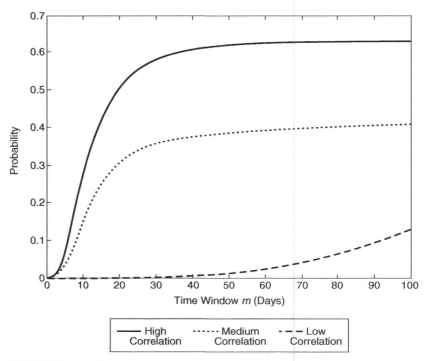

FIGURE 8.4 Portfolio Default Intensities
Note: The figure shows the probability of an *m*-day interval within 10 years experiencing four or more defaults (base case).
Source: Duffie and Singleton (1998).

difficult for banks to recapitalize within one year of experiencing defaults on the loans in their portfolios (see Carey [2001b]).

SUMMARY

Modern portfolio theory (MPT) provides an extremely useful framework for a loan portfolio manager considering risk/return trade-offs. The lower the correlation among loans in a portfolio, the greater the potential for a manager to reduce a bank's risk exposure through diversification. Furthermore, to the extent that a VAR-based capital requirement reflects the concentration risk and default correlations of the loan portfolio, such a portfolio may have lower credit risk than when loan exposures are considered independently additive.

In this chapter, we describe the methodologies used to measure default correlations in commercial models such as Moody's KMV and Kamakura's reduced form model. These models are derived from the academic literature that implemented the MPT using the capital asset pricing model (CAPM). Application of the CAPM to credit risk measurement has been expanded to incorporate multifactor asset pricing models to estimate the sensitivity of default risk to underlying macroeconomic and other risk factors. The default correlations for any pair of assets then can be computed using the factor loadings (the beta estimates) for each asset.

Putting the Parameters Together

The VAR Approach: CreditMetrics and Other Models

INTRODUCTION

In the previous two parts of this book, we provided objective empirical models that can be used to estimate the critical parameters of credit risk assessment: PD and LGD, and their correlations. Now, we can put them all together in an integrated model that incorporates these parameters in order to assess credit risk.

Since 1993, when the Bank for International Settlements (BIS) announced its intention to introduce a capital requirement for market risk, great strides have been made in developing and testing value at risk (VAR) methodologies. The incentive to develop internal VAR models was given a further boost in 1996, when the BIS amended its market risk proposal and agreed to allow certain banks to use their own internal models, rather than the standardized model proposed by regulators, to calculate their market risk exposures. Since the end of 1996 in the European Union and 1998 in the United States, the largest banks (subject to regulatory approval) have been able to use their internal models to calculate VAR exposures for their trading book and, thus, capital requirements for market risk.[1]

In this chapter, we first review the basic VAR concept and then look at its potential extension to nontradable loans and its use in calculating the capital requirement for loans on the bank's books. Considerable attention will be paid to CreditMetrics, originally developed by J.P. Morgan in conjunction with several other sponsors (including Moody's KMV). CreditMetrics provides a useful benchmark for analyzing the issues and problems of VAR modeling for loans.

THE CONCEPT OF VALUE AT RISK

Essentially, value at risk (VAR) models seek to measure the minimum loss in value of a given asset or liability over a given time period at a given confidence level (e.g., 95 percent, 97.5 percent, 99 percent, and so on.).

A simple example of a tradable instrument such as an equity share will suffice to describe the basic concept of VAR (see Figure 9.1). Suppose the market price (P) of a share today is $80, and the estimated daily standard deviation of its value (σ) is $10. Because the trading book is managed over a relatively short horizon, a trader or risk manager may ask: "If tomorrow is a 'bad day,' what is my VAR (size of loss in value) at some confidence level?"

Assume that the trader is concerned with the value loss on a bad day that occurs, on average, once in every 100 days, and that daily asset values (returns) are normally distributed around the current share price of $80. Statistically speaking, the one bad day has a 1 percent probability of occurring tomorrow. The area under the normal distribution carries information about probabilities. We know that roughly 68 percent of return observations must lie between +1 and –1 standard deviation from the mean, 95 percent of observations lie between +2 and –2 standard deviations from the mean, and 98 percent of observations lie between +2.33 and –2.33 standard deviations from the mean. With respect to the last, and in terms of dollars, there is a 1 percent chance that the value of the share will increase to $80 + 2.33\sigma$ (or

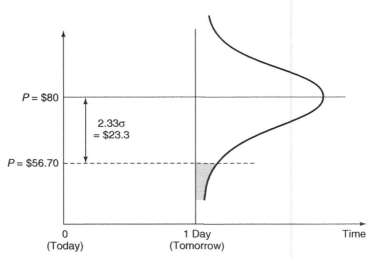

FIGURE 9.1 The VAR of Traded Equity

above) tomorrow, and a 1 percent chance it will fall to a value of $80 − 2.33σ (or below). Because σ is assumed to be $10, this implies that there is a 1 percent chance that the value of the share will fall to $80 − 23.30 = $56.70 or below. Alternatively, there is a 99 percent probability that the equity holder will lose less than $23.30 in value; that is, $23.30 can be viewed as the VAR on the equity share at the 99 percent confidence level. Note that, by implication, there is a 1 percent chance of losing $23.30 *or more* tomorrow. Because asset values are assumed to be normally distributed, the one bad day in every 100 can lead to the loss being placed anywhere in the shaded region below $56.70 in Figure 9.1. (In reality, losses on nonleveraged financial instruments are truncated at 100 percent of value, and the normal curve is at best an approximation to the log-normal distribution.)

Thus, the key inputs in calculating the VAR of a marketable instrument are its current market value (P) and the volatility or standard deviation of that market value ($σ$). Given an assumed risk horizon and a required confidence level (e.g., 99 percent), the VAR can be directly calculated.

Application of this methodology to nontradable loans has some immediate problems. First, P, or the current market value of a loan, is not directly observable because most loans are not traded. Second, because P is not observable, we have no time series to calculate $σ$, the volatility of P. At best, the assumption of a normal distribution for returns on some tradable assets is a rough approximation, and the approximation becomes even less precise when applied to the possible distribution of values for loans. Specifically, as discussed in Chapter 4 in the context of the options pricing approach, loans have both severely truncated upside returns and long downside risks. As a result, even if we can and do measure P and $σ$, we still need to take into account the asymmetry of returns on making a loan.

CreditMetrics

CreditMetrics was first introduced in 1997 by J.P. Morgan and its co-sponsors (Bank of America, KMV, Union Bank of Switzerland, and others) as a value at risk (VAR) framework to apply to the valuation and risk of nontradable assets such as loans and privately placed bonds.[2] RiskMetrics seeks to answer the question: "If tomorrow is a bad day, how much will I lose on tradable assets such as stocks, bonds, and equities?". CreditMetrics asks: "If next year is a bad year, how much will I lose on my loans and loan portfolio?"[3]

As noted previously, because loans are not publicly traded, we observe neither P (the loan's market value) nor $σ$ (the volatility of the loan value over the horizon of interest). However, using (1) available data on a borrower's credit rating, (2) the probability that the rating will change over the next year (the rating transition matrix), (3) recovery rates on defaulted loans, and (4) credit spreads and yields in the bond (or loan) market, it is possible to calculate a hypothetical P and σ for any nontraded loan or bond, and thus a VAR number for individual loans and the loan portfolio.[4]

We first examine a simple example of calculating the VAR on a loan, and subsequently discuss technical issues surrounding this calculation. Consider as an example a five-year fixed-rate loan of $100 million made at 6 percent annual interest.[5] The borrower is rated BBB.

Rating Migration

Based on historical data on publicly traded bonds (or loans) collected by Standard and Poor's (S&P), Moody's, KMV, or other bond or loan analysts, the probability that a BBB borrower will stay at BBB over the next year is estimated at 86.93 percent.[6] There is also some probability that the borrower will be upgraded (e.g., to A) or will be downgraded (e.g., to CCC or even to default, D). Indeed, eight transitions are possible for the borrower during the next year. Seven involve upgrades, downgrades, or no rating change, and one involves default.[7] The estimated probabilities of these transitions are shown in Table 9.1.[8]

Valuation

The effect of rating upgrades and downgrades is to impact the required credit risk spreads or premiums on the loan's remaining cash flows and thus the implied market (or present) value of the loan. If a loan is downgraded, the required credit spread should increase (remember that the contractual

TABLE 9.1   One-Year Transition Probabilities for BBB-Rated Borrower

AAA	0.02%	
AA	0.33	
A	5.95	
BBB	86.93	⟵———— Most likely to stay in the same class
BB	5.30	
B	1.17	
CCC	0.12	
Default	0.18	

Source: Gupton et al., *"CreditMetrics—Technical Document, RiskMetrics—Technical Document,"* J.P. Morgan, April 2, 1997, page 11.

loan rate in our example is assumed fixed at 6 percent) so that the present value of the loan to the financial institution (FI) should fall. A credit rating upgrade has the opposite effect. Technically, because we are revaluing the five-year, $100 million, 6 percent loan at the end of the first year (the credit horizon), after a *credit event* has occurred during that year, then (measured in $ millions):[9]

$$P = 6 + \frac{6}{(1 +_1r_1 + s_1)} + \frac{6}{(1 +_1r_2 + s_2)^2} + \frac{6}{(1 +_1r_3 + s_3)^3} + \frac{106}{(1 +_1r_4 + s_4)^4} \quad (9.1)$$

where r_i are the risk-free rates (so called forward zero rates) on zero-coupon U. S. Treasury bonds *expected* to exist one year into the future.[10] The one-year forward zero rates are calculated from the current Treasury yield curve (see Appendix 9.1). Furthermore, s_i is the annual credit spread on (zero-coupon) loans of a particular rating class for one-year, two-year, three-year, and four-year maturities (the latter are derived from observed spreads in the corporate bond market over Treasuries).[11] In this example, the first year's coupon or interest payment of $6 million (to be received on the valuation date at the end of the first year) is undiscounted and can be regarded as equivalent to accrued interest earned on the bond or the loan.

In CreditMetrics, interest rates are assumed to be deterministic.[12] Thus, the risk-free rates, r_i, are obtained by decomposing the current spot yield curve to obtain the one-year forward zero curve, following the procedure outlined in Appendix 9.1 in which fixed credit spreads are added to the forward zero-coupon Treasury yield curve. An example is shown in Table 9.2. The risk-free zero-coupon yield curve is first derived using U.S. Treasury securities in order to obtain the pure discount equivalent of the risk-free rates. Then the zero-coupon yield curve is used to derive the forward risk-free rates for U.S. Treasury securities of varying maturities expected to prevail one year into the future: $r_1, r_2, \ldots r_T$ (Note that $T = 4$ in the example shown in equation 9.1). Finally, a fixed credit spread, s_i, for each maturity i is added to the one-year forward risk-free discount rate (see, for example, Table 9.11 in Appendix 9.1). We obtain one forward yield curve for each of the seven ratings, as shown in Table 9.2. Each coupon and principal payment on the risky loan is discounted at the rate chosen from Table 9.2 that matches the coupon's maturity and the loan's rating.

Suppose that, during the first year, the borrower is upgraded from BBB to A. That is, a favorable credit event occurs during the first year of the loan's life (see Figure 9.2). The present value, or market value, of the loan to the financial institution (FI) at the end of the one-year risk horizon (in millions) including the first year's $6 million of accrued interest is then:[13]

TABLE 9.2 One-Year Forward Zero Curves Plus Credit Spreads by Credit Rating Category (Percent)

Category	Year 1	Year 2	Year 3	Year 4
AAA	3.60	4.17	4.73	5.12
AA	3.65	4.22	4.78	5.17
A	3.72	4.32	4.93	5.32
BBB	4.10	4.67	5.25	5.63
BB	5.55	6.02	6.78	7.27
B	6.05	7.02	8.03	8.52
CCC	15.05	15.02	14.03	13.52

Source: Gupton et al., *"CreditMetrics—Technical Document, Risk-Metrics—Technical Document,"* J.P. Morgan, April 2, 1997, page 27.

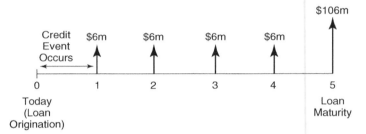

FIGURE 9.2 Cash Flows on the Five-Year BBB Loan—Credit Events Are Upgrades, Downgrades, or Defaults

$$P = 6 + \frac{6}{(1.0372)} + \frac{6}{(1.0432)^2} + \frac{6}{(1.0493)^3} + \frac{106}{(1.0532)^4} = \$108.66 \quad (9.2)$$

At the end of the first year, if the borrower is upgraded from BBB to A, the $100 million (book value) loan has a market value of $108.66 million. This is the value the FI would theoretically be able to obtain at the year 1 horizon if it sold the loan in the loan sales market to another FI at the fair market price or value, inclusive of the first year's coupon payment of $6 million.[14] Table 9.3 shows the value of the loan if other credit events occur. Note that the loan has a maximum market value of $109.37 million (if the borrower is upgraded from BBB to AAA) and a minimum value of $51.13 million if the borrower defaults. The latter is the estimated recovery value of the loan (or one minus the loss given default, LGD if the borrower defaults).[15]

The actual probability distribution of loan values is shown in Figure 9.3. The value of the loan has a relatively fixed upside and a long downside

TABLE 9.3 Value of the Loan at the End of Year 1 for Different Ratings (Including First-Year Coupon)

Year-End Rating	Value (Millions)
AAA	$109.37
AA	109.19
A	108.66
BBB	107.55
BB	102.02
B	98.10
CCC	83.64
Default	51.13

Source: Gupton et al., *"CreditMetrics—Technical Document, RiskMetrics—Technical Document,"* J.P. Morgan, April 2, 1997, page 10.

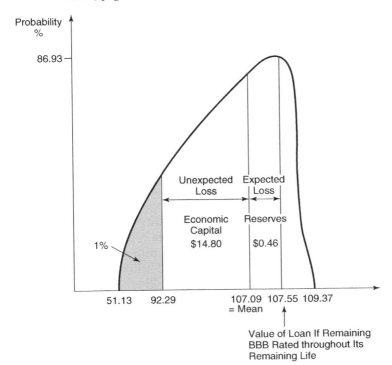

FIGURE 9.3 Actual Distribution of Loan Values on Five-Year BBB Loan at the End of Year 1 (Including First-Year Coupon Payment)

(i.e., a negative skew). The value of the loan therefore is not symmetrically (or normally) distributed. In order to take this into account, CreditMetrics produces two VAR measures:

1. A VAR measure based on the normal distribution of loan values.
2. A VAR measure based on the actual distribution of loan values.

Calculation of VAR

Table 9.4 shows the calculation of the VAR, based on each approach, for both the 5 percent and 1 percent worst-case scenarios around the mean loan value. The first step in determining VAR is to calculate the mean of the loan's value, or its expected value, at year 1. This is the sum of each possible loan value, at the end of year 1, multiplied by its transition probability over the year. The mean value of the loan is $107.09 (see also Figure 9.3). However, the FI is concerned about unexpected losses or volatility in value. In particular, if next year is a bad year, how much can it expect to lose with a certain probability? We could define a *bad year* as occurring once every 20 years (the 5 percent VAR) or once every 100 years (the 1 percent VAR). This definition is similar to market risk VAR except that for credit risk the risk horizon is longer relative to equity—one year rather than one day.

Assuming that loan values are normally distributed, the variance (σ^2) of loan value (in millions) around its mean is $8.9477, and its standard deviation σ, or volatility, is the square root of the variance, equal to $2.99. Thus, the 5 percent VAR for the loan is $1.65 \times \$2.99 = \$4.93$ million. The 1 percent VAR is $2.33 \times \$2.99 = \$6.97$ million. However, this likely underestimates the actual or true VAR of the loan because, as shown in Figure 9.3, the distribution of the loan's value is clearly non-normal. In particular, it demonstrates a negative skew or a long-tailed downside risk.

Using the actual distribution of loan values and probabilities in Table 9.4, we can see that there is a 6.77 percent probability that the loan value will fall below $102.02, implying an approximate 5 percent actual VAR of $5.07 million ($107.09 − $102.02 = $5.07 million), and there is a 1.47 percent probability that the loan value will fall below $98.10, implying an approximate 1 percent actual VAR of $8.99 million ($107.09 − $98.10 = $8.99). These actual VARs could be made more precise by using linear interpolation to get at the 5 percent and 1 percent VAR measures. For example, because the 1.47 percentile equals $98.10 and the 0.3 percentile equals $83.64, using linear interpolation, the 1.00 percentile equals approximately $92.29. This suggests an actual 1 percent VAR of $107.09 − $92.29 = $14.80.[16]

TABLE 9.4 VAR Calculations for the BBB Loan (Benchmark Is Mean Value of Loan)

Year-End Rating	Probability of State (%)	New Loan Value Plus Coupon (millions)	Probability Weighted Value (S)	Difference of Value from Mean ($)	Probability Weighted Difference Squared
AAA	0.02	$109.37	0.02	2.30	0.0010
AA	0.33	109.19	0.36	2.10	0.0146
A	5.95	108.66	6.47	1.57	0.1474
BBB	86.93	107.55	93.49	0.46	0.1853
BB	5.30	102.02	5.41	(5.06)	1.3592
B	1.17	98.10	1.15	(8.99)	0.9446
CCC	0.12	83.64	1.10	(23.45)	0.6598
Default	0.18	51.13	0.09	(55.96)	5.6358
			$107.09 = Mean Value		$8.9477 = Variance of Value

σ = Standard deviation = $2.99

Assuming normal distribution
$$5 \text{ Percent VAR} = 1.65 \times \sigma = \$4.93$$
$$1 \text{ Percent VAR} = 2.33 \times \sigma = \$6.97$$

Assuming actual distribution*
6.77 Percent VAR = 93.23 percent of = $107.09 − $102.02 = $5.07 actual distribution
1.47 Percent VAR = 98.53 percent of = $107.09 − $98.10 = $8.99 actual distribution
1 Percent VAR = 99 percent of actual = $107.09 − $92.29 = $14.80 distribution

Note: Calculation of 6.77 percent VAR (i.e., 5.3% + 1.17% + 0.12% + 0.18%) and 1.47 percent VAR (i.e., 1. 17% + 0.12% + 0.18%). The 1 percent VAR is interpolated from the actual distribution of the loan's values under different rating migrations.

Source: Gupton et al., *"CreditMetrics—Technical Document, RiskMetrics—Technical Document,"* J.P. Morgan, April 2, 1997, page 28.

CAPITAL REQUIREMENTS

It is interesting to compare these VAR numbers with international bank capital requirements under the Basel Accords (see Chapter 13). For a $100 million face (book) value BBB loan to a private-sector borrower, the capital requirement under both Basel I and the Standardized Approach of Basel II (100 percent risk bucket) would be $8 million. Note the contrast with the two VAR measures developed previously. Using the 1 percent VAR based on the normal distribution, the capital requirement against unexpected losses on the loan (i.e., economic capital) would be $6.97 million (i.e., less than the Basel capital requirement).[17] Under the VAR approach, loan loss reserves are also held to meet expected loan losses, which in the case of the BBB loan are $0.46 million, or $107.55 million (the value of the BBB loan if no rating changes or default occurs) minus $107.09 million (the expected value of the BBB loan taking into account transition and default probabilities). Adding the expected losses of $0.46 million to $6.97 million results in a total capital requirement (for both expected and unexpected losses) of $7.43 million (see Figure 9.3 for a breakdown of the capital requirement). Using the 1 percent VAR based on the interpolated value from the actual distribution shown in Table 9.4, the economic capital requirement would be $14.80 million for unexpected losses plus the loan loss reserve for expected losses of $0.46 million (an amount much greater than the Basel capital requirement).

Using CreditMetrics to set capital requirements tells us nothing about the potential size of losses that exceed the VAR measure. That is, the VAR measure is the *minimum* loss that will occur with a certain probability. Extreme value theory (EVT) examines the tail of the loss distribution conditional on the expectation that the size of the loss exceeds VAR.[18] Tail events are those loss events that occur rarely, but when they do, they have dramatic consequences, as the catastrophic events of 2007–2009 clearly demonstrate.[19] Figure 9.4 depicts the size of unexpected losses when catastrophic events occur.[20] Using the estimates from Table 9.4 based on a normal distribution, the 5 percent VAR for unexpected losses is $4.93 million. We set this to be the threshold level; that is, EVT considers only the distribution of unexpected losses that exceed $4.93 million.

However, Figure 9.4 assumes that unexpected losses beyond the 95 percent threshold level follow a generalized Pareto distribution (GPD) with fat tails (see Appendix 9.2 for a derivation of the values shown in Figure 9.4). Thus, the estimated 1 percent VAR distributed according to the GPD is larger than the normally distributed 1 percent VAR of $6.97 million (from Table 9.4). Under the parameter assumptions described in Appendix 9.2, the 1 percent VAR for the GPD, denoted $\overline{VAR}_{.99}$, is $22.23 million. The expected shortfall, denoted $\overline{ES}_{.99}$, is calculated as the mean of the excess distribution of unexpected losses beyond the threshold $\overline{VAR}_{.99}$, which is shown as $53.53 million in Figure 9.4. This would be the capital charge for the mean of the most extreme events (i.e., those in the 1 percent tail of the distribution). As such, the $\overline{ES}_{.99}$ amount can be viewed as the capital charge that would incorporate risks posed by extreme or catastrophic events or,

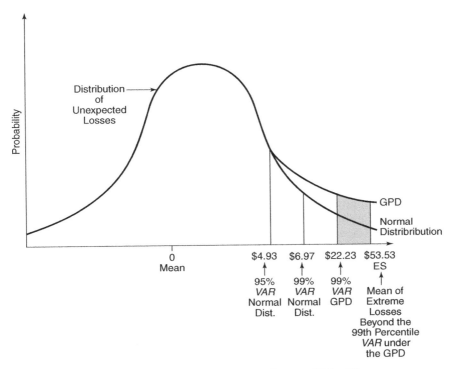

FIGURE 9.4   Estimating Unexpected Losses Using Extreme Value Theory
Note: ES is the expected shortfall assuming a Generalized Pareto Distribution (GPD) with fat tails.

alternatively, a capital charge that internally incorporates an extreme, catastrophic stress-test multiplier. Since the GPD is fat tailed, the increase in losses is quite large at high confidence levels; that is, the extreme values of $\overline{ES}_q$ (for high values of q, where q is a risk percentile) correspond to extremely rare catastrophic events that result in enormous losses.

Some have argued that the use of EVT may result in unrealistically large capital requirements (see Cruz et al. [1998]). In contrast, Ebnother and Vanini (2007) argue that EVT and VAR techniques underestimate credit risk because they focus on only one year and ignore the autocorrelation in economic cycles. They propose a time-conditional expected shortfall method that is estimated over a five-year time horizon so as to determine whether the firm can remain solvent over several years of economic downturns.

TECHNICAL ISSUES AND PROBLEMS

In this section, we address some of the main technical issues surrounding CreditMetrics. Some of these issues (and assumptions) can be incorporated quite smoothly into the basic model; others are less easy to deal with.

Rating Migration

A number of issues arise when we use the bond-rating transitions assumed in Table 9.1 to calculate the probabilities of moving to different rating categories (or to default) over the one-year horizon.

First, underlying the calculation of the transition numbers, which involves averaging one-year transitions over a past data period (e.g., 20 years), is an important assumption about the way defaults and transitions occur.[21] Specifically, we assume that the transition probabilities follow a stable Markov process (see Altman and Kao [1992]), which means that the probability that a bond or loan will move to any particular state during this period is independent of (or uncorrelated with) any outcome in the past period. However, there is evidence that rating transitions are autocorrelated over time. For example, a bond or loan that was downgraded in the previous period has a higher probability (compared to a loan that was not downgraded) of being downgraded in the current period (see, for example, the results in Nickell et al. [2001a]). This suggests that a second or higher Markov process may better describe rating transitions over time.[22]

The second issue involves transition matrix stability. The use of a single transition matrix assumes that transitions do not differ across borrower types (e.g., industrial firms versus banks, or the United States versus Japan) or across time (e.g., peaks versus troughs in the business cycle). Indeed, there is considerable evidence to suggest that important industry factors, country factors, and business cycle factors impact rating transitions (see Nickell et al. [2001a] and Bangia et al. [2000]). For example, when we examine a loan to a Japanese industrial company, we may need to use a rating transition matrix built around data for that country and industry.

In 1999, CreditMetrics introduced modifications to allow for cyclicality to be incorporated into the transition matrix. Kim (1999) and Finger (1999) consider a market factor (the credit cycle index), denoted as Z, such that all debt instruments are independent and conditional on the market factor.[23] Figure 9.5 shows the conditional default probability, $p(Z)$, such that the entire distribution shifts down when Z is negative (i.e., the market declines during a bad year), thereby increasing the probability of default; when Z is positive (in a good year), the entire $p(Z)$ distribution shifts upward, thereby decreasing the default probability. The impact of market forces on the

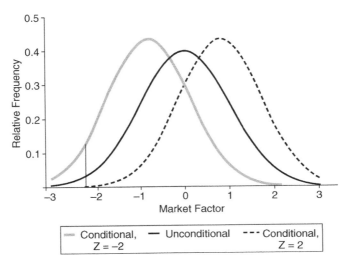

FIGURE 9.5 Unconditional Asset Distribution and Conditional Distributions with Positive and Negative Z
Source: Finger (1999), page 16.

conditional default probability depends on the index weight w, such that when w is close to one (zero), values are highly correlated (uncorrelated) with the market factor, and the conditional default probability is highly dependent upon (independent of) market forces.

The third issue relates to the portfolio of bonds used in calculating the transition matrix. Altman and Kishore (1997) found noticeable impact of bond "aging" on the probabilities calculated in the transition matrix. Indeed, a material difference is noted, depending on whether the bond sample used to calculate transitions is based on new bonds or on all bonds outstanding in a rating class at a particular moment in time. This undermines the assumption of credit risk homogeneity for all bonds in the same ratings classification. Kealhofer, Kwok, and Weng (1998) show that default rates are skewed within each ratings class, so that the mean default rates may be twice as large as median default rates. Simulating Moody's bond ratings transition matrices 50,000 times using Monte Carlo simulation techniques, they find that approximately 75 percent of borrowers within a rating grade may have default rates below the mean, leading to adverse selection among borrowers; that is, only the riskiest 25 percent of all borrowers within each rating classification obtain loans if they are priced at the mean default spread. Moreover, there was such an overlap in the range of default probabilities for each class that a bond rated BBB may have a default probability in the AAA rating class range.

The fourth issue relates to the general problem of using bond transition matrices to value loans. As noted earlier, to the extent that collateral, covenants and other features make loans behave differently from bonds, using bond transition matrices may result in an inherent valuation bias. Moreover, bond ratings lag market-based measures of default risk, such as Moody's KMV EDF^{TM}, in forecasting default probabilities (see Chapter 4). This suggests that the internal development of loan rating transitions by banks to replace problematic external credit ratings (see the discussion in Chapter 3) based on EDF^{TM}s and historic loan databases might be viewed as crucial in improving the accuracy of VAR measures of loan risk.[24]

Valuation

In the VAR calculation shown earlier in this chapter, the amount recoverable on default (assumed to be $51.13 per $100 of face value), the forward zero interest rates (r_t), and the credit spreads (s_t) are all nonstochastic (or at least hedged). Making any or all of them stochastic generally will increase any VAR calculation and capital requirement. In particular, loan recovery rates have quite substantial variability (see Carty and Lieberman [1996]), and the credit spread on, say, an AA loan might be expected to vary within the same rating class at any moment in time (e.g., AA+ and AA– bonds or loans are likely to have different credit spreads). More generally, credit spreads and interest rates are likely to vary over time, with the credit cycle, and with shifts in the term structure, rather than being deterministic.

One reason for assuming that interest rates are nonstochastic or deterministic is to separate market risk from credit risk.[25] But this remains highly controversial, especially to those who feel that their measurement should be integrated rather than separated and that credit risk is positively correlated with the interest rate cycle (see Crouhy et al. [2001]). Kiesel et al. (2001) incorporate spread risk into CreditMetrics, arguing that stochastically varying spreads are strongly correlated across different exposures and thus are not diversified away, and find spread risks of about 7 percent of asset values for a portfolio of five-year maturity bonds. However, Kim (2000) contends, in the limited context of market VAR, that time horizon mismatches (up to 10 days for market risk and up to one year for credit risk) create problems in integrating spread risk and credit migration risk that may lead to overestimation of economic capital requirements.

Regarding recovery rates, if the standard deviation of recovery rates is $25.45 around a mean value of $51.13 per $100 of face value, it can be shown that the 99 percent VAR for the BBB loan in our example under the normal distribution will increase to 2.33 × $3.18 million = $7.41 million, or a VAR-based capital requirement of 7.41 percent of the face value of the

BBB loan (as compared to $6.97 million under the fixed LGD assumption) for unexpected losses only.[26] A related question is whether the volatility of the LGDs of bonds is the same as for loans, given the greater contract flexibility of the latter.[26]

Mark-to-Market Model versus Default Model

By allowing for the effects of credit rating changes (and hence, spread changes) on loan values as well as default, CreditMetrics can be viewed as a mark-to-market (MTM) model. Other models view spread risk as part of market risk and concentrate on expected and unexpected loss calculations rather than on expected and unexpected changes in value (or VAR) as in CreditMetrics. This alternative approach is often called the default model or default mode (DM).

It is useful to compare the effects of the MTM model and the DM model by calculating the expected and, more importantly, the unexpected losses for the same example (the BBB loan) considered earlier. Table 9.1 shows that in a two-state, default/no-default world, the probability of default is $p = 0.18$ percent and the probability of no default $(1 - p)$ is 99.82 percent. In case of default, the recovery rate is $51.13 per $100 (see Table 9.3), and the loss given default (LGD) is 1 minus the recovery rate, or $48.87 per $100. The book value exposure amount of the BBB loan is $100 million.

Given these numbers, the expected loss on the loan is:

$$\text{Expected loss} = p \times \text{LGD} \times \text{Exposure}$$
$$= .0018 \times .4887 \times \$100,000,000 \qquad (9.3)$$
$$= \$87,966$$

To calculate the unexpected loss, we have to make some assumptions regarding the distribution of default probabilities and recoveries. The simplest assumption is that recoveries are fixed and are independent of the distribution of default probabilities. Moreover, because the borrower either defaults or does not default, the probability of default can (most simply) be assumed to be binomially distributed with a standard deviation of:

$$\sigma = \sqrt{p(1 - p)} \qquad (9.4)$$

Given a fixed recovery rate and exposure amount, the unexpected loss on the loan is:

$$\text{Unexpected loss} = \sqrt{p(1 - p)} \times \text{LGD} \times \text{Exposure}$$
$$= \sqrt{(.0018)(.9982)} \times .4887 \times \$100,000,000 \qquad (9.5)$$
$$= \$2,071,512$$

To make this number comparable with the VAR number calculated under CreditMetrics for the normal distribution, we can see that the one standard deviation loss of value (VAR) on the loan is $2.99 million versus $2.07 million under the DM approach.[28] This difference occurs partly because the MTM approach allows for an upside as well as a downside to the loan's value, and the DM approach fixes the maximum upside value of the loan to its book or face value of $100 million. Thus, economic capital under the DM approach is more closely related to book value accounting concepts than to the market value accounting concepts used in the MTM approach.

THE PORTFOLIO APPROACH IN CREDITMETRICS

As discussed in Chapter 8, modern portfolio theory (MPT) asserts that diversification reduces risk. Until a return dimension was added, CreditMetrics could be viewed more as a loan portfolio VAR model (for economic capital calculations) rather than a full-fledged MPT risk/return optimization model.[29] Here, we concentrate on the measurement of correlations and the VAR for a loan portfolio. As with individual loans, two approaches to measuring portfolio VAR are considered:[30]

1. Loan portfolios are assumed to have normally distributed asset values.
2. The actual loan portfolio value distribution exhibits a long-tailed downside or negative skew.

We first consider the normal distribution case, which produces a direct analytic solution to VAR calculations using conventional MPT techniques.

CreditMetrics: Portfolio VAR Under the Normal Distribution

In the normal distribution model, a two-loan case provides a useful benchmark. A two-loan case is readily generalizable to the N-loan case; that is, the risk of a portfolio of N loans can be shown to depend on the risk of each pair of loans in the portfolio and on the risk of each individual loan (see the later discussion and Appendix 9.3).

To calculate the VAR of a portfolio of two loans, we need to calculate (1) the joint migration probabilities for each loan (assumed to be the $100 million face value BBB loan discussed earlier in this chapter, and an A-rated loan of $100 million face value); and (2) the joint payoffs or values of the loans for each possible one-year joint migration probability.

TABLE 9.5   Joint Migration Probabilities with 0.30 Asset Correlation (Percent)

		Obligor 2 (A)							
		AAA	AA	A	BBB	BB	B	CCC	Default
Obligor 1 (BBB)		0.09	2.27	91.05	5.52	0.74	0.26	0.01	0.06
AAA	0.02	0.00	0.00	0.02	0.00	0.00	0.00	0.00	0.00
AA	0.33	0.00	0.04	0.29	0.00	0.00	0.00	0.00	0.00
A	5.95	0.02	0.39	5.44	0.08	0.01	0.00	0.00	0.00
BBB	86.93	0.07	1.81	79.69	4.55	0.57	0.19	0.01	0.04
BB	5.30	0.00	0.02	4.47	0.64	0.11	0.04	0.00	0.01
B	1.17	0.00	0.00	0.92	0.18	0.04	0.02	0.00	0.00
CCC	0.12	0.00	0.00	0.09	0.02	0.00	0.00	0.00	0.00
Default	0.18	0.00	0.00	0.13	0.04	0.01	0.00	0.00	0.00

Source: Gupton et al., *"CreditMetrics—Technical Document, RiskMetrics—Technical Document,"* J.P. Morgan, April 2, 1997, page 38.

Joint Migration Probabilities

Table 9.5 shows the one-year individual and joint migration probabilities for BBB and A loans.[31] Given eight possible credit states for the BBB-rated borrower and eight possible credit states for the A-rated borrower over the next year (the one-year horizon), there are 64 joint migration probabilities (see the cells in Table 9.5). Importantly, the joint migration probabilities are not simply the product of the two individual migration probabilities, but should also reflect the correlation. This can be seen by looking at the independent probabilities that the BBB loan will remain BBB (0.8693) and the A loan will remain A (0.9105) over the next year. The joint probability, assuming the correlation between the two migration probabilities is zero, would be:

$$0.8693 \times 0.9105 = 0.7915 \text{ or } 79.15\%$$

Note that the joint probability in Table 9.5 is slightly higher, at 79.69 percent, because the (assumed) correlation between the two borrowers is 0.3.

Adjusting the migration table to reflect correlations is a two-step process. First, an economic model is needed to motivate migration transitions. In CreditMetrics, a Merton-type model is used to link asset value or return volatility to discrete rating migrations for individual borrowers. Second, a model is needed to calculate the correlations among the asset value volatilities of individual borrowers. Similar to KMV, asset values of borrowers are unobservable, as are correlations among those asset values. The correlations among the individual borrowers are therefore estimated from multifactor models driving borrowers' stock returns.

An Example of the Link between Asset Volatilities and Rating Transitions

To see the link between asset volatilities and rating transitions, consider Figure 9.6, which links standardized normal asset return changes (measured in standard deviations) of a BB-rated borrower to rating transitions.[32] If the unobservable (standardized) changes in asset values of the firm are assumed to be normally distributed around the firm's current asset value, we can calculate how many standard deviations asset values would have to change to move the firm from BB into default. For example, the historic one-year default probability of this type of BB borrower is 1.06 percent. Using the standardized normal distribution tables, asset values would have to fall by 2.3σ for the firm to default. Also, there is a 1 percent probability that the BB firm will move to a C rating over the year. Asset values would have to fall by at least 2.04σ to change the BB borrower's rating to C or below.[33] The full range of possibilities is graphed in Figure 9.6. Similar figures could be constructed for a BBB-rated borrower, an A-rated borrower, and so on. The links between asset volatility and rating changes for an A-rated borrower are shown in Table 9.6.

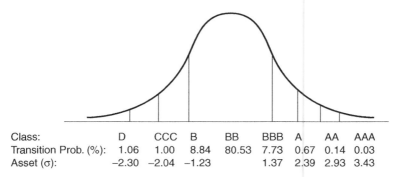

Class:	D	CCC	B	BB	BBB	A	AA	AAA
Transition Prob. (%):	1.06	1.00	8.84	80.53	7.73	0.67	0.14	0.03
Asset (σ):		−2.30	−2.04	−1.23		1.37	2.39	2.93	3.43

FIGURE 9.6   The Link between Asset Value Volatility (σ) and Rating Transitions for a BB-Rated Borrower

TABLE 9.6 The Link between Asset Value Volatility (σ) and Rating Transitions for an A-Rated Borrower

Class	Default	CCC	B	BB	BBB	A	AA	AAA
Transition probability	0.06	0.01	0.26	0.74	5.52	91.05	2.27	0.09
Asset (σ)	-3.24	-3.19	-2.72	-2.30	-1.51		1.98	3.12

From Figure 9.6, we can see that a BB-rated borrower will remain BB as long as the standardized normal asset returns of the borrowing firm fluctuate between -1.23σ and $+1.37\sigma$. The A borrower's rating (see Table 9.6) will remain unchanged as long as the asset returns of the firm vary within the -1.51σ and $+1.98\sigma$ range. Assume that the correlation (ρ) between those two firms' asset returns is 0.2 (to be calculated in more detail below). The joint probability (Pr) that both borrowers will remain in the same rating class during the next year can be found by integrating the bivariate normal density function as follows:

$$Pr(-1.23\sigma < BB < 1.37\sigma, -1.51\sigma < A < 1.98\sigma) = \int_{-1.23\sigma}^{1.37\sigma} \int_{-1.51\sigma}^{1.98\sigma} f(Y_1 Y_2; \rho) dY_2 dY_1$$

$$= .7365$$

$$(9.6)$$

where Y_1 and Y_2 are random variables representing the borrowers' asset values, f is the joint probability distribution of asset values, and $\rho = 0.30$.

In equation (9.6), the ρ (correlation coefficient's value) was assumed to be equal to 0.30. As described next, these correlations, in general, are calculated in CreditMetrics from multifactor models of stock returns for individual borrowers.[34] This contrasts with Moody's KMV, which deleverages equity returns in order to derive implied asset values and thus returns for individual borrowers (see Chapter 8).

Calculating Correlations Using CreditMetrics

Consider two firms, A and Z. We do not observe their asset values or returns, but we do observe their stock returns. Both are publicly traded companies. The returns (R_A) on the stock of company A, a chemical company, are driven by a single industry index factor (R_{CHEM}, the returns on the chemical industry index) and some idiosyncratic risk (U_A) assumed to be diversifiable in a portfolio context. The estimated sensitivity of firm A's stock returns to the chemical industry's returns is 0.9. Thus:[35]

$$R_A = .9R_{CHEM} + U_A \tag{9.7}$$

Firm Z represents a German universal bank. It has return sensitivity to two factors: the German banking industry return index (R_{BANK}) and the German insurance industry return index (R_{INS}). The estimated independent factor sensitivities are, respectively, 0.15 and 0.74. Thus:

$$R_Z = .74R_{INS} + .15R_{BANK} + U_Z \tag{9.8}$$

The correlation between the two firms, A and Z, will depend on the correlation between the chemical industry return index and the insurance industry return index and on the correlation between the chemical industry index and the banking industry index:[36]

$$\rho_{AZ} = (.9)(.74)\left(\rho_{CHEM,INS}\right) + (.9)(.15)\left(\rho_{CHEM,BANK}\right) \tag{9.9}$$

If the correlations $\rho_{CHEM,INS}$ and $\rho_{CHEM,BANK}$ are, respectively, 0.16 and 0.08, we have:

$$\rho_{AZ} = [(.9)(.74)(.16) + (.9)(.15)(.08)] = 0.1174$$

Firms A and Z have a low but positive default correlation, and correlation values calculated in a similar fashion are inserted into equation (9.6) to solve the bivariate normal density function and thus the joint migration probability in tables such as Table 9.5.

Joint Loan Values

In addition to the example described earlier of 64 joint migration probabilities, we can calculate 64 joint loan values in the two-loan case. The market value for each loan in each credit state is calculated as in the individual loan example earlier in this chapter. Individual loan values are then added to get a portfolio loan value, as shown in Table 9.7. Thus, if over the year both loans get upgraded to AAA, then the market value of the loan portfolio at the one-year horizon becomes $215.96 million. By comparison, if both loans default, the value of the loan portfolio becomes $102.26 million.

With 64 possible joint probabilities, p_i, and 64 possible loan values, V_i, the mean value of the portfolio and its variance are as computed in equations (9.10) and (9.11):

$$\begin{aligned} \text{Mean} &= p_1V_1 + p_2V_2 + \ldots + p_{64}V_{64} \\ &= \$213.63 \text{ million} \end{aligned} \tag{9.10}$$

TABLE 9.7 Loan Portfolio Values

All Possible 64 Year-End Values for a Two-Loan Portfolio ($)

Obligor 1 (BBB)		Obligor 2 (A)							
		AAA	AA	A	BBB	BB	B	CCC	Default
		106.59	106.49	106.30	105.64	103.15	101.39	88.71	51.13
AAA	109.37	215.96	215.86	215.67	215.01	212.52	210.76	198.08	160.50
AA	109.19	215.78	215.68	215.49	214.83	212.34	210.58	197.90	160.32
A	108.66	215.25	215.15	214.96	214.30	211.81	210.05	197.37	159.79
BBB	107.55	214.14	214.04	213.85	213.19	210.70	208.94	196.26	158.68
BB	102.02	208.61	208.51	208.33	207.66	205.17	203.41	190.73	153.15
B	98.10	204.69	204.59	204.40	203.74	210.25	199.49	186.81	149.23
CCC	83.64	190.23	190.13	189.94	189.28	186.79	185.03	172.35	134.77
Default	51.13	157.72	157.62	157.43	156.77	154.28	152.52	139.84	102.26

Source: Gupton et al., "*CreditMetrics—Technical Document, RiskMetrics—Technical Document,*" J.P. Morgan, April 2, 1997, page 12.

$$\begin{aligned}\text{Variance} &= p_1(V_1 - \text{Mean})^2 + p_2(V_2 - \text{Mean})^2 + \ldots + p_{64}(V_{64} - \text{Mean})^2 \\ &= \$11.22 \text{ million}\end{aligned} \tag{9.11}$$

Taking the square root of the solution to equation (9.11), the σ of the loan portfolio value is $3.35 million and the 99 percent VAR under the normal distribution is:

$$2.33 \times \$3.35 = \$7.81 \text{ million} \tag{9.12}$$

Interestingly, comparing this value of $7.81 million for a loan portfolio of $200 million with the 99 percent VAR-based capital requirement of $6.97 million for the single BBB loan of $100 million in this chapter, we can see that although the loan portfolio has doubled in face value, the VAR-based capital requirement (based on the 99th percentile of the loan portfolio's value distribution) has increased by only $7.81 million minus $6.97 million, which is $0.84 million. Perhaps even more illustrative of the diversification effects is that the bank's capital ratio falls from 6.97 percent to $7.81/$200, or 3.91 percent. The reason for this is portfolio diversification. Specifically, built into the joint transition probability matrix in

Table 9.5 is an assumed correlation of 0.3 between the default risks of the two loans.

CreditMetrics: Portfolio VAR Using the Actual Distribution

Unfortunately, the capital requirement under the normal distribution is likely to underestimate the true 99 percent VAR because of the skewness in the actual distribution of loan values. Using Table 9.5 in conjunction with Table 9.7, the 99 percent (worst) loan value for the portfolio is $204.40 million.[37] Thus, the unexpected change in value of the portfolio from its mean value is:

$$\$213.63 \text{ million} - \$204.40 \text{ million} = \$9.23 \text{ million}$$

This is higher than the capital requirement under the normal distribution discussed earlier ($9.23 million versus $7.81 million), but the benefits of portfolio diversification are clear. In particular, the capital requirement of $9.23 million for the combined $200 million face value portfolio can be favorably compared to the $8.99 million 99 percent VAR using the actual distribution for the single BBB loan of $100 million face value calculated earlier in this chapter.[37]

CreditMetrics with N Loans The normal distribution model can be extended in either of two directions. The first option is to keep expanding the loans' joint transition matrix by directly or analytically computing the mean and standard deviation of the portfolio. This, however, rapidly becomes computationally difficult. For example, in a five loan portfolio, there are 8^5 possible joint transition probabilities, or over 32,000 joint transitions. The second option is to manipulate the equation for the variance of a loan portfolio. It can be shown that the risk of a portfolio of N loans depends on the risk of each pair-wise combination of loans in the portfolio as well as the risk of each loan individually. To estimate the risk of a portfolio of N loans, we only need to calculate the risks of subportfolios containing two assets and of each individual asset, as shown in Appendix 9.3 to this chapter.

In order to compute the distribution of loan values in the large sample case where loan values are not normally distributed, CreditMetrics uses Monte Carlo simulation.[39] Consider the portfolio of 20 loans in Table 9.8 and the correlations among those loans (borrowers) in Table 9.9.

For each loan, 20,000 (or more) different underlying borrower asset values are simulated, based on the original rating of the loan, the joint

TABLE 9.8 Example Portfolio

Credit Asset	Principal Rating	Maturity Amount	Market (Years)	Value
1	AAA	$ 7,000,000	3	$7,821,049
2	AA	1,000,000	4	1,177,268
3	A	1,000,000	3	1,120,831
4	BBB	1,000,000	4	1,189,432
5	BB	1,000,000	3	1,154,641
6	B	1,000,000	4	1,263,523
7	CCC	1,000,000	2	1,127,628
8	A	10,000,000	8	14,229,071
9	BB	5,000,000	2	5,386,603
10	A	3,000,000	2	3,181,246
11	A	1,000,000	4	1,181,246
12	A	2,000,000	5	2,483,322
13	B	600,000	3	705,409
14	B	1,000,000	2	1,087,841
15	B	3,000,000	2	3,263,523
16	B	2,000,000	4	2,527,046
17	BBB	1,000,000	6	1,315,720
18	BBB	8,000,000	5	10,020,611
19	BBB	1,000,000	3	1,118,178
20	AA	5,000,000	5	6,181,784

Source: Gupton et al., *"CreditMetrics—Technical Document, RiskMetrics— Technical Document,"* J.P. Morgan, April 2, 1997, page 121.

transition probabilities to other rating classes, and the historical correlations among the loans.[40] The loan (or borrower) can either stay in its original rating class or migrate to another rating class (see the earlier discussion and Figure 9.6). Each loan is then revalued after each simulation (and rating transition). Adding across the simulated values for the 20 loans produces 20,000 different values for the loan portfolio as a whole.[41] A VAR for the loan portfolio, based on the 99 percent worst case, can be calculated as the value of the loan portfolio that has the 200th worst value out of 20,000 possible loan portfolio values. In conjunction with the mean loan portfolio value, a capital requirement (VAR) can then be calculated.

TABLE 9.9 Asset Correlation for Example Portfolio

	1	2	3	4	5	6	7	8	9	10	11	12	13	14	15	16	17	18	19	20
1	1	0.45	0.45	0.45	0.15	0.15	0.15	0.15	0.15	0.15	0.1	0.1	0.1	0.1	0.1	0.1	0.1	0.1	0.1	0.1
2	0.45	1	0.45	0.45	0.15	0.15	0.15	0.15	0.15	0.15	0.1	0.1	0.1	0.1	0.1	0.1	0.1	0.1	0.1	0.1
3	0.45	0.45	1	0.45	0.15	0.15	0.15	0.15	0.15	0.15	0.1	0.1	0.1	0.1	0.1	0.1	0.1	0.1	0.1	0.1
4	0.45	0.45	0.45	1	0.15	0.15	0.15	0.15	0.15	0.15	0.1	0.1	0.1	0.1	0.1	0.1	0.1	0.1	0.1	0.1
5	0.15	0.15	0.15	0.15	1	0.35	0.35	0.35	0.35	0.35	0.2	0.2	0.2	0.2	0.2	0.15	0.15	0.15	0.1	0.1
6	0.15	0.15	0.15	0.15	0.35	1	0.35	0.35	0.35	0.35	0.2	0.2	0.2	0.2	0.2	0.15	0.15	0.15	0.1	0.1
7	0.15	0.15	0.15	0.15	0.35	0.35	1	0.35	0.35	0.35	0.2	0.2	0.2	0.2	0.2	0.15	0.15	0.15	0.1	0.1
8	0.15	0.15	0.15	0.15	0.35	0.35	0.35	1	0.35	0.35	0.2	0.2	0.2	0.2	0.2	0.15	0.15	0.15	0.1	0.1
9	0.15	0.15	0.15	0.15	0.35	0.35	0.35	0.35	1	0.35	0.2	0.2	0.2	0.2	0.2	0.15	0.15	0.15	0.1	0.1
10	0.15	0.15	0.15	0.15	0.35	0.35	0.35	0.35	0.35	1	0.2	0.2	0.2	0.2	0.2	0.15	0.15	0.15	0.1	0.1
11	0.1	0.1	0.1	0.1	0.2	0.2	0.2	0.2	0.2	0.2	1	0.45	0.45	0.45	0.45	0.2	0.2	0.2	0.1	0.1
12	0.1	0.1	0.1	0.1	0.2	0.2	0.2	0.2	0.2	0.2	0.45	1	0.45	0.45	0.45	0.2	0.2	0.2	0.1	0.1
13	0.1	0.1	0.1	0.1	0.2	0.2	0.2	0.2	0.2	0.2	0.45	0.45	1	0.45	0.45	0.2	0.2	0.2	0.1	0.1
14	0.1	0.1	0.1	0.1	0.2	0.2	0.2	0.2	0.2	0.2	0.45	0.45	0.45	1	0.45	0.2	0.2	0.2	0.1	0.1
15	0.1	0.1	0.1	0.1	0.2	0.2	0.2	0.2	0.2	0.2	0.45	0.45	0.45	0.45	1	0.2	0.2	0.2	0.1	0.1
16	0.1	0.1	0.1	0.1	0.15	0.15	0.15	0.15	0.15	0.15	0.2	0.2	0.2	0.2	0.2	1	0.55	0.55	0.25	0.25
17	0.1	0.1	0.1	0.1	0.15	0.15	0.15	0.15	0.15	0.15	0.2	0.2	0.2	0.2	0.2	0.55	1	0.55	0.25	0.25
18	0.1	0.1	0.1	0.1	0.15	0.15	0.15	0.15	0.15	0.15	0.2	0.2	0.2	0.2	0.2	0.55	0.55	1	0.25	0.25
19	0.1	0.1	0.1	0.1	0.1	0.1	0.1	0.1	0.1	0.1	0.1	0.1	0.1	0.1	0.1	0.25	0.25	0.25	1	0.65
20	0.1	0.1	0.1	0.1	0.1	0.1	0.1	0.1	0.1	0.1	0.1	0.1	0.1	0.1	0.1	0.25	0.25	0.25	0.65	1

Source: Gupton et al., "CreditMetrics—Technical Document, RiskMetrics—Technical Document," J.P. Morgan, April 2, 1997, page 122.

The CreditMetrics portfolio methodology can also be used to calculate the marginal risk contribution for individual loans—that is, for loan transfer pricing. Unlike the KMV-type approach, funds are viewed as being flexibly adjustable to accommodate an expanded loan supply, and the word *marginal* means loans are either made or not made to a borrower (rather than having an incremental amount of new loans made to a current borrower). Thus, CreditMetrics defines the risk contribution of an asset to a portfolio as the change in the portfolio's standard deviation due to the addition of the asset into the portfolio. In contrast, Moody's KMV defines the asset's risk contribution as the change in the portfolio standard deviation due to a small change in the weight of the asset in the portfolio (see equation (8.15) in Chapter 8 for the definition of MRC_i).

Table 9.10 shows the stand-alone and marginal risk contributions of 20 loans in a hypothetical loan portfolio based on a standard deviation (σ) measure of risk. The stand-alone columns reflect the dollar and percentage risk of each loan, viewed separately. The stand-alone percentage risk for the CCC-rated asset (number 7) is 22.67 percent, and for the B-rated asset (number 15) it is 18.72 percent. The marginal risk contribution columns in Table 9.10 reflect the risk of adding each loan to a portfolio of the remaining 19 loans (the standard deviation risk of a 20-loan portfolio minus the standard deviation risk of a 19-loan portfolio). Interestingly, Table 9.10 shows that, on a stand-alone basis, asset 7 (CCC) is riskier than asset 15 (B), but when risk is measured in a portfolio context (by its marginal risk contribution), asset 15 is riskier. The reason can be seen from the correlation matrix in Table 9.9, where the B-rated loan (asset 15) has a high correlation level of .45 with assets 11, 12, 13, and 14. By comparison, the highest correlations of the CCC-rated loan (asset 7) are with assets 5, 6, 8, 9, and 10 at the .35 level.

One policy implication is immediate and is shown in Figure 9.7, where the total risk (in a portfolio context) of a loan is broken down into two components: (1) its percentage marginal standard deviation (vertical axis) and (2) the dollar amount of credit exposure (horizontal axis). We then have:

$$\text{Total risk of a loan (\$)} = \text{Marginal standard deviation (\%)}$$
$$\times \text{Credit exposure (\$)}$$

For example, using the credit exposure value for loan 15 (a B-rated loan) shown in Table 9.9 and the marginal standard deviation for loan 15 shown in Table 9.10, the total risk of loan 15 can be calculated as follows:

$$\$270,000 = 8.27\% \times \$3,263,523$$

TABLE 9.10 Standard Deviation of Value Change

Asset	Credit Rating	Stand-Alone Absolute ($)	Stand-Alone Percent	Marginal Absolute ($)	Marginal Percent
1	AAA	4,905	0.06	239	0.00
2	AA	2,007	0.17	114	0.01
3	A	17,523	1.56	693	0.06
4	BBB	40,043	3.37	2,934	0.25
5	BB	99,607	8.63	16,046	1.39
6	B	162,251	12.84	37,664	2.98
7	CCC	255,680	<u>22.67</u>	73,079	<u>6.48</u>
8	A	197,152	1.39	35,104	0.25
9	BB	380,141	7.06	105,949	1.97
10	A	63,207	1.99	5,068	0.16
11	A	15,360	1.30	1,232	0.10
12	A	43,085	1.73	4,531	0.18
13	B	107,314	15.21	25,684	3.64
14	B	167,511	15.40	44,827	4.12
15	B	610,900	<u>18.72</u>	270,000	<u>8.27</u>
16	B	322,720	12.77	89,190	3.53
17	BBB	28,051	2.13	2,775	0.21
18	BBB	306,892	3.06	69,624	0.69
19	BBB	1,837	0.16	120	0.01
20	AA	9,916	0.16	389	0.01

Source: Gupton et al., *"CreditMetrics—Technical Document, RiskMetrics—Technical Document,"* J.P. Morgan, April 2, 1997, page 130.

Also plotted in Figure 9.7 is an equal-risk "isoquant" of $70,000. Suppose managers wish to impose total credit risk exposure limits of $70,000 on each loan measured in a portfolio context. Then asset 15 (the B-rated loan) and assets 16 and 9 are clear outliers. One possible solution would be for the bank to sell asset 15 to another bank, or to swap it for another B-rated asset that has a lower correlation with the other loans (assets) in the bank's portfolio. In doing so, its expected returns may remain approximately unchanged, but the bank's loan portfolio risk is likely to decrease.[42]

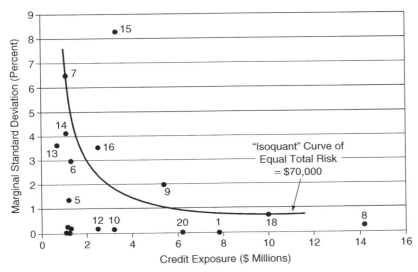

FIGURE 9.7   Credit Limits and Loan Selection in CreditMetrics

SUMMARY

In this chapter, we have outlined the VAR approach to calculating the capital requirement on a loan or a bond. We have used one application of the VAR methodology—CreditMetrics—to illustrate the approach and discuss the technical issues involved. Its key characteristics are: (1) it involves a full valuation or MTM approach in which both an upside and a downside to loan values are considered, and (2) the analyst can consider the actual distribution of estimated future loan values in calculating a capital requirement on a loan. We have also incorporated potential portfolio diversification benefits and correlation analysis into the VAR methodology and used Credit-Metrics to calculate the VAR and capital requirements for a loan portfolio.

APPENDIX 9.1: CALCULATING THE FORWARD ZERO CURVE FOR LOAN VALUATION

Yields on U.S. Treasury securities can be used as the foundation for the valuation of risky debt because U.S. Treasury note and bond markets are more liquid than corporate debt markets. To derive the credit-risk-adjusted discount factor, CreditMetrics uses the following procedure:

1. Obtain the current yield curve, denoted CYC_{RF}, on risk-free (U.S. Treasury) coupon-bearing instruments.
2. Decompose CYC_{RF} into a zero yield curve, denoted ZYC_{RF}, using a no-arbitrage condition.
3. Solve for the one-year forward zero risk-free yield curve, FYC_{RF}.
4. Add fixed credit spreads obtained from historical loss experience in order to obtain the one-year forward zero risky debt yield curve, FYC_R.[43]

The following example illustrates the CreditMetrics approach.

The Current Yield Curve on Risk-Free (U.S. Treasury) Coupon-Bearing Instruments

From the current yield curve (CYC_{RF}) for risk-free coupon bonds, shown in Figure 9.8, a zero yield curve for risk-free bonds (ZYC_{RF}) can be derived using *no-arbitrage* pricing relationships between coupon bonds and zero-coupon bonds, and solving by successive substitution.

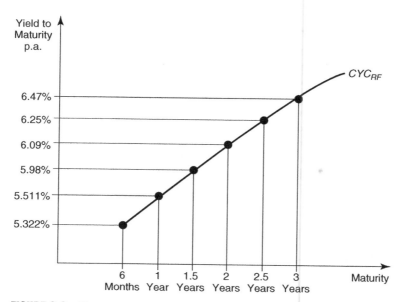

FIGURE 9.8 The Current Yield Curve on Risk-Free U.S. Treasury Coupon-Bearing Instruments

Calculation of the Current Zero Risk-Free Curve Using No Arbitrage

U.S. Treasury notes and bonds carry semiannual coupon payments; therefore all yields are divided by two to reflect semiannual rates.[44] We utilize the double subscript notation introduced in Chapter 5, with the exception that the semiannual, rather than annual periods are numbered consecutively; thus, $_0r_1$ is the spot (current) rate on the risk-free U.S. Treasury security maturing in six months, $_0r_2$ is the spot (current) rate on the risk-free U.S. Treasury security maturing in one year, $_2r_1$ is the one-year forward rate on a six-month U.S. Treasury security, and so on. Thus, for a bond with a face value F of 100 and semi-annual coupon payments C, $_0z_1$ follows from:

$$\text{Six-month zero}: \quad 100 = \frac{C+F}{1+_0r_1} = \frac{C+F}{1+_0z_1} = \frac{100+(5.322/2)}{1+(.05322/2)}$$

Therefore, the six-month zero risk-free rate is $_0z_1 = 5.322$ percent per annum.

$$\text{One-year zero}: \quad 100 = \frac{C}{1+_0r_2} + \frac{C+F}{(1+_0r_2)^2} = \frac{C}{1+_0z_1} + \frac{C+F}{(1+_0z_2)^2}$$

$$100 = \frac{(5.511/2)}{1+(.05511/2)} + \frac{100+(5.511/2)}{(1+.05511/2)^2}$$

$$= \frac{(5.511/2)}{1+(.05322/2)} + \frac{100+(5.511/2)}{(1+.055136/2)^2}$$

Therefore, the one-year zero risk-free rate is $_0z_2 = 5.5136$ percent per annum.

The process continues to trace out the zero yield curve for risk-free U.S. Treasury securities—shown as ZYC_{RF} in Figure 9.9. The next step is to trace out the risk-free forward yield curve, denoted FYC_{RF}, using ZYC_{RF}.

Derivation of the One-Year Forward Government Yield Curve Using the Current Risk-Free Zero Yield Curve

We can use the expectations hypothesis of the yield curve in order to derive the risk-free ZYC_{RF} expected next year, or the risk-free one-year forward zero yield curve, FYC_{RF}, shown in Figure 9.10. But, first we derive a series of six-month forward rates using the rates on the ZYC_{RF} curve as follows:[45]

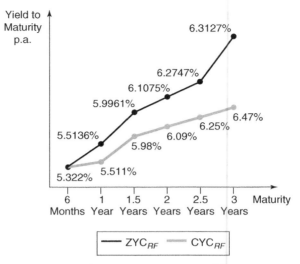

FIGURE 9.9 Zero-Coupon Risk-Free U.S. Treasury Yield Curve

$$(1 + {}_0z_2)^2 = (1 + {}_0z_1)(1 + {}_1z_1)$$
$$[1 + (.055136/2)]^2 = (1 + .05322/2)(1 + {}_1z_1)$$

Therefore, the rate for six-months forward delivery of six-month maturity U.S. Treasury securities is expected to be ${}_1z_1 = 5.7054$ percent per annum.

$$(1 + {}_0z_3)^3 = (1 + {}_0z_2)^2(1 + {}_2z_1)$$
$$[1 + (.059961/2)]^3 = (1 + .055136/2)^2(1 + {}_2z_1)$$

Therefore, the rate for one-year forward delivery of six-month maturity U.S. Treasury securities is expected to be ${}_2z_1 = 6.9645$ percent per annum.

$$(1 + {}_0z_4)^4 = (1 + {}_0z_3)^3(1 + {}_3z_1)$$
$$[1 + (.061075/2)]^4 = (1 + .059961/2)^3(1 + {}_3z_1)$$

Therefore, the rate for six-month maturity U.S. Treasury securities to be delivered in 1.5 years is ${}_3z_1 = 6.4419$ percent per annum.

$$(1 + {}_0z_5)^5 = (1 + {}_0z_4)^4(1 + {}_4z_1)$$
$$[1 + (.062747/2)]^5 = (1 + .061075/2)^4(1 + {}_4z_1)$$

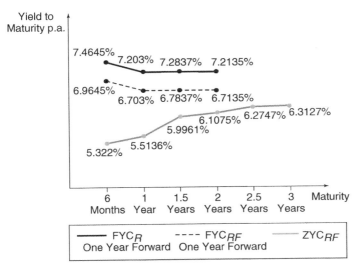

FIGURE 9.10 Derivation of the One-Year Forward Risky Debt Yield Curve

Therefore, the rate for six-month maturity U.S. Treasury securities to be delivered in two years is $_4z_1 = 6.9452$ percent per annum.

Now we can use these forward rates on six-month-maturity U.S. Treasury securities to obtain the one-year forward risk-free yield curve FYC$_{RF}$ shown in Figure 9.10 as follows:

$$(1 + {}_2z_2)^2 = (1 + {}_2z_1)(1 + {}_3z_1)$$

Therefore, the yield for one-year maturity U.S. Treasury securities to be delivered in one year is $_2z_2 = 6.703$ percent per annum.

$$(1 + {}_2z_3)^3 = (1 + {}_2z_1)(1 + {}_3z_1)(1 + {}_4z_1)$$

Therefore, the yield for 18-month maturity U.S. Treasury securities to be delivered in one year is: $_2z_3 = 6.7837$ percent per annum.

$$(1 + {}_2z_4)^4 = (1 + {}_2z_1)(1 + {}_3z_1)(1 + {}_4z_1)(1 + {}_5z_1)$$

Therefore, the yield for two-year maturity U.S. Treasury securities to be delivered in one year is: $_2z_4 = 6.7135$ percent per annum.

TABLE 9.11   Credit Spreads for AAA Bonds

Maturity (in Years, Compounded Annually)	Credit Spread, s_i
2	0.007071
3	0.008660
5	0.011180
10	0.015811
15	0.019365
20	0.022361

Source: Gupton et al., *"CreditMetrics—Technical Document, RiskMetrics—Technical Document,"* J.P. Morgan, April 2, 1997, page 164; from Bridge Information Systems, February 15, 1997.

Derivation of One-Year Forward Risky Yield Curve—FYC$_R$

CreditMetrics adds a fixed credit spread (s_i) to the risk-free forward zero yield curve in order to obtain the risky debt forward yield curve, FYC$_R$, shown in Figure 9.10. Table 9.11 shows credit spreads provided by commercial firms such as Bridge Information Systems for different maturities. Typically, commercially provided credit spreads are calculated using historical averages. The one-year forward yield curve for risky debt, FYC$_R$ in Figure 9.10, is illustrated assuming a fixed 50 basis point credit spread.

A Last Methodological Word

The methodology presented in this Appendix has been criticized for, among other reasons, its assumptions of deterministic interest rates (fixed yield curves) and constant credit spreads, s_i. The second criticism could be addressed by decomposing risky debt yield curves directly rather than decomposing the risk-free U.S. Treasury yield curve and then adding on a fixed credit spread. However, this approach injects noise into valuations if risky debt markets are illiquid and prices are subject to error (see the discussion in Chapter 5).

APPENDIX 9.2: ESTIMATING UNEXPECTED LOSSES USING EXTREME VALUE THEORY

The generalized pareto distribution (GPD) is a two-parameter distribution with the following functional form:

$$G_{\xi,\beta}(x) = 1 - (1 + \xi x/\beta)^{-1/\xi} \text{ if } \xi \neq 0$$
$$= 1 - e^{-x/\beta} \text{ if } \xi = 0$$

The two parameters that describe the GPD are ξ (the shape parameter) and β (the scaling parameter). If $\xi > 0$, then the GPD is characterized by fat tails.[46]

Suppose that the GPD describes the portion of the distribution of unexpected losses that exceeds the 5 percent VAR, and assume that a normal distribution best describes the distribution of values for the BBB-rated loan described in Table 9.4 up to the 95th percentile, denoted as the threshold value $u = \$4.93$ million. If we had 10,000 observations of unexpected losses on this loan, denoted by $n = 10,000$, the 95 percent threshold is set by the 500 observations with the largest unexpected losses denoted as $N_u = 500$; that is $(10,000 - 500)/10,000 = 95$ percent. Suppose that fitting the GPD parameters to the data yields $\xi = 0.5$ and $\beta = 7$.[47] McNeil (1999) shows that the estimate of a VAR beyond the 95th percentile, taking into account the heaviness of the tails in the GPD (denoted $\overline{VAR}_q$) can be calculated as follows:

$$\overline{VAR}_q = u + (\beta/\xi)\left[(n(1-q)/N_u)^{-\xi} - 1\right]$$

Substituting in the parameters of this example for the 99th percentile VAR, or $\overline{VAR}_{.99}$, yields:

$$\$22.23 = \$4.93 + (7/.5)\left[(10,000(1 - .99)/500)^{-.5} - 1\right]$$

McNeil (1999) also shows that the expected shortfall (i.e., the mean of the credit losses exceeding $\overline{VAR}_{.99}$) can be estimated as follows:

$$\overline{ES}_q = \overline{VAR}_q/(1 - \xi) + (\beta - \xi u)/(1 - \xi)$$

where q is set equal to the 99th percentile. Thus,

$$\overline{ES}_q = (\$22.23/.5) + (7 - .5(4.93))/.5 = \$53.53$$

to obtain the values shown in Figure 9.4.

As can be seen, the ratio of the extreme (shortfall) loss to the 99th percentile loss is quite high:

$$\overline{ES}_{.99}/\overline{VAR}_{.99} = \$53.53/\$22.23 = 2.4$$

This means that nearly 2.5 times more capital would be needed to secure the bank against catastrophic credit losses compared to unexpected losses occurring up to the 99th percentile level, even when allowing for "fat tails" in the VAR.99 measure. It also suggests that a catastrophic credit stress-test multiplier of between 2 and 3 would be appropriate in this case.

APPENDIX 9.3: THE SIMPLIFIED TWO-ASSET SUBPORTFOLIO SOLUTION TO THE N-ASSET PORTFOLIO CASE

The standard formula for the risk of a portfolio with equally weighted assets i and j is:

$$\sigma_p^2 = \sum_{i=1}^{n} \sigma^2(V_i) + 2 \sum_{i=1}^{n-1} \sum_{\substack{j=1 \\ j \neq i}}^{n} Cov(V_i, V_j) \tag{9.13}$$

Alternatively, we may relate the covariance terms to the variances of pairs of assets, where

$$\sigma^2(V_i + V_j) = \sigma^2(V_i) + 2\, Cov(V_i, V_j) + \sigma^2(V_j) \tag{9.14}$$

and thus

$$2\, Cov(V_i, V_j) = \sigma^2(V_i + V_j) - \sigma^2(V_i) - \sigma^2(V_j) \tag{9.15}$$

substituting the equation for $2\, Cov(V_i, V_j)$ into equation (9.13), we can express the portfolio standard deviation in terms of the risk of individual assets and the standard deviations of subportfolio containing two assets.

$$\sigma_p^2 = \sum_{i=1}^{n-1} \sum_{\substack{j=1 \\ j \neq i}}^{n} \sigma^2(V_i + V_j) - (n-2) \sum_{i=1}^{n} \sigma^2(V_i) \tag{9.16}$$

APPENDIX 9.4: CREDITMETRICS AND SWAP CREDIT RISK

Assuming some credit event occurs during the next year, how will the value of a swap be affected during its remaining life? Conceptually, the value of a swap is the difference between two components. The first component is the net present value (NPV) of a swap between two default-risk-free counterparties. This involves valuing the swap at the year 1 horizon, based on fixed and expected (forward) government rates, and discounting by the forward zero curve (see Appendix 9.1).

For example, in a three-year plain-vanilla fixed for floating interest rate swap, the expected net present value at the one-year horizon (hereafter, *swap future value* FV) would be:

$$FV = \frac{\left(\overline{F} - \overline{f}_2\right)}{(1 + {}_1z_1)} + \frac{\left(\overline{F} - \overline{f}_3\right)}{(1 + {}_1z_2)^2}$$

where $\overline{F}$ = fixed rate on swap
$\overline{f}_i$ = forward rates (expected floating rates) in period i
${}_1z_i$ = forward zero-coupon rates in period i

Note that any positive (or negative) FV reflects movements in government yield curves and thus interest rate (or market) risk on the swap rather than the default risk on the swap—although, as noted earlier and in what follows, it is difficult to separate the two because the more out-of-the-money a contract becomes to any given party, the greater is the incentive to default.[48]

The second component is an adjustment for credit risk. CreditMetrics deducts from the FV of any swap an expected loss amount reflecting credit risk. This expected loss amount will vary by the end of the year 1 horizon rating category of the counterparty (e.g., AAA versus C) and by default (D). Thus, as described in applying CreditMetrics to loans, eight different expected losses will be associated with the eight different transition states over the one-year horizon (including the counterparty's credit rating remaining unchanged). Hence:

Value of swap at year 1 for rating class R	=	FV (risk-free future value in year 1)	−	Expected loss rating class R (year 1 through to maturity)

In turn, for each of the seven nondefault ratings, the expected loss is calculated as the product of three variables:

Expected loss (rating class R)	=	Average exposure (year 1 through year N)	×	Cumulative probability of default (year 1 through year N)	×	Loss given default

We discuss each variable in the next section.

Average Exposure

As is well known, two general forces drive the default risk exposure on a fixed/floating swap. The first is what may be called the interest-rate diffusion effect—the tendency of floating rates to drift apart from fixed rates with the passage of time. The degree of drift depends on the type of interest rate model employed (e.g., mean reversion or no mean reversion) but, in general, the diffusion effect on exposure may be seen as increasing with the term of the swap.

Offsetting the diffusion effect, in terms of replacement cost, is the maturity effect. As time passes and the swap gets closer to maturity, the number of payment periods a replacement contract must cover declines. Thus, the maturity effect tends to reduce exposure as the time remaining to swap maturity shrinks. Adding the diffusion effect and the maturity effect, the overall effect of the two forces on future replacement cost (exposure) suggests that future exposure levels rise, reach a maximum, and then decline. To measure exposure amounts each year into the future, two approaches are normally followed: (1) a Monte Carlo simulation method or (2) an option pricing method.[49]

Cumulative Probability of Default

As discussed in Chapter 6, the cumulative mortality rate (CMR) over N years is linked to marginal (annual) mortality rates (MMRs) by

$$CMR = 1 - \prod_{i=1}^{N} (1 - MMR_i)$$

Assuming that transition probabilities follow a stationary Markov process, then the CMRs for any given rating can be found by either (1) using a methodology similar to Altman (1989)—that is, calculating the annual MMRs and then the appropriate CMR for the remaining life of the swap; or (2) multiplying the annual transition matrix by itself N times (where N is the remaining years of the swap contract at the one-year horizon).[50] In the three-year swap, the cumulative mortality rates would be the last column calculated from the matrix:

$$[\text{One-year transition matrix}]^2$$

Loss Given Default (LGD)

The loss given default (or 1 minus the recovery rate) should not only reflect the loss per contract, but, where relevant (as under the Basel II rules), take netting into account.

The product of average exposure (AE), the cumulative probability of default (CMR), and the loss given default (LGD) gives the expected loss for each of the seven nondefault rating transitions. For the transition at the credit horizon to default (i.e., during year 1 of the swap), the expected loss is given as:

$$\text{Expected loss on default} = \text{Expected exposure in year } 1 \times \text{LGD}$$

Specifically, in the three-year swap, where default is assumed to occur at the end of year 1, exposure will be measured by the total replacement cost over the remaining two years of the swap.[51]

An Example

Following CreditMetrics, consider the example of a three-year fixed/floating swap with a notional value of $10 million, an LGD of 50 percent, and an average exposure, measured at the end of year 1, of $61,627. Based on historical (bond) transition matrices (and CMRs calculated from them) for a counterparty rated AA at the end of the one-year credit-event horizon, the value of the swap is as follows:

$$
\begin{aligned}
\text{Value of swap at credit horizon} &= \text{FV} - \text{Expected loss} \\
&= \text{FV} - (\text{AE} \times \text{CMR}_{AA} \times \text{LGD}) \\
&= \text{FV} - (\$61,627 \times .0002 \times .5) \\
&= \text{FV} - \$6
\end{aligned}
$$

where FV is the expected future value of the default-free swap at the end of the year. For a three-year swap where the counterparty is rated CCC at the end of the one-year credit horizon:

$$
\begin{aligned}
\text{Value of swap at credit horizon} &= \text{FV} - (\$61,627 \times .3344 \times .5) \\
&= \text{FV} - \$10,304
\end{aligned}
$$

The lower value of the CCC counterparty swap reflects the higher CMR of that type of counterparty over the remaining two years of the swap. Note also that the lower-rated counterparty may also have a higher LGD, although in this example, it is assumed to be the same as the LGD for the AA-rated counterparty. If the CCC-rated counterparty had a lower LGD than 50 percent, then the swap value would be even lower.

For a swap where the counterparty defaults during the one-year horizon, expected exposure (EE or replacement cost) over the remaining two years is assumed to be $101,721. Thus:

TABLE 9.12 Value of Three-Year Swap at the End of Year 1

Rating of Counterparty	Value ($)
AAA	FV – 1
AA	FV – 6
A	FV – 46
BBB	FV – 148
BB	FV – 797
B	FV – 3,209
CCC	FV – 10,304
D	FV – 50,860

Source: Gupton et al., *"CreditMetrics—Technical Document, RiskMetrics—Technical Document,"* J.P. Morgan, April 2, 1997, page 51.

$$\text{Value of swap at the one-year horizon} = \text{FV} - (\text{EE} \times \text{LGD})$$
$$= \text{FV} - (\$101,721 \times .5)$$
$$= \text{FV} - \$50,860$$

Table 9.12 summarizes the expected swap values at the end of year 1 under the seven possible rating transitions and the one default state. The size of the expected and unexpected loss of value on a swap will depend on the initial rating of the counterparty at time 0 (today), the one-year transition probabilities during the first year, and the one-year forward or expected future values (FV) calculated in Table 9.13, where the counterparty is rated as AA today (time 0).

Table 9.13 shows that the credit-related expected loss of value on the swap is $21.80, and the 99 percent unexpected loss of value (VAR) is approximately $126.20. If the original rating of the swap counterparty is lower, the expected and unexpected losses of value are likely to be higher.

A similar methodology could be used to calculate the credit VAR of forwards (swaps can be viewed as a succession of forward contracts) as well as interest rate options and caps. For example, the average exposure on a three-year interest rate cap, as measured at the end of the one-year horizon, would be the average of the replacement cost of the cap (the fair value of the cap premium under an appropriate interest rate model) measured at the beginning of year 2 and the beginning of year 3.[52] As with swaps, replacement costs tend to reflect a similar inverted U-shape, because of the offsetting effects of the interest rate diffusion effect and the maturity effect.[53]

TABLE 9.13 Expected and Unexpected Loss on a Three-Year $10 Million Swap to an AA Counterparty

Rating at Year 1	One-Year Transition Probability (%)	Value of Swap at One-Year Horizon ($)
AAA	0.7	FV – 1
AA	90.65	FV – 6
A	7.65	FV – 46
BBB	0.77	FV – 148
BB	0.06	FV – 797
B	0.14	FV – 3,209
CCC	0.02	FV – 10,304
D	0.01	FV – 50,860
	100.00	Expected FV – 21.80
		99% Value FV – 148

99% unexpected loss of value = [Expected value – 99 percent value] = $126.20

Source: Gupton et al., *"CreditMetrics—Technical Document, RiskMetrics—Technical Document,"* J.P. Morgan, April 2, 1997.

CHAPTER **10**

Stress Testing Credit Risk Models: Algorithmics Mark-to-Future

INTRODUCTION

A key issue for bankers and regulators is internal model validation and predictive accuracy. In the context of market models, this issue has led to numerous efforts to back-test models to ascertain their predictive accuracy. The second pillar of the Basel II capital accords states that bank regulators must evaluate how well banks are assessing their capital needs relative to their risk, thereby requiring bank examiners to validate the accuracy of bank risk measurement models. Currently, under the Basel market risk-based capital requirements, a bank must back-test its internal market model over a minimum of 250 past days if it is used for capital requirement calculations. If the forecast VAR errors on those 250 days are too large, implying that the risk is underestimated on too many days, a system of penalties is imposed by regulators to create incentives for bankers to get their models right.[1]

Many observers, however, have argued that back-testing over 250 days is simply not enough, given the high standard errors that are likely to occur if the period is not representative of true market conditions. To reduce errors of this type, one suggestion has been to increase the number of past daily observations over which a back-test of a model is conducted. For example, using at least 1,000 past daily observations is commonly considered to be adequate to ensure that the period chosen is representative in terms of testing the predictive accuracy of any given model.[2] Unfortunately, even for traded financial assets such as currencies, a period of 1,000 past days requires going back in time over four years and may involve covering a wide and unrepresentative range of forex regimes.

In response to these criticisms, bank regulators conducted a stress test of the 19 largest U.S. banks (each with year-end assets exceeding $100 billion as of December 2008) that was forward looking. The test required the banks "to project their credit losses and revenues for the two years 2009 and 2010, including the level of reserves that would be needed at the end of 2010 to cover expected losses in 2011, under two alternative economic scenarios" (Board of Governors of the Federal Reserve System, April 2009). In this chapter, we discuss the design and results of the Federal Reserve stress tests of major banks in 2009.

BACK-TESTING CREDIT RISK MODELS

To appropriately back-test or stress test market-risk models, 250 observations may be regarded as too few, but it is unlikely that a bank would be able to generate anywhere near that many past time-series observations for back-testing its internal credit-risk models. For example, with annual observations (which are the most likely to be available), a bank might be able to generate only 40 past observations that cover five or six credit cycles.[3] A banker or regulator is then severely hampered from performing time-series back-testing similar to that currently available for market risk models.[4]

Even when available for back-testing of credit risk models, loan databases are often subject to substantial error in classifications. In order to compute the loss distribution for a loan portfolio, individual loans must be classified according to their default probabilities. Carey and Hrycay (2001) compare three methodologies to accomplish this:

1. The internal ratings method.
2. Mapping to external ratings.
3. Credit scoring (see Chapter 6).

These methodologies have biases that may undermine the accuracy of the estimated loss distribution. For example, the internal ratings method may be unstable if ratings criteria have changed over time or if there are insufficient data to estimate a time-invariant historical average default rate for each internal rating classification. In contrast, the efficacy of the external ratings mapping method is undermined by possible judgmental biases in assigning each individual loan to a particular external ratings classification. Finally, credit scoring models suffer from biases in model estimates that are exacerbated across different credit cycles. Carey and Hrycay (2001) find that the classification model does well in quantifying rating grades, but correctly identifies only one third of defaulting firms. Moreover, the biases introduced by errors in classification differ for investment-grade as opposed to non-investment-grade debt instruments. Some, but not all, of these problems can be alleviated if long panels of loan data are collected.[5]

Benchmarking and Accuracy Ratios

Traditionally, back-testing approaches employed by regulators have been to evaluate or stress test a given bank's model by comparing that bank's loan rating system with that of similar size banks. For example, suppose that IBM has drawn-down loans from 10 banks, each of which has an internal rating system. As discussed in more detail in the Appendix to Chapter 13, bank internal rating systems rate the credit risk of the borrower on a numerical scale (e.g., 1 to 10, where 1 is the best credit and 10 is the worst). The internal rating is based on the bank's assessment, supported by historical data, of either the probability of default, PD (unitary scale), or both PD and the loss given default, LGD (dual scale). A regulator can stress test the accuracy of the bank's internal rating process by comparing the rating of a particular company, say IBM, using 10 different banks' internal ratings (normalized to the same scale). In this way, an extreme outlier can be identified and the bank regulator can then penalize the bank by rejecting the accuracy of the bank's internal ratings model. This may cause the bank to lose the ability to use its internal ratings to calculate its capital for credit risk capital requirements, as specified in the Basel II Capital Accord (see Chapter 13). This will also increase the penalized bank's capital requirement.

The accuracy of internal ratings models is difficult to assess, however, because of the potential for either highly rated borrowers to default or borrowers with low ratings to repay their loans. That is, there is an overlap between the defaulting and nondefaulting internal ratings, as shown in Figure 10.1.

A banker may choose the cut-off point C so that all loan applicants with scores below C will be denied loans because they are expected to default, and all applicants with scores above C will be granted loans. However, Figure 10.1 shows that some successful loan applicants will default, whereas some denied loans (the cross-hatched area) would not have defaulted. The question is to determine the correct cut-off point C that will maximize the hit rate while minimizing the false alarm rate. The hit rate for a cut-off point C, HR(C) is calculated as

$$HR(C) = H(C)/ND$$

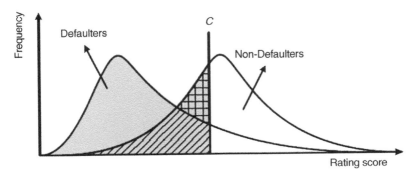

FIGURE 10.1 The Overlap in Internal Ratings Systems
Source: BIS (2005), page 37.

where H(C) is the number of defaulters correctly predicted using cut-off point C, and ND is the number of defaulters in the data sample. The false alarm rate is

$$FAR(C) = F(C)/NND$$

where F(C) is the number of nondefaulters incorrectly forecast as defaulters using cut-off point C (i.e., the cross-hatched area in Figure 10.1) and NND is the number of nondefaulters in the sample.

Figure 10.2 shows how the accuracy of an internal ratings model can be determined by comparing the hit rate to the false alarm rate. The *receiver operating characteristic* (ROC) curve is drawn by plotting the hit rate and false alarm rate for each cut-off point C. The perfect model always has a hit rate of 100 percent and a 0 percent false alarm rate for any cut-off point C. The random model (a 45 degree line) has the accuracy of tossing a coin: 50 percent hit rate and 50 percent false alarm rate. Actual internal ratings models are somewhere between these two extremes, as shown in Figure 10.2. The larger the area under the ROC curve, the more accurate the internal ratings model.[6]

Time-Series versus Cross-Sectional Stress Testing

In a recent set of papers, Granger and Huang (1997), at a theoretical level, and Carey (1998, 2000) and Lopez and Saidenberg (1998), at a simulation/empirical level, show that stress tests similar to those conducted across time for market risk models can be conducted using cross-sectional or panel data for credit risk models. In particular, suppose that in any given year a bank has a sample of N loans in its portfolio, where N is large. By repeated subsampling of the total loan portfolio, it is possible to build up a cross-

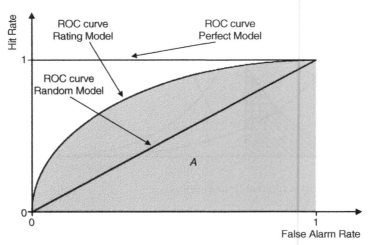

FIGURE 10.2 Measuring the Accuracy of Internal Ratings Models
Source: Bank for International Settlements (2005), page 38.

sectional distribution of expected losses, unexpected losses, and the full probability density function of losses. By comparing cross-sectional sub-portfolio loss distributions with the actual full-portfolio loss distribution, it is possible to generate an idea of the predictive accuracy of a credit risk model. For example, if the model is a good predictor or forecaster, the mean average loss rate and the mean 99th percentile loss rate from 10,000 randomly drawn sub-portfolios of the total loan portfolio should be pretty close to the actual average and 99th percentile loss rates on the full loan portfolio experienced in that year. Indeed, different models may have different prediction errors, and the relative size of the prediction errors can be used to judge the best model (see Lopez and Saidenberg [2000] and Carey [2000]).

A number of statistical issues arise with cross-sectional stress testing, but these are generally similar to those that arise with time-series stress testing (or back-testing). The first issue is that the number of loans in the portfolio has to be large. For example, Carey's (2000) sample is based on 30,000 privately placed bonds held by a dozen life insurance companies during 1986 to 1992, a period during which over 300 credit-related events (defaults, debt restructurings, and so on) occurred for the issuers of the bonds. The subsamples chosen varied in size; for example, portfolios of $0.5 billion to $15 billion in size containing no more than 3 percent of the bonds of any one issuer. Table 10.1 shows simulated loss rates from 50,000 subsample portfolios drawn from the 30,000 bond population. Sub-portfolios were limited to $1 billion in size. Using a Moody's database of

TABLE 10.1 Loss Rate Distribution When Monte Carlo Draws Are From Good versus Bad Years

Portfolio Characteristics		Simulated Portfolio Loss Rates Percent						
Percent Rated Below BBB	Years Used in Monte Carlo	Mean	At Loss Distribution Percentiles					
			95	97.5	99	99.5	99.9	99.95
0%	Good: 1986–1989	0.09	0.53	0.74	1.40	1.46	1.98	2.14
0%	Bad: 1990–1992	0.15	0.87	1.26	1.45	1.59	2.22	2.28
0%	Very bad: 1991	0.16	0.91	1.40	1.54	1.67	2.28	2.36
100%	Good: 1986–1989	1.73	4.18	4.63	5.11	5.43	5.91	6.05
100%	Bad: 1990–1992	2.53	5.59	6.31	7.19	7.82	8.95	9.33
100%	Very bad: 1991	3.76	6.68	7.30	8.04	8.55	9.72	10.19

Source: Carey (1998).

bond ratings and defaults during 1970–1998, Carey (2000) constructs $5 billion subportfolios composed of around 500 bonds and estimates loss distributions under a default mode (DM) model.

The loss rates in Table 10.1 vary by year. In 1991, which was the trough of the last U.S. recession, 50,000 simulated portfolios containing below-investment-grade (rated lower than BBB) bonds produced a (mean) 99 percent loss rate of 8.04 percent, which is quite close to the BIS 8 percent risk-based capital requirement. However, notice that in relatively good years (e.g., 1986–1989), the 99 percent loss rate was much lower at 5.11 percent. Carey (2000) also shows that capital ratios in bad years must be about 175 percent of those in good years if capital is set to cover unexpected losses computed at the 99 percent VAR level.[7]

A related issue is the representativeness of any given year or subperiod chosen to evaluate statistical moments such as the mean (expected) loss rate and the 99 percent unexpected loss rate. Suppose we look at 1991, a recession year. A set of systematic and unsystematic risk factors likely determined the intensity of the recession. The more a recession year reflects systematic rather than unsystematic recession risk factors, the more representative the loss experience of that year is, in a predictive sense, for future bad recession years. This suggests that some type of screening tests need to be conducted on various recession years before a given year's loss experience is chosen as a benchmark for testing predictive accuracy among credit risk models and for calculating capital requirements.[8]

A second issue is the effect of outliers on simulated loss distributions. A few extreme outliers can seriously affect the mean, variance, skewness, and kurtosis of an estimated distribution, as well as the correlations among the loans implied in the portfolio. In a market risk model context, Stahl (1998) has shown how only 5 outliers out of 1,000, in terms of foreign currency exchange rates, can have a major impact on estimated correlations among key currencies. With respect to credit risk, the danger is that a few big defaults in any given year could seriously bias the predictive power of any cross-sectional test of a given model.

Carey (2000) demonstrates the importance of portfolio *granularity* (large disparities in loan sizes within the portfolio) on unexpected loss distributions. Table 10.2 shows that expected losses are relatively unaffected, but that unexpected losses, particularly in the extreme 99.9 percent extreme tails of the distribution, are sensitive to both the size disparity across loans (see rows 1 and 2 of Table 10.2) and large loans to single borrowers (See rows 3 and 4 of Table 10.2).

A third issue deals with variability in LGDs across time and across debt instruments.[9] Table 10.3 shows the wide range of weighted-average LGDs over the period 1978–2001. LGD also varies across industry sectors over time. For example, the telecommunications sector experienced a historically high 88 percent LGD during the second quarter of 2001 (see Altman and Karlin [2001b]). Carey (2000) finds that assumptions about LGD significantly affect the loan portfolio's loss distribution. For example, allowing LGD to vary causes unexpected losses at the 99 percent tail of the loss

TABLE 10.2 The Impact of Loan Size Distribution on Portfolio Losses

Simulation Parameters	Mean	95%	99%	99.5%	99.9%
Base case, 500 loans, random sizes	0.67	2.01	2.98	3.39	4.34
Base case, 500 loans, equal sizes	0.65	1.73	2.37	2.58	2.98
Base case, no one-borrower limit	0.66	2.09	3.38	4.16	7.81
Base case, 5% limit on lending to a single borrower	0.66	2.11	3.14	3.55	4.43

Source: Carey (2001b), Tables 6 and 7.

distribution to increase from 0.64 percent (assuming a fixed LGD of 10 percent for all senior debt and a fixed LGD of 5 percent for all senior debt restructurings) to 3.18 percent for variable LGDs (assuming a mean LGD of 44 percent for senior debt and a mean LGD of 22 percent for senior debt restructurings). Moreover, Fraser (2000) uses CreditMetrics to stress test a portfolio of 331 liquid Eurobonds for LGD sensitivity, finding a significant 0.048 percent increase in portfolio 99 percent VAR for every 1 percent increase in expected LGD.

Stress tests of other model parameters show less sensitivity. For example, Fraser (2000) finds that a 1 percent increase in constant correlations assumed for a Eurobond portfolio causes a 0.026 percent increase in Credit-Metrics' estimate of 99 percent VAR, but that the impact was non-monotonic; for certain ranges, as correlations increased, some risk measures actually decreased. Moreover, Carey (2000) finds that the distribution of obligors across industries (with different cross-correlations) does not have much of an impact on unexpected loss estimates.

USING THE ALGORITHMICS MARK-TO-FUTURE MODEL

Back-testing often takes the form of scenario analysis. That is, how will a credit risk model perform under different market scenarios? Stress testing, in particular, focuses on the extreme crisis scenarios. Algorithmics Mark-to-Future (MtF) is a scenario-based model that focuses on estimating each asset's risk and return characteristics under thousands of different scenarios corresponding to all major risk factors, ranging from market risk to operational risk to credit risk. For example, Algorithmics MtF can create 5 to 20 extreme scenarios corresponding to historical market crashes using 50 to 200 systemic market and credit factors in order to conduct credit risk stress tests over time horizons between 1 and 10 years. MtF differs from other credit risk measurement models in that it views market risk and credit risk as inseparable.[10] Stress tests show that credit risk measures are quite sensitive to market risk factors.[11] Indeed, it is the systemic risk parameters that drive creditworthiness in MtF.[12]

Dembo et al. (2000) offer an example of credit risk stress testing using MtF for a BB-rated swap obligation (see Figure 10.3). The firm's credit risk is estimated using a Merton model of default; that is, a creditworthiness index (CWI) is defined that specifies the distance to default as the distance between the value of the firm's assets and a (non-constant) default boundary.[13] Figure 10.3 shows the scenario simulation of the CWI,

TABLE 10.3 Weighted Average (By Issue) Recovery Rates On Defaulted Debt By Seniority Per $100 Face Amount (1978–2009, (3Q))

Default Year	Senior Secured			Senior Unsecured			Senior Subordinated			Subordinated			Discount and Zero Coupon			All Seniorities	
	No.	%	$	No.	%	$	No.	%	$	No.	%	$	No.	%	$	No.	$
2009	27	11%	$38.74	173	73%	$25.90	28	12%	$14.39	4	2%	$12.57	4	2%	$12.23	236	$26.03
2008	18	14%	$30.52	79	63%	$49.56	23	18%	$30.25	4	3%	$21.09	1	1%	$2.71	125	$42.52
2007	10	36%	$87.24	10	36%	$47.70	6	21%	$63.98	2	7%	$46.53	0	0%	$0.00	28	$66.65
2006	9	18%	$90.60	26	52%	$60.90	8	16%	$50.24	1	2%	$60.33	6	12%	$78.31	50	$65.32
2005	67	54%	$76.50	44	36%	$45.88	7	6%	$32.67	0	0%	$0.00	5	4%	$74.21	123	$61.10
2004	27	39%	$63.67	33	48%	$56.77	2	3%	$37.44	0	0%	$0.00	7	10%	$43.06	69	$57.72
2003	57	28%	$53.51	108	53%	$45.40	29	14%	$35.98	0	0%	$38.00	8	4%	$32.27	203	$45.58
2002	37	11%	$52.81	254	75%	$21.82	21	6%	$32.79	0	0%	$0.00	28	8%	$26.47	340	$25.30
2001	9	3%	$40.95	187	67%	$28.84	48	17%	$18.37	0	0%	$0.00	37	13%	$15.05	281	$25.62
2000	13	8%	$39.58	47	29%	$25.40	61	37%	$25.96	26	16%	$26.62	17	10%	$23.61	164	$26.74
1999	14	11%	$26.90	60	47%	$42.54	40	31%	$23.56	2	2%	$13.88	11	9%	$17.30	127	$27.90
1998	6	18%	$70.38	21	62%	$39.57	6	18%	$17.54	0	0%	0.00	1	3%	$17.00	34	$40.46
1997	4	16%	$74.90	12	48%	$70.94	6	24%	$31.89	1	4%	$60.00	2	8%	$19.00	25	$57.61
1996	4	17%	$59.08	4	17%	$50.11	9	38%	$48.99	4	17%	$44.23	3	13%	$11.99	24	$45.44
1995	5	15%	$44.64	9	27%	$50.50	17	52%	$39.01	1	3%	$20.00	1	3%	$17.50	33	$41.77
1994	5	23%	$48.66	8	36%	$51.14	5	23%	$19.81	3	14%	$37.04	1	5%	$5.00	22	$39.44
1993	2	6%	$55.75	7	22%	$33.38	10	31%	$51.50	9	28%	$28.38	4	13%	$31.75	32	$38.83

Year																Total	
1992	15	22%	$59.85	8	12%	$35.61	17	25%	$58.20	22	33%	$49.13	5	7%	$19.82	67	$50.03
1991	4	3%	$44.12	69	44%	$55.84	37	24%	$31.91	38	24%	$24.30	9	6%	$27.89	157	$40.67
1990	12	10%	$32.18	31	27%	$29.02	38	33%	$25.01	24	21%	$18.83	11	9%	$15.63	116	$24.66
1989	9	12%	$82.69	16	21%	$53.70	21	28%	$19.60	30	39%	$23.95				76	$35.97
1988	13	21%	$67.96	19	31%	$41.99	10	16%	$30.70	20	32%	$35.27				62	$43.45
1987	4	13%	$90.68	17	55%	$72.02	6	19%	$56.24	4	13%	$35.25				31	$66.63
1986	8	14%	$48.32	11	20%	$37.72	7	13%	$35.20	30	54%	$33.39				56	$36.60
1985	2	7%	$74.25	3	11%	$34.81	7	26%	$36.18	15	56%	$41.45				27	$41.78
1984	4	29%	$53.42	1	7%	$50.50	2	14%	$65.88	7	50%	$44.68				14	$50.62
1983	1	13%	$71.00	3	38%	$67.72				4	50%	$41.79				8	$55.17
1982							16	80%	$39.31	4	20%	$32.91				20	$38.03
1981	1	100%	$72.00													1	$72.00
1980				2	50%	$26.71				2	50%	$16.63				4	$21.67
1979										1	100%	$31.00				1	$31.00
1978										1	100%	$60.00				1	$60.00
Total/ Average	387	15%	$57.55	1279	50%	$36.24	471	18%	$30.04	259	10%	$30.85	161	6%	$25.49	2,557	$36.72
Standard Dev*			$18.39			$13.74			$14.62			$17.46			$20.49		$14.19
Median			$57.42			$45.64			$32.73			$29.69			$18.25		$41.77

*Standard deviations are calculated based on the yearly averages.

Source: Authors' Compilations from Various Dealer Quotes.

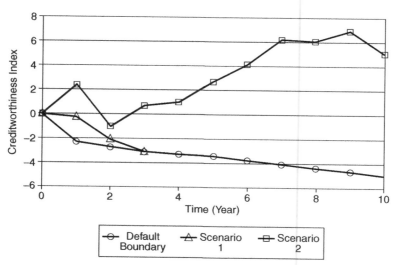

FIGURE 10.3 Merton Model of Default
Source: Dembo et al., (2000), page 68.

illustrating two possible scenarios of firm asset values: In scenario 1 the firm defaults in year 3, while in scenario 2 the firm remains solvent for the next 10 years. The default date under each scenario is represented by the point at which the firm's asset value first hits the default boundary.[14]

MtF assumes that the CWI follows a geometric Brownian motion standardized to have a mean of zero and a variance of one. The basic building block of the CWI is the unconditional cumulative default probability for typical BB-rated firms, obtained using the Merton model (as discussed in Chapter 4). Using the unconditional default probabilities as a foundation, a conditional cumulative default probability distribution is generated for each scenario. That is, the sensitivity of the default probability to scenario risk factors is estimated in the following manner. For example, suppose that the unconditional likelihood of default within five years for a BB firm is 9.6 percent. Choose a particular scenario of the time path of the S&P 500 and six-month U.S. Treasury rates over the next 10 years. This is the credit driver. Suppose that in this particular scenario (call it scenario 9, or S9), the credit driver decreases about 1.2 standard deviations in five years. What is the impact of the decline in the credit driver represented in S9 on the default risk of this BB-rated firm?

MtF estimates all BB-rated firms' historical sensitivity to the credit driver using a multifactor model that incorporates both systemic and

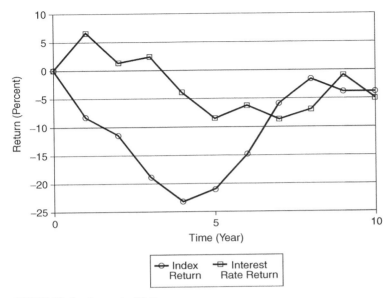

FIGURE 10.4   Scenario S9 Returns
Source: Dembo et al., (2000), page 70.

idiosyncratic credit factors. If the results of the multifactor model suggest that the obligor has a positive correlation to the credit driver, then the swap's credit quality is expected to decrease under this scenario. The conditional cumulative default probability is calculated based on the results of the multifactor model. In this example, the BB firm's five-year probability of default increases from 9.6 percent to 11.4 percent under scenario S9. Figure 10.4 shows the return on the BB swap obligation over the next 10 years using the conditional default probabilities obtained for S9. This process is replicated for several scenarios. Figure 10.5 shows the conditional default probabilities for 10 different credit driver scenarios. A return distribution can be derived using the full range of possible scenarios.

The results for scenario S9 depend on the assumption that systemic risk explains 5 percent of the total variance of the CWI, with idiosyncratic risk explaining the remaining 95 percent. If, by contrast, systemic risk accounted for 80 percent of the variance, the five-year conditional default probability under scenario S9 would have been 44.4 percent instead of 11.4 percent. Therefore, conditional default probabilities have higher volatility when the systemic risk component is greater.

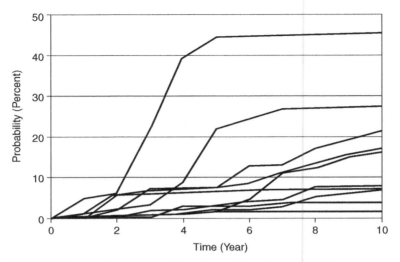

FIGURE 10.5   Ten Scenarios of Conditional Default Probabilities
Source: Dembo et al., (2000), page 70.

STRESS TESTING U.S. BANKS IN 2009

Concerns about the stability of the U.S. banking system in the wake of
the financial crisis of 2007–2009 led the Federal Reserve, together with
the Federal Deposit Insurance Corporation (FDIC) and the Office of the
Comptroller of the Currency (OCC), to require the 19 largest U.S. banks
to conduct an unprecedented stress test exercise from February through
April 2009 (formally called the Supervisory Capital Assessment Program,
or SCAP). All banks with more than $100 billion in year-end assets as of
December 2008 were required to participate, representing two-thirds of
the assets and more than one half of the loans in the U.S. banking system
at the time. Banks were required to conduct a "what if" exercise to forecast their credit losses and revenues under two alternative economic
scenarios:

1. The baseline scenario, set equal to the average projections published by
   Consensus Forecasts, the Blue Chip Survey, and the Survey of Professional Forecasters as of the start of the stress test.
2. The adverse scenario, set by banking supervisors to reflect a longer and
   deeper recession than expected by market forecasters.

TABLE 10.4 Economic Scenarios: Baseline and More Adverse Alternatives

	2009	2010
Real GDP[a]		
Average Baseline[b]	−2.0	2.1
Consensus Forecasts	−2.1	2.0
Blue Chip	−1.9	2.1
Survey of Professional Forecasters	−2.0	2.2
Alternates More Adverse	−3.3	0.5
Civilian unemployment rate[c]		
Average Baseline[b]	8.4	8.8
Consensus Forecasts	8.4	9.0
Blue Chip	8.3	8.7
Survey of Professional Forecasters	8.4	8.8
Alternative More Adverse	8.9	10.3
House prices[d]		
Baseline	−14	−4
Alternative More Adverse	−22	−7

[a]Percent change in annual average.

[b]Baseline forecasts for real GDP and the unemployment rate equal the average of projections released by Consensus Forecasts, Blue Chip, and Survey of Professional Forecasters in February.

[c]Annual average.

[d]Case-Shiller 10-City Composite, percent change, fourth quarter of the previous year to fourth quarter of the year indicated.

Source: Board of Governors of the Federal Reserve System, *The Supervisory Capital Assessment Program: Design and Implementation*, April 24, 2009, 6.

Table 10.4 shows the macroeconomic assumption in the two alternative scenarios.[15] Figure 10.6 shows the assumed distribution of macroeconomic scenario changes over the two-year forecasting period.

Banks were instructed to calculate their projected losses going forward, not including losses already booked until the end of 2008.[16] They were told to forecast expected losses under the loss reserve provisions of accrual accounting, which require the bank to write down the loan value if repayment becomes doubtful, but not to reflect liquidity-driven declines in market values.[17] There were 12 separate loan categories covered in the stress test: three types of first lien mortgages (prime, Alt-A, and subprime); two types of second/junior lien mortgages (closed-end and home equity lines of

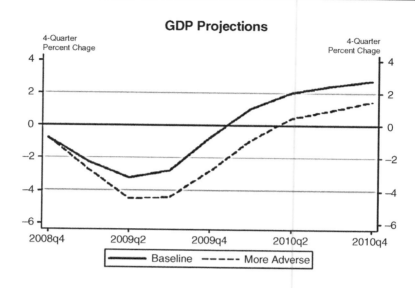

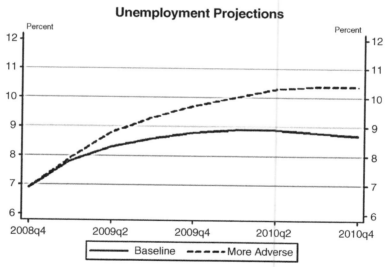

FIGURE 10.6 GDP and Unemployment Projections

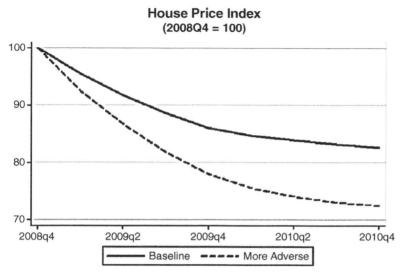

House Price Index
(2008Q4 = 100)

FIGURE 10.6 (*Continued*)
Source: Board of Governors of the Federal Reserve System, *The Supervisory Capital Assessment Program: Design and Implementation*, April 24, 2009, 7.

credit, or HELOCs); commercial and industrial (C&I) loans; three types of commercial real estate (CRE) loans (construction, multifamily, and non-farm nonresidential); credit cards; other consumer loans; and other loans. For example, the banks were required to provide to regulators detailed data for their residential loan portfolio (separating first mortgages, HELOCs, and closed-end second mortgages) on loan-to-value ratios, FICO scores, geography, documentation level, year of origination, and so on.

Banks were also required to forecast the resources available to cover projected losses. These resources consist of pre-provision net revenue (PPNR) and allowances for loan and lease losses (ALLL) combined with existing capital. The test specified that resources must exceed anticipated losses under both scenarios and still leave sufficient capital to exceed minimum regulatory capital standards. To determine capital requirements, the stress test focused on common stockholders' equity and Tier 1 capital, consisting of common stockholders' equity, qualifying perpetual preferred stock, and certain other assets (subject to limits). The focus of the recommendations was on ascertaining whether the banks had sufficient Tier 1 common stockholders' equity capital to withstand a substantial economic downturn.

TABLE 10.5   Capital Assessment Program for 19 U.S. Bank Holding Companies ($ Billions)

	AmEx	BofA	BB&T	BNYM	CapOne	Citi	FifthThird
Tier 1 capital	10.1	173.2	13.4	15.4	16.8	118.8	11.9
Tier 1 common capital	10.1	74.5	7.8	11.0	12.0	22.9	4.9
Risk-weighted assets	104.4	1,633.8	109.8	115.8	131.8	996.2	112.6
Estimated for 2009 and 2010 for the more adverse scenario							
Total less estimates (before purchase accounting adjustments)	11.2	136.6	8.7	5.4	13.4	104.7	9.1
First lien mortgages	-na-	22.1	1.1	0.2	1.8	15.3	1.1
Second/Junior lien mortgages	-na-	21.4	0.7	-na-	0.7	12.2	1.1
Commercial and industrial loans	-na-	15.7	0.7	0.4	1.5	8.9	2.8
Commercial real estate loans	-na-	9.4	4.5	0.2	1.1	2.7	2.9
Credit card loans	8.5	19.1	0.2	-na-	3.6	19.9	0.4
Securities (AFS and HTM)	-na-	8.5	0.2	4.2	0.4	2.9	0.0
Trading and counterparty	-na-	24.1	-na-	-na-	-na-	22.4	-na-
Other[a] *	2.7	16.4	1.3	0.4	4.3	20.4	0.9
Total Less Rate on Loans[b]	14.3%	10.0%	8.6%	2.6%	11.7%	10.9%	10.5%
First lien morgages	-na-	6.8%	4.5%	5.0%	10.7%	8.0%	10.3%
Second/Junior lien mortgages	-na-	13.5%	8.6%	-na-	19.9%	19.5%	8.7%
Commercial and industrial loans	-na-	7.0%	4.5%	5.0%	9.7%	5.8%	11.0%
Commercial real estate loans	-na-	9.1%	12.6%	9.9%	6.0%	7.4%	13.9%
Credit card loans	20.2%	23.5%	18.2%	-na-	18.2%	23.0%	22.3%
Memo: Purchase accounting adjustments	0.0	13.3	0.0	0.0	1.5	0.0	0.0
Resources other than capital to aboard losses in the more adverse scenario[c]	11.9	74.5	5.5	6.7	9.0	49.0	5.5
SCAP buffer added for more adverse scenario							
(SCAP buffer is defined as additional Tier 1 common/contingent common)							
Indicated SCAP buffer as of December 31, 2008	0.0	46.5	0.0	0.0	0.0	92.6	2.6
Less: Capital actions and effects of Q1 2009 results[d,e,f,g]	0.2	12.7	0.1	−0.2	−0.3	87.1	1.5
SCAP buffer[h,i,j]	0.0	33.9	0.0	0.0	0.0	5.5	1.1

[a] Includes other consumer and non-consumer loans and miscellaneous commitments and obligations

[b] Includes losses on other consumer and non-consumer loans

[c] Resources to aboard losses include pre-provision net revenue less the change in the allowance for loan and lease losses

[d] Capital actions include completed or contracted transactions since Q4 2008

[e] For BofA, includes capital benefit from risk-weighted asset impact of eligible asset guarantee

[f] For Chi, includes impact of preferred exchange offers announced on February 27, 2009

[g] Total includes only capital actions and effects of Q1 2009 results for firms that need to establish a SCAP buffer

[h] There may be a need to establish an additional Tier 1 capital buffer, but this would be satisfied by the additional Tier 2 Common capital buffer unless otherwise specified for a particular BHC

[i] GMAC needs to augment the capital buffer with $11.5 billion of Tier 1 Common/contingent Common of which $9.1 billion must be new Tier 1 capital

[j] Regions needs to augment the capital buffer with $2.5 billion of Tier 2 Common/contingent Common of which $400 million must be new Tier 2 capital

Note: Numbers may not sum up to 1 due to rounding.

Source: Board of Governors of the Federal Reserve System, *The Supervisory Capital Assessment Program: Design and Implementation,* April 24, 2009, 9.

	GMAC	Goldman	JPMC	KeyCorp	MetLife	Morgan Stanley	PNC	Regions	State St	SunTrust	USB	Wells	Total
	17.4	55.9	136.2	11.6	30.1	47.2	24.1	12.1	14.1	17.6	24.4	85.4	836.7
	11.1	34.4	87.0	6.0	27.8	17.8	11.7	7.6	10.8	9.4	11.8	33.9	412.5
	172.7	464.8	1,337.5	106.7	326.4	310.6	250.9	116.3	69.6	162.0	230.6	1,082.3	7,814.8
	9.2	17.8	97.4	6.7	9.6	19.7	18.8	9.2	8.2	11.8	15.7	86.1	599.2
	2.0	-na-	18.8	0.1	0.0	-na-	2.4	1.0	-na-	2.2	1.8	32.4	102.3
	1.1	-na-	20.1	0.6	0.0	-na-	4.6	1.1	-na-	3.1	1.7	14.7	83.2
	1.0	0.0	10.3	1.7	0.0	0.1	3.2	1.2	0.0	1.5	2.3	9.0	60.1
	0.6	-na-	3.7	2.3	0.8	0.6	4.5	4.9	0.3	2.8	3.2	8.4	53.0
	-na-	-na-	21.2	0.0	-na-	-na-	0.4	-na-	-na-	0.1	2.8	6.1	82.4
	0.5	0.1	1.2	0.1	8.3	-na-	1.3	0.2	1.8	0.0	1.3	4.2	35.2
	-na-	17.4	16.7	-na-	-na-	18.7	-na-	-na-	-na-	-na-	-na-	-na-	99.3
	4.0	0.3	5.3	1.8	0.5	0.2	2.3	0.8	6.0	2.1	2.8	11.3	83.7
	6.6%	0.9%	10.0%	8.5%	2.1%	0.4%	9.0%	9.1%	4.4%	8.3%	7.8%	8.8%	9.1%
	10.2%	-na-	10.2%	3.4%	5.0%	-na-	8.1%	4.1%	-na-	8.2%	5.7%	11.9%	8.8%
	21.2%	-na-	13.9%	6.3%	14.1%	-na-	12.7%	11.9%	-na-	13.7%	8.8%	13.2%	13.8%
	2.7%	1.2%	6.8%	7.9%	0.0%	2.4%	6.0%	7.0%	22.8%	5.2%	5.4%	4.8%	6.1%
	33.3%	-na-	5.5%	12.5%	2.1%	45.2%	11.2%	13.7%	35.5%	10.6%	10.2%	5.9%	8.5%
	-na-	-na-	22.4%	37.9%	-na-	-na-	22.3%	-na-	-na-	17.4%	20.3%	26.0%	22.5%
	0.0	0.0	19.9	0.0	0.0	0.0	5.9	0.0	0.0	0.0	0.0	23.7	64.3
	−0.5	18.5	72.4	2.1	5.6	7.1	9.6	3.3	4.3	4.7	13.7	60.0	362.9
	6.7	0.0	0.0	2.5	0.0	8.3	2.3	2.9	0.0	3.4	0.0	17.3	185.0
	−4.8	7.0	2.5	0.6	0.6	6.5	1.7	0.4	0.2	1.3	0.3	3.6	110.4
	11.5	0.0	0.0	1.8	0.0	1.8	0.6	2.5	0.0	2.2	0.0	13.7	74.6

The results of the stress test show that the aggregate losses at the top 19 U.S. banks could equal $600 billion during 2009 and 2010 under the adverse economic scenario. Although the aggregate resources available to meet these losses was estimated at $835 billion, additional capital totaling $74.6 billion was required for 10 of the 19 banks. Therefore, 9 of the banks were found to have sufficient capital to withstand the adverse economic scenario, and the banking system as a whole (as measured by the largest 19 banks) was found to be fundamentally solvent.

Table 10.5 shows the results of the stress test for each of the 19 banks. The banks that passed the stress test (i.e., those which required no additional SCAP buffer as shown in the last row of Table 10.5) were American Express, BB&T Corporation, Bank of New York Mellon, Capital One Financial Corporation, Goldman Sachs Group, JPMorgan Chase, MetLife, State Street Corporation and U.S. Bancorp. Figure 10.7 shows each bank's total projected losses as a fraction of year-end 2008 risk-weighted assets.[18]

Banks with capital deficiencies, according to the stress test scenario, were required to provide a plan for resolving their deficiencies within 30 days, to be implemented within six months. The banks that passed the stress test quickly (as of June 2009) repaid the funds granted to them in October 2008 under the Troubled Asset Relief Program (TARP), see Chapter 3. However, companies such as JPMorgan Chase and Morgan Stanley have to

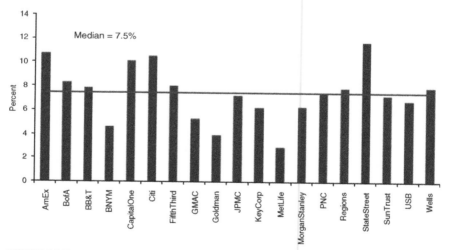

FIGURE 10.7 Supervisor Estimates of Total Losses to Risk-Weighted Assets for More Adverse Scenario
Source: Board of Governors of the Federal Reserve System, *The Supervisory Capital Assessment Program: Overview of Results*, May 7, 2009, 10.

find a price to repurchase the warrants issued to the government in order to completely exit the TARP.

It might be noted that this stress test exercise has not been without its critics. In particular, by defining capital measures that include perpetual preferred stock and various intangibles and "other assets," the capital measures were in all probability biased upwards. Moreover, the risk-weighted assets denominator had credit risk weights reflecting the precrisis exposures of securitized assets as per the 2006 Basel II model. This would have biased the denominator of the Tier 1 capital ratio downwards and the calculated capital ratios upwards.

SUMMARY

A key measure of the usefulness of internal credit risk models is their predictive ability. Tests of predictive ability, such as back-testing, are difficult for credit risk models because of the lack of data for a sufficiently long time series. Nevertheless, given a large and representative (in a default risk sense) loan portfolio, it is possible to stress test credit risk models by using cross-sectional subportfolio sampling techniques that provide predictive information on average loss rates and unexpected loss rates. Moreover, the predictive accuracy, in a cross-sectional sense, of different models can be used to choose among different models. In the future, wider-panel data sets and even time-series of loan loss experience are likely to be developed by banks and/or consortia of banks.

Another approach to credit risk stress testing that avoids the problem of data limitations is the scenario analysis approach, such as that adopted by Algorithmics Mark-to-Future. Credit drivers, composed of market risk factors, are used to estimate conditional default probabilities. Varying the credit driver scenario causes changes in conditional default probabilities which are then used to determine a creditworthiness index. Scenarios can also be chosen to replicate extreme events in order to stress test the portfolio's credit risk exposure.

The stress tests conducted by bank regulators during the early part of 2009 consisted of a forward-looking forecast of credit losses and revenues under several economic scenarios. The results showed that the aggregate worst-case losses under adverse economic conditions could be met by resources (revenues and shareholders' equity) for the largest 19 companies in the U.S. banking system. However, 9 out of 19 banks were required to raise additional capital totaling $75 billion.

CHAPTER 11

RAROC Models

INTRODUCTION

Today, virtually all major banks and financial institutions (FIs) have developed risk-adjusted return on capital (RAROC) models to evaluate the profitability of various business lines, including their lending. The RAROC concept was first introduced by Bankers Trust in the 1970s. The recent surge among banks and other FIs to adopt proprietary forms of the RAROC approach can be explained by two major forces: (1) the demand by stockholders for improved performance, especially the maximization of shareholder value, and (2) the growth of FI conglomerates built around separate business units (or profit centers).[1] These two developments have been the impetus for banks to develop a measure of performance that is comparable across business units, especially when the capital of the bank is both costly and limited.

WHAT IS RAROC?

In terms of modern portfolio theory (MPT), RAROC can best be thought of as a Sharpe ratio for business units, including lending. Its numerator, as explained below, is some measure of adjusted income over either a future period (the next year) or a past period (the previous year). The denominator is a measure of the unexpected loss or economic capital at risk (VAR) as a result of that activity. Thus:

$$RAROC = \frac{\text{Adjusted income}}{\text{Capital at risk}} \qquad (11.1)$$

In this chapter, we concentrate on the measurement of RAROC in terms of lending, although, as noted earlier, it can be applied across all areas of the bank.[2] Once calculated, the RAROC of a loan can be compared with some hurdle rate reflecting the bank's cost of funds or the opportunity cost to stockholders for holding equity in the bank. Thus, in some RAROC models, the hurdle rate is the bank stockholders' required return on equity (ROE); in others, it is some measure of the weighted-average cost of capital (WACC).[3]

If

$$\text{RAROC} > \text{Hurdle rate} \tag{11.2}$$

then the loan is viewed as value-adding, and scarce bank capital should be allocated to the activity.[4]

Because RAROC historically has been calculated on a stand-alone basis, without incorporating correlations among activities, the number of projects/activities satisfying equation (11.2) often exceeds the available (economic) capital of the bank. It may take time to raise new equity to fund all valuable projects (in a RAROC sense), so a second-round allocation of economic capital usually takes place (see Dermine [1998] and Crouhy, Turnbull, and Wakeman [1998]).[5] This is to calculate a weight (w_i) for activity i such that:

$$w_i = \frac{EC_B}{\sum\limits_{i=1}^{n} EC_i} \tag{11.3}$$

where EC_B is the available economic capital of the bank and EC_i is the stand-alone economic capital allocation to the viable (acceptable) projects under equation (11.2).[6] Marginal economic capital allocated for the ith business unit is $w_i EC_i$ and across all business units the following holds:

$$\sum_{i=1}^{n} w_i EC_i = EC_B$$

RAROC, ROA, AND RORAC

Before looking at the different forms that RAROC can take, it is worthwhile to briefly compare RAROC with return on assets (ROA) and return on risk-adjusted capital (RORAC). The formulas for these alternative (loan) performance measures are:

$$\text{ROA} = \frac{\text{Adjusted income}}{\text{Assets lent}} \tag{11.4}$$

$$\text{RORAC} = \frac{\text{Adjusted income}}{\text{BIS risk-based capital requirement}} \qquad (11.5)$$

All three measures—RAROC, ROA, and RORAC—calculate income in a similar fashion, but they differ in the calculation of the denominator. Thus, ROA, a traditional measure of performance, completely ignores the risk of the activity of lending, and uses assets lent as the denominator. RORAC uses the Bank for International Settlements (BIS) regulatory capital requirement as a measure of the capital at risk from the activity. Under BIS I for private-sector loans, this meant taking the book value of the outstanding loan and multiplying it by 8 percent. Under Basel II the relevant capital amount will depend on the model used (standardized or internal ratings-based) and potentially the PD, LGD, and maturity of the loan. By comparison, the alternative forms of RAROC discussed in the next section seek to more accurately measure the economic or VAR exposure from lending activity. To the extent that the BIS II regulatory proposals are successful at more accurately assessing a capital requirement that covers the credit risk of the loan portfolio, RORAC measures should approach RAROC measures upon adoption of the new capital standards.

ALTERNATIVE FORMS OF RAROC

We subsequently discuss the two components of the RAROC ratio: the numerator and the denominator.

The Numerator

As shown in equation (11.1), the numerator reflects the adjusted expected one-year income on a loan. The numerator can reflect all or a subset of the factors in equation (11.6):

$$\text{Adjusted income} = [\text{Spread} + \text{Fees} - \text{Expected loss} - \text{Operating costs}](1 - \tau)$$
$$(11.6)$$

The spread term reflects the direct income earned on the loan—essentially, the difference between the loan rate and the bank's cost of funds. To this should be added fees directly attributable to the loan over the next year. For example, loan origination fees would be added, as would commitment fees. There are, however, a number of gray areas. Suppose, in making a loan to a small business, the small business brings its asset management business to the bank (the customer relationship effect) and that business also generates annual fees. A lending officer may view these asset management fees as part of the loan's profitability, and thus include it in the loan's RAROC calculation. The banks asset manager will also claim some of the fees, as part of his RAROC calculation for the asset management unit. The danger is that fees will be double- or triple-counted. A very careful allocation of fees via some allocation matrix is needed, so as to avoid the double-counting problem.[7]

In many RAROC models, two deductions are commonly made from the spread and fees, in order to calculate adjusted income. The first recognizes that expected losses are part of normal banking business and therefore should be deducted from direct income. One way to do this would be to use a KMV-type model where:

$$\text{Expected loss}_i = \text{EDF}_i \times \text{LGD}_i \tag{11.7}$$

Alternatively, some annual accounting-based loss reserves can be allocated to the loan. As Dermine (1998) notes, this can bias the calculation if there is a link between the loan's maturity and the size of annual loss reserves. Finally, some RAROC models deduct measures of a loan's operating costs, such as a loan officer's time and resources in originating and monitoring the loan. In practice, a precise allocation of such costs across loans has proved to be very difficult.

Finally, equation (11.6) computes the asset's after-tax adjusted income, where τ is often set equal to the statutory tax rate. However, Nakada et al. (1999) use the effective corporate tax rate to measure the tax penalty associated with the double taxation of returns—once at the corporate level and again at the shareholder level.[8] More precisely, however, the appropriate tax rate should be the asset's effective marginal tax rate. That is, all else being equal, shareholders would prefer the project with the lower effective tax rate if different earning streams are subject to differential tax treatments.

The Denominator

Historically, two approaches have emerged to measure the denominator of the RAROC equation or economic capital at risk.[9] The first approach, following Bankers Trust, develops a market-based measure. The second, following Bank of America, among others, develops an experiential or historically based measure.

The original Bankers Trust approach was to measure capital at risk as being equal to the maximum (adverse) change in the market value of a loan (L)

over the next year. Starting with the duration equation:

$$\frac{\Delta L}{L} = -D_L \frac{\Delta R}{1 + R_L} \qquad (11.8)$$

where $\Delta L/L$ is the percentage change in the market value of a loan expected over the next year, D_L is the Macauley duration of the loan, and $\Delta R/(1 + R_L)$ is the expected maximum discounted change in the credit-risk premium on the loan during the next year.[10] We can rewrite the duration equation with the following interpretation:

$$\Delta L \quad = -D_L \quad \times \quad L \quad \times \quad \left(\frac{\Delta R}{1 + R_L}\right) \quad (11.9)$$

Dollar capital risk exposure or loss amount	=	Duration of the loan	×	Risk amount or loan exposure	×	Expected discounted change in the credit factor on the loan

The loan's duration (say, 2.7 years) and the loan amount (say, $1 million) are easily estimated. It is more difficult to estimate the maximum change in the credit risk premium on the loan expected over the next year. Publicly available data on loan risk premiums are scarce, so users of this approach turn to publicly available corporate bond market data to estimate credit risk premiums. First, a Standard and Poor's (S&P) or other rating agency's credit rating (AAA, AA, and so on) is assigned to a borrower. Thereafter, the risk premium changes for all the bonds traded in that particular rating class over the past year are analyzed. The ΔR in the RAROC equation is then:

$$\Delta R = \text{Max}[\Delta(R_i - R_G) > 0] \qquad (11.10)$$

where $\Delta(R_i - R_G)$ is the change in the yield spread between corporate bonds of credit rating class i (R_i) and matched-duration U.S. Treasury bonds (R_G) over the past year. To consider only the worst-case scenario, the maximum change in yield spread is chosen, as opposed to the average change.

As an example, let us evaluate the credit risk of a loan to an AAA-rated borrower. Assume there are currently 400 publicly traded bonds in that class (the bonds were issued by firms whose rating type is similar to that of the borrower). The first step is to evaluate the actual changes in the credit risk premiums ($R_i - R_G$) on each bond for the past year. These

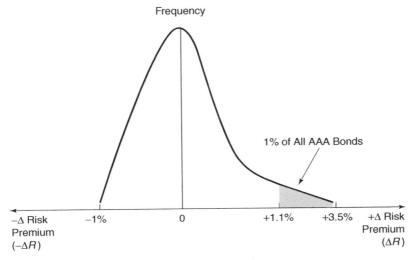

FIGURE 11.1 Estimating the Change in the Risk Premium

(hypothetical) changes are plotted in the frequency curve of Figure 11.1. They range from a fall in the risk premium of 1 percent to an increase of 3.5 percent. Because the largest increase may be a very extreme (unrepresentative) number, the 99 percent worst-case scenario is chosen (only 4 bonds out of 400 have risk premium increases exceeding the 99 percent worst case). For the example shown in Figure 11.1, this is equal to 1.1 percent.

The estimate of loan (or capital) risk, assuming that the current average level of rates on AAA bonds is 10 percent, is:

$$
\begin{aligned}
\Delta L &= D_L \times L \times \frac{\Delta R}{1 + R_L} \\
&= -(2.7)(\$1 \text{ million})\left(\frac{.011}{1.10}\right) \\
&= -\$27,000
\end{aligned}
\tag{11.11}
$$

Thus, although the face value of the loan amount is $1 million, the risk amount, or change in the loan's market value due to a decline in its credit quality, is $27,000.

To determine whether the loan is worth making, the estimated loan risk is compared to the loan's adjusted income. For simplicity, we ignore operating costs and marginal corporate tax rates here (although estimates of these could be made). Suppose the annual projected adjusted income is as follows:

$$
\begin{array}{rcll}
\text{Spread} = 0.2\% \times \$1\,\text{million} & = & \$2,000 \\
\text{Fees} = 0.15\% \times \$1\,\text{million} & = & \$1,500 \\
\text{Expected loss} = 0.1\% \times \$0.5\,\text{million} & = & \dfrac{\$\ (500)}{\$3,000}
\end{array}
\tag{11.12}
$$

The loan's RAROC can then be calculated as:

$$
\text{RAROC} = \frac{\text{One-year adjusted income on loan}}{\text{Capital at risk}(\Delta L)} = \frac{\$3,000}{\$27,000} = 11.1\%
$$

If this number exceeds the bank's hurdle rate, the loan should be made.[11]

Most banks, however, have adopted a different way to calculate the denominator of the RAROC equation or capital at risk (unexpected loss). The calculation usually involves experiential modeling based on a historic database of loan (or bond) defaults. Essentially, for each type of borrower the adjusted one-year income is divided by an unexpected default rate, and the result is multiplied by the loss given default (LGD), where the unexpected default rate is some multiple of the historic standard deviation of default rates for such borrowers. The multiple of σ used will reflect both the desired credit rating of the bank and the actual distribution of losses. For example, suppose the bank wants to achieve an AA rating and, on average, only 0.03 percent of AA-quality firms default in a year. Consequently, the amount of capital needed has to cover up to 99.97 percent of loan (asset) losses. Based on the standardized normal distribution, the standard deviation of losses (σ) would have to be multiplied by 3.4. That is,[12]

$$
\text{Unexpected loss}_i = 3.4 \times \sigma_i \times \text{LGD}_i \times \text{Exposure}_i
\tag{11.13}
$$

However, as discussed in Chapters 4 through 8, loan loss distributions tend to be skewed and have fat tails. Therefore, depending on the fatness of the tail, the multiplier of σ is increased. For example, Zaik, Walter, and Kelling (1996) reported that Bank of America uses a multiplier of 6:

$$
\text{Unexpected loss}_i = 6 \times \sigma_i \times \text{LGD}_i \times \text{Exposure}_i
\tag{11.14}
$$

Others have argued for a multiplier as high as 10 if a bank wants to achieve AAA status.[13]

THE RAROC DENOMINATOR AND CORRELATIONS

Neither the market-based version nor the experientially based version of the RAROC denominator (depicted in equation (11.8) and (11.13), respectively) allows for correlations (and thus diversification) among business line risks, including lending.[14] That the RAROC equation should take such correlations into account can be seen by calculating the RAROC from a one-factor capital asset pricing model (CAPM) that describes the equilibrium risk/return trade-offs among assets and implicitly assumes that loans are tradable assets like equities. This theoretical RAROC includes an adjustment for correlation in its denominator. Specifically, following James (1996), Crouhy, Turnbull, and Wakeman (1998), and Ho (1999), the CAPM states:

$$R_i - r_f = \beta_i (R_M - r_f) \tag{11.15}$$

where
R_i = the return on a risky asset i
r_f = the risk-free rate[15]
R_M = the return on the market portfolio
β_i = the risk of the asset

and

$$\beta_i = \frac{\sigma_{iM}}{\sigma_M^2} = \frac{\rho_{iM}\sigma_i\sigma_M}{\sigma_M^2} = \frac{\rho_{iM}\sigma_i}{\sigma_M} \tag{11.16}$$

where
σ_{iM} = covariance between the returns on risky asset i and the market portfolio M
σ_M = standard deviation of the return on the market portfolio
ρ_{iM} = correlation between the returns on the risky asset i and the market portfolio, where $\rho_{iM}\sigma_i\sigma_M = \sigma_{iM}$ by definition.

Substituting equation (11.16) into equation (11.15), we have:

$$R_i - r_f = \rho_{iM}\sigma_{iM}(R_M - r_f)/\sigma_M \tag{11.17}$$

And, rearranging the equation, we have:

$$\frac{R_i - r_f}{\rho_{iM}\sigma_i} = \frac{R_M - r_f}{\sigma_M} \tag{11.18}$$

$$\text{RAROC} = \text{Hurdle rate}$$

The left-hand side of equation (11.18) is the theoretical RAROC; the right-hand side is the hurdle rate, the excess return on the market per unit of market risk (or the market price of risk). As can be seen by setting

$\rho_{iM} = 1$, the theoretical RAROC takes the stand-alone form employed by most banks, which is also the traditional Sharpe ratio, $(R_i - r_f)/\sigma_i$, for a risky asset.

This will clearly bias against projects for which (excess) returns $(R_i - r_f)$ may be low but which have low correlations (ρ_{iM}) with the market portfolio. Reportedly, some banks are building correlations into their RAROC denominators. That is, they are measuring the unexpected loss as:

$$\text{Unexpected loss}_i = \rho_{iM} \times \text{Multiplier} \times \sigma_i \times \text{LGD}_i \times \text{Exposure}_i \quad (11.19)$$

In doing so, two issues arise. First, looking at the correlation of the loan's return with the market (even if it can be estimated) may be erroneous unless the bank is holding a very well-diversified portfolio of tradable assets (i.e., liquid and marketable assets).[16] Second, the RAROC formula in (11.19) becomes non-implementable if ρ_{iM} lies in the range $-1 \leq \rho_{iM} \leq 0$.

Flaws in the preceding analysis emanate from the implied CAPM assumption that once the loan's unsystematic risk is diversified away, all that remains is the loan's systematic risk exposure to market risk. However, if that were true, then the loan's market risk might be more efficiently managed and hedged using derivatives and there would be no need to allocate capital using RAROC since risk, by implication, would largely be diversified away (at least for traded derivatives or organized exchanges and where the basis risk is small). That is, the RAROC approach was developed to deal with the risk of *untraded* and *unhedgeable* assets, such as loans, for which the CAPM does not generally apply.

Banks specialize in information-intensive relationship lending activities that cannot be efficiently offered by capital markets.[17] Only a fraction of the risk of these loans can be hedged using fairly priced currency and interest rate derivatives. The remainder is often an illiquid credit risk component, although the recent growth in the market for credit derivatives has reduced this illiquid portion somewhat. The bank prices these two components of risk differently. The market portion of the loan's risk is priced in the capital market and is based only on the loan's correlation with systematic market risk factors, as stated previously. However, the nontraded or illiquid credit risk component of the loan must be evaluated by each bank individually, with the risk pricing based on the loan's correlation with the credit risk of the bank's own portfolio. Since each bank's portfolio will have a different credit risk exposure, each bank will price a loan differently. That is, a bank with a loan portfolio uncorrelated with the credit risk of the proposed loan will offer the borrower more attractive terms than would a bank with a portfolio of loans that is highly correlated with the credit risk of the new loan. Froot and Stein (1998) decompose loan risk into tradable and nontradable risk components using a two-factor model.

Suppose that a bank has an opportunity to either accept or reject a loan of a small amount relative to the total portfolio size.[18] Froot and Stein (1998) and James (1996) decompose the loan's total risk ε into a tradable, market risk component, denoted ε_T, and a nontradable, illiquid credit risk component, denoted ε_N, as follows:

$$\varepsilon = \varepsilon_T + \varepsilon_N$$

By construction, the nontradable risk component ε_N is uncorrelated with the market portfolio. In contrast, the tradable risk component ε_T is fully priced using the CAPM. Froot and Stein (1998) show that the hurdle rate, the required return on the loan, denoted μ^*, can be expressed as:[19]

$$\mu^* = g\, cov(\varepsilon_T, M) + G\, cov(\varepsilon_N, \varepsilon_p) \tag{11.20}$$

where $\mu^* =$ the loan's hurdle rate

$\varepsilon_T =$ the tradable, market risk portion of the loan's total risk

$\varepsilon_N =$ the nontradable, illiquid credit risk portion of the loan's total risk

$\varepsilon_p =$ the nontradable, illiquid credit risk portion of the entire loan portfolio

$M =$ the systematic market risk factor

$g =$ the market unit price of systematic risk

$G =$ the bank's level of risk aversion

It can be shown that g is simply the CAPM hurdle rate from equation (11.18). That is,

$$g = \frac{R_M - r_f}{\sigma_M}$$

Thus, the first term in equation (11.20), $g\, cov(\varepsilon_T, M)$, is the market price of the loan's tradable risk component where the $cov(\varepsilon_T, M)$ term incorporates the covariance (implicitly the correlation) of the tradable risk on the loan with the market.

Moreover, in the second additional term, G measures the impact on shareholder wealth of marginal changes in the value of the bank's portfolio. If it is costly for the bank to raise external funds on short notice, then the bank's shareholders will be risk averse with respect to fluctuations in the portfolio's value.[20] Thus, the second term in equation (11.20) is the cost to bank shareholders in terms of capital at risk due to volatility stemming from the loan's untradable risk component.[21] Equation (11.20) can then be restated as:

$$\text{Hurdle rate} = \begin{array}{c} \text{Market price} \\ \text{of the loan's} \\ \text{traded risk} \end{array} + \begin{array}{c} \text{Bank shareholders' cost} \\ \text{of capital to cover} \\ \text{nontradable risk} \end{array} \qquad (11.20')$$

The bank will make the loan only if the expected return on the loan (the adjusted income) exceeds the risk-adjusted hurdle rate in equation (11.20').

RAROC AND EVA

Equation (11.20') illustrates the link between RAROC and economic value added (EVA), which is a risk-adjusted performance measure increasingly used by banks and other firms. In the context of lending, EVA requires a loan to be made only if it adds to the economic value of the bank from the shareholders' perspective. In fact, an EVA formula can be directly developed from the RAROC formula.

Assume ROE is the hurdle rate for RAROC. Then a loan should be made if:

$$\text{RAROC} > \text{ROE} \qquad (11.21)$$

or

$$\frac{(\text{Spread} + \text{Fees} - \text{Expected loss} - \text{Operating costs})}{\text{Capital at risk or economic capital } (K)} > \text{ROE}$$

Rearranging, the EVA per dollar of the loan is positive if the net dollar profit of loan returns exceeds the total dollar capital cost of funding; that is,

$$(\text{Spread} + \text{Fees} - \text{Expected loss} - \text{Operating costs}) - \text{ROE} \times K \geq 0$$

SUMMARY

This chapter has discussed the RAROC model of lending (and other business-unit) performance. RAROC is similar to a Sharpe ratio commonly analyzed in assessing the performance of risky assets and portfolios of risky assets (such as mutual funds). There are two different approaches to calculating RAROC: (1) the market-based approach and (2) the experiential approach. A major weakness of the RAROC model is its explicit failure to account for correlations. To correct this, we examine a two-factor model that incorporates the loan's correlation with the bank portfolio's illiquid credit risk exposure. This implies that bank capital is costly and therefore that shareholders are averse to unhedgeable, illiquid credit risks. This is supported by the prevalence of RAROC-type models introduced in response to shareholder initiatives.

Five

Credit Risk Transfer Mechanisms

CHAPTER 12

Credit Derivatives

INTRODUCTION

Credit derivatives, such as asset securitization and credit default swaps, allow investors to separate the credit risk exposure from the lending process itself. That is, banks can assess the creditworthiness of loan applicants, originate loans, fund loans, and even monitor and service loans without retaining exposure to loss from credit events, such as default or missed payments. This decoupling of the risk from the lending activity allows the market to efficiently transfer risk across counterparties. However, it also loosens the incentives to carefully perform each of the steps in the lending process. This loosening of incentives has been an important factor leading to the global financial crisis of 2007–2009, which has witnessed the aftereffects of poor loan underwriting, shoddy documentation and due diligence, failure to monitor borrower activity, and fraudulent activity on the part of both lenders and borrowers.

Warren Buffett has termed derivatives "financial weapons of mass destruction."[1] He has decried the "daisy chain of risk" that is facilitated by derivatives that require little payment up front but can represent large and uncertain obligations in the future. This point of view has led some to call for a ban on certain derivatives, although Warren Buffett admits that "the derivatives genie is out of the bottle, and these instruments will almost certainly multiply in variety and number until some event makes their toxicity clear." However, the fundamental question is whether derivatives are the cause of this "toxic" behavior, or merely the vehicle for excessive risk taking. If it is the latter, there will always be financial players who exploit the system for personal gain, whether they have derivatives to accomplish their nefarious goals.

In this chapter, we describe these controversial but important products and discuss mechanisms for measuring and managing their risk exposures. Financial securities in general, and credit instruments in particular, comprise a bundle of risks—for example, interest rate risk through duration and convexity, credit risk through default and volatility of credit spreads, and liquidity risk through embedded call options and market price volatility.[2] It would clearly be inefficient if the only way to manage some portion of these risk exposures was to sell the entire bond. Credit derivatives (as well as other types of derivatives) improve financial outcomes by allowing investors to separately manage each individual risk exposure. But, because these instruments are powerful risk management tools, their power can be abused. We should be able to retain the economic benefits of prudent use of credit derivatives, while policing abuses.

CREDIT DEFAULT SWAPS

A credit default swap (CDS) is essentially an insurance policy on the face value (notional value) of corporate debt (a bond or a loan) such that the CDS buyer pays a premium in exchange for protection against loss from credit events (e.g., default) on the underlying (reference) debt instrument.[3] That is, in the event of default, the CDS seller must either pay the CDS buyer some cash amount or transfer physical securities, depending upon the method of settlement. Credit default swaps are customizable, over-the-counter (OTC) contracts, although standardization enhances the tradability (liquidity) of the contract.[4] Thus, 5-year CDS contracts are most prevalent, although 1-, 3-, 7-, and 10-year contracts are also traded.[5]

In contrast to actual insurance policies, there is no requirement that the CDS buyer actually owns the underlying reference securities, and therefore the notional value of CDS contracts in recent years has exceeded the total value of the outstanding debt instruments. For example, Helwege et al. (2009) report that the numerical amount of General Motors' outstanding debt was $20 billion less than the $65 billion CDS notional value. As of the end of 2006, the Bank of England estimated total global corporate debt instruments (bonds plus loans) outstanding at $17.1 trillion. In contrast, the BIS reported that single-name CDSs outstanding during the first half of 2007 had a total notional value exceeding $20 trillion.[6] This has implications both for settlement of the CDS contract and systemic risk exposure.

The credit derivatives market has grown from an ad hoc attempt by banks to transfer their risk exposure to an innovative dealer system that has evolved into a standardized global market.[7] Since 2007, the size of the OTC derivatives market has grown, albeit at a reduced pace in the second half of the year 2008. Figure 12.1 shows the size of the global OTC derivatives market for the years 2006 through 2008. Although the market has grown over this time frame, the second half of 2008 witnessed the first ever decline

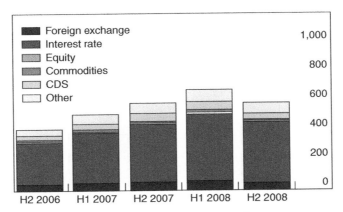

FIGURE 12.1 Notational Amounts Outstanding
Note: The BIS tables show the gross amount of CDSs and are not adjusted for interdealer double counting.
Source: Bank for International Settlements, www.bis.org.

in notional value from $683.7 trillion to $592 trillion as of the end of 2008. Out of this, CDSs represented $41.9 trillion, with $25.7 trillion in single-name CDSs outstanding (a decline of 22.8 percent from six months prior) and $16.1 trillion in multiname (basket) CDSs outstanding (a decline of 32.7 percent; see Figure 12.2).[8] Table 12.1 shows the different credit derivative products in use over the 2000–2006 period. Figure 12.2 shows that multiname CDSs surpassed single name CDSs, but have since retrenched during the financial crisis of 2007–2009. However, as will be discussed later in this chapter, increasingly popular multiname CDS vehicles are indexed CDSs and synthetic CDOs, which use an index of corporate entities as the reference securities.[9]

Similar to options, but different from non-credit-related swaps, the risks on a credit swap are not symmetrical. That is, the protection buyer (i.e., the buyer of the CDS) receives a payment upon the occurrence of a credit event trigger, but the swap expires worthless if no trigger occurs.[10] In that event, the protection seller (i.e., the seller of the CDS) keeps the periodic premiums paid for the swap, similar to the convex cash flows that characterize options (see the discussion in Chapter 4). Thus, the protection buyer transfers the credit risk to the protection seller in exchange for a premium. The size of the premium, known as the *swap spread*, is the internal rate of return that equates the present value of the periodic premium payments to the expected payments in the event of a credit event trigger. The spread is quoted per annum, but paid quarterly throughout the year.[11]

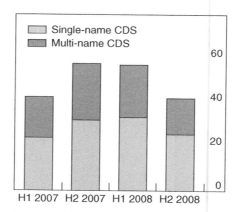

FIGURE 12.2   Global OTC Derivatives Volume, 2006–2008
Source: Bank for International Settlements, www.bis.org.

Although the credit protection buyer hedges exposure to default risk, there is still counterparty credit risk in the event that the seller fails to perform its obligations under the terms of the contract (as was the concern in September 2008 with regard to AIG, an active CDS seller).[12] The growth of the CDS market worldwide has made counterparty credit risk a source of contagion. Jorion and Zhang (2009) empirically find that bankruptcy announcements cause negative abnormal equity returns and increases in

TABLE 12.1   Credit Derivative Product Mix

	2000	2002	2004	2006
Single-name credit default swaps	38	45	51	33
Basket products	6	6	4	2
Full index trades	—	—	9	30
Tranched index trades	—	—	2	8
Synthetic CDOs—fully funded	—	—	6	4
Synthetic CDOs—partially funded	—	—	10	13
Credit-linked notes (funded CDSs)	10	8	6	3
Credit spread options	5	5	2	1
Equity-linked credit products	—	—	1	0
Swaptions	—	—	1	1
Others	41	36	8	6

Source: Mengle (2007), page 8.

CDS spreads for creditors. The credit contagion is larger if the creditor's exposure to the bankrupt entity is larger.

There are two major types of CDS: the total return swap and the pure credit default swap. Hirtle (2009) states that as of 2006, 97 percent of all credit derivatives held by U.S. commercial banks were pure CDSs, with the remainder being total return swaps. We therefore focus on these instruments.[13]

The Total Return Swap

A total return swap involves swapping an obligation to pay interest at a specified fixed or floating rate for payments representing the total return on a loan or a bond. For example, suppose that a bank lends $100 million to a firm at a fixed rate of 10 percent. If the firm's credit risk increases unexpectedly over the life of the loan, the market value of the loan will fall. The bank can seek to hedge an unexpected increase in the borrower's credit risk by entering into a total return swap in which it agrees to pay a counterparty (say, an insurance company) the total return based on an annual rate equal to the promised interest (and fees) on the loan, plus the change in the market value of the loan as estimated by some independent third party or parties. In return, the bank receives a variable market rate payment of interest annually—for example, the one-year LIBOR (London Interbank Offered Rate)—from the insuring counterparty (in this example, the insurance company). If the loan decreases in value over the payment period, the bank pays the insurance company a relatively small (possibly negative) amount equal to the fixed payment on the swap minus the capital loss on the loan.

For example, Figure 12.3 shows the payout on a total return swap. Suppose the loan was priced at par ($100) at the beginning of the swap period, denoted P_0. At the end of the swap period (or on the first payment date), the loan has an estimated market value of $90 (90 cents on the dollar, denoted P_T) due to an increase in the borrower's credit risk. Suppose that the fixed rate payment as part of the total return swap, denoted $\bar{F}$, is 12 percent. The bank would pay to the insurance company (swap counterparty) the fixed rate of 12 percent minus 10 percent (the capital loss on the loan), or a total of 2 percent, and would receive in return a floating payment (e.g., LIBOR, say equal to 11 percent in this hypothetical example) from the CDS seller, as shown in Figure 12.3. Thus, the net profit on the swap to the bank/lender is 9 percent (11 percent minus 2 percent) times the notional amount of the swap contract. This gain can be used to offset the loss in market value of the loan held on the bank's balance sheet over that period. Thus, the seller of credit protection (the insurance company) would compensate the buyer of credit protection (the bank) when there is an adverse credit event. If there

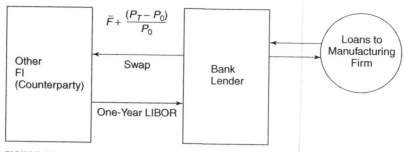

FIGURE 12.3   Cash Flows on a Total Return Swap

is no credit event, then the insurance buyer (the bank) simply pays the CDS seller a variable premium equal to 1 percent in this example (the 12 percent fixed rate minus the 11 percent LIBOR)—just as in an insurance contract, with the premium varying over time as the market value of the loan as well as LIBOR both fluctuate.

Pure Credit Default Swaps

Total return swaps can be used to hedge credit risk exposure, but they contain an element of interest rate (or market) risk as well as credit risk. For example, in the previous example, if LIBOR changes, then the *net* cash flows on the total return swap will also change, even though the credit risk of the underlying loans has not changed. Moreover, if the price of the loan changes due to interest rate or liquidity risk considerations, then the payout on the total return swap will also be affected, even if there is no change in the borrower's credit risk exposure.

To strip out the interest-rate-sensitive element from total return swaps, an alternative swap called a *pure* credit default swap was developed and has since dominated the market for credit protection. The CDS is characterized by the following four terms:

1. The identity of the reference loan—that is, the notional value, maturity, and the credit spread (over LIBOR) on a risky loan issued by the reference obligor.[14]
2. The definition of a credit event, usually any one of the following: bankruptcy, prepayment, default, failure to pay, repudiation/moratorium, or restructuring.
3. The compensation that the protection seller (e.g., the insurance company) will pay the protection buyer (e.g., the bank) if a credit event occurs.

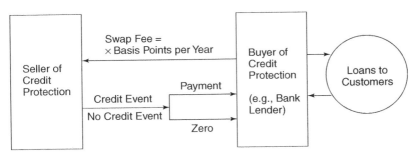

FIGURE 12.4 A Credit Default Swap

4. Specification of either physical settlement (delivery of agreed debt instruments) or cash settlement. Early credit swaps were cash settled, but now physical delivery is the most common settlement method. Physical delivery is preferred because it gives the CDS seller more time to recoup the settlement payment through recovery of the value of the reference loan. However, the borrower's consent may be needed to transfer the loan if the credit derivative specifies physical delivery upon occurrence of a credit event.

Figure 12.4 shows that the protection buyer on a CDS (say, a bank) will pay (in each swap period) a fixed fee or payment (similar to a premium on an insurance policy) to the protection seller swap counterparty (say, an insurance company). If the CDS reference loan (or loans) does not default, the protection buyer will receive nothing back from the swap counterparty. However, if the loan (or loans) defaults, Figure 12.4 shows that the CDS seller will cover the default loss by making a default payment equal to the par value of the original loan minus the secondary market value of the defaulted loan. For example, if the loan's price falls to $40 per $100 of face value upon the borrower's default, then the insurance company selling the CDS will pay the CDS buyer $60 and receive in return the claim on the defaulted loan.[15] Thus, the CDS seller pays out par minus the recovery value of the loan in the event of default.

CDS Indices

In September 2003, the Dow Jones CDX (DJ CDX) North American Investment Grade Index was introduced. In November 2004, Markit initiated a credit index data service that included the DJ CDX (which also includes indices covering emerging market credit derivatives) and the International Index Company's (IIC) iTraxx (which covers the European Union, Japan, and non-Japan Asia). Both sets of indices are made up of 125 of the most liquid, investment-grade credits in the form of CDSs. For example, the DJ CDX consists of a basket of 125 CDS contracts on U.S. firms with liquid, investment-grade corporate debt. The identity of the components in the index changes every six months—every March and September for the DJ CDX. Companies may be dropped from the index if they are downgraded or become illiquid. For example, Ford and General Motors were dropped from the DJ CDX in September 2005 when their debt fell below investment-grade. The index is equally weighted, and so each CDS component makes up 0.8 percent of the index value.

Using indexed CDSs to hedge credit risk may be less expensive because of the liquidity of these instruments, although it does expose the hedger to basis risk.[16] As will be discussed later in this chapter, synthetic CDOs are composed of tranches of indexed CDSs.

Swap Settlement Upon Trigger of Credit Event

As may be clear from the previous discussion, a CDS is similar to buying multiperiod credit insurance. Therefore, if default occurs, the CDS seller (the insurer) frequently ends up holding the reference loan. This is the case if the CDS specifies physical settlement. However, often there is no lending relationship between the CDS seller and the borrower that would place the insurer in the position formerly held by the bank lender (the CDS buyer). Indeed, if the CDS would have specified cash settlement, there would have been no transfer of the loan at all to the CDS seller—there would simply have been a cash payment made by the CDS seller to the CDS buyer. Thus, the physical delivery of a reference loan upon settlement of a CDS after a default event is simply a policy payment-in-kind on a credit risk insurance policy. As noted earlier, this settlement methodology is often chosen because of the absence of mark-to-market debt prices during the time period around defaults and other credit events. Instead, the CDS seller plays the role of an insurer and, as in any insurance policy, steps into the shoes of the CDS buyer (the insured), thereby indemnifying them against loss.

However, as the market grew, physical settlement became problematic as the notional value of CDSs exceeded the supply of debt instruments available, particularly with the growth of indexed CDSs. For example, Helwege et al. (2009) state that only a third of the Lehman CDS contracts outstanding in September 2008 were written to hedge debt positions, with the remaining two-thirds being pure derivatives positions. There were simply not enough bonds to go around for physical settlement of the CDS claims.[17] However, the absence of a transparent, reliable price for the reference security often makes cash settlement difficult. Recently, since the Delphi auction of 2005, the market has turned to the auction mechanism in order to determine a uniform price for settlement of CDS contracts.[18] Under the auction procedure, each CDS seller can choose whether to undertake cash or physical settlement at a uniform price. That is, investors can choose whether to provide debt instruments to the auction (physical settlement) or not (cash settlement).

Gross and Saperia (2008) provide the following example of a CDS settlement auction. Suppose that investor A buys $10 million of CDSs (long protection) on a reference bond.[19] Investor A provides the bonds to the auction. Suppose that their value is $4 million, representing a 40 percent recovery rate. Investor A gets $4 million from the auction sale of the bonds and $6 million from the protection seller in cash. Now, suppose that investor B sells the $10 million of CDSs to investor A. Investor B can buy the bonds at auction by submitting a bid to the auction. If investor B does submit a bid to buy $10 million face value of bonds, then the CDS is physically settled, since investor B pays investor A $10 million for bonds worth $4 million, and investor B gets to keep the bonds. If, however, investor B prefers cash settlement, then no bid to purchase the bonds is submitted to the auction and investor B will simply pay investor A $10 million in cash to settle the CDS obligation. Thus, the auction allows each CDS seller to choose whether to settle their obligation through cash or physical settlement.[20]

Helwege et al. (2009) examine the performance of 43 CDS auctions held since 2005 and find that they efficiently settle the contracts at prices close to the observed prices in secondary bond markets. They illustrate the working of the CDS auction with the auction for Lehman senior bonds that took place on October 10, 2008.[21] Table 12.2 shows that 14 securities dealers participated in the auction, placing orders to sell a total of $4.92 billion Lehman senior bonds. The first stage of the auction examines the bids and removes both bids if the highest bid is greater than or equal to the lowest offer. Thus, both the Barclays and HSBC bids are removed from the pool.[22] The rest of the bids are ranked in order of size and divided into two groups: (1) the highest bid (lower shaded box in Table 12.2) and (2) the lowest offer prices (upper shaded box). The average of the highest bid (lowest offer) group was 9.25 (10.3125). Averaging these and rounding to the nearest eighth results in an *inside market midpoint* of 9.75. This is the first-stage auction price.

There is no need for a second stage if the market clears in the first stage—that is, if the open interest is equal to zero at the end of the first stage—and the inside market midpoint would be the final auction price. However, at the end of the first stage in the Lehman auction described in Table 12.2, there was open interest of more than $5 billion to sell (i.e., negative open interest). Thus, a second stage of the auction must be conducted

TABLE 12.2 CDS Auction for Lehman Bonds, October 10, 2008

Securities Dealer	Bid	Offer	Physical Settlement Request ($ millions)
Barclays Bank PLC	8	10	Sell: 130
Credit Suisse Securities (USA) LLC	8	10	Sell: 755
Deutsche Bank AG	8	10	Sell: 870
Merrill Lynch, Pierce, Fenner & Smith Inc.	8	10	Sell: 141
Morgan Stanley & Co. Inc.	8.25	10.25	Sell: 480
UBS Securities LLC	8.75	10.75	Sell: 464
Goldman Sachs & Co.	8.875	10.875	Sell: 1470
BNP Paribas	9	11	Sell: 390
JPMorgan Chase Bank, N.A.	9	11	Buy: 612
Citigroup Global Markets Inc.	9.25	11	Sell: 574
The Royal Bank of Scotland PLC	9.25	11.25	Sell: 191
Banc of America Securities LLC	9.5	11.5	Sell: 170
Dresdner Bank AG	9.5	11.5	Buy: 30
HSBC Bank USA, N.A.	10	12	Sell: 187

Note: All bids are based on $100 face value.
Source: Helwege et al., (2009), 20.

within 30 minutes of the end of the first stage. In the second stage, dealers submit limit orders to meet any portion of the open interest at any price, capped at the one above (below) the inside market midpoint for negative (positive) open interest, or in this case 10.75. In the Lehman auction, the second-stage limit orders were to buy (since the open interest was to sell); there were 453 offers to buy at prices ranging from 0.125 to 10.75 (the cap price). The market cleared at prices of 8.625 or higher. Therefore, the final auction price was set at 8.625 for Lehman senior bonds on October 10, 2008.

Helwege et al. (2009) judge the Lehman auction to be efficient, citing that $72 billion of gross notional value of CDSs was settled with a net cash payment of $5.2 billion from CDS sellers to buyers. Further, they conclude that the market is satisfied with the auction process in general, as evidenced by the participation of 95 percent of all eligible parties. However, only a small number of auctions have been conducted to date.

Basel I Model of Credit Risk for Swaps

Under the Basel I risk-based capital ratio rules, a major distinction is made between exchange-traded derivative security contracts (e.g., Chicago Board of Trade exchange-traded options) and OTC-traded instruments (e.g., forwards, swaps, caps, and floors).[23] The credit or default risk of exchange-traded derivatives is approximately zero because when a counterparty defaults on its obligations, the exchange itself adopts the counterparty's obligations in full. However, no such guarantee exists for bilaterally negotiated OTC contracts originated and traded outside organized exchanges. Hence, most off-balance-sheet (OBS) futures and options positions have no capital requirements for a bank, although most forwards, swaps, caps, and floors do.[24]

For the purposes of capital regulation under the Basel I codes, the calculation of the risk-adjusted asset values of OBS market contracts requires a two-step approach: (1) credit equivalent amounts are calculated for each contract, and (2) the credit equivalent amounts are multiplied by an appropriate risk weight.

Specifically, the notional or face values of all non-exchange-traded swap, forward, and other derivative contracts are first converted into credit equivalent amounts (i.e., *as if* they are on-balance-sheet credit instruments). The credit equivalent amount itself is divided into a *potential exposure* element and a *current exposure* element:

$$
\begin{array}{c}
\text{Credit equivalent amount} \\
\text{of OBS derivative} \\
\text{security items (\$)}
\end{array}
=
\begin{array}{c}
\text{Potential} \\
\text{exposure (\$)}
\end{array}
+
\begin{array}{c}
\text{Current} \\
\text{exposure (\$)}
\end{array}
\qquad (12.1)
$$

The potential exposure component reflects the credit risk if the counterparty to the contract defaults in the future. The probability of such an occurrence is modeled as depending on the future volatility of interest rates/exchange rates. Based on a Federal Reserve Bank of England Monte Carlo simulation exercise, Basel I came up with a set of conversion factors that varied by type of contract (e.g., interest rate or foreign exchange) and by maturity bucket (see Table 12.3). The potential exposure conversion factors in Table 12.3 are larger for foreign exchange contracts than for interest rate contracts. Also, note the larger potential exposure factors for longer-term contracts of both types.

In addition to calculating the potential exposure of an OBS market instrument, a bank must calculate its current exposure to the instrument: the cost of replacing a contract if a counterparty defaults today. The bank calculates this replacement cost or current exposure by replacing the rate or

TABLE 12.3 Basel I Credit Conversion Factors for Interest Rate and Foreign Exchange Contracts in Calculating Potential Exposure (as a Percent of Nominal Contract Value)

Remaining Maturity	Conversion Factors For	
	Interest Rate Contracts (%)	Exchange Rate Contracts (%)
1. One year or less	0.0	1.0
2. One to five years	0.5	5.0
3. Over five years	1.5	7.5

Source: Federal Reserve Board of Governors press release, August 1995, Section IL.

price that was initially in the contract with the current rate or price for a similar contract, and then recalculates all the current and future cash flows to obtain a current present-value measure of the replacement cost of the contract.

If the net present value (NPV) is greater than 0, then the replacement value equals current exposure. However, if the NPV is less than 0, then current exposure is set to zero because a bank cannot be allowed to gain by defaulting on an out-of-the-money contract.

After the current and potential exposure amounts are summed to produce the credit equivalent amount of each contract, this dollar number is multiplied by a risk weight to produce the final risk-adjusted asset amount for OBS market contracts. In general, the appropriate risk weight under Basel I is .5, or 50 percent. That is,

$$\begin{matrix} \text{Risk-adjusted asset value} \\ \text{of OBS market contracts} \end{matrix} = \begin{matrix} \text{Total credit equivalent} \\ \text{amount} \times .5 \ (\text{risk weight}) \end{matrix} \qquad (12.2)$$

An Example

Suppose that the bank had taken one interest-rate hedging position in the fixed/floating interest rate swap market for four years with a notional dollar amount of $100 million, and one two-year forward US$/£ foreign exchange contract for $40 million. The credit-equivalent amount for each item or contract is shown in Table 12.4.

TABLE 12.4 Potential Exposure + Current Exposure ($ Millions)

Type of Contract (Remaining Maturity)	Notional Principal	×	Potential Exposure Conversion Factor =	Potential Exposure ($)	Replacement Cost	Current Exposure	=	Credit Equivalent Amount
Four-year fixed-floating interest rate swap	$100	×	.005 =	.5	3	3	=	$3.5
Two-year forward foreign exchange contract	$40	×	.05 =	2	−1	0	=	$2

A_{gross} = $2.5	Net current exposure = $2	Current exposure = $3

For the four-year fixed/floating interest rate swap, the notional value (contract face value) of the swap is $100 million. Because this is a long-term, over one-year, less than five-year interest rate contract, its face value is multiplied by .005 to get a potential exposure or credit risk equivalent value of $0.5 million (see Table 12.4). We add this potential exposure to the replacement cost (current exposure) of this contract to the bank. The replacement cost reflects the cost of having to enter into a new fixed/floating swap agreement, at today's interest rates, for the remaining life of the swap. Assuming that interest rates today are less favorable, on a present value basis, the cost of replacing the existing contract for its remaining life would be $3 million. Thus, the total credit equivalent amount (current plus potential exposure for the interest rate swap) is $3.5 million.

Next, we can look at the foreign exchange two-year forward contract of $40 million face value. Because this is an over one-year, less than five-year foreign exchange contract, the potential (future) credit risk is $40 million times .05, or $2 million (see Table 12.4). However, its replacement cost is minus $1 million and, as discussed earlier, when the replacement cost of a contract is negative, the current exposure has to be set equal to zero (as shown). Thus, the sum of potential exposure ($2 million) and current exposure ($0) produces a total credit equivalent amount of $2 million for this contract.

Because the bank in this example has just two OBS derivative contracts, summing the two credit equivalent amounts produces a total credit equivalent amount of $3.5 million + $2 million = $5.5 million for the bank's OBS market contracts. The next step is to multiply this credit equivalent amount by the appropriate risk weight. Specifically, to calculate the risk-adjusted asset value for the bank's OBS derivative or market contracts, we multiply the credit equivalent amount by the appropriate risk weight, which for virtually all over-the-counter derivative security products is .5, or 50 percent:[25]

$$\begin{array}{l}\text{Risk-adjusted} \\ \text{asset value of} \\ \text{OBS derivatives}\end{array} = \begin{array}{l}\$5.5 \text{ million (credit} \\ \text{equivalent amount)}\end{array} \times \begin{array}{l}0.5 \text{ (risk} \\ \text{weight)}\end{array} = \$2.75 \text{ million}$$

As with the risk-based capital requirement for loans, the Basel I regulations do not directly take into account potential reductions in credit risk from holding a diversified portfolio of OBS contracts. As Hendricks (1994) and others have shown, a portfolio of 50 pay-floating and 50 pay-fixed swap contracts will be less risky than a portfolio of 100 pay-fixed (or floating) contracts. Nevertheless, although portfolio diversification is not recognized directly, it has been recognized indirectly since October 1995, when banks were allowed to net contracts with the same counterparty under standard master agreements.

The post-1995 Basel netting rules define *net current exposure* as the net sum of all positive and negative replacement costs (or mark-to-market values of the individual derivative contracts). The net potential exposure is defined by a formula that adjusts the gross potential exposure estimated earlier:

$$A_{net} = \left(0.4 \times A_{gross}\right) + \left(0.6 \times NGR \times A_{gross}\right)$$

where A_{net} is the net potential exposure (or adjusted sum of potential future credit exposures), A_{gross} is the sum of the potential exposures of each contract, and NGR is the ratio of net current exposure to gross current exposure, or *net to gross ratio*. The 0.6 is the amount of potential exposure that is reduced as a result of netting.[26]

The same example (with netting) will be used to show the effects of netting on the total credit equivalent amount. Here we assume both contracts are with the same counterparty (see Table 12.4).

The net current exposure is the sum of the positive and negative replacement costs; that is, $3 million plus a negative $1 million equals $2 million. The total current exposure is $3 million and the gross potential exposure (A_{gross}) is $2.5 million. To determine the net potential exposure, the following formula is used:

$$NGR = \frac{\text{Net current exposure}}{\text{Current exposure}} = \frac{\$2 \text{ million}}{\$3 \text{ million}} = \frac{2}{3}$$

$$A_{net} = (0.4 \times 2.5) + \left(0.6 \times \frac{2}{3} \times 2.5\right) \qquad (12.3)$$

$$= \$2 \text{ million}$$

Total credit equivalent amount	=	Net potential exposure	+	Net current exposure
$4 million	=	$2 million	+	$2 million

Risk-adjusted asset value of OBS market contracts	=	Total credit equivalent amount	×	0.5 (risk weight)
$2 million	=	$4 million	×	0.5

As can be seen, using netting reduces the risk-adjusted asset value from $2.75 million to $2 million. And, given the BIS 8 percent capital requirement, the capital required against the OBS contracts is reduced from $220,000 to $160,000.[27] This capital requirement may be reduced even further under Basel II, which takes credit mitigation into account by adjusting the exposure to reflect the value of collateral, credit guarantees, or netting.

Basel II Capital Requirements for CDSs

The Basel II regulations cover CDSs under the category of credit risk mitigation, such that capital requirements may be reduced if CDSs are used to reduce the credit risk exposure of the banking book. These transactions fall under the category of "collateralized transactions" defined to be transactions that meet two criteria:

1. Banks have a credit exposure or potential credit exposure.
2. That credit exposure or potential credit exposure is hedged in whole or in part by collateral posted by a counterparty or by a third party on behalf of the counterparty (Basel II Accord, June 2006, paragraph 119).

This definition includes OTC credit derivatives, such as CDSs.[28] In general, the risk weight of the counterparty is substituted for the underlying exposure's risk weight subject to a minimum 20 percent floor. Thus, for

TABLE 12.5   Basel II Standard Supervisory Haircuts

Issue Rating for Debt Securities	Residual Maturity	Sovereigns	Other issuers
AAA to AA−/A-1	≤ 1 year	0.5	1
	>1 year, ≤ 5 years	2	4
	> 5 years	4	8
A+ to BBB−/ A-2/A-3/P-3 and unrated bank securities per para. 145(d)	≤ 1 year	1	2
	>1 year, ≤ 5 years	3	6
	> 5 years	6	12
BB+ to BB−	All	15	
Main index equities (including convertible bonds) and gold		15	
Other equities (including convertible bonds) listed on a recognized exchange		25	
UCITS/Mutual funds		Highest haircut applicable to any security in which the fund can invest	
Cash in the same currency		0	

Note: Supervisors may permit banks to calculate haircuts using their own internal estimates of market price volatility and foreign exchange rate volatility.

Source: Basel II (June 2006), paragraph 151.

example, if a bank made a loan to a BBB-rated company and then fully hedged that risk with a CDS in which the counterparty was an A-rated bank, the risk weight would decline from 100 percent to 50 percent.[29]

Under the comprehensive approach, Basel II focuses on adjustments to the exposure amount, and retains the Basel I methodology. That is, credit risk mitigation reduces the exposure at default (EAD) that is at risk, thereby reducing the capital requirement, even though the risk weight is unchanged. The methodology of Basel II, therefore, reduces the exposure level to reflect the safeguard afforded by the credit protection for CDS buyers and then applies the Basel I risk weights to the EAD.[30] To use the previous example shown in equation (12.3), if the OBS position was 25 percent collateralized, then the risk-adjusted asset value would be reduced to $1.5 million, that is, $4m × .5 × (1 − .25).

To determine the collateral weight, haircuts are applied to the value of collateral in order to protect against volatility in collateral prices. Table 12.5 shows the standard supervisory haircuts proposed under Basel II.[31]

The haircuts shown in Table 12.5 are used to calculate the adjusted value of EAD as follows:

$$E^* = \max\{0, [E \times (1 + He) - C \times (1 - Hc - Hfx)]\} \qquad (12.4)$$

where
E^* = The exposure value after risk mitigation
E = Current value of the exposure
He = Haircut appropriate to the exposure
C = The current value of the collateral received
Hc = Haircut appropriate to the collateral
Hfx = Haircut appropriate for currency mismatch between the collateral and exposure

With some exceptions, under both the simple and comprehensive approaches, there is a 20 percent risk weight floor. Thus, even if the exposure is fully collateralized, there is a floor (that is, $.20E$) capital requirement. For example, a fully collateralized $4 million exposure would have an adjusted exposure value E^* equal to $800,000 (.20 times $4 million) for a floor capital level (assuming a 50 percent risk weight and an 8 percent capital requirement) of $32,000 (that is, $600,000 × .5 × .08). If, however, the exposure was not fully collateralized, then the adjusted exposure E^* would be calculated using equation (12.4), with a floor haircut of 20 percent. For example, if the adjusted collateral value was $1 million on the $4 million exposure, then the adjusted exposure value E^* would be $3.2 million (that is, $4 million – (1 − .20) × $1 million) for a $128,000 capital charge (which is $3.2 million × .5 × .08, assuming a 50 percent risk weight and an 8 percent capital requirement).

There are certain restrictions to the credit substitution process. In particular, a credit derivative must be a direct claim on the CDS seller and be "unconditional and irrevocable." Since a loan restructuring may be viewed as an adverse credit event, the extent to which restructuring events are covered by the CDS may limit the degree of hedging. Thus, capital regulations do not permit full credit mitigation of loan exposures using CDS.[32]

CREDIT SECURITIZATIONS

In Chapter 1, we described the process of asset-backed securitization and how abuses in the process contributed to the global financial crisis of

2007–2009. While most familiar in terms of mortgage-backed securities (pools of mortgage loans), the same securitization process was applied to other types of loans as well. For example, a collateralized debt obligation (CDO) is a financial claim on the cash flows generated by a pool of debt securities, usually corporate debt obligations. Before the credit bubble began to build, the growth of commercial credit or loan securitization (as in the case of loan sales and trading) had been hampered by concerns about negative customer relationship effects if loans were removed from the balance sheet and packaged and sold as collateralized loan obligations (CLOs) to outside investors.[33] Thus, some loan securitizations were conducted in which loans remained on the balance sheet, and asset-backed securities (credit-linked notes, or CLNs) were issued against the loan portfolio.[34] Moreover, synthetic CDOs represent claims on a portfolio of CDS contracts, rather than actual loans or debt instruments, and thus CDOs can be written on CDS indices, such as the DJ CDX. Indeed, a CDO-squared (CDO^2) is a CDO of other CDO securities.

A huge variety of these products has emerged, but the differences among them relate to the way in which credit risk is transferred from the loan-originating bank to the note investor. In general, a subportfolio of commercial loans is segmented on the asset side of the balance sheet or in an off-balance-sheet vehicle (such as a special-purpose vehicle, SPV, or a structured investment vehicle, SIV), and an issue of a CDO, CLO or CLN is made. The return and risk of investors vary by type of issue. Some investors are promised a high yield on the underlying loans in return for bearing all the default risk; other investors are offered lower yields in return for partial default protection (i.e., a shared credit risk with the bank). In general, the bank issuer takes the first tranche of default risk but is protected against catastrophic risk (which is borne by the CLN investor).

Just as for mortgage-backed securities, the CDO typically contains several tranches, each tied to a specific attachment point. For example, synthetic CDOs based on CDS indices such as the DJ CDX have the following standardized attachment points: 3 percent, 7 percent, 10 percent, 15 percent and 30 percent. The equity tranche (most junior, highest risk security) attaches at the 0 to 3 percent level. Thus, the equity tranche absorbs the first 3 percent of credit losses. To illustrate, Table 12.6 shows a $100 million cash CDO comprising a diversified portfolio of 100 equal-size five-year par corporate bonds. Assume that the equity tranche represents $3 million in notional value (3 percent of the total portfolio value), and pays a coupon rate of 500 basis points over LIBOR.[35] Suppose that one of the bonds defaults and that there is no recovery (LGD is 100 percent). The equity tranche of the CDO loses $1 million, with a remaining notional value of $2 million. After the default, future coupon payments are paid on $2 million

TABLE 12.6 CDO Tranches Using Standardized Attachment Points

Tranche	Attachment Points	Notional Value	Credit Loss Absorption	Average Coupon Spread 2003–2005
Equity	0 to 3%	$3 million	First $3 million	1,759 bp
Junior mezzanine	3% to 7%	$4 million	$3 to $7 million	240 bp
Senior mezzanine	7% to 10%	$3 million	$7 to $10 million	82 bp
Super senior mezzanine	10% to 15%	$5 million	$10 to $15 million	34 bp
Senior B	15% to 30%	$15 million	$15 to $30 million	12 bp
Senior A	30% to 100%	$70 million	Any above $30 million	0

Note: This example uses a hypothetical CDO with notional value of $100 million. The attachment points are the standardized attachment points for synthetic CDOs based on the DJ CDX North American Investment Grade Index.

The average coupon spreads are obtained from Longstaff and Rajan (2008). The equity tranche spread includes an up-front premium averaging 39.34 over the period from October 2003 to October 2005.

Source: Longstaff and Rajan (2008), 538.

notional value, rather than the original $3 million. If the portfolio sustains credit losses of $3 million, then the equity tranche is completely wiped out. Thus, the equity tranche investor is essentially leveraged $33\frac{1}{3}$ to 1 since a 3 percent loss in the portfolio translates into a 100 percent loss on the equity tranche of the CDO.[36]

Just above the equity tranche is a junior mezzanine tranche with a total notional amount of 4 percent of the portfolio value, or $4 million. It attaches at 3 percent, since the equity tranche absorbs the first 3 percent of the losses. Thus, the junior mezzanine tranche will only realize credit losses if the defaults exceed $3 million. Since this tranche has a width of 4 percent, it will absorb any losses between $3 and $7 million. A senior mezzanine tranche will then attach at 7 percent. Suppose (using the standardized attachment points for the synthetic CDO mentioned earlier) that this tranche had a $3 million notional value, or 3 percent of the portfolio amount. The senior mezzanine tranche absorbs losses between $7 and $10 million. The next, super-senior mezzanine tranche attaches at 10 percent and extends to 15 percent, with a notional value of $5 million (5 percent of total portfolio value). Any credit losses between $10 and $15 million are charged to these security holders. Finally, the two senior tranches are the B tranche (attaching at the 15 percent level) and the A tranche (attaching at the 30 percent level). Using these standardized attachment points, the notional value of the B (A) tranche is $15 ($70) million. Thus, the most senior, A tranche absorbs credit losses only if they exceed $30 million. If this is unlikely to occur, the A tranche will be considered very low risk and have a high credit rating.[37]

During the buildup of the credit bubble that burst in 2007, the CDO market grew rapidly, especially in terms of synthetic CDOs. Longstaff and Rajan (2008) state that at the end of 2006, the market size was almost $2 trillion, having grown by 20 percent from the previous year. An example of the synthetic securitization structure is the BISTRO (Broad Index Secured Trust Offering), illustrated in Figure 12.5. In this structure, the originating bank purchases credit protection from the intermediary bank (e.g., the bank originator, JP Morgan Chase) via a CDS subject to a "threshold." That is, the CDS will not pay off unless credit losses on the reference loan portfolio exceed a certain level, 1.50 percent in this example.[38] The intermediary buys credit protection on the same portfolio from a SPV. The BISTRO SPV is collateralized with government securities which it funds by issuing credit-tranched notes to capital market investors. However, the BISTRO collateral is substantially smaller than the notional value of the portfolio. In the example shown in Figure 12.5, only $700 million of collateral backs a $10 billion loan portfolio (7 percent collateralization).[39] This is possible because the portfolio is structured to have enough investment grade loans and diversification that make it unlikely that losses on the loan portfolio would exceed $850 million ($700 million in BISTRO collateral plus the bank's absorption of the first $150 million in possible losses, i.e., 1.5 percent of the portfolio's notional value.) This structure significantly reduces the legal, systems, personnel, and client relationship costs associated with a traditional ABS. It permits much greater diversity in the portfolio underlying the BISTRO than is possible for a CLO or CLN. For example, unfunded credit exposures, such as loan commitments, letters of credit and trade receivables can be included in the BISTRO portfolio, whereas CLOs are limited to portfolios of funded loans. Moreover, since the BISTRO is unrelated in any way to the originating bank, there should be no reputational risk effects, thereby further reducing capital charges.

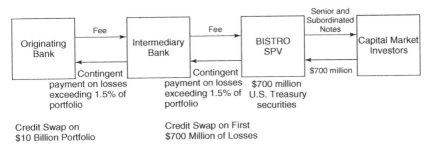

FIGURE 12.5 BISTRO structure.
Note: Under BIS I market risk capital rules, the intermediary bank can use VAR to determine the capital requirements of its residual risk position.

Basel II Capital Requirements for Asset-Backed Securities

To be eligible for recognition of risk transference (and therefore not subject to *bank* capital requirements), the asset-backed security (ABS) must be completely independent of the originating bank, such that:[40]

- ▪ *Significant credit risk associated with the securitized exposures has been transferred to third parties.*
- ▪ *The transferor does not maintain effective or indirect control over the transferred exposures. The assets are legally isolated from the transferor in such a way . . . that the exposures are put beyond the reach of the transferor and its creditors, even in bankruptcy or receivership. . . .*
- ▪ *The securities issues are not obligations of the transferor. . . .*
- ▪ *The transferee is a special purpose entity (SPE). . . .*

(Basel II [2006], paragraph 554)

Even when the conditions for a *clean break* are met, the originating bank may still be required to hold capital against the assets in the ABS pool if regulators believe that the bank is subject to reputational risk. That is, to prevent damage to the originating bank's reputation, the bank might offer *implicit recourse*, which may take the form of the following possible responses to credit deterioration in the asset pool underlying the ABS: the bank may repurchase or substitute credit-impaired assets in the pool, loans may be made to the special-purpose vehicle, or fee income associated with the ABS structure may be deferred. Under such circumstances, regulators may force the bank to hold capital against *all* assets in *all* ABSs issued, even those for which implicit recourse was not granted, as if all assets in all ABS pools remained on the bank's balance sheet. Thus, the finding of the provision of implicit recourse engenders punitive regulatory action that is made public by bank regulators.

The Securitization Framework states that bank capital requirements may be computed using either the standardized method or the ratings-based approach.[41] Panel A (B) of Table 12.7 provides the risk weights under the standardized (ratings-based) approach. The ratings-based approach adjusts the risk weight obtained using the external credit rating to reflect maturity, tranche seniority, and granularity of the asset pool.[42]

A simple example illustrates the impact of the Securitization Framework on bank capital requirements. Figure 12.6 shows a bank with $100 million of BBB loans on the balance sheet which paid a capital charge of $8 million. Suppose these loans were placed in an SPV and two tranches of bonds were issued, as shown in Figure 12.6. The first tranche of $80 million was rated AA because it was structured to absorb default losses only after the first 3 percent of losses on the entire $100 million loan portfolio (corresponding to the historical default rate of bonds with a BBB rating) were borne by the second tranche of $20 million. Because of the low quality of the second tranche it was rated B. Suppose that the high-quality tranche was sold to outside investors, but the bank or its subsidiaries (as commonly the case) ended up owning (buying) the second, B-rated tranche.

Because Basel I treated all commercial credit risks with equal weight, the capital requirement on the $20 million of purchased bonds (that have

TABLE 12.7 Panel A: Long-Term Rating Category

Long-Term Rating Category				
External Credit Assessment	AAA to AA−	A+ to A−	BBB+ to BBB−	BB+ to BB−	B+ and Below or Unrated
Risk Weight	20%	50%	100%	350%	Deduction

Short-Term Rating Category			
External Credit Assessment	A-1/P-1	A-2/P-2	A-3/P-3	All Other Ratings or Unrated
Risk Weight	20%	50%	100%	Deduction

Source: Basel II, June 2006, paragraph 567.

TABLE 12.7 Panel B: RBA Risk Weights When the External Assessment Represents a Long-Term Credit Rating and/or an Inferred Rating Derived from a Long-Term Assessment

External Rating (Illustrative)	Risk Weights for Senior Positions and Eligible Senior IAA Exposures	Base Risk Weights	Risk Weights for Tranches Backed by Non-Granular Pools
AAA	7%	12%	20%
AA	8%	15%	25%
A+	10%	18%	35%
A	12%	20%	
A−	20%	35%	
BBB+	35%		50%
BBB	60%		75%
BBB−		100%	
BB+		250%	
BB		425%	
BB−		650%	
Below BB− and unrated		Deduction	

Source: Basel II, June 2006, paragraph 615.

virtually the same credit risk as the original $100 million BBB portfolio) would be subject to a capital charge of only $20 million times 8 percent, or $1.6 million. That is, the bank has *arbitraged* a capital savings of $8 million minus $1.6 million, or $6.4 million, through the securitization. Under the standardized approach of Basel II, the risk weight on the B-rated tranche would be 350 percent (see Panel A of Table 12.7), and therefore the capital charge on the $20 million tranche would be $5.6 million, (that is, $20 million × 8 percent × 3.5), thereby mitigating arbitrage incentives. However, securitizations originated during the 2006–2007 precrash period were more likely to have a 3 percent equity tranche than the 20 percent equity tranche shown in Figure 12.6.

January 2009 Proposals for Changes in Basel II

The global financial crisis of 2007–2009 has led the Basel Committee to propose changes in Basel II's treatment of securitization instruments, with a

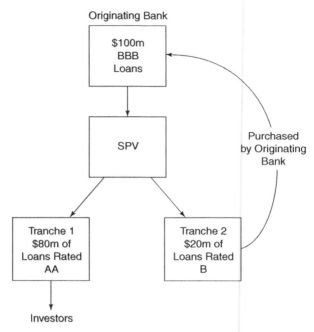

FIGURE 12.6 Regulatory Arbitrage under Basel I

particular focus on *resecuritizations*, such as CDOs of ABSs, CDO²s, and asset-backed commercial paper (ABCPs). The January 2009 proposal defines a resecuritization as an exposure where one or more of the underlying exposures is a securitization. The following five changes are to be implemented in December 2010:

1. Higher risk weights are applied on resecuritizations for IRB users, as shown in Panel C of Table 12.7. The floor risk weight has been increased from 7 percent to 20 percent for resecuritizations.
2. Altered risk weights are applied on resecuritizations for standardized model users, as shown in Panel D of Table 12.7. The floor risk weight has been increased from 20 percent to 40 percent for resecuritizations.
3. External credit ratings cannot be used if the guarantee is provided by the bank itself. The January 2009 document notes that banks avoided lending to their SIVs on lines of credit by buying the ABCPs that could not be sold in the market during the summer and fall of 2007. The banks then held capital against the ABCPs using the inflated external credit ratings. This proposal would eliminate this loophole.

TABLE 12.7 Panel C: January 2009 Alterations to Basel II

Long-Term Rating	Securitization Exposures			Resecuritization Exposures	
	Senior, Granular	Non-Senior, Granular	Non-Granular	Senior	Non-Senior
AAA	7	12	20	20	30
AA	8	15	25	25	40
A+	10	18	35	35	50
A	12	20	35	40	65
A−	20	35	35	60	100
BBB+	35	50	50	100	150
BBB	60	75	75	150	225
BBB−	100	100	100	200	350
BB+	250	250	250	300	500
BB	425	425	425	500	650
BB−	650	650	650	750	550
Below	Deduction				

Short-Term Rating	Securitization Exposures			Resecuritization Exposures	
	Senior, Granular	Non-Senior, Granular	Non-Granular	Senior	Non-Senior
A1	7	12	20	20	30
A2	12	20	35	40	65
A3	60	75	75	150	225
Below	Deduction				

Source: Basel II Alterations, January 2009, 2.

4. Banks are required to have procedures to perform their own due diligence on securitizations and not just rely on credit ratings.
5. Changes are made to treatment of liquidity facilities in the standardized approach. Basel II permitted off-balance-sheet securitizations to have a credit conversion factor of 20 percent if they have an original maturity up to one year and 50 percent if over one year. The proposal would change that to 50 percent for all securitizations. Moreover, liquidity

TABLE 12.7 Panel D

Long-Term Rating	Securitization Exposures	Resecuritization Exposures
AAA to AA−	20	40
A+ to A−	50	100
BBB+ to BBB−	100	225
BB+ to BB−	350	650
B− and below or unrated	Deduction	

Short-Term Rating	Securitization Exposures	Resecuritization Exposures
A-1/P-1	20	40
A-2/P-2	50	100
A-3/P-3	100	225
All other ratings or unrated	Deduction	

Source: Basel II Alterations, January 2009, page 4.

facilities (e.g., backup lines of credit) that can be taken down only under conditions of general market disruption would see their credit conversion factor increase from 0 percent to 20 percent.

The January 2009 proposals also proposed revisions to pillar 2 (supervisory oversight) and pillar 3 (market discipline), reflecting the growth of credit-based securitizations. Supervisors were urged to improve their risk oversight by analyzing the bank on an integrated, fully consolidated basis and conducting stress tests (see Chapter 10). The Basel Committee opined that "the major causes of serious banking problems continue to be lax credit standards for borrowers and counterparties, poor portfolio risk management, and a lack of attention to changes in economic and other circumstances that can lead to deterioration in the credit standing of a bank's counterparties." It is the bank supervisor's responsibility to make sure that banks have in place adequate risk controls to measure and manage risk even as markets evolve and grow.

Pillar 3 is intended to complement pillars 1 (minimum capital requirements) and 2 (supervisory oversight) in promoting bank safety and soundness. In order to improve market disclosure, the January 2009 proposals stated that "banks are responsible for conveying their actual risk profile to market participants." More disclosure regarding securitizations would be required.[43]

FINANCIAL FIRMS' USE OF CREDIT DERIVATIVES

Credit derivatives are remarkably versatile and customizable products, allowing counterparties to effectively manage their credit risk exposure (either by hedging or speculating) at relatively low cost. Protection buyers are said to take short positions in the credit risk of the reference entity, whereas protection sellers take long positions. Table 12.8 shows the breakdown of market participants buying and selling protection against credit risk. Typically, banks, securities firms and corporate FIs are net buyers of credit protection, whereas insurance companies, hedge funds, mutual funds and pension funds are net sellers.[44] However, some financial firms are market makers in the market for credit derivatives, and therefore take both long and short positions. The growing participation of hedge funds as both buyers and sellers of credit derivatives is shown in Table 12.8.

Hirtle (2009) shows that U.S. commercial banks were net protection buyers, particularly in the years 2004–2007. This could be consistent with the increase in the bank supply of credit. Hirtle (2009) also shows that the supply of credit to small business borrowers actually decreases when banks increase their use of credit derivatives as hedging instruments. However, the availability of credit to large corporate borrowers, most likely to be the direct object of CDS hedges (i.e., *named credits*, or firms issuing reference securities) increases when banks increase their CDS activity, suggesting that risk hedging may allow banks to expand their lending activity. That is, banks can recycle their capital and increase their risk-taking activities to the extent that a bank can transfer that risk (i.e., for large corporate borrowers) via credit derivatives.

CDS SPREADS AND RATING AGENCY RATING SYSTEMS

As the CDS market has grown in depth and importance, discontent with the through-the-cycle approach of traditional rating systems has also grown. As a result, rating agencies such as Fitch and Moody's have moved toward developing *point-in-time* ratings for corporate, bank and sovereign borrowers based on CDS spreads. The essential idea is to produce short-term forward-looking measures of a counterparty's credit exposure risk. For example, Fitch utilizes a CDS database back to 1999 that covers over 2,500 ratings in more than 80 countries. Because different countries and CDS contracts treat restructuring triggers for CDS contracts differently—varying from no restructuring to modified restructuring (covering debt obligations that

TABLE 12.8   Buyers of Protection by Institution Type

Buyers of Protection by Institution Type				
Type of Institution	2000	2002	2004	2006
Banks (including securities firms)	81	73	67	50
Banks—trading activities	—	—	—	90
Banks—loan portfolio	—	—	—	20
Insurers	7	6	7	6
Monoline insurers	—	3*	2	2
Reinsurers	—		3	2
Other insurance companies	—	3	2	2
Hedge funds	3	12	16	28
Pension funds	1	1	3	2
Mutual funds	1	2	3	2
Corporates	6	4	3	2
Other	1	2	1	1

Sellers of Protection by Institution Type				
Type of Institution	2000	2002	2004	2006
Banks (including securities firms)	63	55	54	44
Banks—trading activities	—	—	—	35
Banks—loan portfolio	—	—	—	9
Insurers	23	33	20	17
Monoline insurers	—	21*	10	8
Reinsurers	—		7	4
Other insurance companies	—	12	3	5
Hedge funds	5	5	15	32
Pension funds	3	2	4	4
Mutual funds	2	3	4	3
Corporates	3	2	2	1
Other	1	0	1	1

*Monoline insurers and reinsures combined

Source: Mengle (2007), page 9.

mature up to 30 months after an event) to modified restructuring (covering debt obligations that mature up to 60 months after an event) and full restructuring (i.e., all debt restructurings), Fitch identifies three major rating regions: America and Oceania (modified restructuring), Europe and Africa (modified modified restructuring), and Asia (full restructuring).

Essentially, CDS implied rating systems use traditional rating grades (AAA, AA+, and so on) into which CDS spreads are mapped. The data is usually exponentially smoothed out over a window as long as a year, and then rating boundaries are fitted to the CDS smoothed data using a sum of squared differences fitting technique.

The implied ratings for any borrower can differ substantially from traditional ratings. Fitch has found that implied ratings lead traditional rating changes by one month in 64 percent of cases examined and by three months in 52 percent of cases. This can produce some drastic effects. For example, Evans (2007) shows that Moody's CDS implied ratings for MBIA during the early stages of the crisis were CAA1, whereas the firm has an AAA traditional rating, some 15 notches higher.

At this time it is hard to tell whether CDS implied ratings will come to replace traditional ratings. There are at least two reasons for this. First, they reflect overtly short-term investor sentiments that may result in short-term bubble effects in the ratings. Second, there have been concerns about the efficiency of the OTC CDS market and especially over the transparency of prices in the market. If the current Obama-Geithner Plan for CDS market reform gets adopted and CDSs have to be traded on organized exchanges, this may enhance the chances of implied ratings challenging the current dominance of traditional ratings.

SUMMARY

This chapter looks at the role that credit derivatives are playing in allowing banks to hedge the credit risk of their loan portfolios. The market has evolved so that the dominant credit derivatives are single-name credit default swaps (CDSs), multiname CDSs (particularly indexed CDSs), and tranched synthetic CDOs. However, there has been some retrenchment in these instruments in the wake of the global financial crisis of 2007–2009. Innovative solutions, such as auctions, have been devised to address problems such as the inadequate supply of debt instruments for physical delivery in the settlement of CDSs in a default event. Basel capital requirements have been amended to address the evolution of the CDS market.

APPENDIX 12.1: PRICING THE CDS SPREAD WITH COUNTERPARTY CREDIT RISK EXPOSURE

Observed CDS premia typically exceed credit spreads. However, a counter-vailing factor that reduces this differential by reducing swap premia is counterparty credit risk. That is, the protection buyer is exposed to possible default by the protection seller, particularly if the protection seller defaults at the same time as a credit event occurs. Since this possibility makes the CDS's credit protection less valuable, the swap premium will generally carry a counterparty credit charge that is deducted from the credit spread. This credit charge will depend on the counterparty's credit risk exposure as well as the correlation between the counterparty's PD and the reference entity's PD. The greater the counterparty credit charge, the lower the CDS premium is relative to the reference loan's credit spread.

Hull and White (2001) use a reduced form model to price CDS premia with counterparty credit risk. Table 12.9 shows that the CDS premium varies from 194.4 basis points for an AAA-rated counterparty uncorrelated to the reference entity's PD down to 145.2 basis points for a BBB-rated counterparty with a PD that has a correlation of 0.08 with the reference entity's PD.

Hull and White (2001) use an approximation of the reduced form model to estimate the CDS premium with counterparty default risk. If CS_0 is the CDS premium without counterparty default risk, then:

$$CS = CS_0(1 - g)/(1 - h) \qquad (12.5)$$

where CS = the CDS premium with counterparty credit risk

g = the proportional reduction in the present value of the expected payoff on the CDS to the buyer of credit protection arising from counterparty defaults

h = the proportional reduction in the present value of expected payments on the CDS to the seller of credit protection arising from counterparty defaults

Arbitrarily assuming that there is a 50 percent chance that the counterparty default occurs before or after the reference entity defaults, then:

$$g = 0.5\, P_{rc}/Q_r \qquad (12.6)$$

where P_{rc} = the joint probability of default by the counterparty and the reference entity between time 0 and the maturity date of the CDS

Q_r = the probability of default by the reference entity between time 0 and the maturity date of the CDS

TABLE 12.9 CDS Spreads for Different Counterparties

Correlation between the Counterparty and Reference Entity	Counterparty Credit Ratings			
	AAA	AA	A	BBB
0.0	194.4	194.4	194.4	194.4
0.2	191.6	190.7	189.3	186.6
0.4	188.1	186.2	182.7	176.7
0.6	184.2	180.8	174.5	163.5
0.8	181.3	176.0	164.7	145.2

Notes: CDS spreads are in basis points. The reference loan is BBB-rated, has a maturity of five years, and requires semiannual payments of 10 percent per annum with an expected recovery rate of 30 percent. Results are based on 500,000 Monte Carlo trials for each set of parameter values.

Source: Hull and White (2001).

Moreover, under the assumption of an equal 50 percent probability that either the counterparty or the reference entity defaults first, then the CDS premium payments to the credit protection seller are one-third less than in the no-counterparty default case, and:

$$h = (Q_c/2) - (P_{rc}/3) \tag{12.7}$$

where Q_c is the probability of default by the counterparty between time 0 and the maturity date of the CDS. Substituting equations (12.6) and (12.7) into (12.5) yields:

$$CS = CS_0(1 - .5P_{rc}/Q_r)/(1 - .5Q_c + .33P_{rc}) \tag{12.8}$$

Although equation (12.8) incorporates many simplifying assumptions, the estimates of the CDS premiums obtained are quite similar to those shown in Table 12.9. For example, when the correlation between the counterparty and the reference entity is 0.4 or less, then the analytic approximation in equation (12.8) yields estimates within 1.5 basis points of those obtained in Table 12.9 using 500,000 Monte Carlo simulations.

CHAPTER 13

Capital Regulation

INTRODUCTION

The 1988 Basel Capital Accord (Basel I) was revolutionary in that it sought to develop a single capital requirement for credit risk across the major banking countries of the world.[1,2] A major focus of Basel I was to distinguish the credit risk of sovereign, bank and mortgage obligations (accorded lower risk weights) from nonbank private sector or commercial loan obligations (accorded the highest risk weight). There was little or no attempt to differentiate the credit risk exposure within the commercial loan classification. All commercial loans implicitly required an 8 percent total capital requirement (Tier 1 plus Tier 2), regardless of the inherent creditworthiness of the borrower, its external credit rating, the collateral offered, or the covenants extended.[3,4] Since the capital requirement was set too low for high-risk/low-quality business loans and too high for low-risk/high-quality loans, the mispricing of commercial lending risk created an incentive for banks to shift portfolios toward those loans that were more underpriced from a regulatory risk capital perspective; for example, banks tended to retain the most risky tranches of securitized loan portfolios (see Jones [2000] for a discussion of these regulatory capital arbitrage activities). Thus, the 1988 Basel Capital Accord had the unintended consequence of encouraging a long-term deterioration in the overall credit quality of bank portfolios.[5]

The proposed goal of the new Basel Capital Accord (known as Basel II or BIS II) is to correct the mispricing inherent in Basel I (or BIS I) and incorporate more risk-sensitive credit exposure measures into bank capital requirements, without changing aggregate capital requirements.[6] However, the global financial crisis of 2007–2009 has prompted some rethinking of the Basel II proposals.[7]

THE 2006 BASEL II PLAN

The Basel Committee on Banking Supervision of the Bank for International Settlements (BIS) seeks to establish best practices in risk-based capital regulation by consulting with supervisors, practitioners and academics so as to propose plans for potential adoption by national bank regulators throughout the world. The final version of Basel II was proposed in June 2006 in order to address shortcomings in the original Basel I plan (adopted in 1992) and to enhance the risk sensitivity of capital requirements.[8] The Basel II framework consists of three pillars: (1) minimum capital requirements, (2) the supervisory review process, and (3) market discipline, as shown in Figure 13.1 Most of the details in the June 2006 proposals relate to pillar 1, whereas pillars 2 and 3 are generally left to the discretion of national bank regulators.

Pillar 1 of Basel II follows a three-step (potentially evolutionary) paradigm. Banks can choose among—or, for less sophisticated banks, are expected to evolve from—(1) the basic standardized approach, (2) the internal ratings-based model foundation approach, and (3) the internal ratings-based

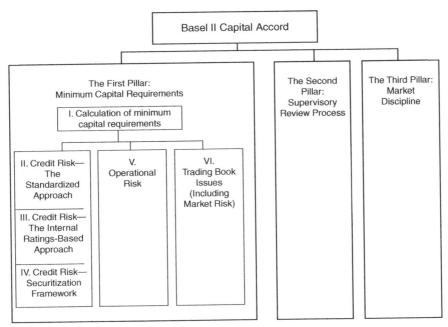

FIGURE 13.1   The Structure of the Basel II Capital Accords
Source: Bank for International Settlements, www.bis.org.

advanced approach. The standardized approach is based on external credit ratings assigned by independent ratings agencies (such as Moody's, Standard & Poor's and Fitch). Both internal ratings approaches require the bank to formulate and use its own internal ratings system based on the bank's own implementation of a credit risk measurement model. The risk weight assigned to each commercial obligation is based on the ratings assignment (either external or internal), so that higher (lower) rated, high (low) credit quality obligations have lower (higher) risk weights and therefore lower (higher) capital requirements, thereby mitigating the incentives to engage in risk shifting and regulatory arbitrage.

Whichever of the three models is chosen, the Basel II proposal requires that overall capital adequacy be measured as follows:[9]

$$
\begin{aligned}
\text{Regulatory total capital} = \ &\text{Credit risk capital requirement} \\
&+ \text{Market risk capital requirement} \\
&+ \text{Operational risk capital requirement}
\end{aligned}
$$

where

1. The credit risk capital requirement depends on the bank's choice of either the standardized or the internal ratings-based (foundation or advanced) approaches.
2. The market risk capital requirement depends on the bank's choice of either the standardized or the internal model approach (e.g., RiskMetrics, historical simulation or Monte Carlo simulation). This capital requirement was introduced in 1996 in the European Union and in 1998 in the United States.
3. An operational risk capital requirement depends on the bank's choice between a basic indicator approach, a standardized approach, and an advanced measurement approach (AMA).[10] While part of the 8 percent ratio under Basel I was viewed as capital allocated to absorb operational risk, the proposed new operational risk requirement aims to separate out operational risk from credit risk in order to better measure this risk. (See Chapter 6 of Allen et al. [2004] for a discussion of the operational risk component of Basel II.)

The Three Tiers of Capital Designations

Bank capital is divided into three classes: Tier 1, Tier 2, and Tier 3 (see Table 13.1).[11] Tier 1 capital is considered to be a higher form of capital than Tier 2, because it is composed of more patient, long-term funds that can serve as a cushion against losses. Residual claims are capital securities

TABLE 13.1 Definition of Qualifying Capital for Bank Holding Companies

Components	Minimum Requirements
Core capital (Tier 1)	Must equal or exceed 4 percent of weighted-risk assets
Common stockholders' equity	No limit
Qualifying cumulative and noncumulative perpetual preferred stock	Limited to 25 percent of the sum of common stock, minority interest, and qualifying perpetual preferred stock
Minority interest in equity accounts of consolidated subsidiaries	Organizations should avoid using minority interests to introduce elements not otherwise qualifying for Tier 1 capital
Less: Goodwill*	
Supplementary capital (Tier 2)	Total of Tier 2 is limited to 100 percent of Tier 1[†]
Allowance for loan and lease losses	Limited to 1.25 percent of weighted-risk assets
Nonqualifying perpetual preferred stock	No limit within Tier 2
Hybrid capital instruments, perpetual debt, and mandatory convertible securities	No limit within Tier 2
Subordinated debt and intermediate-term preferred stock (original weighted-average maturity of five years or more)	Subordinated debt and intermediate-term preferred stock are limited to 50 percent of Tier I; amortized for capital purposes as they approach maturity[†]
Revaluation reserves (equity and buildings)	Not included; organizations encouraged to disclose; may be evaluated on a case-by-case basis for international comparisons and taken into account in making an overall assessment of capital
Deductions (from sum of Tier 1 and Tier 2)	
Investments in unconsolidated subsidiaries	
Reciprocal holdings of banking organizations' capital securities	As a general rule, one-half of the aggregate investments would be deducted from Tier 1 capital and one-half from Tier 2 capital[‡]
Other deductions (such as other subsidiaries or joint ventures) as determined by supervisory authority	On a case-by-case basis or as a matter of policy after formal rule making
Total capital (Tier 1 + Tier 2 − Deductions)	Must equal or exceed 8 percent of weighted-risk assets

*Goodwill on the books of bank holding companies before March 12, 1988, would be grandfathered.
[†]Amounts in excess of limitations are permitted but do not qualify as capital.
[‡]A proportionately greater amount may be deducted from Tier 1 capital if the risks associated with the subsidiary so warrant.
Source: A. Saunders and M. Cornett, *Financial Institutions Management: A Risk Management Approach*, 6th ed. (Boston: McGraw-Hill Irwin, 2008), Table 20-6, page 600.

that receive cash flows only after all other claimants (creditors) are fully paid. The subordinated place in the priority structure of residual claimants gives them the capital-like feature. Thus, common stock is the purest form of capital (considered Tier 1) since equity holders are the very last in line to receive payment.

The Federal Reserve stress tests of 2009 (see Chapter 10) focused on Tier 1 capital in general, and tangible common stockholders' equity in particular.[12] That is, the Supervisory Capital Assessment Program's (SCAP) capital buffer required for each of the 19 banks that were required to take part in the stress test was a Tier 1 risk-based ratio of at least 6 percent and a Tier 1 common stock risk-based ratio of at least 4 percent.

Basel II's Standardized Model

The Standardized Model of credit risk measurement for pillar 1 of Basel II enhances the risk sensitivity of capital requirements by dividing the commercial obligor designation into gradations of risk classifications (risk buckets) dependent upon external credit ratings. Under the original Basel I system, all commercial loans were viewed as having the same credit risk (and thus the same risk weight).[13] Essentially, the book value of each loan was multiplied by a risk weight of 100 percent and then by 8 percent in order to generate the Tier 1 plus Tier 2 minimum capital requirement of 8 percent of risk-adjusted assets, the so-called 8 percent rule. Table 13.2 compares the risk weights for corporate obligations under the proposed new standardized model to the original Basel I risk weights. Under Basel II, the bank's assets are classified into each of the five risk buckets according to the credit rating assigned the obligor by independent rating agencies. In order to

TABLE 13.2 Total Capital Requirements on Corporate Obligations under the Standardized Model of BIS II

External Credit Rating	AAA to AA−	A+ to A−	BBB+ to BB−	Below BB−	Unrated
Risk weight under BIS II	20%	50%	100%	150%	100%
Capital requirement under BIS II	1.6%	4%	8%	12%	8%
Risk weight under BIS I	100%	100%	100%	100%	100%
Capital requirement under BIS I	8%	8%	8%	8%	8%

obtain the minimum capital requirement for credit risk purposes, all credit exposures (known as the exposure at default, EAD) in each risk weight bucket are summed up, weighted by the appropriate risk weight from Table 13.2, and then multiplied by the overall total capital requirement of 8 percent.[14]

The standardized approach takes into account credit risk mitigation by adjusting the transaction's EAD to reflect collateral, credit derivatives or guarantees, and offsetting on-balance-sheet netting. However, any collateral value is reduced by a haircut to adjust for the volatility of the instrument's market value. Moreover, a floor capital level assures that the credit quality of the borrower will always impact capital requirements. Such mitigation estimates based on the supposed market value of collateral have proven totally inadequate in the current crisis.

The risk weights for claims on sovereign countries and their central banks are shown in Table 13.3. The new weights allow for differentiation of credit risk within the classification of OECD nations. Under Basel I, all OECD nations carried preferential risk weights of 0 percent on their government obligations. Basel II levies a risk weight that depends on the sovereign country's external rating, not on its political affiliation.[15] However,

TABLE 13.3 Total Capital Requirements on Sovereigns under the Standardized Model of BIS II

External Credit Rating	AAA to AA– or ECA Rating 1	A+ to A– or ECA Rating 2	BBB+ to BBB– or ECA Rating 3	BB+ to B– or ECA Rating 4 to 6	Below B– or ECA Rating 7
Risk weight under BIS II	0%	20%	50%	100%	150%
Capital requirement under BIS II	0%	1.6%	4%	8%	12%

Notes: ECA denotes *export credit agency*. To qualify, the ECA must publish its risk scores and use the OECD methodology. If there are two different assessments by ECAs, then the higher risk weight is used. Sovereigns also have an unrated category with a 100 percent risk weight (not shown). Under BIS I, the risk weight for OECD government obligations is 0 percent. OECD interbank deposits and guaranteed claims, as well as some non-OECD bank and government deposits and securities, carry a 20 percent risk weight under BIS I. All other claims on non-OECD governments and banks carry a 100 percent risk weight under BIS I.

claims on the BIS, the IMF, the European Central Bank and the European Community all carry a 0 percent risk weight.

There are two options for standardized risk weighting of claims on banks and securities firms. Under option 1, all banks incorporated in a given country are assigned a risk weight one category less favorable than the sovereign country's risk weight. Thus, the risk weights for option 1 shown in Table 13.4 pertain to the *sovereign country's* risk weight. For example, a bank that is incorporated in a country with an AAA rating will have a 20 percent risk weight under option 1, resulting in a 1.6 percent capital requirement.[16] Option 2 uses the external credit rating of the bank itself to set the risk weight. Thus, the risk weights for option 2 shown in Table 13.4 pertain to the *bank's* credit rating. For example, a bank with an AAA rating receives a 20 percent risk weight (and a 1.6 percent capital requirement) no matter what the sovereign country's credit rating. Table 13.4 also shows that Basel II reduced the risk weights for all bank claims with original maturity of three months or less.[17] The choice of which option applies is left to national bank regulators and must be uniformly adopted for all banks in the country.

Assessment of the Standardized Model

Basel II is a step in the right direction in that it adds risk sensitivity to the regulatory treatment of capital requirements to absorb credit losses. However, Altman and Saunders (2001a, b) and the Institute of International

TABLE 13.4 Total Capital Requirements on Banks under the Standardized Model of Basel II

External Credit Rating	AAA to AA−	A+ to A−	BBB+ to BBB−	BB+ to B−	Below B−	Unrated
Risk weight under Basel II option 1	20%	50%	100%	100%	150%	100%
Capital requirement under Basel II option 1	1.6%	4%	8%	8%	12%	8%
Risk weight under Basel II option 2	20%	50%	50%	100%	150%	50%
Risk weight for short-term claims under Basel II option 2	20%	20%	20%	50%	150%	20%

Note: The capital requirements for option 2 can be calculated by multiplying the risk weight by the 8 percent capital requirement.

Finance (2000) find insufficient risk sensitivity in the proposed risk buckets of the standardized model, especially in the lowest-rated bucket for corporates (rated below BB-) which will require a risk weight three times greater than proposed under Basel II to cover unexpected losses, based on empirical evidence on corporate bond loss data.[18] By contrast, the risk weight in the first two corporate loan buckets may be too high. Indeed, Resti and Sironi (2007) use 7,232 Eurobonds issued during 1991–2003 and find that the risk weights under the standardized model are not sufficiently convex (steep). They advocate breaking the BBB+ to BB- risk class into two separate risk weights so as to increase risk sensitivity. Moreover, they find no difference in the relationship between ratings and bond spreads for financial and nonfinancial firms, and suggest that the differential risk weight schedules be eliminated.

The unrated risk bucket (of 100 percent) has also been criticized since the majority of obligations held by the world's banks are not rated (see Ferri et al. [2001]). For example, it is estimated that less than 1,000 European companies are rated, so the retention of an unrated risk bucket is a major lapse that threatens to undermine the risk sensitivity of Basel II.[19,20] Specifically, actual default data on nonrated loans puts them closer to the 150 percent bucket risk weight than the specified 100 percent risk weight. In addition, low-quality borrowers that anticipate receiving an external credit rating below BB- have an incentive to avoid independent rating agencies altogether, choosing to reduce their costs of borrowing by remaining unrated, but thereby reducing the availability of credit information available to the market.[21]

More fundamentally, however, basing capital requirements on external credit ratings is problematic if the ratings themselves are inaccurate and biased upward. As discussed in Chapter 1, credit ratings are lagging indicators that are beset with conflicts of interest stemming from the fact that the ratings agencies are dependent upon the issuers for a substantial share of their revenue.[22] In June 2009, the Basel Committee took note of (and expressed the concern of some regulatory authorities about) the ubiquitous use of credit ratings in the banking and securities sectors, as well as in the insurance industry. In addition to capital requirements, external credit ratings are used to classify assets so as to designate permissible activities, set asset concentration limits, determine risk and evaluate disclosure requirements.

As already noted, significant shortcomings of external credit ratings have become apparent during the global 2007–2009 financial crisis, as well as during the Enron and WorldCom debacles in 2001 and 2002 (see the discussion in Chapter 1). Since the obligors are free to choose their rating agency, moral hazard may lead rating agencies to shade their ratings upward in a bid to obtain business, thereby understating required capital levels. Moreover, since there is no single, universally accepted standard for credit ratings, they may not be comparable across rating agencies and across countries (see the discussions in White [2001], Cantor [2001], and Griep and De Stefano [2001]). This is likely to distort capital requirements more in less developed countries (LDC), because of greater volatility in LDC sovereign ratings, less transparent financial reporting in those countries, and the greater impact of the sovereign rating as a de facto ceiling for the private sector in LDCs.[23]

Finally, banks are also considered "delegated monitors" (see Diamond [1984] and the discussion in Chapter 1) who have a comparative advantage in assessing and monitoring the credit risks of their borrowers. Indeed, this function is viewed as making banks "special". This appears to be inconsistent with the concept underlying the standardized model, which essentially attributes this bank monitoring function to external rating agencies for the purposes of setting capital requirements. Adoption of this approach may well reduce banks' incentives to invest time and effort in monitoring, thereby reducing the availability of information and further undermining the value of the banking franchise. Indeed, the recent financial crisis resulted, in large part, from the failure of banks to perform their delegated monitoring and screening functions.

The Internal Ratings-Based Models for Credit Risk

Under the internal ratings-based (IRB) approach, each bank is required to establish an internal ratings model to classify the credit risk exposure of each activity (e.g., commercial lending, consumer lending, etc.), whether on or off the balance sheet. For the foundation IRB approach, the required outputs obtained from the internal ratings model are estimates of one year probability of default (PD) and exposure at default (EAD) for each transaction.[24] In addition to these estimates, independent estimates of both the loss given default (LGD) and maturity (M) are required to implement the advanced IRB approach.[25] The bank computes risk weights for each individual exposure (e.g., corporate loan) by incorporating its estimates of PD, EAD, LGD and M obtained from its internal ratings model and its own internal data systems. The model also assumes that the average default correlation among individual corporate borrowers, denoted R, is between 12 and 24 percent with the correlation specified as a decreasing function of PD.[26] Recent research by Moody's KMV, however, has shown that correlations appear to actually increase with PD.

Expected losses upon default (EL) can be calculated as follows:

$$EL = PD \times LGD$$

where PD is the probability of default and LGD is the loss given default.[27] However, this considers only one possible credit event—default—and ignores the possibility of losses resulting from credit rating downgrades. That is, deterioration in credit quality caused by increases in PD or LGD will cause the market value of the loan to fall even prior to default, thereby resulting in portfolio losses. Thus, credit risk measurement models can be differentiated on the basis of whether the definition of a *credit event* includes only default (the default mode or DM models) or whether it also includes nondefault credit quality deterioration (the mark-to-market or MTM models). The mark-to-market approach considers the impact of credit downgrades and upgrades on market value, whereas the default mode is only concerned about the economic value of an obligation in the event of default.

There are five elements to any IRB approach:

1. A classification of the obligation by credit risk exposure—the internal ratings model.
2. Internally calculated risk components—PD and EAD for the foundation model and PD, EAD, LGD, and M for the advanced model (other variables specified by the regulator, discussed later).
3. A risk weight function that uses the risk components to calculate the bank's capital for each credit exposure.
4. A set of minimum requirements of eligibility to apply the IRB approach—that is, demonstration that the bank maintains the necessary information systems to accurately implement the IRB approach.
5. Supervisory review of compliance with the minimum requirements.

The scope of the Basel II models encompasses internationally active banks on a consolidated basis. However, insurance subsidiaries owned by banks are not included in the general Basel II proposals for minimum capital requirements. Figure 13.2 shows how the capital accord is to be applied to large, complex financial institutions.

Using VAR in the Basel II IRB Capital Models

The conceptual underpinning for both IRB models is a VAR model used to solve for expected and unexpected losses. Figure 13.3 illustrates a possible loss distribution, used to estimate a VAR model, relating all possible values for security losses/gains to the probability of occurrence for each value (determined by the likelihood that a credit event will occur). In practice, however, loss distributions on loans are likely to be highly skewed. The area under the probability distribution of security losses must sum to one.

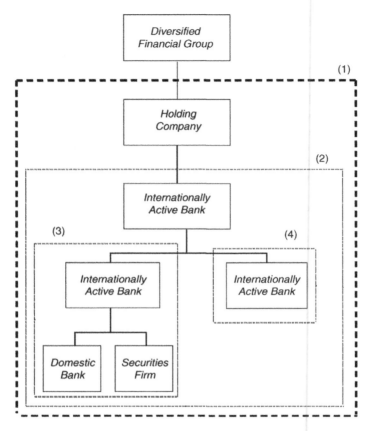

(1) Boundary of predominant banking group. The Framework is to be applied at this level on a consolidated basis, up to holding company level (paragraph 21).

(2), (3) and (4): The Framework is also to be applied at lower levels to all internationally active banks on a consolidated basis.

FIGURE 13.2 Illustration of New Scope of Application of This Framework
Source: Bank for International Settlements, www.bis.org.

For illustrative purposes the probability distribution in Figure 13.3 is assumed to be a normal distribution suggesting that losses/gains are symmetrically distributed around the mean value. Two important loss concepts are illustrated in Figure 13.3. Expected losses (EL) are estimated by the mean of the distribution, whereas unexpected losses (UL) are measured by the chosen percentile cut-off of extreme losses under adverse circumstances. If the loss percentile cut-off is set at 0.1 percent, or at the 99.9 percentile of the distribution (as in Basel II), then UL is the value that just marks off the

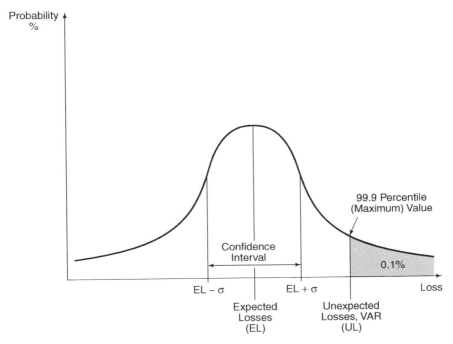

Probability
%

99.9 Percentile
(Maximum) Value

Confidence
Interval

0.1%

EL − σ

EL + σ

Loss

Expected
Losses
(EL)

Unexpected
Losses, VAR
(UL)

FIGURE 13.3 Normal Loss Distribution

shaded area in Figure 13.3 comprising 0.1 percent of the area under the entire loss distribution. That is, there is only 0.1 percent likelihood that losses will exceed UL, or a 99.9 percent chance that losses will be less than this amount. The standard deviation, denoted σ, is a commonly used measure of risk because it measures the loss dispersion around EL weighted by the likelihood of occurrence. For the normal distribution, there is approximately a 67 percent probability that losses will fall within the region from EL − σ to EL + σ, called the *confidence interval*.

The loss distribution shown in Figure 13.3 is normal. However, as noted earlier, most financial loss distributions for loans are skewed with fat tails; that is, there is a greater likelihood of extreme outcomes than implied by the normal distribution. Figure 13.4 shows a skewed loss distribution with the loss measures EL and UL. We can solve for the σ of the loss distribution in Figure 13.4, but since it is not normal, we cannot specify the likelihood that losses will fall within the EL − σ to EL + σ confidence interval unless we have information about the particular shape of the distribution— that is, its *skewness* (lack of symmetry) and its *kurtosis* (the probability of

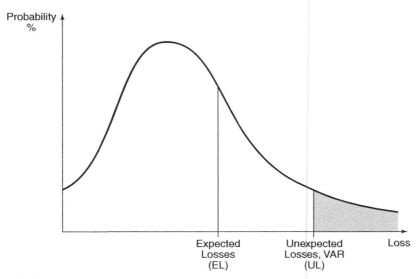

FIGURE 13.4   Skewed Loss Distribution

extreme loss outcomes). For simplicity, therefore, both foundation and advanced IRB models are based on normal distributions.

Figures 13.3 and 13.4 are loss distributions for individual security (loan) investments. However, diversification across different securities causes the risk of a portfolio to be lower than the risk of individual security investments. As noted in Chapter 8, the lower the correlation between pairs of securities, the greater the benefits of diversification in reducing the risk of the portfolio. The correlation coefficient measures the co-movement between pairs of securities on a scale of -1 to $+1$; a correlation coefficient of -1 for perfectly negatively correlated securities (the securities' values move in exactly opposite directions), 0 for uncorrelated, and $+1$ for perfectly positively correlated (the securities' values move together in lockstep). Most securities are positively correlated (thereby preventing the elimination of risk through simple portfolio creation), but not perfectly positively correlated (thereby providing substantial benefits to diversification).

Using this conceptual framework, the 99.9 percentile VAR for a specific asset (e.g., a bank loan) can be stated as

$$VAR_{loan} = EL_{loan} + UL_{loan}$$

The expected loss (EL) on the loan determines the loan loss reserves for such losses. The unexpected loss (UL) protects the financial institution (FI) against unexpected losses, beyond those that are expected. Capital reserves are determined by the level of UL.[28] The sum of loan loss reserves and capital reserves should, therefore, be sufficient to protect the FI from failure (i. e., losses exceeding the sum of the two reserves held by the FI) in all but one year in 1,000, or 99.9 percent of the time. Thus, the capital reserves (UL) can be viewed as the VAR_{loan} minus EL_{loan}. We can rewrite the expression for capital reserves using two definitions: (1) $EL_{loan} = PD \times LGD$, where PD is the expected probability of default under average economic conditions and LGD is the (assumed constant) loss given default, and (2) $UL_{loan} = PD_A \times LGD$, where PD_A is defined to be the probability of default under adverse economic conditions (which reflects in part the current normal PD and the worst year in 1,000-years PD, weighted by the correlation factor R).[29] Thus, the expression for capital reserves (UL) can be rewritten as:

$$\text{Capital reserves}_{loan} = VAR_{loan} - EL_{loan} = (LGD \times PD_A) - (LGD \times PD) \tag{13.1}$$

Under Basel II, the 99.9 percentile VAR for an asset such as a loan is calculated as follows:[30]

$$VAR_{loan} = LGD \times N\left[\frac{G(PD) - RG(0.999)}{(1-R)^{0.5}}\right] \tag{13.2}$$

where $N(\cdot)$ is an area under the standard normal distribution, and $G(\cdot)$ is the inverse of the area under the standard normal distribution. That is, given any PD, it reflects the number of standard deviations with which assets have to decline from their mean value to reach that PD. For example, if PD = 1 percent, then assets would have to decline by 2.33σ from their mean to reach this level. In this case $G(.01) = 2.33\sigma$.

In equation (13.2), R is the loan's default risk correlation, expressed as follows:

$$R = \frac{0.12(1 - e^{-50PD})}{1 - e^{-50}} + 0.12\left[1 - \frac{1 - e^{-50PD}}{1 - e^{-50}}\right]$$

The correlation (R) is assumed to be inversely related to the PD on the loan.[31] Substituting equation (13.2) into equation (13.1) yields equation (13.3):

$$\text{Capital reserves}_{loan} = LGD \times N\left[\frac{G(PD) - RG(0.999)}{(1-R)^{0.5}}\right] - (LGD \times PD) \tag{13.3}$$

where $LGD \times PD = EL$

Since it has been shown that the longer the maturity of the loan, the more likely it is to default, the Basel II IRB model requires that the basic amount of capital computed in equation (13.3) be multiplied by a maturity adjustment factor denoted b derived as follows:

$$b = [0.11852 - 0.05478 \times \ln(\text{PD})]^2 \tag{13.4}$$

Intuitively, b is similar to the slope of a regression line, reflecting the degree to which the default risk increases with the maturity of the loan.

If we now put together the maturity adjustment factor, the expression of the correlation (R), and the basic capital requirement expression, we obtain the full Basel II capital requirement (k) per dollar of credit exposure under the June 2006 proposals of the foundation and advanced IRB models as:

$$k = \left[\text{LGD} \times \text{N} \left(\frac{\text{G(PD)}}{(1-R)^{0.5}} + \frac{\text{G(0.999)}R}{(1-R)^{0.5}} \right) - \text{PD} \times \text{LGD} \right] \times \left\{ \frac{1 + (\text{M} - 2.5)b}{1 - 1.5b} \right\}$$

Where R is the correlation and b the maturity defined above. Note that the term in the first squared bracket can also be written as in equation (13.2) $-\text{PD} \times \text{LGD}$.

This formula shows the amount of required capital (k) per dollar of loans to a given corporate borrower. The dollar amount of capital required for a loan of a particular exposure size would be:

$$\text{Dollar capital requirement} = k \times \text{EAD}$$

where EAD is exposure at default, the net dollar amount of the loan outstanding (adjusted for collateral) at the time of default.

Alternatively, since the Basel II model is calibrated to achieve an overall 8 percent capital requirement, we can compare the actual capital being held against the loan with the required amount (8 percent target). This can be done by computing the amount of risk-weighted assets that the regulatory required capital can support (so as to just meet the 8 percent target). This would be:

$$\text{Risk-weighted assets (RWA)} = k \times 12.5 \times \text{EAD}$$

where 12.5 is the asset multiplier for an 8 percent capital ratio (i.e., $1/.08 = 12.5$).

The issue for capital adequacy is whether

$$\text{Actual capital/RWA} \geq 8\%$$

where actual capital reflects the amount of Tier 1 plus Tier 2 capital currently held by the FI against an unexpected loss on the loan; that is, $k_{actual} \times EAD$.

Thus, the capital adequacy test is whether

$$\frac{\text{Actual capital}}{\text{RWA}} = \frac{k_{\text{actual}} \text{EAD}}{12.5 \times k \times \text{EAD}} = \frac{k_{\text{actual}}}{12.5k} \geq 8\%$$

where k is the required regulatory capital determined earlier.

Clearly, if $k_{actual} = k$, then the 8 percent target is reached; that is,

$$\frac{k_{actual}}{12.5k} = 8\%$$

If k_{actual} equals k, the ks cancel out, leaving $1/12.5 = .08$ or 8 percent. If k_{actual} is greater than k, then the 8 percent minimum target is exceeded, and if k_{actual} is less than k, then the FI will be capital deficient. In this latter situation, the FI would have to either cut back its loans or increase its capital.

There are adjustments to the IRB model's capital requirement previously illustrated for retail exposures and residential mortgages. Table 13.5 shows the different risk weights for exposures to businesses, residential mortgages, retail borrowers and revolving retail accounts.

Comparison of the Foundation and Advanced IRB Models

Loss Given Default From a practical standpoint, the major factor differentiating the foundation from the advanced IRB model is the determination of the loss given default, LGD. Under the foundation approach, the LGD is specified by the regulator, which for senior uncollateralized claims (such as loans) on businesses, sovereigns, and banks is 45 percent. For subordinated claims, the foundation IRB model stipulates a 75 percent LGD. Sophisticated banks are encouraged to move from the foundation to the advanced approach. A primary source for this incentive is the result of the use of the bank's *actual* LGD experience in place of the foundation model's fixed assumption of a 45 or 75 percent LGD. Historical evidence prior to the current crisis suggests that the LGD for bank loans is significantly lower than these loss rates and therefore the shift to the advanced approach is expected to reduce bank capital requirements by 2 to 3 percent; see the discussion in Chapter 7.[32]

However, the quid pro quo for permission to use actual LGD is compliance with an additional set of minimum requirements attesting to the

TABLE 13.5 Illustrative IRB Risk Weights for Unexpected Losses

Asset Class (Maturity: 2.5 years)	Corporate Exposures		Residential Mortgages		Other Retail Exposures		Qualifying Revolving Retail Exposure	
LGD	(Big) 45%	(SME) 45%	45%	25%	45%	85%	45%	85%
PD:								
0.03%	14.44%	11.30%	4.15%	2.30%	4.45%	8.41%	0.98%	1.85%
0.05%	19.65%	15.39%	6.23%	3.46%	6.63%	12.52%	1.51%	2.86%
0.10%	29.65%	23.30%	10.69%	5.94%	11.16%	21.08%	2.71%	5.12%
0.25%	49.47%	39.01%	21.30%	11.83%	21.15%	39.96%	5.76%	10.88%
0.40%	62.72%	49.49%	29.94%	16.64%	28.42%	53.69%	8.41%	15.88%
0.50%	69.61%	54.91%	35.08%	19.49%	32.36%	61.13%	10.04%	18.97%
0.75%	82.78%	65.14%	46.46%	25.81%	40.10%	75.74%	13.80%	26.06%
1.00%	92.32%	72.40%	56.40%	31.33%	45.77%	86.46%	17.22%	32.53%
1.30%	100.95%	78.77%	67.00%	37.22%	50.80%	95.95%	21.02%	39.70%
1.50%	105.59%	82.11%	73.45%	40.80%	53.37%	100.81%	23.40%	44.19%
2.00%	114,86%	88.55%	87.95%	48.85%	57.99%	109.81%	28.92%	54.63%
2.50%	122.16%	93.43%	100.64%	55.91%	60.90%	115.03%	33.98%	64.18%
3.00%	128.44%	97.58%	111.99%	62.22%	62.79%	118.61%	38.66%	73.03%
4.00%	139.58%	105.04%	131.63%	73.13%	65.01%	122.80%	47.16%	89.08%

efficacy of the bank's information systems in maintaining data on LGD and updating these data over a seven-year back-casting window. Clearly, under the current crisis, the down or adverse condition LGD estimates will rise substantially.

Maturity   Another adjustment to the foundation approach's capital requirement for FIs using the advanced IRB model is the incorporation of a maturity adjustment factor reflecting the transaction's effective maturity rather than the stipulated maturity. The foundations model sets effective maturity M at 2.5 years for all loans. The advanced IRB model stipulates that the maturity measure is the greater of either one year or actual effective maturity, which is the weighted average life:

$$\Sigma_t \, tP_t / \Sigma_t P_t$$

where P_t = the minimum amount of principal contractually payable at time t, for all instruments with a predetermined, minimum amortization schedule. The maturity is capped at seven years in order to avoid overstating the impact of maturity on credit risk exposure.

Probability of Default   For both the foundations and advanced models, the PD has to be based on historic-based loan ratings systems with a minimum of six categories and PD-associated estimates based on five years of historic data.

A full discussion of loan rating systems can be found in Appendix 13.1.

Exposure at Default   Under the IRB model, both the foundation model and the advanced model allow a bank to calculate the individual exposure at default (EAD) for each loan that takes into account netting, collateral, and other offsets.

Correlation   A crucial misconception about the IRB model relates to the correlation factor (R). The factor R is a measure of a loan's systematic risk vis-à-vis a single factor (implicitly a measure of economic/market performance). As such, it is more akin to the beta (β) for the single-factor capital asset pricing model (CAPM) rather than a correlation (ρ) across loans in the loan portfolio that may well reflect high concentration risk in the loan portfolio.

The Basel II model specifies an explicit functional equation for R that is to be applied to each individual loan and cannot be self-determined by even the most sophisticated banks. As specified, R lies between 12 percent and 24 percent, suggesting a low degree of correlation in the context of a single-factor model, and the value of R varies inversely with PD. That is, the higher the R, the lower the PD. This implies that high-default-risk borrowers will have relatively low R values and, ceteris paribus, lower capital requirements. The key assumption here is that most loan defaults occur because of a borrower's unsystematic risk due to factors such as poor management, poor product choice, and so on. As noted earlier, there is considerable empirical evidence that suggests the opposite—that is, R and PD should be positively related. Clearly, this issue is highly contentious given the rise in default rates during the current crisis. Indeed, future research is needed to see what proportion of corporate defaults over the 2007–2009 period were due to systematic risk rather than unsystematic risk factors.

Summary In sum, the IRB model foundations approach allows banks to input two of the five factors that drive the dollar amount of capital required by qualifying banks (i.e., PD and EAD) while the advanced model allows banks to input four of the five factors (PD, EAD, M, and LGD). Under both approaches, R is set by bank regulators.

The advanced IRB approach entails the estimation of parameters requiring long histories of data that are unavailable to most banks. Given the costs of developing these models and databases, there is the possibility of dichotomizing the banking industry into haves and have-nots. For example, some anecdotal estimates suggest that no more than 15 U.S. banks' ratings systems meet the criteria to qualify to use either of the IRB approaches. Moreover, capital requirements are highly sensitive to the accuracy of certain input values; in particular, estimates of LGD and the granularity in PD are important (see Gordy [2000] and Carey [2000]).[33] Since credit losses are affected by economic conditions, the model parameters should also be adjusted to reflect expected levels of economic activity. Many of these assumptions will have to be revised in light of experiences during the 2007–2009 crisis. Thus, the data requirements are so substantial that full implementation of the advanced IRB approach may be difficult even for the most sophisticated banks. Similarly, regulators have commensurate challenges in obtaining the necessary data to validate the banks' models.

Assessment of the IRB Models

The IRB models of Basel II are a potential improvement over Basel I and the standardized model of Basel II in terms of sophistication in measuring credit risk. Moreover, the IRB approaches move regulatory capital in the direction of economic capital and VAR measures of risk. However, they are far from an integrated portfolio management approach to credit risk measurement. Focus on individual ratings classifications (whether using external credit ratings under the standardized model or internal risk scoring models under

IRB) prevents an aggregated view of credit risk across all transactions, with regulatory concerns about systemic risk, as reflected in the systematic risk correlation (R), preventing full consideration of cross-asset correlations. Thus, capital requirements are likely to be lower than economically necessary when considering actual portfolio correlations or concentrations.[34]

Moreover, incompatible approaches to assessing the capital adequacy of insurance companies and other nonbanking firms may obscure their impact on financial system stability. In the United States and Europe, the insurance industry, the securities industry, and government-sponsored enterprises (such as Fannie Mae and Freddie Mac) all use a variety of models, ranging from minimum ratios, to stress test survivorship requirements, to dynamic risk-of-ruin scenario analysis that includes both the asset and liability sides of the balance sheet, in order to measure capital requirements for these instructions. All of these have been found to be lacking during the recent crisis.

Basel II is based on a prespecified threshold insolvency level. That is, capital levels are set so that the estimated probability of insolvency of each bank is lower than a threshold level such as 99.9 percent (i.e., 0.1 percent probability of failure per year, or one bank insolvency every 1,000 years).[35] However, there are two potential shortcomings to this approach from the regulator's point of view. First, without considering the relationship between individual banks' insolvency probabilities, Basel II cannot specify an aggregate, systemwide insolvency risk threshold; see, for example, Acharya (2001). Second, there is no information about the magnitude of loss given bank insolvency. The deposit insurer, for example, may be concerned about the cost to the deposit insurance fund in the event that the bank's capital is exhausted and a bank has to be liquidated under adverse conditions. (See Gordy [2000] for a discussion of the estimation of the "expected tail loss.") Basel II addresses neither of these concerns. However, there is evidence that banks hold capital in excess of the regulatory minimum in response to market pressure. For example, in order to participate in the swap market, the bank's credit quality must be higher than would be induced by complying with either Basel I or II.[36] Thus, regulatory capital requirements may be considered lower bounds that do not obviate the need for more precise credit risk measurement.

Adoption of Basel II throughout the World

The EU and Basel Committee member states (Belgium, Canada, France, Germany, Italy, Japan, Luxembourg, the Netherlands, Spain, Sweden, Switzerland, the United Kingdom and the United States) adopted the full Basel II accord for implementation as of the end of 2007. Although U.S. bank regulators were at the forefront of designing Basel II, U.S.

regulators initially decided not to adopt the regulations for the vast majority of the banks in the United States. That is, on December 7, 2007, U.S. bank regulators announced that banks with more than $250 billion in assets or at least $10 billion of on-balance-sheet foreign exposures would be required to use the advanced IRB approach.[37] Only if a bank met "substantial risk measurement and management infrastructure requirements" would it be permitted to opt into the advanced IRB model (Board of Governors [2007]). All other banks could adopt the standardized model of Basel II, if they so chose. Otherwise, they would remain under the Basel I requirements.

Concerns were expressed about the bifurcation of U.S. bank capital regulations. U.S. bank regulators pointed to a proposal (advanced in December 2006) to create a more risk-sensitive version of Basel I (dubbed Basel IA) that would increase the number of risk weights, use loan-to-value (LTV) ratios to risk-weight residential mortgages, and recognize the role of collateral and guarantors, among other proposals. However, in July 2008, U.S. bank regulators decided not to adopt Basel IA, and instead apply the standardized model of Basel II to U.S. banks on the grounds that this would harmonize international bank capital requirements.[38] Thus, U.S. bank regulators essentially chose to adopt Basel II, with an exception relating to residential mortgages. In doing so, U.S. bank regulators implicitly chose to replace the standardized model with Basel IA for residential mortgages, thereby applying an LTV test to determine the loan's risk weight. In the United States, therefore, first (junior) lien mortgages have risk weights ranging from 20 percent (75 percent) to 150 percent, depending upon whether the LTV is less than 60 percent or greater than 95 percent (90 percent).[39]

U.S. bank regulators also chose to maintain a supplementary capital requirement: the traditional leverage requirement, which requires well-capitalized banks to maintain at least a 5 percent ratio of Tier 1 capital to total non-risk-weighted, on-balance-sheet assets. Gilbert (2006) describes how the maintenance of the leverage requirement is essential to mitigate competitive pressures if the United States does not adopt Basel II for all banks. Since Basel II adoption is expected to reduce capital requirements on individual institutions (see Powell [2005]) and since capital is the bank's most costly source of funds, non-adopting banks would be at a competitive disadvantage vis-à-vis banks that adopted Basel II, particularly the advanced IRB model.

Because of concerns about reduced capital protection, U.S. regulators adopted a transitional period which restricts a bank's capital requirement from falling below 95 percent, 90 percent, and 85 percent of the bank's Basel II transitional first, second, and third floor periods, scheduled to begin in 2010, at the earliest at the very largest U.S. bank organizations such as J.P. Morgan Chase. Moreover, the financial crisis of 2007–2009 led U.S. bank regulators to impose additional capital requirements based on Tier 1 and tangible capital (leverage) ratio on the largest 19 U.S. banks that were required to participate in the stress tests conducted during February–March 2009 (see the discussion in Chapter 10). Philipp Hildebrand (2008) has, like many regulators, described the importance of a leverage ratio in addition to the Basel II capital requirement. His arguments are that bank regulators must control bank leverage, since high leverage has made the global banking system fragile and prone to repeated crises, and that the two largest Swiss banks (UBS and Credit Suisse) were among the most highly capitalized banks in the world (according to Basel capital standards), but were among the worst capitalized in terms of the leverage ratio.

Nevertheless, one of the shortcomings of a simple leverage ratio capital requirement is that it fails to consider off-balance-sheet positions. As discussed in Chapter 1, off-balance-sheet activity was the primary mechanism for excessive risk taking during the period preceding the global crisis of 2007–2009.[40] Moreover, leverage ratios are highly procyclical, thereby exacerbating business cycles. Finally, they can be distorted by the inclusion of preferred stock and other nonstandard types of real capital, such as common equity and retained earnings. There has been discussion of a countercyclical capital requirement that would automatically increase capital requirements in good times and decrease them in bad times. The intuition is simple. In good times, banks have retained profits and access to the equity market, which allows them to build up excess capital reserves. By contrast, in bad times, profits disappear and banks' access to the equity market might be limited. These proposals have not been put into practice, with the possible exception of Spain.[41] Heid (2007) argues that the capital buffer held over and above the minimum capital requirement would play an important role in mitigating the volatility and procyclicality inherent in capital regulations under Basel I, but will exacerbate procyclicality under Basel II. That is, under Basel I, banks cut back on their capital buffer during economic downturns due to reduced lending, but under Basel II the increased risk weights overcompensate for the reduction in lending and lead to an increase in the capital buffer during downturns, thereby exacerbating procyclicality.

Because of concerns about procyclicality and fear of exacerbating economic distress, there has been a consensus agreement among the Basel Committee not to raise capital requirements during the ongoing global banking crisis of 2007–2009. The focus instead has been toward the *composition* rather than the *quantity* of bank capital. That is, innovations in capital markets have led to the inclusion in bank capital (both Tier 1 and 2) of hybrid instruments (such as auction-rate preferred stock). The June 2009 Obama-Geithner Plan (see Chapter 3) calls for the Basel Committee to harmonize the definition of bank capital, improve regulatory procedures for measurement of the risk of the trading book and securitization exposures, and implement a "simple, transparent, non-model based measure of leverage, as recommended by the G-20 Leaders."[42] Finally, the Obama-Geithner Plan calls for proposals to mitigate the procyclicality of capital requirements so that capital buffers would be required during good economic periods, so as to build an excess capital reserve to support adequate capital during economic downturns.

An innovative proposal to accomplish this has been put forth in Kashyap, Rajan, and Stein (2008). They compare a fixed capital standard to requiring a homeowner to hold a fixed fraction of the house value in a savings account without permitting any expenditure from the account to repair the house when it is damaged in a storm. They advocate a countercyclical capital standard on a marketwide basis. Instead of requiring the banks to hold additional capital in good times, they suggest the creation of a systemic risk insurance policy provided by sovereign wealth funds, pension funds, or market investors to supplement traditional bank capital. These investors would place, say, $10 billion into a "lock box," in exchange for a premium paid by the bank. The insurance policy would pay off only if the overall banking sector is in crisis. Otherwise, the insurers would receive their money back plus the premium. To avoid manipulation and moral hazard concerns, the crisis payout would be equal to the losses of all other banks except the covered bank. Only large, systemically important banks would participate. Although there are many difficulties with this plan (not the least of which are the incentives for herding behavior that may exacerbate banking crises, and whether nonbanks could ever collectively build a sufficiently large fund to be a credible tool in a crisis), the proposal has the potential of using a market solution to recapitalize the banking system during a crisis without incurring the regulatory policy costs and deadweight losses associated with fire sale liquidation of bank portfolios.

SUMMARY

The Basel Accord on bank capital (Basel II) makes capital requirements more sensitive to credit risk exposure. Regulations governing minimum capital requirements allow the bank to evolve through three steps: (1) the standardized model, (2) the internal ratings-based (IRB) foundation approach, and (3) the advanced IRB approach. In the standardized model, credit risk weights are determined using external ratings assigned by independent credit rating agencies. For commercial loans, there are four risk buckets (plus an unrated classification) corresponding to prespecified corporate credit ratings.

The IRB approaches require banks to formulate their own internal ratings models in order to classify the credit risk of their activities. The foundation approach requires that the bank estimate only the probability of default (PD) and the exposure at default (EAD). There are two additional parameter estimates required to implement the advanced approach: the loss given default (LGD) and the maturity (M). Basel II requires supervisors to validate the internal models developed by the banks, in conjunction with enhanced disclosure requirements that reveal more detailed credit risk information to the market.

APPENDIX 13.1 LOAN RATING SYSTEMS

One of the oldest rating systems for loans was developed by the U.S. Office of the Comptroller of the Currency (OCC). The system has been used in the United States and abroad by regulators and bankers to assess the adequacy of their loan loss reserves. The OCC rating systems places an existing loan portfolio into five categories: four low-quality ratings and one high-quality rating. In Table 13.6 the minimum required loss reserve appears next to each category.

In the United States, the National Association of Insurance Commissioners (NAIC) utilizes a six-grade regulatory classification scheme, as shown in Table 13.7. NAIC regulatory ratings have been used to assess capital requirements for U.S. insurance companies since the mid-1990s. Insurance companies' internal ratings, as examined by Carey (2001a) for private

TABLE 13.6 Loss Reserves

	Percent
Low-quality ratings:	
Other assets especially mentioned (OAEM)	0
Substandard assets	20
Doubtful assets	50
Loss assets	100
High-quality rating:	
Pass/performing	0

Note: Technically speaking, the 0 percent loss reserves for OAEM and pass loans are lower bounds. In practice, the reserve rates on these categories are determined by the bank in consultation with examiners, depending on some type of historical analysis of charge-off rates for the bank.

TABLE 13.7 NAIC Ratings

NAIC Ratings	Rating Agency Equivalent	Insurance Company Internal Ratings	Required Capital for Life Insurance Companies
1	AAA, AA, A	1, 2, 3	0.3%
2	BBB	4	1.0
3	BB	5	4.0
4	B	6	9.0
5	Less than B	7	20.0
6	Default	7	30.0
Cash and U.S. government bonds		1	0.0
Residential mortgages			0.5
Commercial mortgages			3.0
Common stock			30.0
Preferred stock			NAIC Rating Capital Factor Plus 2.0

Source: Carey (2001a), Kupiec et al. (2001). The factors are multiplied by the book value of the life insurance company's year-end principal balances in each NAIC rating category in order to calculate the preliminary dollar capital requirement.

placements, are highly consistent with the external regulatory ratings. They are consistent in 76.1 percent of the cases and vary by one grade or less in 96.7 percent of the cases. Moreover, internal ratings of debt (bonds) are highly consistent across insurance companies. There is complete correspondence in 64.2 percent of the cases and variation by one grade or less in 90.5 percent of the cases. However, Carey (2001a) finds less consistency across insurance company internal ratings for below-investment-grade debt. That is, when one insurance company rates an obligation as BB or lower, other insurance companies holding the loan assign the same rating in only 37 percent of the cases. This inconsistency is potentially damaging to the case for internal ratings models at banks because, whereas only 13 percent of the private placements at insurance companies were below investment grade, typically more than 50 percent of large bank portfolios were below investment grade as of year-end 1997 (see Treacy and Carey [2000]).

Internal Ratings at Banks

Over the years, bankers have extended the OCC ratings systems by developing internal rating systems that subdivide the pass/performing rating category in more detail. For example, at any given moment, there is always a chance that some pass or performing loans will go into default, and that some reserves, even if very low, should be held against these loans. Currently, it is estimated that a majority of U.S. bank holding companies have developed internal rating systems for loans on a 1 to 9 or 1 to 10 scale, including the top 50 FIs in the United States. An example of a 1 to 10 loan rating system and its mapping into equivalent bond ratings is shown in Table 13.8 (and also earlier, in Chapter 4, as Table 4.1).

In Table 13.8 the OCC pass grade is divided into six different categories (ratings 1 to 6). Ratings 7 to 10 correspond to the OCC's four low-quality loan ratings. These loan rating systems do not exactly map into bond rating systems, especially at the lower-quality end. One reason is that bond rating systems are supposed to rate an individual loan (including its covenants and collateral backing), whereas loan rating systems are more oriented to rating the overall borrower. This lack of one-to-one mapping between bond ratings and loan ratings raises a flag as to (1) the merits of newer models that rely on bond data to value loans, and (2) the proposed new standardized model of the Basel II capital requirements that ties capital requirements to external ratings.

Treacy and Carey (2000), in their survey of the 50 largest U.S. bank holding companies, and the BIS (2000) survey of 30 FIs across the G-10 countries find considerable diversity in internal ratings models. Although all the FIs used similar financial risk factors, there were differences across FIs with regard to the relative importance of each of the factors, as well as the weight assigned to statistically based processes according to expert judgment. Treacy and Carey (2000) find that qualitative factors played a greater role in determining the ratings of loans to small and medium-size firms when the loan officer was chiefly responsible for the ratings. This finding does not apply to loans to large firms, in which the credit staff primarily sets the ratings, using quantitative methods such as credit scoring models. Typically, ratings were set with a one-year time horizon, although data were often available for three to five years.

The architecture of the internal rating system can be one-dimensional (an overall rating is assigned to each loan) or two-dimensional; in the latter, each borrower's overall creditworthiness (the probability of default, PD) is assessed separately from the loss severity of the individual loan (the loss given default, LGD, taking into account any collateral or guarantees). Treacy and Carey (2000), who recommend a two-dimensional rating

TABLE 13.8   An Example of a Loan Rating System and Bond Rating Mapping

Bond Rating	Score	Risk Level	Description
AAA	1	Minimal	Excellent business credit, superior asset quality, excellent debt capacity and coverage; excellent management with depth. Company is a market leader and has access to capital markets.
AA	2	Modest	Good business credit, very good asset quality and liquidity, strong debt capacity and coverage, very good management in all positions. Company is highly regarded in industry and has a very strong market share.
A	3	Average	Average business credit, within normal credit standards: satisfactory asset quality and liquidity, good debt capacity and coverage; good management in all critical positions. Company is of average size and position within the industry.
BBB	4	Acceptable	Acceptable business credit, but with more than average risk: acceptable asset quality, little excess liquidity, modest debt capacity. May be highly or fully leveraged. Requires above-average levels of supervision and attention from lender. Company is not strong enough to sustain major setbacks. Loans are highly leveraged transactions due to regulatory constraints.
BB	5	Acceptable with care	Acceptable business credit, but with considerable risk: acceptable asset quality, smaller and/or less diverse asset base, very little liquidity, limited debt capacity. Covenants structured to ensure adequate protection. May be highly or fully leveraged. May be of below-average size or a lower-tier competitor. Requires significant supervision and attention from lender. Company is not strong enough to sustain major setbacks. Loans are highly leveraged transactions due to the obligor's financial status.
B	6	Management attention	Watch list credit: generally acceptable asset quality, somewhat strained liquidity, fully leveraged. Some management weakness.

TABLE 13.8 (*Continued*)

Bond Rating	Score	Risk Level	Description
			Requires continual supervision and attention from lender.
CCC	7	Special mention (OAEM)	Marginally acceptable business credit; some weakness. Generally undesirable business constituting an undue and unwarranted credit risk but not to the point of justifying a substandard classification. Although the asset is currently protected, it is potentially weak. No loss of principal or interest is envisioned. Potential weaknesses might include a weakening financial condition; an unrealistic repayment program; inadequate sources of funds; or lack of adequate collateral, credit information, or documentation. Company is undistinguished and mediocre.
CC	8	Substandard	Unacceptable business credit; normal repayment in jeopardy. Although no loss of principal or interest is envisioned, a positive and well-defined weakness jeopardizes collection of debt. The asset is inadequately protected by the current sound net worth and paying capacity of the obligor or pledged collateral. There may already have been a partial loss of interest.
C	9	Doubtful	Full repayment questionable. Serious problems exist to the point where a partial loss of principal is likely. Weaknesses are so pronounced that, on the basis of current information, conditions, and values, collection in full is highly improbable.
D	10	Loss	Expected total loss. An uncollectible asset or one of such little value that it does not warrant classification as an active asset. Such an asset may, however, have recovery or salvage value, but not to the point where a write-off should be deferred, even though a partial recovery may occur in the future.

system, estimate that 60 percent of the FIs in their survey had one-dimensional systems. Moreover, BIS (2000) finds that banks are better able to assess the PD of their borrowers relative to estimating LGD.

More banks can be expected to adopt internal ratings systems in response to the incentives built into the proposed new Basel Capital Accord. Therefore, some words of caution are in order. Adoption of internal ratings for the purpose of assessing regulatory capital requirements has the potential to distort the integrity of the rating system, especially if banks view capital as costly and wish to minimize that cost. Supervisors will have to validate the accuracy of a wide variety of internal ratings (see the discussion on stress testing and back-testing in Chapter 10). Moreover, reliance on internal ratings raises concerns about (1) the ongoing integrity of each system; (2) the consistency and comparability of the ratings, particularly across national boundaries; and (3) the evolution and disclosure of best-practices methods that become international standards. (See Griep and De Stefano [2001].)

Notes

CHAPTER 1   Setting the Stage for Financial Meltdown

1. Bank of England, *Financial Stability Report* no. 22, October 2007, 32.
2. Collateralized debt obligations (CDOs) are securities created by pooling asset-backed securities (ABSs), mortgage-backed securities (MBSs) such as collateralized mortgage obligations (CMOs), loans, and corporate bonds, and dividing the pool's promised income into tranches that are distinguished by risk and return. Collateralized loan obligations (CLOs) are CDOs predominantly backed by leveraged bank loans. Synthetic CDOs obtain the credit risk on an underlying portfolio of credit instruments using pools of credit default swaps, rather than owning the underlying cash assets.
3. The arranger purchases the assets to be placed in the pool, obtains the credit rating, structures the deals, files with the SEC, and underwrites the asset-backed securities to be issued by the SPV. Thus, the arranger must fund the loans over the period (typically three months or less) after origination and before the asset-backed securities are issued. Bank arrangers use their own funds to finance the loans over this period, but nonbank arrangers typically use third-party warehouse lenders. Indeed, an early step in the credit crisis of 2007 occurred in January 2007 when warehouse lenders pulled back and demanded more collateral to finance the loans of nonbank arrangers. (See the discussion in Chapter 2.)
4. The transformation of the securitization technology from pro rata pass-through to tranched CMOs in the 1980s is described in Allen (1997), 718–720.
5. In fact, during the summer and fall of 2007 when the ABCP market stopped functioning, several large banks (e.g., Citibank) absorbed their insolvent SIV's ABSs, even though they were not legally obligated to do so, because of reputational concerns.
6. A repurchase agreement (repo) allows a bank to borrow against collateral (securities) transferred to a counterparty. This transaction is typically reversed within a short time period—from a week to three months. Moreover, the collateral is marked-to-market on a daily basis.
7. In large syndications, there may be several lead banks. Moreover, the duties of the lead bank may be split up into the following titles: administrative agent (transfers all interest and principal payments), syndication agent (the syndicate underwriter), and documentation agent (handles the legal aspects).
8. Credit rating agencies such as Moody's, Standard & Poor's, and Fitch rank borrowers on a scale from AAA (most creditworthy) to D (default), where all

ratings at or above BBB–/Baa3 are considered investment-grade and all ratings below BBB–/Baa3 are considered below investment-grade (junk) status.

9. A basis point is 0.01 percent; there are 100 basis points in a percent. As we show in Chapter 2, the spreads during the 2007–2009 financial crisis were abnormally high, with investment-grade spreads over LIBOR of more than 500 basis points.

10. However, the lead arranger typically retains a substantial stake in the loan in order to induce it to provide monitoring and market-making services to the rest of the syndicate (see Allen and Gottesman [2006]).

11. "Anatomy of a Global Credit Crisis," *New Zealand Herald*, August 22, 2007, 2.

12. Bank for International Settlements (BIS), Monetary and Economic Department, "OTC Derivatives Market Activity in the Second Half of 2006," www.bis.org, Table 1.

13. Functionally, CDS contracts have the same economic function as insurance policies, despite the fact that insurance is regulated by the individual states and the CDS market is largely self-regulated under the auspices of the International Swaps and Derivatives Association (ISDA) and Britain's Financial Services Authority (FSA). Another distinction between a CDS contract and insurance is that buyers of insurance are required to have an insurable interest (the insured owns the home or automobile being insured), whereas buyers of CDS contracts do not have to own the CDS's underlying risky reference security. Neither of these distinctions negates the financial function of CDSs as credit risk credit insurance policies.

14. The Basel Committee consists of senior supervisory representatives from Belgium, Canada, France, Germany, Italy, Japan, Luxembourg, the Netherlands, Sweden, Switzerland, the United Kingdom, and the United States. It usually meets at the Bank for International Settlements (BIS) in Basel, where its permanent Secretariat is located.

15. More than 100 countries have adopted Basel I. Morrison and White (2009) examine the costs and benefits of creating a level playing field through international bank capital standards. The disadvantage is that since capital regulations substitute for high-quality regulatory oversight, international bank capital requirements must be set to the weakest regulatory standard. However, in a world of mobile capital, a level playing field avoids the cherry-picking effect that reduces the size and efficiency of banks in weaker economies.

16. The SEC's adoption of Regulation FD in October 2000 mandated fair disclosure of any material and forward-looking information to the market as a whole, rather than to a favored institution. That is, it "compelled companies to disseminate all material information to both the public and Wall Street at the same time, preventing issuers from tipping off selected analysts or institutional investors." ("SEC Report Urges Improvements to U.S. Fair Disclosure Laws," *International Financial Law Review*, London, January 2002, page 5.)

17. See also Boot et al. (2006) for a discussion of the central role of credit ratings in financial markets and regulation.

18. Appendix 1.1 shows how credit ratings provided by the three major rating agencies are mapped on a comparable basis.
19. Beaver, Shakespeare, Soliman (2006), 4.
20. Concerns about the accuracy and timeliness of external credit ratings predate the recent crisis. For example, Reisen and von Maltzan (1999) and Reinhart (2001) discuss lags in sovereign credit ratings, Kealhofer (2000) and Altman and Saunders (2001a) discuss lags in publicly traded corporate ratings, and Bongini et al. (2001) discuss lags in credit ratings of banks. As ratings change over time, the transaction may be shifted from one risk bucket to another, thereby injecting excessive volatility into capital requirements (see Linnell 2001) and may lead to an increase in systemic risk since, with increased downgrades in a recession, banks may find their capital requirements peaking at the worst time (i.e., in the middle of a recession when earnings are relatively weak)— just as during the recent financial crisis. Indeed, there is evidence (Ferri et al. [2001]; Monfort and Mulder [2000]; Altman and Saunders, [2001b]) that ratings agencies behave procyclically since ratings are downgraded in a financial crisis, thereby increasing capital requirements at just the point in the business cycle that stimulation in lending and bank asset growth is required (see Reisen [2000]). Thus, pegging capital requirements to external ratings may exacerbate systemic risk concerns. Further, concern about systemic risk may lead to regulatory attempts to influence ratings agencies, thereby undermining their independence and credibility.

CHAPTER 2   The Three Phases of the Credit Crisis

1. Countrywide did not discontinue Alt-A mortgages until March 2007.
2. R. Brooks and C.M. Ford, "The United States of Subprime," *Wall Street Journal*, October 11, 2007, A1, A16.
3. J. McDermott, "Healthy CLO Issuance to Continue . . . For Now," *LSTA Loan Market Chronicle*, 2005, 64–65.
4. Standard & Poor's, "Record Setting Leveraged Loan Market Shows No Signs of Slowing (Yet)," January 3, 2007.
5. This included loans with payment-in-kind (PIK) toggles which enabled the borrower to substitute monetary interest payments for increases in the principal balance on the loan. Thus, if the borrower could not pay the coupon payment on the loan when it came due, the amount would simply be added to the loan balance.
6. "Anatomy of a Global Credit Crisis," *New Zealand Herald*, August 22, 2007, 2.
7. R. Brooks and C. M. Ford, "The United States of Subprime," *Wall Street Journal*, October 11, 2007, A1, A16.
8. J. Shenn, "Subprime Loan Defaults Pass 2001 Peak," *Bloomberg Markets*, February 2, 2007.
9. S. Ng, and C. Mollenkamp, "Fresh Credit Worries Grip Market," *Wall Street Journal*, November 2, 2007, A1.
10. K. Howley, "Realtor Group Lowers Forecast for Home Sales," *Miami Herald*, October 10, 2007.

11. Loeffler (2008) uses an AR(1), or one-period lag model using quarterly seasonally adjusted housing price changes estimated as of August 2005 to predict subsequent worst-case scenarios (at both 1 percent and 0.1 percent VAR). However, the model generates overly optimistic forecasts of housing prices when the S&P Case-Shiller index is used in place of the OFHEO index. Loeffler (2008) claims that is the result of the shorter estimation time horizon since the S&P Case-Shiller index dates back only to 1987, whereas the OFHEO index dates back to 1975. However, another explanation is that the S&P Case-Shiller index turns down sooner in 2006 than the OFHEO index. If the OFHEO index provides a more optimistic measure of housing prices, the model forecasts may be more likely to fall within the range of observed values.

12. Flight-to-quality episodes are common components of financial and macroeconomic volatility, as in the Penn Central default of 1970, the stock market crash of 1987, the Russian default/LTCM debacle in 1998, and the 9/11 attack. See Caballero and Krishnamurthy (2008) for a theoretical explanation for recurrent crises and the flight to quality generated by unanticipated events, increased uncertainty, and decreases in aggregate liquidity. Under such circumstances, central bank intervention is warranted.

13. "Bank's Struggles Show Fallibility of Models," *Wall Street Journal*, November 5, 2007, C2.

14. Bank of England, *Financial Stability Report* no. 22, October 2007, 19.

15. Northern Rock's mortgage portfolio was not exposed to the subprime market, and the five-year credit default swap premium on Northern Rock stayed relatively low until the end of July. However, the bank was vulnerable because it depended on purchased funds for the bulk of its liabilities. Thus, according to the Bank of England, it was the shutdown of the securitization market and turmoil in the short-term funding market (i.e., liquidity risk) that brought down Northern Rock, not credit risk in the bank's mortgage portfolio (see Bank of England [2007], 10–12).

16. Figure 2.6 shows the spread between LIBOR (the London Interbank Offer Rate) for both one-month and three-months terms minus the overnight indexed swap rate (OIS), which is the geometric average of overnight interest rates over the same term period. The Fed uses this spread to measure stress in money markets, such that the wider the spread, the less willing banks are to lend to one another over the short term. Although at historically high levels during the fall of 2007, spreads rose to unprecedented heights during the period following the Lehman bankruptcy on September 15, 2008. The LIBOR-OIS spread historically averaged 10 basis points, but Figure 2.6 shows that it hit 364 basis points in October 2008.

17. G. Tett, P. J. Davies, and S. Ishmael, "New Fears over Subprime Fallout," *Financial Times*, November 2, 2007, 1.

18. Brunnermeier and Yogo (2009) show how firms preserve liquidity when they are in good health and manage their debt maturity over several refinancing cycles.

19. For example, "Funds specializing in distressed investments earned annual returns of more than 30 percent in the early 1990s as the economy pulled out of recession," as stated in Michael de la Merced and Azchery Kouwe, "'Vulture' Investors Eye Bad Assets, But Warily," *New York Times*, February 11, 2009, A1, A22.
20. The LCDX is a tradable index comprising 100 single-name CDSs maintained by Reuters Loan Pricing Corporation. The higher the spread, the greater the premium for credit risk exposure. See the discussion of indexed CDSs in Chapter 12.
21. Gretchen Morgenson, "A Paper Trail That Often Leads Nowhere," *New York Times*, December 28, 2008, C1, C2.
22. G. Morgenson, "Guess What Got Lost in the Pool?" *New York Times*, March 1, 2009, C1, C2.
23. "The CBOE Volatility Index—VIX," CBOE white paper, 2003, www.cboe.com/micro/vix/vixwhite.pdf.
24. See Hakkio and Keeton (2009).
25. To calculate the interquartile range (IQR), the data are divided into quartiles: top 25 percent observations, middle 50 percent observations, bottom 25 percent observations. The first quartile delineates the bottom 25 percent of the observations and the third quartile delineates the top 25 percent of the observations. The IQR is the difference between the third quartile and the first quartile, and measures the range of uncertainty.

CHAPTER 3 The Crisis and Regulatory Failure

1. It is perhaps not surprising that the Fed took an aggressive, activist policy stance in addressing the financial crisis. Boyd, Kwak, and Smith (2005) find that the economic output losses of financial crises range from 63 to 302 percent of real per capital GDP in the last precrisis year, and may persist for decades.
2. www.frbdiscountwindow.org/.
3. The Fed undertook these unprecedented steps under the "unusual and exigent circumstances" provisions of Section 13(3) of the Federal Reserve Act.
4. Philippon and Schnabl (2009) examine the impact of three different bailout mechanisms: government purchase of bank equity, government purchase of risky assets, and the provision of debt guarantees. With compulsory participation, they find that all interventions are equivalent. However, if participation is voluntary, then government purchase of equity is the most efficient bailout mechanism since it quickly restarts lending and spurs new investment.
5. Clawbacks allow employers to recoup executive compensation and bonuses if it is subsequently found that the executive acted improperly. Allen and Li (2009) discuss the clawback system that has been in place for Chinese banks since 1998, and find that the policy may have contributed to the recent decline in cronyism and more prudent lending practices at the Big Four Chinese banks.
6. Although this sounds like self-dealing, such a plan would have offered a direct credit guarantee to banks so that they could use the bank's private information

to work out the loans without concern about capital impairment. Thus, it is similar in effect to direct governmental guarantees and equity infusions.

7. British government bailout plans have also been unsuccessful at generating bank participation. For example, a government guarantee program for ABSs introduced in January 2009 had no participants because bankers claimed that it was too expensive. In addition, a small-business loan guarantee program was unpopular because it required small business owners to pledge their personal assets as collateral.

8. In addition, from 1986 to 1989, the Federal Savings and Loan Insurance Corporation (FSLIC, absorbed by the RTC) took over an additional 296 thrifts with total assets of $125 billion (see Curry and Shibut [2000]).

9. Another countercyclical proposal along these lines is advanced by Kashyap, Rajan, and Stein (2008), who advocate the creation of an insurance policy against systemic risk that would pay off only in large-scale banking crises. See Chapter 13 for a discussion.

10. http://www.ustreas.gov/press/releases/tg72.htm.

11. Ibid.

12. Department of the Treasury press release, June 17, 2009, 10.

13. Historically, there have been concerns about overconcentration of financial power in the United States, explaining the creation of 12 regional Federal Reserve banks when the central bank was created in 1914.

14. F. Norris, "Derivatives Tug of War Takes Shape," *New York Times*, June 26, 2009, B1, B5.

15. However, Duffie and Zhu (2009) show that introduction of a centralized clearinghouse may actually reduce settlement efficiency and increase risk exposures unless the number of dealers is exceptionally high. Moreover, the introduction of multiple clearinghouses makes it more likely that the required scale would not be reached, and that netting efficiency would actually decline.

16. H. W. Jenkins, "Too Bernanke to Fail?" *Wall Street Journal*, July 1, 2009, A11.

17. Brown et al. (2008) examine the value of disclosure through hedge fund registration and find that information about past legal and regulatory problems contained in the filings is potentially useful in detecting conflicts of interest. However, they find evidence suggesting that lenders and equity investors obtain this information through means other than regulatory filings.

18. Of course, the impact of such a plan on bank profitability, and potential disincentives to provide critically needed financial services, must be considered carefully.

CHAPTER 4   Loans as Options: The Moody's KMV Model

1. In many cases, the models can also be applied to private firms by proprietary *mapping* models, such as Moody's KMV RiskCalc™ Private Firm model, which uses an industry-level distance-to-default structural model together with firm-specific financial statement analysis (see Dwyer [2005]). Moody's KMV

has data on 16,268 publicly traded U.S. firms over the period 1981–2006; (see Zhang, Zhu, and Lee [2008]).

2. In fact, if there are direct and indirect costs of bankruptcy (e.g., legal costs), the lender's loss on a loan may exceed principal and interest. This makes the payoff in Figure 4.1 even more similar to that shown in Figure 4.2 (i.e., the loan may have a negative payoff).

3. Historically, corporate bond pricing data have been unavailable to the public and are often quoted at artificial *matrix* prices, making it difficult to estimate the structural model in equation (4.2). However, Transaction Reporting and Compliance Engine (TRACE), requiring the reporting of all trades of all publicly traded corporate bonds to NASD, was introduced in July 2002. Bessembinder, Maxwell, and Venkataraman (2006) show that after the introduction of TRACE, the bond market became more competitive, with an approximately 50 percent decrease in trade execution costs for TRACE-eligible bonds. In addition, Hotchkiss and Jostova (2007) use bond trade data that insurance companies are required to report to the National Association of Insurance Commissioners (NAIC).

4. In April 2002, KMV was purchased by Moody's for $210 million in an all-cash transaction. Currently, Moody's KMV is known as Moody's Analytics. Dwyer and Stein (2006) describe how the merger of historical default databases held by Moody's and KMV resulted in an enhanced data set of small firm defaults available to Moody's KMV.

5. This could happen, for example, if the assets are liquidated at current market values and the resulting funds are used to meet borrowing obligations.

6. In the event of liquidation of the firm's assets, the model assumes that the shareholders receive nothing. In practice, however, more than 75 percent of all bankrupt firms' debt structures are renegotiated so as to allow some deviation from absolute priority, in which the equity holders receive some payment even if the bondholders are not fully paid. Acharya et. al. (2000) extend the Merton model to include renegotiation in the event of default. However, Bharath et al. (2007) find this high incidence of deviations from absolute priority has declined after 1990 to 22 percent, falling as low as 9 percent during the period 2000–2005.

7. The volatility of a firm's equity value, σ, may be calculated using historical equity prices or backed out of option prices. Swidler and Wilcox (2001) solve for the implied volatility of large bank equity prices using option prices.

8. If the Black-Scholes options pricing model is used, the form of equation (4.4) is:

$$\sigma = (A/E)N(d_1)\sigma_A$$

where $N(\cdot)$ is the normal probability distribution, and

$$d_1 = \frac{\ln\left(\frac{A}{B}\right) + \left(r + .5\sigma^2\right)T}{\sigma\sqrt{T}}$$

which is solved using an iterative process. For example, Crosbie and Bohn (2003) and Vassalou and Xing (2004) assume values of

$$\sigma_A = \sigma(E/(E + B))$$

which are substituted into equation (4.3) until an iterative solution is reached. That is, the assumed value of σ_A is used to calculate daily values of A over a time period of, say, 12 months. The volatility of these estimates of asset values is compared to the assumed value of σ_A. The model is reestimated iteratively until the volatility of the estimated asset values, A, converges to σ_A.

9. Moody's KMV has found that most firms do not default immediately upon reaching the technical insolvency point when the market value of assets has declined to equal the firm's total liabilities. The firm may have lines of credit or other cash-generating mechanisms that permit the servicing of debt even after the technical point of insolvency is reached. However, Mella-Barral and Perraudin (1997) suggest that default may begin before technical insolvency is reached because shareholders can extract concessions on coupon payments. Vassalou and Xing (2004) find that the default probability forecasts are not impacted by varying the percent of long-term debt included in the definition of the default boundary.

10. Moody's KMV also doesn't make distinctions in the liability structure as to seniority, collateral, or covenants. Convertible debt and preferred stock are treated as long-term liabilities. It might be noted, however, that the user can input whatever value of B he feels is economically appropriate. Geske (1977) has extended the Merton model to include coupon payments, covenants, and so on.

11. Bongini et al. (2001) show that external credit ratings lagged behind default-risk-adjusted Ronn and Verma deposit insurance premiums in forecasting the 1998 Asian banking crisis.

12. Keep in mind that σ_A is the annual standard deviation of asset values expressed in dollar terms, or percentage standard deviation times the market value of assets.

13. Distance to default $= [A(1 + g) - B]/\sigma_A = (\$110 - \$80)/\$10 = 3$ standard deviations. Moody's KMV uses a constant asset growth assumption for all firms in the same market, which is the expected growth rate of the market as a whole. The rationale for this assumption is that in an efficient market, differences in growth rates between the market and individual firms are fully discounted (i.e., arbitraged away) and incorporated in the stock prices (and hence into the asset value) of the firm. Thus, in equilibrium, there is no difference between asset growth of individual firms and the market. The only other adjustment to this constant (across-the-board) asset growth rate is for firm-specific payouts such as dividends or interest payments. The adjusted number is then applied to the implied current asset value in the distance to default formula.

14. Under the assumption of normality, half of the 9,500 firms in KMV's North American database have a distance to default of 4.0 or more, implying that

more than half of the firms are AAA-rated—a conclusion at odds with actual ratings (see KMV [2000]). In reality, asset values have considerably fatter tails than those that characterize the normal or lognormal distributions.

15. Of course, there is something unappealing about using the normality assumption to back out estimates of A and σ_A in order to get to this point in the model and then dropping the assumption when it comes to the final step (see Sundaram [2001]).

16. In addition to the public firm model, Moody's KMV offers RiskCalc^{TM}, which measures the credit risk of private firms (see Appendix 4.2).

17. However, this methodology raises the question whether KMV's empirical EDF measures firm-specific default or is, rather, a composite measure particular to the database used. This criticism does not apply to Moody's empirical EDF scores because the influence of each key variable is determined for each firm individually at each point in time.

18. Dwyer and Qu (2007) describe recent improvements in the calibration of the Moody's KMV model that result in fewer observations hitting the floor and the ceiling on EDF scores. For example, better modeling of distressed firms enabled the raising of the EDF score ceiling to 35 percent from 20 percent.

19. For simplicity, interest rates are assumed constant in the Merton model, although Acharya and Carpenter (2000) show that declines in interest rates may trigger default. Longstaff and Schwartz (1995b) model stochastic interest rates.

20. Although all the rating agencies offer opinions about creditworthiness, there are subtle but significant differences across agencies. For example, S&P ratings represent estimates of the probability of default, whereas Moody's ratings estimate expected loss, which can be calculated as the probability of default times the loss given default. Thus, Moody's does not have a default rating "D," but S&P does (see Hamilton, Cantor, and Ou [2002]).

21. Most of the firms in the sample are U.S. firms, representing 1,127,452 out of a total of 1,287,987 observations. As of the end of 2006, Moody's had data on about 7,900 public defaults, 5,600 of which were in North America.

22. Longstaff et al. (2005) show that Enron's credit default swap spreads did not start to increase until September 2001, just three months prior to Enron's default declaration.

23. Stein (2005) shows how a power curve can be used to set a cost-minimizing lending cutoff point, as well as to determine loan prices.

24. Crosbie and Bohn (2003) claim that Moody's KMV EDF scores forecast credit risk for financial institutions despite the fact that it is difficult to observe the assets and liabilities of opaque banks and financial firms, as well as the possibility that default will not occur when the market value of assets falls below balance sheet liabilities.

25. Another reason for the better predictability of KMV scores over the short horizon is that Standard & Poor's and Moody's calibrate their ratings to default experience over the past 30 years. Their probabilities therefore reflect a "cycle average" view. By comparison, KMV's EDFs reflect strong cyclicality over the

business cycle. Some studies have shown that EDFs do not offer any advantage for time horizons over two years (see Miller [1998]).

26. If the assets have no systematic risk, then the two probabilities (KMV EDF and risk-neutral EDF) are identical. Anderson and Sundaresan (2000) show that the risk-adjusted EDF performs better than the risk-neutral EDF in replicating historical bond defaults, and that fluctuations in leverage and asset volatility explain most of the variations in bond spreads over time. Bohn (2000a) finds that KMV empirical EDFs explain 60 percent of credit spread volatility.

27. Bond spreads for low-credit-risk issues are higher than would be implied by KMV empirical EDFs alone because the market Sharpe ratio scaling parameter tends to increase with the bond's term, thereby increasing observed bond spreads (see Kealhofer [2000]). Bohn (1999) finds that low-credit-quality bond issues have humped-shape or downward-sloping credit spread term structures, whereas high-credit-quality bond issues have upward-sloping credit spread term structures. Maclachlan (1999) asserts that credit spread levels fluctuate over the business cycle and display a tendency for short maturity credit spreads to increase the most during recessions. KMV's Portfolio Manager estimates this macroeconomic effect using a multifactor model (see Chapter 8).

28. For instance, the likelihood function exploits known interrelationships among the two unobservable variables, A and σ_A, and the two observable variables, E and σ, such as the fact that equity values are strictly increasing in asset values.

29. The three structural models used by Ericsson and Reneby (2005) are: (1) the traditional Merton (1974) model, (2) Briys and de Varenne (1997), and (3) Leland and Toft (1996). Briys and de Varenne (1997) incorporate early default and interest rate risk into the traditional Merton model, whereas Leland and Toft (1996) endogenize the firm's capital structure.

30. See, for example, Jones, Mason, and Rosenfeld (1984).

31. Longstaff and Schwartz (1995a) obtain wider credit spreads in their model of an exogenously determined but stochastic default boundary by incorporating the costs associated with asset liquidation. However, Huang and Huang (2003) argue that firms can continue operating with negative net worth, and therefore specify a default boundary that is some fraction β (<1) of the debt's face value.

32. For example, an insider might sell a large block if he has private information about the adverse nature of future prospects for the firm, although the time between the sale and actual default will likely be short, thereby mitigating the benefits of a KMV-type model as an early warning system.

33. As noted earlier, S&P credit ratings are forecasts of PD, whereas Moody's credit ratings estimate PD × LGD.

34. Agrawal et al. (2008) use a structural model, Moody's KMV CreditMark methodology, to estimate loan values and find that their estimates perform well when compared to quotes from the secondary market in syndicated bank leveraged loans over the period 2002–2006.

35. In this chapter, we focus on one-year EDF scores to predict the probability of default over the following year. However, Moody's KMV estimates multiyear default probabilities by constructing a term structure of forward EDF scores,

annually for a period up to five years. Dwyer and Qu (2007) present a methodology to extend the model beyond five years.

36. However, Tang and Yan (2007) find an estimated liquidity premium in CDS spreads that is on par with that in Treasury and corporate bonds, resulting from search and agency costs in the over-the-counter CDS market. Arora et al. (2005) offer another justification for the testing of credit risk model accuracy using CDS spreads. They note that since none of the credit risk models are calibrated using CDS data, the test represents a "fair, out-of-sample test...that avoids the pitfalls of testing models on data similar to data used to fit the models" (page 5).

37. The naïve version of the structural model assumes that the past year's equity returns determine the asset drift term (expected asset value at the end of the next year), sets asset volatility equal to a constant weighted average of observed equity and assumed debt volatilities, and assumes that the default boundary point equals the face value of the firm's debt. Despite these simplifications, the naïve model in Bharath et al. (2008) slightly outperforms the traditional Merton model in out-of-sample classification of defaulting firms. Both models outperform a simple classification based on the market value of equity, as well as a reduced form model using the same data inputs but without the function form of the structural model.

38. Kealhofer (2000) claims that the KMV model can incorporate multiple debt and nondebt fixed liabilities, debt with embedded options, maturity differences, dividend payouts, and coupon payments. The way this is accomplished is by converting a complex debt structure into a zero-coupon-equivalent single default point value B. Bohn (2000a) surveys different specifications of structural models that vary with respect to their assumptions about asset value, the default-free rate, the default point, and recovery rates (LGD).

39. Since asset values have a positive drift term, whereas leverage is assumed constant, Merton models imply a negative slope of the term structure of credit spreads—in other words, default risk approaches zero as the debt's maturity increases because asset values drift higher than the fixed default point. In general, this is not observed in actual risky bond spreads.

40. Moody's KMV RiskCalc^{TM} is based on the KMV Private Firm Model, which generates an imputed stock price series for private firms by using comparable public firms, and then solving for the distance to default directly. In the complete version of RiskCalc^{TM}, the public firm distance to default is input as an adjustment factor, and firm-specific ratios are used in a probit estimation.

CHAPTER 5   Reduced Form Models: Kamakura's Risk Manager

1. Reduced form models can be estimated using options prices as well as debt prices. For example, Camara, Popova and Simkins (2009) decompose stock options prices in order to estimate the probability of default for financial companies and building construction firms during the financial crisis of 2007–2009.

They find that during the crisis the average PD for financial (building construction) firms increases from 1 percent to 7 percent (15 percent). In this chapter, we focus on the decomposition of debt prices in reduced form models.

2. For the pricing of derivatives, when the underlying asset is traded, the risk-neutral price is the correct one, irrespective of investor preferences. This is because, with an underlying asset, the derivative can be perfectly hedged to create a riskless portfolio. When a portfolio is riskless, it has an expected return equal to the risk-free rate.

3. Parlour and Plantin (2008) show theoretically that a liquidity premium arises from the bank's trade-off between holding and monitoring the loan until maturity, and selling the loan so as to recycle capital into other investment opportunities.

4. This assumes that the default probability is independent of the security's price, something that does not hold for swaps with asymmetric counterparty credit risk, for example. Duffie and Singleton (1999) specify that one should use a "pure" default-free rate r that reflects repo specials and other effects. The U.S. Treasury short rate, typically used as the empirical proxy for r, may be above or below the pure default-free rate.

5. To illustrate the double subscript notation, the yield on a B-rated two-year zero-coupon bond to be received one year from now would be denoted $_1y_2$. This bond would mature three years from today—one year until it is delivered on the forward contract and then two years until maturity from then. Spot rates are for transactions with immediate delivery; the first subscript of a spot rate is always zero.

6. The tree diagram shows only five possible transition ratings: A, B+, B, C, or D (default), and thus is considerably simpler than reality in which there are 18 possible ratings transitions alone. Moreover, default need not be an absorbing state in reality if restructuring is possible.

7. Using the credit rating agencies' transition matrices to estimate the default probability inserts error into the model since the empirically observed ("natural") default rates are lower than risk-neutral default rates. See the discussion in Chapter 4 on converting KMV empirical EDFs to risk-neutral EDFs by adjusting for expected asset returns. KPMG obtains risk-neutral default rates by solving for the credit spreads for one-year option-free term loans and using iterative arbitrage pricing methods to price two-state (default or non-default) reference loans as contingent claims on the one-year loans.

8. In practice, the other possibilities could include exercise of embedded options, prepayments, restructuring, as well as finer gradations of ratings migrations.

9. Thus, the PD in the first period is the probability that the B-rated loan will default, 5 percent. In the second period, it is the sum of the probabilities that the A-rated loan defaults, 0.34 percent, plus the PD for the B-rated loan, 5 percent, to arrive at the 5.34 percent PD we found in the solution to equation (5.6).

10. Recall that the one-year risk-free forward rate is obtained using the 8 percent one-year spot yield and the 10 percent two-year spot yield shown in Figure 5.1 so that

$$(1 + .10)^2 = (1 + .08)(1 + _1r_1)$$

to obtain

$$_1r_1 = 12.04 \text{ percent per annum}$$

11. In this example, we follow Belkin et al. (1998b) and assume that the risk premium has a flat term structure. In practice, however, this assumption does not hold (see Chen and Huang [2000]).

12. Note that the credit spread, CS, is assumed to be constant over time—that is, in years 1 and 2 in this example.

13. Not only is the risk-neutral PD higher than the natural PD, but Duffee (1999) finds that the risk-neutral PD is nonstationary, whereas the natural PD is mean-reverting.

14. Typically, the binomial tree model assumes LGD of 100 percent, although LGD may be less than 100 percent, as long as it is fixed for the maturity of the debt instrument.

15. Although most intensity-based models assume that LGD is fixed, Unal et al. (2001) find that LGD varies intertemporally and cross-sectionally.

16. Duffie and Singleton (1999) show that PD and LGD cannot be separately identified in defaultable bond prices because risky debt is priced on the credit spread, PD × LGD.

17. Structural models can be viewed as a special case of reduced form models in which the default process is endogenously determined by the relationship between stochastic asset values and the default point if asset values are assumed to follow a jump process that makes it possible for assets to jump past the default point. See Duffie and Lando (2001), which specifies the hazard rate in terms of asset value volatility that is known only imperfectly through past and present accounting data. Imperfect information about asset values allows the default stopping time to be modeled as a jump process. Cathcart and El-Jahel (1998) achieve this by assuming that default occurs when a stochastic signaling process hits the default barrier.

18. A Poisson distribution describes the random arrival through time such that the exponentially distributed intensity of the Poisson process jumps by a certain amount at each arrival time (corresponding to default or credit migration); the inter-arrival times are assumed to be statistically independent.

19. Duffee (1998) finds misspecification in these models, particularly for below-investment-grade bonds.

20. They break their sample of firms into four industry groups: (1) finance, insurance, and real estate; (2) transportation, communication, and utilities; (3) manufacturing and mineral; and (4) other.

21. However, Campbell, Hilscher, and Szilagyi (2008) find evidence of a distress risk anomaly, such that the equities of firms with high PD have lower returns, but higher volatilities than low PD stocks. This suggests that equity prices do

not include a distress risk premium, and therefore do not compensate investors for exposure to default risk.

22. Since reduced form models are purely empirical, they cannot be evaluated by interpreting their economic assumptions and implications. They are data-driven and should therefore provide results that conform to the data better than do structural models. However, if there is noise in the credit spreads data (see the discussion later on the determinants of bond spreads), then the reduced form model may be tailored to a somewhat fickle standard (see Anderson and Sundaresan [2000]).

23. Kamakura also estimates PD using the Merton options-theoretic model, as well as a private firm model. In October 2008, Kamakura introduced Kamakura Risk Manager Version 7.0, to "allow major financial institutions and corporations to parse the incremental risk of each asset and liability on the balance sheet into liquidity risk, credit risk, and interest rate risk components and simulate it forward in a realistic way." *Marketwire* press release, October 9, 2008.

24. Jarrow (2001) makes the interesting point that, prior to this work, structural models used only equity prices, eschewing debt prices as too noisy, whereas reduced form models used only debt prices. This is claimed to be the first model to combine both debt and equity prices in an intensity-based format.

25. As expected, the private firm model (estimated entirely using industry- and firm-specific accounting data because of the absence of market prices) has a lower accuracy rate of 88.12 percent area under the ROC curve and 79.94 percent for the first two deciles.

26. The March 2009 Troubled Company Index value of 24.3 percent was the worst for the current recession as of this writing. As of July 1, 2009, the index had fallen to 16.4 percent of public firms in distress, as defined by a short-term default probability in excess of 1 percent.

27. In this chapter, we focus on credit spreads for corporate borrowers. Duffie, Pederson, and Singleton (2000) use a reduced form model to estimate the credit risk of Russian dollar-denominated debt.

28. Huang and Huang (2000) use the Longstaff-Schwartz structural model to find average yield spreads (credit risk spreads) for 10-year corporate bonds as follows: Aaa: 63 bp (10.2 bp); Aa: 91 bp (13.5 bp); A: 123 bp (20 bp); Baa: 194 bp (46 bp); Ba: 299 bp (174 bp); B: 408 bp (373.6 bp). Moreover, they find that the credit spread is even lower for investment-grade bonds with shorter maturities.

29. On April 27, 2007, the NYSE launched an online trading platform for U.S. corporate bonds using its electronic equity trading facility Arca. In November 2006, the NYSE won an exemption from the Securities and Exchange Commission to trade unlisted bonds if they are issued by exchange-listed companies, thereby increasing the potential number of bonds traded electronically from 1,000 (on the old ABS system) to 6,000. The dominant player in online corporate bond trading, MarketAxess Holdings, uses a request-for-quote system where institutional investors can ask for prices from several dealers to buy or sell bonds.

30. Data availability on TRACE was phased in over the period 2002–2006. For example, prior to April 2004, transactions data were available only for bonds rated A or better and over $100 million. It was not until January 9, 2006, that transaction data on all non-144A (private placement) bonds were disseminated on TRACE (see Goldstein and Hotchkiss [2007]). However, the system ultimately provided price data within 15 minutes of trade for 95 percent of the dollar value traded of corporate bonds (not including private placements) (see Edwards et al. [2007]).

31. The overnight swap rate is the interbank rate for unsecured lending, repriced every day for the relevant time period. LIBOR (the London Interbank Offer Rate) is the unsecured interbank (fixed) rate for term loans of either one month or three month (as shown in Figure 2.6).

32. Chang and Sundaresan (1999) endogenize the relationship between the PD and economic conditions by noting that when default risk increases during economic downturns, investors become more risk-averse (they exhibit a *flight to quality*), thereby causing risk-free rates to decline and building in an inverse relationship between default risk and the default-free term structure.

33. This example was adapted from Duffie and Singleton (1998).

34. Using equation (5.7) to calculate the PD over a five-year time horizon, we obtain a PD of .005 for the A-rated firm and .2212 for the B-rated firm.

35. The intensity of the sum of independent Poisson processes is just the sum of the individual processes' intensities; therefore, the portfolio's total intensity is

$$(1,000 \times .001) + (100 \times .05) = 6 \text{ defaults per year}$$

We discuss portfolio correlations in Chapter 11.

36. Indeed, with constant intensity, the two terms are synonymous.

37. For risk-neutral investors, this expression for survival probabilities, particularly in its continuous-time form, is mathematically equivalent to the current price of a zero-coupon bond with maturity t discounted at interest rate h.

38. The parameters would have to be adjusted to remove the risk premium in order to obtain the risk-neutral credit spread.

39. Moody's computes that the average default rate of B (Baa) rated corporate issues over the period 1920–1997 was 442 (32) basis points.

CHAPTER 6   Other Credit Risk Models

1. However, Mester (1997) reports that only 8 percent of banks with up to $5 billion in assets used scoring for small business loans. In March 1995, in order to make credit scoring of small business loans available to small banks, Fair Isaac introduced its Small Business Scoring Service, based on five years of data on small business loans collected from 17 banks.

2. Other popular credit scoring models are the O score model by Ohlson (1980) and the Zmijewski (1984) model.

3. Astebro and Rucker (2000) demonstrate the economic implications of the choice of a cutoff point in a credit scoring model of European cell phone customers. If economic conditions are ignored, then the cutoff point is the Z value midway between the average Z of the failed (bankrupt) group and the average Z of the matched sample of nonfailing firms.

4. The Z'' model adds an intercept term of 3.25 so that a D-rated firm calibrates to a zero Z'' score.

5. In comparing the accuracy of internal ratings and credit scoring models, Carey and Hrycay (2001) find that long time periods of data across several points of the business cycle must be utilized in order to reduce the models' distortions.

6. Combining the volatility of annual MMRs with LGDs can produce unexpected loss calculations as well (see Altman and Saunders [1997]).

7. That is, a mortality rate is binomially distributed (see McAllister and Mingo [1994] for further discussion).

8. As a basis of comparison, Table 6.2 is based on 1,719 bond issues. In most published studies to date, mortality tables have been built on total samples of around 4,000 bonds and loans (see Altman [1989] and Altman and Suggitt [1997]). However, the Central Bank of Argentina has recently built transition matrices and mortality tables based on over 5 million loan observations, although fewer than 20,000 of these observations are usable (see Inter-American Development Bank study [2001]). These Argentinean credit registry data are available on the Central Bank's web site.

9. A Type 1 error misclassifies a bad loan as good. A Type 2 error misclassifies a good loan as bad.

10. The maximal fully connected two-layer network with 10 input variables and 12 hidden units has a maximum number of weights of

$$1 + 12(10 + 2) = 145$$

All possible combinations of these weights within the two layers (treating the ordering of the connections as unique) is

$$2^{145} = 4.46 \times 10^{43}$$

11. Shumway (2001) shows that a multiperiod, nonstatic discriminant model is theoretically equivalent to a discrete reduced form model (see Chapter 5 for a description of discrete-time hazard models).

12. Similarly, Campbell et al. (2008) find that the KMV Moody's default estimate adds little additional explanatory power to a reduced form model.

13. The O score model is a discriminant model similar to the Z-score model (see Ohlson [1980]) and Griffin and Lemmon [2002].

14. The sample consists of all public firms with size greater than $30 million dollars. The accuracy ratios for the EDF measure and Z score are 0.81 and 0.60, respectively.

CHAPTER 7   A Critical Parameter: Loss Given Default (LGD)

1. Contingent value rights (CVRs) can also be used as a means of payment in acquisitions and other settlements.
2. Recovery of face value (RFV) is an appropriate assumption for the sovereign CDS market since settlement of a CDS contract takes the form of physical delivery of another bond with a value equivalent to the underlying original face value of the CDS contract. Early CDSs were cash settled (consistent with the RMV scenario), but now physical delivery is the most common settlement method. Physical delivery is preferred because it gives the CDS seller more time to recoup the settlement payment through recovery of the value of the underlying reference security.
3. There is no default credit event on sovereign CDSs because there is no international bankruptcy court with jurisdiction over sovereign borrowers.
4. Version 3.0 of the Moody's KMV LossCalc™ model utilizes a linear link regression approach that ensures that the LGD is between 0 and 1 and that the average estimated LGD is equal to the observed average LGD for selected subsamples. Other models incorporate nonlinear functional forms (such as a beta distribution), which may be a more accurate representation of the functional form (particularly at extremely high or low LGDs), but which will not force the average estimated LGD to be equal to the observed average LGD for subsamples of the database.
5. Galai, Raviv, and Wiener (2007) model the timing between financial distress and liquidation as a function of past distress events and debt structure and covenants.
6. Constructing the lookup table using regression analysis, rather than simply historical average RR, partially alleviates the problems that the lookup table is static and insensitive to the multiple variables that determine LGD.

CHAPTER 8   The Credit Risk of Portfolios and Correlations

1. Moreover, the 1992 Bank for International Settlements (BIS) risk-based capital ratio is linearly additive across individual loans. See Rajan (1992) for an example of the "customer relationship" model.
2. In this chapter, we discuss correlations from the standpoint of measuring the risk of a portfolio. However, exposure to marketwide correlation shocks provides another important motivation for measuring correlations. Driessen, Maenhout and Vilkov (2009) use S&P 100 Index options to show that correlation risk is priced so that a trading strategy that exploits priced correlation risk earns excess returns (high alpha).
3. See Elton and Gruber (1995) for proofs.
4. In practice, KMV finds that portfolio risk can often be reduced by 20 to 50 percent simply by choosing asset allocations that move the portfolio to the efficient

frontier. In many portfolios, as few as 5 percent of the assets account for up to 40 percent of the total risk.

5. In order to distinguish between the different return symbols used in this chapter, we denote the risk-free rate r going forward in this chapter as r_f.

6. It might be noted that in identifying point D, it is assumed that investors (financial institutions) can borrow and lend at the same (risk-free) rate. This unrealistic assumption can be relaxed without changing the fundamentals of the model.

7. Although these assets are not traded on an organized exchange, there is over-the-counter secondary market trading. For example, the Loan Pricing Corporation now tracks secondary market prices on syndicated loans. Currently, over 50,000 loans are included in their database, which contains detailed information about spreads, loan covenants, and maturities. However, the database is not constructed as a time series. Therefore, the loans are not tracked over time; they are only priced as of the loan origination date, thereby making it impossible to update the optimal MPT portfolio over time.

8. Although, arguably, as the number of loans in a portfolio gets bigger, the distribution of returns tends to become more normal. Alternatively, all a manager may care about maximizing is a quadratic utility function, which depends by definition only on the mean and variance of returns.

9. For the seminal work on CAPM, see Sharpe, "Capital Asset Prices: A Theory of Market Equilibrium," *Journal of Finance*, September 1964, 425–442; Lintner, "The Valuation of Risk Assets and the Selection of Risk Investments in Stock Portfolios and Capital Budgets," *Review of Economics and Statistics*, February 1965, 13–37; and Mossin, "Equilibrium in a Capital Asset Market," *Econometrica*, October 1966, 768–783.

10. The structural approach (e.g., Moody's KMV) to correlation estimation is different from the reduced form model (Kamakura) since structural models measure the correlations across asset values, whereas reduced form models focus on the correlation in the default probabilities (hazard functions) themselves. However, Jarrow and Van Deventer (2005) show the consistency between these two methodologies.

11. In contrast, Longstaff, Mithal and Neis (2005) assume that the factors are independent, thereby assuming zero correlation coefficients. Alternatively, Duffie, Pan and Singleton (2000) use a numerical solution that requires them to input parametric values for correlations.

12. CreditMetrics' value at risk (VAR) approach to correlation analysis is described in Chapter 9.

13. One implication of using excess returns instead of gross returns is that the line drawn from the return axis to find the most efficient portfolio (shown in Figure 8.1) would now originate from the origin rather than the r_f point on the return axis (as shown).

14. In the DM model, there are only two possible outcomes—default and no default; hence the binomial probability distribution. Equation (8.9) holds precisely only if the initial loan is valued at par and matures at the credit valuation horizon (say, in one year).

15. KMV's Portfolio Manager assumes that LGD follows a beta distribution with a variance equal to LGD(1 − LGD)/k where k is determined by the distribution's shape parameters.

16. KMV's Portfolio Manager MTM's volatility calculations can be interpreted in a CreditMetrics framework as a mapping of EDFs into score ranges corresponding to different rating classifications. The valuation volatility (VVOL) is then obtained from the migration matrix across all classes except default. Thus, KMV Portfolio Manager and CreditMetrics yield similar estimates for UL. However, the IIF/ISDA (2000) found that the models' results diverged if the risk-neutral pricing method (as opposed to risk-adjusted matrix pricing) was used to obtain the KMV valuations.

17. As discussed previously, Moody's KMV's Portfolio Manager uses a multifactor model to estimate asset correlations.

18. Conditional on the realization of systematic risk, the distribution of portfolio value converges to normal when the portfolio consists of many loans of roughly the same size with relatively low levels of asset correlation. In contrast, Wilson (1998) shows that the loss distribution of undiversified portfolios tends to be bimodal, corresponding to the two events: default and nondefault.

19. If the two assets (Ford and General Electric) were uncorrelated then the concentric circles would be perfectly circular in shape. Figure 8.2 represents them as ellipses, suggesting that asset values are positively correlated; that is, there is greater probability of either a good outcome for both F and G (a move in the northeast direction of Figure 8.2) or a bad outcome for both (a move in the southwest direction) than if the two assets were uncorrelated.

20. If G and F were uncorrelated, then $JDF_{GF} = EDF_G EDF_F$ and ρ_{GF} is 0.

21. Another way that correlations can increase is for the concentric circles to become more elliptical (say, because of greater correlations in migration probabilities), thereby increasing the probability weight in the shaded area, even holding leverage ratios constant.

22. CreditMetrics estimates the sensitivity of equity prices to systematic risk factors (see Chapter 9), whereas Portfolio Manager delevers equity prices and uses asset returns to estimate multifactor systematic risk coefficients. In contrast, Kamakura examines the correlation across hazard functions of default risk. Jarrow and van Deventer (2005) compare these methodologies.

23. Phelan and Alexander (1999) note the opportunities for risk reduction through diversification as a result of the low correlations across bank loans (between 0.5 percent and 2.5 percent) compared to equity correlations of 40 percent and asset correlations which range between 10 to 60 percent. Moreover, debt portfolios tend to be more diverse than equity portfolios with ranges of 300 to 1 in risk differentials across individual assets, as compared to 10 to 1 for equity portfolios.

24. McQuown (1997) asserts that KMV's Portfolio Manager's optimized portfolio weights double the portfolio's Sharpe ratio. However, a substantial portion of this gain may be obtained from the exploitation of mispricing of debt securities.

25. However, gains to diversification are somewhat mitigated in bad economic states because default correlations typically increase as credit quality decreases, thereby exacerbating the portfolio's credit risk as the credit quality of individual assets declines.

26. Barnhill and Maxwell (1999) examine the historical correlation structure from 1987 to 1996 and find that changes in the short U.S. Treasury rate are negatively correlated with returns on the S&P 500 (with a correlation coefficient of -0.33) and are furthermore negatively correlated with 14 out of 15 different industry indices (automotive, banking, chemicals, building, energy, health, insurance, manufacturing, oil and gas, paper, technology, telecommunications, textiles, and utilities), with a slightly positively correlated (with a correlation coefficient of 0.02) with the entertainment industry index.

27. About 100 factors worldwide are used to account for virtually all empirically discernible correlations (see McQuown [1997]).

28. It is used for U.S. loans because "customer relationships" are weaker for its U.S. borrowers than for its Canadian borrowers; in other words, U.S. loans can be viewed as being more commoditized for this bank.

29. Another way of defining the marginal risk contribution in equation (8.15) is $MRC_i = \sigma_{ip}/\sigma_p$. Moody's KMV estimates that the MRC for an individual asset typically ranges from 4 percent to 68 percent of the UL of the portfolio.

30. Note that equation (8.16) can be viewed simply as a restatement of the portfolio risk equation (8.2), where σ_i represents the UL of firm i.

31. Moody's KMV often uses a multiple of 10. That is, Capital = $UL_p \times 10$. However, if the loss distribution was normal and the critical cutoff point was the ninety-ninth percentile, then capital would equal $UL_p \times 2.33$. Clearly, the difference between the multiplicative factors, 2.33 and 10, reflects (1) the degree of skewness in a bank's portfolio loss distribution, and (2) its desired level of capital protection against insolvency (or percentile cutoff point) and thus its desired credit rating. For example, Bank of America uses a multiple of 6 to achieve a 99.97 percent cutoff. Since a 99.97 percent cutoff implies a 0.03 percent probability of default, this has been historically consistent with the one year default probabilities of AA rated firms (see James [1996]). Dvorak (2008) reports that 13 large U.S. financial institutions lost a total of $50 billion from May to November 2007 during the global financial crisis. However, during that same time period, their collective market capitalizations fell a total of $300 billion, suggesting a 6:1 ratio (or a multiplier of 6). Moreover, the range of multipliers was between 1 and 70 across individual financial firms. In place of the multiplier rule of thumb, particularly in the wake of the 2007 global financial crisis, Moody's KMV advocates more accurate modeling of loan transfer pricing (see discussion in this chapter).

32. Duffie and Singleton (1998) also consider another specification of multivariate correlated intensities; that is, all default intensities are modeled as lognormally distributed. In contrast to the example presented in the text, portfolio default losses are relatively insensitive to default intensity correlations under the lognormal specification.

33. The parameter value $h_0 = .001$ reflects an initial mean default arrival rate of one default per thousand years. This is roughly equivalent to the historical average rate of default arrival for bonds rated by Moody's at A or Aa over the period 1920 to 1997.

34. As v approaches zero, the model converges to the independent default intensity model with zero correlations. As v approaches one, the jump intensities become perfectly correlated (identical), thereby eliminating any potential gains to portfolio diversification.

CHAPTER 9   The VAR Approach: CreditMetrics and Other Models

1. The capital requirements for market risk contain a general market risk component and a specific risk component. For example, with respect to corporate bonds that are held in the trading book, an internal model calculation of specific risk would include features such as spread risk, downgrade risk, and concentration risk. Each of these is related to credit risk. Thus, the 1996 BIS market risk capital requirement contains a credit risk component. We discuss the evolution of bank capital requirements and regulation in Chapter 13.

2. See Gupton et al., *CreditMetrics—Technical Document* (New York, J.P. Morgan, April 2, 1997). In 1998, the group developing the RiskMetrics and CreditMetrics products formed a separate company called RiskMetrics Group. Technical information may be obtained from the web site www.riskmetrics. com.

3. The one-year horizon is controversial (see Carey [2001b]). For example, if there is some autocorrelation or trend over time toward default, a longer window (say, two years or more) might be appropriate.

4. As will be discussed in the last section of this chapter, to calculate the VAR of a loan portfolio we also need to calculate default correlations among counterparties.

5. This example is based on the one used in Gupton et al., *CreditMetrics—Technical Document* (1997).

6. As is discussed later in this chapter, the choice of transition matrix has a material effect on the VAR calculations. Moreover, the choice of bond transitions to value loans raises again the question of how closely related bonds and loans are.

7. If the $+/-$ modifiers (*notches*) are utilized, there are 17 different rating categories (see Bahar and Nagpal [2000]).

8. The rating transitions are based on U.S. corporate bond data. For non-U.S. companies a *mapping* is required for the non-U.S. company into a U.S. company, or else the development of a non-U.S. or country-specific rating transition matrix is required.

9. Technically, from a valuation perspective the credit event occurs (by assumption) at the very end of the first year. Currently, CreditMetrics is expanding to allow the credit event window to be as short as three months or as long as five years.

10. Throughout this section the first subscript is suppressed for simplicity; because all valuations take place one year into the future, the first subscript is always one for all terms—for example, $_1r_1$ ($_1r_2$) denotes the zero-coupon risk-free rate on a one-year (two-year) maturity U.S. Treasury to be delivered in one year. See the discussion of the double subscript notation in Chapter 5 and in Appendix 9.1.

11. For notational simplicity, the credit spread (CS) is denoted by s_i in this chapter.

12. The assumption that interest rates are deterministic is particularly unsatisfying for credit derivatives because fluctuations in risk-free rates may cause the counterparty to default as the derivative moves in or out of the money. Thus, the portfolio VAR as well as the VAR for credit derivatives (see for example CIBC's CreditVaR II) assume a stochastic interest rate process that allows the entire risk-free term structure to shift over time (see Crouhy et al. [2000]).

13. In this case, the discount rates reflect the appropriate zero-coupon rates plus credit spreads (s_i) on A-rated loans (bonds). If the borrower's rating were unchanged at BBB, the discount rates would be higher because the credit spreads would reflect the default risk of a BBB borrower. The credit spreads used in CreditMetrics are generated by Bridge Information Systems, a consulting firm, which updates these rates every week.

14. Net of the first year's coupon payment, the loan's price would be $108.66 million − $6 million = $102.66 million.

15. Recent studies have suggested that this LGD may be too high for bank loans. A Citibank study of 831 default corporate loans and 89 asset-based loa s for 1970–1993 find recovery rates of 79 percent (or equivalently LGD equal to 21 percent). Similarly, high recovery rates are found in a Fitch Investor Service report in October 1997 (82 percent) and a Moody's Investor Service Report of June 1998 (87 percent) (see Asarnow [1999]).

16. In the calculation in Table 9.4, we look at the risk of the loan from the perspective of its mean or expected forward value ($107.09). Using an alternative perspective, we would look at the distribution of changes in value around the value of the loan if it continued to be rated BBB over the whole loan period. In Table 9.3, the forward value of the loan, if its rating remains unchanged over the next year, is $107.55. Using this BBB benchmark value, the mean and the variance of the value changes are, respectively: −$0.46 and $2.96. We obtain the mean using the probability-weighted distribution of bond value changes as shown in Table 9.3:

$$.0002(109.37 - 107.55) + .0033(109.19 - 107.55)$$
$$+.0595(108.66 - 107.55) + .053(102.02 - 107.55)$$
$$+.0117(98.10 - 107.55) + .0012(83.64 - 107.55)$$
$$+.0018(51.13 - 107.55) = -0.46$$

Similarly, the variance is:

$$.0002(1.82 + 0.46)^2 + .0033(1.64 + .46)^2 + .0595(1.11 + .46)^2$$
$$+.053(-5.53 + .46)^2 + .0117(-9.45 + .46)^2 + .0012(-23.91 + .46)^2$$
$$+.0018(-56.42 + .46)^2 = 8.77$$

The 1 percent VAR under the normal distribution assumption is then

$$(2.33 \times -\$2.96) + (-\$0.46) = -\$7.36$$

17. In 99 years out of 100, the 1 percent VAR capital requirement would allow the bank to survive unexpected credit losses on loans. Note that under the specific risk component for market risk, which measures spread risk, downgrade risk, and concentration risk for tradable instruments like corporate bonds, the 1 percent one-day VAR has to be multiplied by a factor of 3 or 4 (the stress-test multiplier), and the holding period is 10 days rather than one year; this leads to a $\sqrt{10}$ multiplier of one-day VAR for a liquidity risk adjustment. Boudoukh, Richardson and Whitelaw (1995) have shown (in simulation exercises) that, for some financial assets with normally distributed returns, the 3 to 4 multiplication factor may well pick up extreme losses such as the mean in the tail beyond the 99th percentile. However, they also found that the 3 to 4 multiplication factor badly underestimated extreme losses if there are runs of bad periods (e.g., as might be expected in a major long-term economic contraction). Neftci (2000) used extreme value theory to solve for market VAR and found that the BIS multiplication factor of 3 was excessive; instead, his estimates ranged from 1.02 to 1.33.

18. We discuss EVT from the perspective of assessing additional capital to cover catastrophic risk events. However, Neftci (2000) describes how the VAR itself can be more accurately measured using EVT. An advantage of the EVT approach is that it estimates the positive and negative tails of the underlying parent distribution separately, thereby allowing for distributional asymmetries in long and short positions. Longin and Solnik (2001) use EVT and find correlation increases across assets in bear markets (negative tails), but not in bull markets (positive tails).

19. Because of this property, EVT can also be used to measure operational risk (see Allen et al. [2002]).

20. For large samples of identically distributed observations, Block Maxima Models (generalized extreme value [GEV] distributions) are most appropriate for extreme values estimation. However, the peaks-over-threshold (POT) models make more efficient use of limited data on extreme values. Within the POT class of models is the generalized Pareto distribution (GPD) (see Appendix 9.2, McNeil [1999], and Neftci [2000]). Bali (2001) uses a more general functional form that encompasses both the GPD and the GEV—the Box-Cox-GEV.

21. Using the simple approach to calculating a transition matrix, suppose we have data for 1997 and 1998. In 1997, 5.0 percent of bonds rated BBB were downgraded to B. In 1998, 5.6 percent of bonds rated BBB were downgraded to B. The average transition probability of being downgraded from BBB to B is therefore 5.3 percent. In practice, however, historical average default rates are not accurate measures of the default probability; that is, average historical default probability typically overstates the default rate (see Crouhy et al. [2000]).

22. Finger (2000a) uses both an extended CreditMetrics model and an intensity-based model to examine correlated default probabilities over varying time horizons and finds considerable impact on economic capital requirements.

23. The credit cycle index, Z, is constructed from the default probabilities on speculative grade bonds (equal to and lower than Moody's Ba rating) regressed (using a probit model) on four factors: (1) the credit spread between Aaa and Baa; (2) the yield on 10-year Treasury bonds; (3) the quarterly consumer price index; and (4) the quarterly growth of GDP. To obtain Z, the model parameters are estimated using historical quarterly data, then projected forward to the next quarter and transformed into a standard normal distribution. Kim (1999) back-tests this specification and finds that it decreases forecasting errors by more than 30 percent when compared to the historical average. Bangia et al. (2000) use National Bureau of Economic Research (NBER) designations of contractions and expansions to obtain conditional probabilities of default. Using 1 percent VAR, they find that economic capital is nearly 30 percent higher for a contraction year than for an expansion year (see also Nickell et al. [2001a]).

24. That is, the transition matrix can be built around KMV's EDF scores rather than bond ratings. The correlation between KMV's transitions and rating agencies' transitions is low. In the December 2001 version of CreditMetrics, risk-neutral probabilities are used instead of historical migration probabilities. Alternatively, Algorithmics Mark to Future™ VAR uses scenario analysis as an alternative to valuations based on ratings transition matrixes.

25. The assumption of nonstochastic interest rates is also consistent with Merton (1974). Nevertheless, Shimko, Tejima and van Deventer (1993) have extended the Merton model to include stochastic interest rates.

26. Gupton et al., *CreditMetrics—Technical Document* (1997), 30. Whether recovery rates are constant, an additional capital requirement of $0.46 million, in our example, must be held as reserves against expected losses.

27. Unal et al. (2001) show that LGDs on bonds are extremely volatile across time and cross-sectionally.

28. Or, using the 99th percentile comparison, $2.33 \times \$2.99 = \$6.97$ million, versus $2.33 \times \$2.07 = \$4.82$ million.

29. Returns are calculated as the loan value on the horizon date (net of the bank's cost of funds) divided by the current loan value. However, returns may be undefined, particularly if the maturity of the loan exceeds the horizon date or if the horizon period is more than one year.

30. In all models, exposures are assumed to be independent of default risk. Finger (2000a) extends CreditMetrics to consider marketwide credit events (such as the 1997 Asian crisis) which can impact exposure values, as for credit derivatives.

31. Table 9.5 shows the transition matrix using historical migration probabilities. As of the December 2001 version of CreditMetrics, risk-neutral probabilities are used instead.

32. A standardized return is an actual return that is divided by its estimated standard deviation after subtracting the mean return. Thus, a standardized normal distribution has a mean of zero and a standard deviation of unity.

33. There is a 2.06 percent probability (1.06 percent + 1.00 percent) that the BB-rated borrower will be downgraded to C or below.

34. Arguably, we should be measuring correlations between loans and not borrowers. For example, a low-quality borrower with a highly secured loan would find the loan rated more highly than the borrower as a whole.

35. CreditMetrics requires the user to input the factor sensitivity coefficients.

36. By construction of the factor sensitivities, the bank and insurance indices are independent of each other. Note the correlation between the unsystematic return components U_A and U_Z is zero by assumption.

37. To find this number, the probabilities have to be counted backwards: the worst loan outcome, then the next worst, and so on until one reaches the loan value where the cumulative probability (starting from the worst case) is 1 percent—that is, the 99th percentile VAR.

38. In this case, the bank's capital requirement falls from 8.99 percent to $9.23/$200 million = 4.62 percent.

39. This approach can be computationally intensive, particularly for large portfolios. Nagpal and Bahar (1999) suggest an analytic solution that transforms correlated defaults into mutually exclusive scenarios with independent default probabilities. The number of scenarios is independent of the number of assets in the portfolio, thereby making their method computationally efficient for large portfolios. However, the methodology is not always feasible because it may generate negative probabilities.

40. Technically, decompose the correlation matrix (Σ) among the loans using the Cholesky factorization process, which finds two matrixes, A and A' (its transpose), such that I = AA'. Asset return scenarios (y) are generated by multiplying the matrix A' (which contains memory relating to historical correlation relationships) by a random number vector z, that is, $y = A'z$.

41. This can be quite computationally intensive. In the December 2001 version of CreditMetrics, variance-reduction techniques are used to cut down the number of required simulations by a factor of between 10 and 100. Rather than sampling the distribution around the origin, the new version of CreditMetrics extrapolates the entire distribution from concentrated sampling in the tails.

42. Appendix 9.4 demonstrates how CreditMetrics can be used to measure the risk of swaps.

43. The assumption of fixed credit spreads is quite contentious, as discussed in Appendix 9.1.

44. We abstract here from variations in the length of each semiannual coupon payment period that may range from 180 to 184 days. All risk-free rates are denoted r, all risky corporate bond rates are denoted y, and all zero-coupon risk-free rates are denoted z.

45. All one-year forward rates deliver in two half years; hence the first subscript 2 for all one-year forward yields.

46. If $\xi = 0$, then the distribution is exponential; if $\xi < 0$ it is the Pareto type II distribution.

47. These estimates are obtained from McNeil (1999), who estimates the parameters of the GPD using a database of Danish fire insurance claims. The scale and shape parameters may be calculated using maximum likelihood estimation in fitting the (distribution) function to the observations in the extreme tail of the distribution.

48. Finger (2000a) proposes an extension of CreditMetrics that would incorporate the correlation between credit exposure size and counterparty credit risk on derivatives instruments. In June 1999, the Counterparty Risk Management Policy Group called for the development of stress tests to estimate "wrong-way credit exposure" such as experienced by U.S. banks during the Asian currency crises. That is, credit exposure to Asian counterparties increased just as foreign currency declines caused FX losses on derivatives positions.

49. See Smith, Smithson, and Wilford (1990). The intuition behind using a Black-Scholes-type model to measure potential exposure can be seen by looking at the five variables that would determine the option value to default on a swap: the original interest rate on the swap (the strike price), the current interest rate (the current underlying price), the volatility of interest rates, the short-term interest rate, and the time to maturity of the swap.

50. The question, of course, is which transition matrix to use. Arguably, because the cash flows on swaps are similar to the coupon flows on bonds, a bond transition matrix may prove to be adequate.

51. This is an approximation. Default can occur at any time between time 0 and the end of the one-year credit-event horizon.

52. A cap can be valued as a call option on interest rates or a put on the price of a bond.

53. CreditMetrics allows for the estimation of the VAR for other off-balance sheet (OBS) activities, such as loan commitments, asset-backed securities, and credit guarantees (such as letters of credit).

CHAPTER 10   Stress Testing Credit Risk Models: Algorithmics Mark-to-Future

1. Under the internal model rules of the BIS for market risk, the bank's internal VAR has to be multiplied by a minimum value of 3. Intuitively, this 3 can be viewed as a stress test multiplier accommodating outliers in the 99 percent tail of the distribution. If, in back-testing a model, regulators/auditors find that the model underestimated VAR on fewer than 4 days out of the past 250 days, it is placed in a green zone and the VAR multiplier remains at its minimum value of 3. If risk is found to be underestimated anywhere between 4 days and 9 days of underestimated risk is found (out of 250 days), the model is placed in the yellow zone and the multiplier is increased to a range from 3.4 to 3.85. If more than 10

daily errors are found, the model is placed in the red zone and the multiplication factor for the internal VAR is set at 4. Some observers have labeled this regulatory punishment system the "traffic light" system.

2. Kupiec (1995) describes how a minimum of 1,000 observations is necessary to stress test a market VAR model if the underlying loss function is assumed to be symmetric. If, as is the case, the distribution is not symmetric, even more data are required. For example, McNeil's (1999) extreme value theory back-tests for market risk use more than 5,000 daily observations (see Appendix 9.2 for a discussion of extreme value theory).

3. Even this is somewhat optimistic; not even the rating agencies have default histories going back that far. Currently, most banks have perhaps two or three years of usable data (see Carey and Hrycay [2001]).

4. For example, Nickell et al. (2001b) conclude that their results suggesting that both KMV and CreditMetrics underestimate the credit risk of Eurobonds should be treated with caution since they only have 10 years of data.

5. Only active monitoring can reduce classification gaming designed either to minimize bank capital requirements or to maximize loan officer bonuses.

6. The cumulative accuracy ratio is one of many alternative statistical measures of historic ratings accuracy (see Bank for International Settlements [2006]).

7. Some models may perform better at different points in the credit cycle. Keswani (1999) uses Brady bond prices and finds that structural models outperformed (underperformed) reduced form models in the period before (after) the 1994 Mexican peso crisis.

8. The analogy with back-testing market risk models using time-series data is linked to how representative the past period is (i.e., the past 250 days under the BIS rules).

9. Altman and Karlin (2001b) average bond defaults over 1978–2001 and find that LGD is inversely related to bond seniority; that is, the median LGD is lowest (42.58 percent) for senior secured debt, next for senior unsecured (57.73 percent), and highest (68.04 percent) for subordinated debt. However, that effect has been somewhat unstable in recent years (see Table 10.3).

10. Finger (2000a) proposes an extension of CreditMetrics that would incorporate the correlation between market risk factors and credit exposure size. This is particularly relevant for the measurement of counterparty credit risk on derivatives instruments because the derivative can move in or out of the money as market factors fluctuate. In June 1999, the Counterparty Risk Management Policy Group called for the development of stress tests to estimate "wrong-way credit exposure" such as experienced by U.S. banks during the Asian currency crises; credit exposure to Asian counterparties increased just as the foreign currency declines caused FX losses on derivatives positions.

11. Fraser (2000) finds that a doubling of the spread between Baa-rated bonds over U.S. Treasury securities from 150 basis points to 300 basis points increases the 99 percent VAR measure from 1.77 percent to 3.25 percent for a Eurobond portfolio.

12. Since other models assume credit risk to be independent of market risk (e.g., see Chapter 9 for a discussion of CreditMetrics' assumption of fixed credit spreads), the MtF estimates must be compared to the sum of market risk and credit risk exposures obtained in other models.

13. Although the default boundary is not observable, it can be computed from the (unconditional) default probability term structure observed for BB-rated firms.

14. Default is assumed to be an absorbing state, so Figure 10.1 shows that the curve representing the firm's asset value in scenario 1 coincides with the default boundary for all periods after year 3.

15. During the months it took to implement the stress test, the economy deteriorated further so that the baseline scenario had already been breached by the date of publication of the results (March 7, 2009). For example, the consensus unemployment rate was 9.3 percent, rather than the 8.9 percent in the baseline scenario.

16. Although each bank constructed its own loss and revenue forecasts, they were required to submit detailed documentation and backup data to bank regulators for extensive review. The forecasts were compared to independent benchmarks that estimated indicative loan loss rates for each type of loan using micro data. Approval of the banks' forecasts occurred after a period of negotiation between the banks and the regulators about the implications of the stress test and the required additions to each bank's capital base.

17. However, firms with trading assets of $100 billion or more were additionally asked to estimate potential losses from trading and counterparty credit risk under a market stress scenario similar to the market shocks of the second half of 2008.

18. Risk-weighted assets are calculated under the conditions established by the Basel Accord on Bank Capital Requirements. See Chapter 13 for a discussion.

CHAPTER 11   RAROC Models

1. The second motivation is consistent with academic studies showing that bank holding companies establish internal capital markets to allocate scarce capital across various subsidiaries (see Houston et al. [1997]). Even when structured to be bankruptcy-remote, capital constraints at these subsidiaries have imposed real costs at the holding company level, as evidenced during the 2007–2009 financial crisis.

2. According to Zaik, Walter and Kelling (1996), Bank of America applies its RAROC model to 46 different business units within the bank.

3. In general, WACC will be less than ROE.

4. The RAROC approach essentially assumes that all assets are either perpetuities or pure discount instruments with the same maturity date. To adjust for differences across assets in the timing of cash flows, capital budgeting's net present value approach should be used with the discount rate adjusted for the risk of each individual asset. Analyzing RAROC for property and insurance companies, Nakada et al. (1999) use the present value of all cash flows (discounted at the insurer's marginal borrowing rate) in both the numerator and denominator of equation (11.1).

5. Turnbull (2000) defines the term structure of economic capital as the schedule of required capital over the long-term planning horizon, which is determined by the timing and risk of project cash flows.
6. However, Machlachlan (1998) notes a circularity in valuing projects and investment allocations using economic capital (EC) when the project's market value itself must be used to obtain the measure of EC.
7. Nevertheless, some banks take a "customer relationship" approach and calculate the RAROC for the whole relationship.
8. In applying RAROC to the investment decisions of insurance companies, Nakada et al. (1999) solve for a combined RAROC that balances the diversification effects against the tax penalty. Similarly, the tax penalty in Turnbull (2000) is the tax that bank shareholders pay on the risk-free interest received from the interim investment of economic capital until it is needed, either in the event of default or at the maturity of the loan, to repurchase equity. Alternatively, the tax penalty may be viewed as the debt tax shield forgone because of the use of economic capital (equity) rather than debt to finance part of the loan.
9. The economic capital required in the initial period of the loan is used in the denominator even if economic capital requirements vary over the life of the loan. Some (e.g., Nakada et al. [1999]) have argued that the present value of economic capital over the life of the project should be used in the denominator, but Turnbull (2000) shows that any adjustment for the stream of economic capital should instead be included in the numerator.
10. Credit risk is distinguished from market risk in that the interest rate on the loan can be decomposed into: $R_L = r_f + R$ where R_L is the loan rate, r_f is the risk-free rate (Treasury rate) on a similar duration bond, and R is the credit spread. Here, we are not concerned with changes in r_f (Δr_f) that affect the loan's market value, but rather with the effects of shifts in R (ΔR), the credit spread.
11. Suppose the bank's hurdle was its ROE of 10 percent. Then the loan would be profitable and should be made under the RAROC criterion.
12. As discussed earlier, one simple way to calculate σ is to use the binomial model. Based on N years of data, where p_i is the default rate in year i for this borrower type:

$$\sigma = (1/N)\sqrt{\sum_{i=1}^{n} p_i(1 - p_i)}$$

13. As of August 2009, no bank had AAA status in the United States.
14. Maclachlan (1998) shows that maximizing RAROC may not produce efficient portfolio allocations, particularly in the event of increases in the tail density of return distributions; in other words, since RAROC is a point estimate of the reward to risk, it may result in overinvestment in correlated risky outlier assets. Therefore, Dvorak (2008) suggests a move from RAROC toward loan transfer pricing (see the discussion in Chapter 8).

15. In order to distinguish between the different return symbols used in this chapter, we denote the risk-free rate r going forward as r_f.

16. Some multifactor specification of equation (11.15) may be more appropriate in many cases.

17. Indeed, without a comparative advantage in providing monitoring and information services, there would be no reason for banks to exist in private economies.

18. If this assumption is relaxed, then the required return (hurdle rate) cannot be expressed as a constant, as in the standard RAROC formulation, but rather as an increasing function of the amount invested in the loan. The form of the Froot and Stein (1998) result differs from the standard RAROC formulation shown in equation (11.1). Instead, Froot and Stein solve for the optimal level of investment in the new project (the loan) as a function of the bank's risk aversion, the loan's unhedgeable risk, and the loan's expected return.

19. In Froot and Stein (1998), the result in equation (11.20) is driven by the assumption of convex costs of issuing equity to meet the bank's economic capital requirements. Turnbull (2000) achieves the same result assuming that the role of economic capital is to lower any particular loan's default probability to a desired level (say, commensurate with the bank's chosen credit rating). Therefore, for any marginal loan, the economic capital is calculated on a marginal, not a stand-alone basis. Thus, diversification of the loan portfolio may reduce the amount of economic capital required for any particular loan; capital can be considered subadditive and the result in equation (11.20) obtains.

20. James (1996) offers empirical evidence documenting the sensitivity of loan growth to bank financing constraints and capital costs. Ho (1999) uses typical insurance company data to simulate the cost of capital adjustments and finds an S&P convexity charge of 34.7 basis points, where the S&P convexity charge is defined to be the price shock (capital charge) in the event of a 300 basis point parallel shift in the yield curve for a bond with negative convexity compared to an option-free bond of the same duration.

21. This term can be viewed as the cost per unit of bank capital times the amount of capital that may be lost due to unhedgeable fluctuations in the loan's value.

CHAPTER 12   Credit Derivatives

1. Warren Buffett's quotes have been taken from the 2002 Berkshire Hathaway annual report.

2. Garmaise and Moskowitz (2009) connect risk of natural catastrophes (e.g., earthquakes) with credit risk in the real estate market. Inefficiencies in the supply of insurance against natural disasters can distort bank credit availability, further expanding the range of risks bundled into credit markets. Almeida and Philippon (2007) show that the marginal costs of financial distress during bad times are about as large as the debt tax shield.

3. The credit event can be specified as default, failure to pay, restructuring, and so on. However, the use of restructuring as a credit event is ambiguous when the reference security is a loan, since loan restructuring is a fairly common

occurrence that may be triggered by something other than the borrower's financial distress. Thus, restructuring is known as a *soft* credit event. Repudiation or a moratorium is used as a credit event for credit derivatives based on government obligations.

4. As discussed in Chapter 3, there have been several proposals to move credit derivatives trading to organized exchanges. It is unclear whether the benefits of exchange trading (enhanced transparency and liquidity) will be offset by the costs of basis risk and lack of customization as the standardized contracts diverge from the underlying risks to be hedged.

5. The increased presence of hedge funds led to an agreement that enhanced the liquidity of the CDS market in 2006. Liquidating a CDS position typically required either offsetting transactions or an agreement by both counterparties to terminate (tear up) the transaction. However, hedge funds preferred to transfer their shares via assignment—a process known as *novation*. Unfortunately, there were problems in coordinating novation agreements and getting confirmation. In September 2006, the ISDA Novation Protocol was announced to standardize novation procedures, requiring parties to obtain prior consent, which could be communicated electronically. The results were to dramatically reduce confirmation backlogs.

6. Single-name CDSs specify a single reference security. In contrast, multiname CDSs reference more than one name, as in a portfolio or basket CDS or CDS index, such as the Dow Jones CDX. Baskets are credit derivatives based on a small portfolio of loans or bonds, such that all assets included in the underlying pool are individually listed. In contrast, the contents of larger portfolios are described by their characteristics. A basket credit default swap, also known as a first-to-default swap, is structured like a regular CDS, but the reference security consists of several securities. The first reference entity to default triggers a default payment of the par value minus the recovery value and then all payments end. As of the first half of 2007, there was an additional $20 trillion notional value in multiname CDSs.

7. See Smithson (2003) and Mengle (2007) for a discussion of the stages of development of the market for credit derivatives. The standardized contracts, terms, and dispute resolution provided by the International Swap and Derivatives Association (ISDA) played a role in that evolution.

8. Despite the decline in notional value of CDS contracts outstanding, the gross market value for CDSs increased 78.2 percent to $5.7 trillion as of the end of 2008, reflecting turmoil in credit markets during the second half of 2008.

9. The most popular CDS indices consist of 125 corporate entities. Multiname or basket CDSs contain more than one reference security, most commonly between 3 and 10. The most common form of multiname CDS is the first-to-default CDS, which compensates the protection buyer for losses on the first default among the basket of reference entities, after which the swap automatically terminates. As will be shown in this chapter, tranched synthetic collateralized debt obligations (CDOs) comprising indexed CDSs also prioritize credit protection, but are more flexible than first-to-default swaps.

10. In contrast, an interest rate swap (fixed- for floating-rate swap) will entail symmetric payments such that the swap buyer (the fixed-rate leg of the swap) earns positive cash flows when interest rates increase, and the swap seller (the floating-rate leg) earns positive cash flows when interest rates decrease.

11. Over-the-counter CDSs have standardized spread payment dates on March 20, June 20, September 20, and December 20. The spread is constant for the life of the swap, with the exception of a constant maturity CDS in which the spread is reset periodically to the market rate for newly issued CDSs.

12. Swap spreads incorporate counterparty credit risk. For example, Hull and White (2001) find a range of around 50 basis points when they simulate the impact of counterparty credit risk exposure. See Appendix 12.1 for a discussion. Note in Table 12.2 that only Barclays placed a request to sell at the 8/10 bid/offer price.

13. Credit spread options, shown in Table 12.1 to be a vanishing portion of the market (largely replaced by swaptions), give the buyer the right, but not the obligation, to pay a specified credit spread over a specified time period. We consider indexed CDSs and CDOs (listed in Table 12.1) later in this chapter.

14. Both the obligor and the specific reference debt instrument must be specified. The reference instrument is usually a senior unsecured debt obligation, although CDSs can be written on subordinated debt as well.

15. Default payments are usually computed in one of three ways: (1) par minus a final loan price as determined by a poll of dealers (such as Creditex and CreditTrade); (2) payment of par by the counterparty in exchange for physical delivery of the defaulted loan; and (3) a fixed dollar amount contractually agreed to at the swap origination. Increasingly, method 2 is the favored method of settlement because of the difficulty in getting accurate secondary market prices on loans around credit event dates. Gunduz et al. (2007) state that 86 percent of CDS transactions specify physical settlement.

16. Basis risk results when the fluctuations in the value of the reference security underlying the derivative do not move in lockstep with the hedge position. For example, there is basis risk if indexed CDSs are used to hedge a portfolio of loans to firms that are not identical to the 125 firms in the index.

17. This makes the market subject to a squeeze as settling CDS contract holders drive up the demand for the scarce bonds, especially since physical settlement must occur within 30 days of the credit event.

18. The initial auctions were held by Markit and Creditex to determine payment on the iTraxx family of CDS index products covering Europe, Japan, and Asia. For example, the iTraxx Europe index contains 125 of the most liquid CDSs referencing investment-grade debt instruments, which change every six months (see Gross and Saperia [2008]).

19. There are more steps for auctions based on loans, rather than bonds.

20. Indeed, partial cash and partial physical settlement can be chosen, such that investor B can submit a bid to buy any amount of the reference bond from $0 to $10 million in this example.

21. All debt instruments of the same seniority are pooled together and auctioned at the same time, at the same price. Therefore, there is no distinction based on

maturity date, yield, and so on, since in bankruptcy, seniority is the only relevant characteristic determining recovery value.

22. HSBC had to pay a penalty of $12,500 to ISDA because its bid was too high.

23. The 1996 amendment to Basel I incorporated the capital requirements for counterparty credit risk on OBS derivatives discussed in this chapter. Basel II guidelines keep portions of Basel I intact.

24. In this section, we consider all types of swaps (e.g., interest rate, currency), as well as CDSs.

25. The capital requirement under Basel I would then be 8 percent of $2.75 million, or $220,000.

26. See Federal Reserve Board of Governors press release, August 29, 1995, 17.

27. Note that the net to gross current exposure ratio (NGR) will vary across different contracts, whereas the 0.4 and 0.6 weights remain unchanged.

28. However, to be included as a risk mitigation contract, bank regulators required that the CDS specify restructuring as a credit event. To alleviate the ambiguity in this soft credit event, the 2003 ISDA documentation placed some limits on the restructuring trigger (see Mengle [2007]).

29. Chapter 13 describes the Basel II Capital Accord in detail. Banks are required to hold capital in proportion to the risk of their activities (both on and off the balance sheet). The more credit risk exposure, the higher the risk weight and the more capital required. Under the standardized model of Basel II, risk weights range from 0 percent (for government entities) to 150 percent (for below-investment-grade corporate counterparties).

30. The one exception is in the case of a maturity mismatch in which the maturity of the hedge is less than that of the underlying exposure. If the maturity mismatch exceeds one year, then Basel II proposes an adjusted risk weight that is a function of the ratio of the maturities.

31. In November 2001, the Basel Committee on Banking Supervision released potential modifications of the Basel II proposals that could eliminate the collateral weight factor from minimum capital requirements and replace the treatment of residual risks with pillar 2 supervisory oversight. See Bank for International Settlements, November 5 (2001b).

32. See Vinod Kothari's "Credit Derivatives" web site, http://www.credit-deriv .com/.

33. See Dahiya et al. (2001).

34. CLNs were also known as funded CDSs.

35. The junior status of the equity tranche makes it the riskiest and, therefore, the coupon rate will be higher than for the other more senior tranches of the CDO. For all tranches except the equity tranche, CDO pricing data are in terms of the credit spread in the coupon payment paid quarterly on the remaining notional value balance. The equity tranche also includes an up-front premium paid to the CDO buyer in addition to the credit spread in the coupon payment. Longstaff and Rajan (2008) find that CDO pricing includes risk premiums for idiosyncratic or firm-specific default risk, industry default risk, and catastrophic economywide default risk.

36. Implicit leverage declines for the more senior tranches.
37. In the credit bubble buildup, CDO underwriters adjusted the attachment points (and other credit enhancements) to ensure that the top tranches received the highest AAA/Aaa credit rating.
38. This threshold can be viewed as equivalent to the credit enhancement offered by the originating bank in a CLO or CLN.
39. In the early years of the instrument, BISTRO collateralization ranges from 5–15 percent of the notional value of the loan portfolio. However, as the credit markets overheated collateralization and equity tranches on all asset-backed securities declined markedly. For example, a 2006 Goldman Sachs CMO with average LTV of 99.29 percent had only a 3 percent equity tranche. See A. Sloan, "House of Junk," *Fortune*, October 29, 2007.
40. The rules for a *clean break* differ for synthetic securitizations. However, all are intended to insure that ABS holders have neither implicit nor explicit recourse to originators. However, during the 2007–2009 financial crisis, the SIVs held backup lines of credit to their ABCP offerings so that banks such as Citibank ultimately assumed recourse to their ABS holdings, despite meeting legal conditions for a clean break. See the discussion in Chapter 1.
41. If the bank uses the standardized (IRB) method to compute its capital requirement, it must use the standardized (ratings-based) approach under the securitization framework (see Chapter 13).
42. The risk weight for unrated securitizations is calculated using a supervisory formula. See Basel II (June 2006), paragraph 623.
43. Increased risk weighting of market risk was also proposed in January 2009. See "Revisions to the Basel II Market Risk Framework," January 2009. Moreover, in November 2008, the Basel Committee reaffirmed its commitment to fair valuation of bank assets, reiterating the importance of accurate valuation modeling. However, in June 2009, the Financial Accounting Standards Board (FASB) loosened those standards and allowed U.S. banks to use their own discretion in fair value accounting (see the discussion in Chapter 1).
44. DeSantes (1999) describes how insurance companies leverage their high credit ratings and increase earnings by selling credit protection in the credit derivatives market.

CHAPTER 13 Capital Regulation

1. The Basel Committee consists of senior supervisory representatives from Belgium, Canada, France, Germany, Italy, Japan, Luxembourg, the Netherlands, Sweden, Switzerland, the United Kingdom, and the United States. It usually meets at the Bank for International Settlements (BIS) in Basel, Switzerland, where its permanent Secretariat is located.
2. More than 100 countries have adopted the Basel Accords. Morrison and White (2009) examine the costs and benefits of creating a level playing field through international bank capital standards. The disadvantage is that since capital regulations substitute for high-quality regulatory oversight, international bank

capital requirements must be set to the weakest regulatory standard. However, in a world of mobile capital, a level playing field avoids the cherry-picking effect that reduces the size and efficiency of banks in weaker economies.

3. Tier 1 consists of the last, residual claims on the bank's assets, such as common stock and perpetual preferred stock. Tier 2 capital is slightly more senior than Tier 1—for example, preferred stock and subordinated debt. The capital tiers are described in this chapter.

4. An indication of Basel I's mispricing of credit risk for commercial loans is obtained from Flood (2001), who examines the actual loan loss experience for U.S. banks and thrifts from 1984 to 1999. He finds that in 1984 (1996) 10 percent (almost 3 percent) of the institutions had loan losses that exceeded the 8 percent Basel capital requirement. Moreover, Falkenheim and Powell (2001) find that the Basel I capital requirements for Argentine banks were set too low to protect against the banks' credit risk exposures. See ISDA (1998) for an early discussion of the need to reform Basel I.

5. However, Jones (2000) and Mingo (2000) argue that regulatory arbitrage may not be all bad because it set the forces of innovation into motion that will ultimately correct the mispricing errors inherent in the regulations. Moreover, VanHoose (2007) argues that it is unclear whether capital regulation actually promotes the overall safety and soundness of the banking system as a whole. Whether capital requirements induce banks to take more or less risk depends on their risk-aversion levels, among other factors. It is clear, however, that the introduction of capital requirements causes an immediate decline in lending, and a longer-term increase in the capital cushion available to protect depositors and deposit insurers in the event of failure.

6. However, studies show that the introduction of Basel II, particularly the IRB, will reduce capital requirements. For example, Kashyap and Stein (2004) find that capital charges would have been 30 to 45 percent of Basel I requirements using a simulation over the 1998 to 2002 period.

7. In this chapter, we consider only regulatory capital requirements, although there is substantial evidence that banks hold economic capital in excess of regulatory minimums (see Berger et al. [2008]).

8. Earlier versions of the plan date back to 1999.

9. McKinsey estimates that operational risk represents 20 percent, market risk comprises 20 percent, and credit risk 60 percent of the overall risk of a typical commercial bank or investment bank (see Hammes and Shapiro [2001]), page 106.

10. The basic indicator approach levies a single operational risk capital charge for the entire bank; the standardized approach divides the bank into eight lines of business, each with its own operational risk charge; and the advanced measurement approach (AMA) uses the bank's own internal models of operational risk measurement to assess a capital requirement. See Bank for International Settlements (September 2001).

11. At the discretion of national bank regulators, Tier 3 capital consisting of short-term subordinated debt can be used to meet capital requirements against market risks only.

12. Carey (2001b) suggests that since subordinated debt (Tier 2 capital) is not useful in preserving soundness (i.e., impaired subordinated debt triggers bank insolvency), there should be a distinction between equity and loan loss reserves (the buffer against credit risk, denoted Tier A) and subordinated debt (the buffer against market risk, denoted Tier B). Jackson et al. (2001) also show that the proportion of Tier 1 capital should be considered in setting minimum capital requirements.

13. Note that Basel I is still in place in countries that have not yet adopted Basel II.

14. The EAD for on-balance-sheet items is the nominal outstanding amount, whereas EAD for off-balance-sheet items is determined using most of the same credit conversion factors from Basel I, with the exception of loan commitments maturing in less than one year that now have a 20 percent conversion factor rather than the 0 percent under Basel I.

15. Korea and Mexico (both OECD members) will move under the proposals from a zero risk weight to a positive risk weight corresponding to their credit ratings. Powell (2001) uses the standardized approach to estimate that capital requirements for banks lending to Korea (Mexico) will increase by $3.4 billion ($5 billion), resulting in an estimated increase in bond spreads of 74.8 basis points for Korea and 104.5 basis points for Mexico. If the internal ratings-based approach is used, the impact is even greater.

16. That is, an AAA rating would normally warrant a 0 percent risk weight, but instead the risk weight is set one category higher at 20 percent.

17. However, if the contract is expected to roll over upon maturity (e.g., an open repo), then its effective maturity exceeds three months and the bank supervisor may consider it ineligible for the preferential risk weights shown in Table 13.4.

18. For example, Altman and Saunders (2001a,b) compare the historical actual one-year losses on a bond portfolio using a loss distribution (default mode) at the 99.97 percent confidence level and find that the 1.6 percent capital charge for the first risk bucket (AAA to AA− ratings) is too high given the 0 percent historical loss experience. However, the historical one-year loss experience for the lowest-risk bucket (ratings below BB−) is significantly larger than the 12 percent capital requirement. Similarly, Powell (2001) finds insufficient convexity in the standardized approach for sovereign debt.

19. For less developed countries, the proportion of companies with external credit ratings is much lower than for developed countries. Powell (2001) reports that only 150 corporates in Argentina are rated, although the central bank's credit bureau lists 25,000 corporate borrowers. Thus, Ferri et al. (2001) surmise that borrowers in less developed countries are likely to suffer a substantial increase in borrowing costs relative to those in developed countries upon adoption of Basel II. The Basel Committee report (June 2009) documents that external credit ratings are more frequently used in the United States and Canada than in the European Union, Australia, and Japan.

20. Linnell (2001) and Altman and Saunders (2001b) suggest that, at the very least, the unrated classification risk weight should be 150 percent. There is evidence

that the failure ratio on nonrated loans is similar to the failure ratio in the lowest (150 percent) rated bucket (see Altman and Saunders [2001b]).

21. To mitigate this problem, Griep and De Stefano (2001) suggest that more unsolicited ratings be used. German bank associations plan to pool credit data so as to address the problem of unrated small and medium-size businesses. Because of the importance of this market sector to the German economy, Chancellor Schroder threatened to veto the Basel II proposal. See *The Economist*, November 10, 2001.

22. For example, in 2006, Moody's earned 44 percent of its revenues from rating structured finance deals (see Tomlinson and Evans [2007]). Thus, the rating agencies may have been disinclined to scrutinize the quality of the loans in the ABSs, thereby contributing to the large number of defaults on highly rated securities. Perhaps in recognition of these inherent conflicts of interest, U.S. bank regulators in adopting the standardized model in July 2008 stipulated that if there are multiple ratings, the lowest must be used for capital requirements, and that at least two ratings must be obtained for all nontraded assets.

23. Moreover, contagious regional financial crises in confidence may lead to excessive downgrading of sovereign ratings (see Cantor and Packer (1996), Ferri et al. [2001], and Kaminsky and Schmukler [2001]).

24. The use of a one-year time horizon assumes that banks can fully recapitalize any credit losses within a year. Carey (2001b) argues that a two- to three-year time horizon is more realistic. Ebnother and Vanini (2007) specify a five-year time horizon so as to include deep recessions that, according to the National Bureau of Economic Research (NBER), ranged from 35 to 65 months. Under Basel II, the lower bound on PD is 0.03 percent.

25. Maturity is the weighted average life of the loan—that is, the percentage of principal repayments in each year times the year(s) in which these payments are received. For example, a two-year loan of $200 million repaying $100 million principal in year 1 and $100 million principal in year 2 has a weighted average life (WAL) of $[1 \times (100/200)] + [2 \times (100/200)] = 1.5$ years.

26. The correlations specified in the Basel II model are not estimated correlations, as described in Chapter 8, but rather formulaic correlations that are specified as a function of PD.

27. The format of the IRB approaches is to use PD, LGD, and M to determine the loan's risk weight and then to multiply that risk weight times the EAD times 8 percent in order to determine the loan's capital requirement.

28. General provisions to protect the bank against expected losses can be used to satisfy Tier 2 of the Basel II capital requirements under the conditions that (1) they are general loss reserves not charged to any specific loan loss, and (2) they do not exceed 1.25 percent of risk-weighted assets.

29. For UL estimates, the LGD (under the advanced model) should reflect losses in an adverse downturn economy.

30. The format of the Basel II IRB equations is to express PD and LGD in decimals.

31. Allen and Saunders (2004) show that there is no consensus in the literature about whether correlations are either directly or inversely related to PD.

High-PD, less creditworthy firms may be subject to high correlations (particularly in economic downturns), suggesting a direct relationship. Alternatively, low PD firms may be subject to less idiosyncratic risk and therefore higher correlations, suggesting the inverse relationship assumed in the Basel II IRB model.

32. Carty (1998) finds the mean LGD for senior unsecured (secured) bank loans is 21 percent (13 percent), and finds a mean LGD of 36 percent for a portfolio of private placements. Asarnow and Edwards (1995) find a 35 percent LGD for commercial loans. Gupton (2000) finds a 30.5 percent (47.9 percent) LGD for senior secured (unsecured) syndicated bank loans. Gupton et al. (2000) obtain similar estimates for the expected LGD but find substantial variance around the mean.

33. That is, granularity takes into account the number of different rating categories. The more categories, the greater the granularity.

34. Concentration risk is meant to be resolved by supervising case-by-case intervention under pillar 2 of the BIS program.

35. Jackson et al. (2001) show that Basel II is calibrated to achieve a confidence level of 99.96 percent (i.e., an insolvency rate of 0.4 percent), whereas banks choose a solvency standard of 99.9 percent in response to market pressures. This conforms to observations that banks tend to hold capital in excess of regulatory requirements.

36. Jackson et al. (2001) find that a decrease in the bank's credit rating from A+ to A would reduce swap liabilities by approximately £2.3 billion.

37. These banks were also required to use the advanced measurement approach (AMA) to operational risk measurement (see Chapter 5 of Allen et al. [2004]).

38. At the same time, U.S. bank regulators decided to allow U.S. banks to adopt the basic indicator approach (BIA) to operational risk measurement.

39. Similarly, the credit conversion factor for the unfunded portion of home equity lines of credit (HELOCs) was made a function of LTV.

40. There have been proposals for a "managed leverage ratio," which would put off-balance-sheet activity onto the balance sheet and then calculate the leverage ratio (see Mason [2008]).

41. For a survey of the literature on the topic of procyclicality, see Allen and Saunders (2004). For a study examining the relationship between the Spanish business cycle and bank capital, see Ayuso, Perez and Saurina (2004).

42. Obama-Geithner Plan (2009), page 81.

Bibliography

Acharya, V. V. "A Theory of Systemic Risk and Design of Prudential Bank Regulation." *Journal of Financial Stability*, 5(2009), 224–255.

Acharya, V., S. Bharath and A. Srinivasan. "Does Industry-Wide Distress Affect Defaulted Firms? Evidence from Creditor Recoveries" *Journal of Financial Economics* 85(2007): 787–821.

Acharya, V., and J. Carpenter. "Corporate Bond Valuation and Hedging with Stochastic Interest Rates and Endogenous Bankruptcy." *Review of Financial Studies* 15(2002): 1,355–1,383.

Acharya, V. V., J. Huang, M. G. Subrahmanyam, and R. K. Sundaram. "When Does Strategic Debt-Service Affect Debt Spreads?" *Economic Theory*, 2006, 1–16.

Acharya, V., and T. Yorulmazer. "Information Contagion and Bank Herding." *Journal of Money, Credit and Banking*, (2008) 40, no. 1, 215–231.

Agrawal, D., I. Korablev, and D. W. Dwyer. "Valuation of Corporate Loans: A Credit Migration Approach." *Moody's KMV Publication*, January 25, 2008.

Aguais, S. D., L. Forest, S. Krishnamoorthy, and T. Mueller. "Creating Value from Both Loan Structure and Price." *Commercial Lending Review*, Spring 1998, 13–24

Allen, L."Discussion." In *Ratings, Rating Agencies, and the Global Financial System*, R. Levich (ed.). Kluwer Academic Press, 2002.

Allen, L., J. Boudoukh, and A. Saunders.*Value at Risk in Theory and Practice*. Malden, ME: Blackwell Publishing, 2002.

Allen, L., J. Boudoukh, A. Saunders.*Understanding Market, Credit and Operational Risk*. Malden, ME: Blackwell Publishing, 2004.

Allen, L., and G. Li. "Clawbacks and Cronyism: Evidence from China." Baruch College Working Paper, June 2009.

Allen, L., and A. Saunders. "Incorporating Systemic Influences Into Risk Measurements: A Survey of the Literature," *Journal of Financial Services Research* 26, no. 2(2004): 161–191

Allen, L. *Capital Markets and Institutions: A Global View*. New York: John Wiley & Sons, 1997.

Allen, L., and A. Gottesman. "The Informational Efficiency of the Equity Market As Compared to the Syndicated Bank Loan Market,*" Journal of Financial Services Research* 30, no. 1 (August 2006): 5–42.

Almeida, H., and T. Philippon. "The Risk-Adjusted Cost of Financial Distress," *Journal of Finance LXII, no.* 6 (December 2007): 2,557–2,586.

Altman, E. I. "Financial Ratios, Discriminant Analysis and the Prediction of Corporate Bankruptcy." *Journal of Finance.* September 1968, 589–609.

Altman, E. I. "Measuring Corporate Bond Mortality and Performance." *Journal of Finance,* September 1989, 909–922.

Altman, E. I. *Corporate Financial Distress.* 2nd ed., 1983/1990. New York: John Wiley & Sons, 1993.

Altman, E. I. "Predicting Financial Distress of Companies: Revisiting the Z-Score and Zeta Models." Working Paper, Dept. of Finance, NYU., July 2000.

Altman, E. I. et al. "The Z-Metrics Methodology for Estimating Company Credit Ratings and Default Risk Probabilities." Working Paper, March 2010.

Altman, E. I., T. K. N. Baidya, and L. M. R. Dias. "Assessing Potential Financial Problems for Firms in Brazil." *Journal of International Business Studies* 10(2) (1979): 9–24.

Altman, E. I., with B. Brady. "Explaining Aggregate Recovery Rates on Corporate Bond Defaults." Salomon Center Working Paper. November 2001.

Altman, E. I., B. Brady, A. Resti, and A. Sironi. "The Link between Default and Recovery Rates: Theory, Empirical Evidence, and Implications." *Journal of Business* 78, no. 6 (November 2005): 2,203–2,227.

Altman, E. I., and D. L. Kao. "The Implications of Corporate Bond Ratings Drift." *Financial Analysts Journal,* May–June 1992 64–75.

Altman, E. I., and B. Karlin. "Defaults and Returns on High Yield Bonds: Analysis Through 2000 and Default Outlook." Working Paper 10, NYU Salomon Center, February 2001a.

Altman, E., and B. Karlin. "Defaults and Returns on High Yield Bonds: Analysis Through the First Half of 2001 and Default Outlook." NYU Salomon Center, June 2001b.

Altman, E. I., and E. Hotchkiss. "Corporate Credit Scoring—Insolvency Risk Models," in *Corporate Financial Distress and Bankruptcy, 3rd ed.* Wiley Finance: 2006.

Altman, E. I., and V. M. Kishore. "Almost Everything You Wanted to Know About Recoveries on Defaulted Bonds," *Financial Analysts Journal* (1996) November/December, 57–64.

Altman, E. I., G. Marco, and F. Varetto. "Corporate Distress Diagnosis: Comparisons Using Linear Discriminant Analysis and Neural Networks (the Italian Experience)." *Journal of Banking and Finance,* May 1994 505–529.

Altman, E. I., and P. Narayanan. "An International Survey of Business Failure Classification Models." *Financial Markets, Instruments and Institutions* 6(2) (1997).

Altman, E. I., A. Resti, A. Sironi, (eds.). *Recovery Risk.* London: Riskbooks, 2005.

Altman, E. I., and A. Saunders. "Credit Risk Measurement: Developments over the Last Twenty Years." *Journal of Banking and Finance,* December 1997, 1,721–1,742.

Altman, E. I., and A. Saunders. "An Analysis and Critique of the BIS Proposal on Capital Adequacy and Ratings." *Journal of Banking and Finance*, January 2001a, 25–46.

Altman, E. I., and A. Saunders. "Credit Ratings and the BIS Reform Agenda." Paper presented at the Bank of England Conference on Banks and Systemic Risk, London, May 23–25, 2001b.

Altman, E. I., and H. J. Suggitt. "Default Rates in the Syndicated Loan Market: A Mortality Analysis." Working Paper 39, NYU Salomon Center, December 1997.

Amihud, Y., and H. Mendelson. "Liquidity, Maturity and Yields on U.S. Treasury Securities." *Journal of Finance* 46(1991): 1,411–1,425.

"Anatomy of a Global Credit Crisis." *New Zealand Herald*, August 22, 2007, 2.

Anderson, R., S. Sundaresan, and P. Tychon. "Strategic Analysis of Contingent Claims." *European Economic Review*. April 1996, 871–881, April 1996.

Anderson, R., and S. Sundaresan. "A Comparative Study of Structural Models of Corporate Bond Yields: An Exploratory Investigation." *Journal of Banking and Finance*. January 2000, 255–269.

Angbazo, L., J.-P. Mei, and A. Saunders. "Credit Spreads in the Market for Highly Leveraged Transaction Loans." *Journal of Banking and Finance*, October 1998, 1,249–1,282.

Arora, N., J. Bohn, F. Zhu. "Reduced Form vs. Structural Models of Credit Risk: A Case Study of Three Models." *Moody's KMV Publication*, February 17, 2005.

Arrow, K. K. "Le Role des Valeurs Boursieres pour la Repartition de la Meilleure des Risques." *Econometrie* 40(1953): 91–96.

Asarnow, E. "Managing Bank Loan Portfolios for Total Return." Paper presented at a conference on "A New Market Equilibrium for the Credit Business," Frankfurt, Germany, March 11, 1999.

Asarnow, E., and J. Marker. "Historical Performance of the U.S. Corporate Loan Market, 1988–1993." *Journal of Commercial Lending*, Spring 1995, 13–22.

Asarnow, E., and D. Edwards. "Measuring Loss on Defaulted Bank Loans: A 24-Year Study." *Journal of Commercial Lending*, March 1995, 11–23.

Asquith, P., D. W. Mullins, and E. D. Wolff. "Original Issue High Yield Bonds: Aging Analysis of Defaults, Exchanges and Calls." *Journal of Finance*, September 1989, 923–952.

Astebro, T., and F. Rucker. "Foresight Beats Hindsight: Maximizing Portfolio Returns by Optimizing the Cut-Off Credit Score." *RMA Journal*, February 2000, 65–69.

Ayuso, J., D. Perez, and J. Saurina. "Are Capital Buffers Pro-Cyclical? Evidence from Spanish Panel Data," *Journal of Financial Intermediation* 13(2004), 249–264.

Babbel, D. F. "Insuring Banks Against Systematic Credit Risk." *Journal of Futures Markets*, November 6, 1989, 487–506.

Bahar, R., and K. Nagpal. "Modeling the Dynamics." *Credit*, March 2000.

Bali, T. "The Generalized Extreme Value Distribution: Implications for the Value at Risk," Baruch College Working Paper, February 2001.

Bangia, A., F. X. Diebold, and T. Schuermann. "Ratings Migration and the Business Cycle, with Applications to Credit Portfolio Stress Testing." *Journal of Banking and Finance* (2002)26, no. 2/3, 235–264.

Bank for International Settlements, Standardized Model for Market Risk. Basel, Switzerland, 1996.

Bank for International Settlements. "Credit Risk Modeling: Current Practices and Applications." Basel Committee on Banking Supervision. Document no. 49, April 1999a.

Bank for International Settlements. "Sound Practices for Loan Accounting and Disclosure." Basel Committee on Banking Supervision. Document no. 55, July 1999b.

Bank for International Settlements. "Range of Practice in Banks' Internal Ratings Systems." Basel Committee on Banking Supervision, Document no. 66, January 2000.

Bank for International Settlements. "The New Basel Capital Accord." January 2001.

Bank for International Settlements. "Long-term Rating Scales Comparison." April 30, 2001.

Bank for International Settlements. "Working Paper on the Regulatory Treatment of Operational Risk." September 2001.

Bank for International Settlements. "Results of the Second Quantitative Study." November 5, 2001a.

Bank for International Settlements. "Potential Modifications to the Committee's Proposals." November 5, 2001b.

Bank for International Settlements. "Studies on the Validation of Internal Ratings Systems," Working Paper No. 14, May 2005.

Bank for International Settlements, "International Convergence of Capital Measurement and Capital Standards: A Revised Framework Comprehensive Version," June 2006.

Bank of England, Financial Stability Report. Issue 22. October 2007.

Barnhill, T. M. Jr., and W. F. Maxwell. "Modeling Correlated Interest Rate, Spread Risk, and Credit Risk for Fixed Income." *Journal of Banking and Finance, Portfolios* (2002), 26, 347–374.

Barniv, R. and A. Raveh. "Identifying Financial Distress: A New Nonparametric Approach." *Journal of Business, Finance and Accounting*, 16, no. 3 (Summer 1989), 361–383.

Basak, S. and A. Shapiro. "A Model of Credit Risk, Optimal Policies, and Asset Prices." Working Paper, NYU, June 2001.

Basel Committee. "Supervisory Guidance for Assessing Banks' Financial Instrument Fair Value Practices." November 2008.

Basel Committee. "Guidelines for Computing Capital for Incremental Risk in the Trading Book." January 2009.

Basel Committee. "Revisions to the Basel II Market Risk Framework." January 2009.

Basel Committee. "Proposed Enhancements to the Basel II Framework." January 2009.

Basel Committee on Banking Supervision. "International Convergence of Capital Measurement and Capital Standards: A Revised Comprehensive Version." www.bis.org, June 2006.

Basel Committee on Banking Supervision. "Stocktaking on the Use of Credit Ratings." Bank for International Settlements (BIS), June 2009.

Beaver, W. H., C. Shakespeare, and M.T. Soliman. "Differential Properties of Certified vs. Non-Certified Bond Rating Agencies." Stanford University Working Paper, June 2006.

Berger, A. N., R. DeYoung, M. J. Flannery, D. Lee, and O. Oztekin. "How Do Large Banking Organizations Manage Their Capital Ratios?" *Journal of Financial Services Research* 34, pp.123–149, 2008.

Bessembinder, H., W. F. Maxwell, and K. Venkataraman. "Market Transparency Liquidity Externalities, and Institutional Trading Costs in Corporate Bonds," *Journal of Financial Economics* 82 (November 2006): 251–288.

Belkin, B., L. R. Forest, S. D. Aguais, and S. J. Suchower. "Credit Risk Premiums in Commercial Lending (I)." KPMG, New York. August 1998a (mimeo).

Belkin, B., L.R. Forest, S.D. Aguais, and S. J. Suchower. "Credit Risk Premiums in Commercial Lending (II)." New York: KPMG, August 1998b (mimeo).

Belkin, B., S. J. Suchower, and L. R. Forest. "The Effect of Systematic Credit Risk on Loan Portfolio Value at Risk and Loan Pricing." *CreditMetrics Monitor*, Winter 1998c, 17–28.

Belkin, B., S. L. Suchower, D. H. Wagner, and L. R. Forest. "Measures of Credit Risk and Loan Value in LASsm." KPMG Risk Strategy Practice, 1998d (mimeo).

Bharath, S. T., V. Panchapegesan, and I. Werner. "The Changing Nature of Chapter 11" working paper, October 2007.

Bharath, S. T. and T. Shumway. "Forecasting Default with the Merton Distance to Default Model," *Review of Financial Studies* 21, no. 3(2008): 1,339–1,369.

Black, F., and M. Scholes. "The Pricing of Options and Corporate Liabilities." *Journal of Political Economy*, May–June 1973, 637–654.

Black, F. and J. Cox. "Valuing Corporate Securities: Some Effects of Bond Indenture Provisions," *Journal of Finance* 31(1976): 351–367.

Board of Governors of the Federal Reserve System. "The Supervisory Capital Assessment Program: Design and Implementation." April 24, 2009.

Board of Governors of the Federal Reserve System. "The Supervisory Capital Assessment Program: Overview of Results." May 7, 2009.

Board of Governors, Federal Reserve System. "Implementation of Advanced Capital Adequacy Framework (Basel II Draft Final Rule)." October 26, 2007.

Bohn, J. R. "Characterizing Credit Spreads." KMV Corporation, June 1999.

Bohn, J. R. "An Empirical Assessment of a Simple Contingent-Claims Model for the Valuation of Risk Debt."*Journal of Risk Finance* 1, no. 4(2000a): 55–77.

Bohn, J. R. "A Survey of Contingent Claims Approaches to Risky Debt Valuation." *Journal of Risk Finance* 1, no. F 3(2000b): 53–71.

Bohn, J. R., N. Arora, and I. Korablev. "Power and Level Validation of the EDF Credit Measure in North America." *Moody's KMV Publication*, March 18, 2005.

Bongini, P., L. Laeven, and G. Majnoni. "How Good Is the Market at Assessing Bank Fragility: A Horse Race Between Different Indicators." World Bank, Working Paper, January 2001.

Boot, A. W. A., and T. T. Milbourn, and A. Schmeits. "Credit Ratings as Coordination Mechanisms." *Review of Financial Studies* 19, 2006, 81–118.

Boudoukh, J., M. Richardson, and R. Whitelaw. "Expect the Worst." Risk Magazine, September 1995, 101–105.

Boyd, J., S. Kwak, and B. Smith. "The Real Output Losses Associated with Modern Banking Crises." *Journal of Money, Credit and Banking* 37, no. 6 (December 2005): 977–999.

Brenner, M., and Y. H. Eom. "No Arbitrage Option Pricing: New Evidence on the Validity of the Martingale Property." Working Paper 10, NYU Salomon Center, June 1997.

Briys, E., and F. de Varenne. "Valuing Risky Fixed Debt: An Extension." *Journal of Financial and Quantitative Analysis* 32(1997): 239–248.

Brooks, R., and C. M. Ford. "The United States of Subprime," *Wall Street Journal*, October 11, 2007, A1, A16.

Brown, C. O., and I. S. Dinc. "Too Many to Fail? Evidence of Regulatory Reluctance in Bank Failures When the Banking Sector is Weak."*Review of Financial Studies*, forthcoming 2010.

Brown, S., W. Goetzmann, B. Liang, and C. Schwarz. "Mandatory Disclosure and Operational Risk: Evidence from Hedge Fund Registration." *Journal of Finance* LXIII, no. 6 (December 2008): 2,785–2,815.

Brunnermeier, M. "Deciphering the Liquidity and Credit Crunch 2007–2008." *Journal of Economic Perspectives* (2009), 23, no. 1, 77–100.

Brunnermeier, M., and M. Yogo, "A Note on Liquidity Management." *American Economic Review* 99, no. 2(2009).

Caballero, R. J., and Arvind Krishnamurthy. "Collective Risk Management in a Flight to Quality Episode." *Journal of Finance* LXIII, no. 5 (October 2008): 2,195–2,230.

Calem, P. S., and M. LaCour-Little. "Risk-Based Capital Requirements for Mortgage Loans." *Journal of Banking and Finance* 28 (March 2004): 647–672.

Camara, A., I. Popova, and B. J. Simkins. "An Analysis of the Implied Probability of Bankruptcy for Chapter 11 Firms and Global Banks Impacted by the Subprime Crisis." Working paper, February 2, 2009.

Campbell, J., J. Hilscher, and J. Szilagyi. "In Search of Distress Risk," *Journal of Finance* LXIII, no. 6 (December 2008): 2,899–2,939.

Cantor, R. "Moody's Investors Service Response to the Consultative Paper Issued by the Basel Committee on Bank Supervision 'A New Capital Adequacy Approach.'" *Journal of Banking and Finance*, January 2001, 171–186.

Cantor, R., and F. Packer. "Determinants and Impacts of Sovereign Credit Ratings." *Federal Reserve Bank of New York Economic Policy Review*, October 1996, 37–53.

Caouette, J. B., E.J. Altman, and P. Narayanan. *Managing Credit Risk: The Next Great Financial Challenge*. New York: John Wiley & Sons, 1998.

Carty, L. V., and D. Lieberman. "Corporate Bond Defaults and Default Rates 1938–1995." *Moody's Investors Service*, Global Credit Research, January 1996.

Carey, M. "Credit Risk in Private Debt Portfolios." *Journal of Finance*, August 1998, 1,363–1,387.

Carey, M. "Dimensions of Credit Risk and Their Relationship to Economic Capital Requirements." NBER, Working Paper 7629, March 2000.

Carey, M. "Consistency of Internal versus External Credit Ratings and Insurance and Bank Regulatory Capital Requirements." Federal Reserve Board, Working Paper. February 2001a.

Carey, M. "A Policymaker's Guide to Choosing Absolute Bank Capital Requirements." Federal Reserve Board Working Paper, June 3, 2001b.

Carey, M. and M. Hrvcay, "Parameterizing Credit Risk Models with Rating Data." *Journal of Banking and Finance* 2001. 25 no. 1, pp. 197–270.

Carey, M., and M. Gordy. "Measuring LGDs." Federal Reserve Board, Working Paper, 2004.

Carey, M., M. Post, and S. A. Sharpe. "Does Corporate Lending by Banks and Finance Companies Differ? Evidence on Specialization in Private Debt Contracting." *Journal of Finance*, June 1998. 845–878.

Carty, L. V. "Bankrupt Bank Loan Recoveries." *Moody's Investors Service*, Rating Methodology, June 1998.

Carty, L. V., and D. Lieberman. "Defaulted Bank Loan Recoveries." *Moody's Investors Service*, Special Report, November 1996.

Caselli, S., S. Gatti, and F. Querci. "The Sensitivity of the Loss Given Default Rate to Systematic Risk: New Empirical Evidence on Bank Loans." *Journal of Financial Services Research* 34(2008): 1–34.

Cathcart, L., and L. El-Jahel. "Valuation of Defaultable Bonds." *Journal of Fixed Income*, June 1998, 65–78.

Cavallo, M., and G. Majnoni. "Do Banks Provision for Bad Loans in Good Times? Empirical Evidence and Policy Implications." Working Paper 2,691, World Bank, June 2001.

Chakravarty, S., and A. Sarkar. "Trading Costs in Three U.S. Bond Markets." *Journal of Fixed Income* 13(2003): 39–48.

Chang, G., and S. M. Sundaresan. "Asset Prices and Default-Free Term Structure in an Equilibrium Model of Default." Columbia University Working Paper, October 1999.

Chatterjee, S. and A. Yan. "Using Innovative Securities Under Asymmetric Information: Why Do Some Firms Pay with Contingent Value Rights?" *Journal of Financial and Quantitative Analysis* 43, no. 4 (December 2008): 1,001–1,036.

Chava, S. and J. A. Jarrow. "Bankruptcy Prediction with Industry Effects," *Review of Finance*,(2004), 8, 537–569.

Chen, R-R., and J-Z. Huang. "Term Structure of Credit Spreads, Implied Forward Default Probability Curve, and the Valuation of Defaultable Claims." Working Paper, Department of Management, Rutgers University, July 2000.

Chen, R. R., X. Cheng, F. J. Fabozzi, and B. Liu. "An Explicit, Multi-Factor Credit Default Swap Pricing Model with Correlate Factors." *Journal of Financial and Quantitative Analysis* 43, no. 1 (March 2008): 123–160.

Choudhury, S. P. "Choosing the Right Box of Credit Tricks." *Risk Magazine*, November 1997, 17–22.

Clow, R. "Bond Yield." *Institutional Investor*, February 2000, 41–44.

Coates, P. K., and L. F. Fant. "Recognizing Financial Distress Patterns Using a Neural Network Tool." *Financial Management*, Summer 1993, 142–155.

Collin-Dufresne, P., and B. Solnik. "On the Term Structure of Default Premia in the Swap and LIBOR Markets." *Journal of Finance*, June 2001, 1,095–1,115.

Collin-Dufresne, P., and R. Goldstein. "Do Credit Spreads Reflect Stationary Leverage Ratios?" *Journal of Finance*, 56(2001): 1,929–1,957.

Craig, S., J. McCracken, A. Lucchetti, and K. Kelly. "The Weekend That Wall Street Died." *Wall Street Journal*, December 29, 2008 http://online.wsj.com/article/SB123051066413538349.html.

Credit Suisse First Boston. "CreditRisk+: A Credit Risk Management Framework." *Technical Document*, 1997.

Crosbie, P. J., and J. R. Bohn. "Modeling Default Risk." 2003. www.ma.hw.ac.uk/~mcneil/F79CR/Crosbie_Bohn.pdf.

Crouhy, M., and R. Mark. "A Comparative Analysis of Current Credit Risk Models." Paper presented at the Bank of England Conference on Credit Risk Modeling and Regulatory Implications, London. September 21–22, 1998.

Crouhy, M., D. Galai, and R. Mark. "A Comparative Analysis of Current Credit Risk Models." *Journal of Banking and Finance*, January 2000, 57–117.

Crouhy, M., and R. Mark. "Prototype Risk Rating System." *Journal of Banking and Finance*, January 2001, 47–95.

Crouhy, M., S. M. Turnbull, and Lee M. Wakeman. "Measuring Risk-Adjusted Performance." Paper presented at Center for Economic Policy Research (CEPR) Conference, London, September 20, 1998.

Cruz, M., R. Coleman, and G. Salkin. "Modeling and Measuring Operational Risk." *The Journal of Risk* 1, no. 1 (Fall 1998): 63–72.

Cunningham, A. "Bank Credit Risk In Emerging Markets." Moody's Investors Service, Rating Methodology, July 1999.

Curry, T., and L. Shibut. "The Cost of the Savings and Loan Crisis: Truth and Consequences," *FDIC Banking Review* (2000) vol.13 no. 2, 26–35.

Dahiya, S., M. Puri, and A. Saunders. "Bank Borrowers and Loan Sales: New Evidence of the Uniqueness of Bank Loans." *Journal of Business*, 2003.

Das, S., and P. Tufano. "Pricing Credit-Sensitive Debt When Interest Rates, Credit Ratings, and Credit Spreads are Stochastic." *Journal of Financial Engineering,* June 1996, 161–198.

Delianedis, G., and R. Geske. "Credit Risk and Risk-Neutral Default Probabilities: Information About Rating Migrations and Defaults." Paper presented at the Bank of England Conference on Credit Risk Modeling and Regulatory Implications, London, September 21–22, 1998.

Dembo, R. S., A. R. Aziz, D. Rosen, and M. Zerbs. "Mark-to-Future: A Framework for Measuring Risk and Reward."*Algorithmics Publications,* May 2000.

Dermine, J. "Pitfalls in the Application of RAROC in Loan Management." *The Arbitrageur,* Spring 1998, 21–27.

DeSantes, R. "An Appetite for Risk." *CreditRisk,* October 1999, 21–27.

De Stefano, M. T. "Basel Committee's New Capital Standards Could Strengthen Banking." *Standard & Poor's Credit Week,* August 18, 1999, 19–22.

Diamond, D. "Financial Intermediation and Delegated Monitoring" *Review of Economic Studies* 51, 1984, 393–414.

Diebold, F., and R. Mariano. "Comparing Predictive Accuracy." *Journal of Business and Economic Statistics,* May 1995, 253–264.

Driessen, J., P. J. Maenhout, and G. Vilkov. "The Price of Correlation Risk: Evidence from Equity Options." *Journal of Finance* LXIV, no.3, (June 2009): 1,377–1,406.

Duan, J. C. and J. G. Simonato. "Empirical Martingale Simulation for Asset Prices," *Management Science* (1998)44, 1,218–1,233.

Duffee, G. R. "The Relation Between Treasury Yields and Corporate Bond Yield Spreads." *Journal of Finance* 53, 1998, 2,225–2, 242.

Duffee, G. R. "Estimating the Price of Default Risk." *Review of Financial Studies,* Spring 1999, 197–226.

Duffie, D., and H. Zhu. "Does a Central Clearing Counterparty Reduce Clearing Risk?" Working Paper, Stanford University, March 9, 2009.

Duffie, D., and M. Huang. "Swap Rates and Credit Quality." *Journal of Finance,* July 1996, 921–950.

Duffie, D., and D. Lando. "Term Structures of Credit Spreads with Incomplete Accounting Information." *Econometrica* 69, 2001, 633–664.

Duffie, D., J. Pan, and K. J. Singleton. "Transform Analysis and Asset Pricing for Affine Jump Diffusion," *Econometrica* 68, 2000, 1,343–1,376.

Duffie, D., L. H. Pedersen, and K. J. Singleton. "Modeling Sovereign Yield Spreads: A Case Study of Russian Debt." Working Paper, Graduate School of Business, Stanford University, April 2000.

Duffie, D., and K. J. Singleton. "Simulating Correlated Defaults." Paper presented at the Bank of England Conference on Credit Risk Modeling and Regulatory Implications, London, September 21–22, 1998.

Duffie, D., and K. J. Singleton. "Modeling Term Structures of Defaultable Bonds." *Review of Financial Studies* 12(1999): 687–720.

Dullmann, K., and M. Trapp. "Systematic Risk in Recovery Rates—An Empirical Analysis of U.S. Corporate Bonds." Deutsche Bundesbank Working Paper Series No. 2, 2004.

Dvorak, B. "A Brief History of Active Credit Portfolio Management." *Moody's KMV Publication*, March 25, 2008.

Dwyer, D. W. "Examples of Overfitting Encountered When Building Private Firm Default Prediction Models." *Moody's KMV Publication*, April 12, 2005.

Dwyer, D. W. "The Distribution of Defaults and Bayesian Model Validation." *Journal of Risk Model Validation* 1, no. 1(2007): 23–53.

Dwyer, D., and I. Korablev. Moody's KMV LossCalc^{TM} v 3.0. April 9, 2009.

Dwyer, D. W., A. Kocagil, and R. M. Stein. "Moody's KMV RiskCalc v 3.1 Model." *Moody's KMV Publication*, April 5, 2004.

Dwyer, D. W., and R. M. Stein. "Inferring the Default Rate in a Population by Comparing Two Incomplete Default Databases." *Journal of Banking and Finance* 30(2006): 797–810.

Dwyer, D. W., and S. Qu. "EDFTM 8.0 Model Enhancements." *Moody's KMV Publication*, January 29, 2007.

Ebnother, S., and P. Vanini. "Credit Portfolios: What Defines Risk Horizons and Risk Measurement?" *Journal of Banking and Finance* 31(2007): 3,663–3,679.

"Banking Supervision: The Basel Perplex." *The Economist*, November 10, 2001, 65–66.

Edwards, A. K., L. E. Harris, and M. S. Piwowar. "Corporate Bond Market Transaction Costs and Transparency." *Journal of Finance* LXII, no. 3 (June 2007): 1,421–1,451.

Elmer, P. J., and D. M. Borowski. "An Expert System Approach to Financial Analysis: The Case of S&L Bankruptcy." *Financial Management*, Autumn 1988, 66–76.

Elton, E. J., and M. J. Gruber. *Modern Portfolio Theory and Investment Analysis* 5th Ed. New York: John Wiley & Sons, 1995.

Eom, H. Y., J. Helwege, and J-Z Huang. "Structural Models of Corporate Bond Pricing: An Empirical Analysis." *Review of Financial Studies* 17, no. 2 (Summer 2004): 499–544.

Eom, Y. H., J. Helwege, and J-Z Huang. "Structural Models of Corporate Bond Pricing: An Empirical Analysis." Working Paper, January 2001.

Ericsson, J., and J. Reneby. "Estimating Structural Bond Pricing Models." *Journal of Business* 78, no. 2(2005): 707–735.

Ericsson, J., J. Reneby, and H. Wang. "Can Structural Models Price Default Risk? Evidence from Bond and Credit Derivative Markets." Working paper, September 12, 2007.

Estrella, A. "Formulas or Supervision? Remarks on the Future of Regulatory Capital." *Federal Reserve Bank of NY Economic Policy Review*, October 1998.

Evans, David. "Moody's Implied Ratings Show MBIA, Ambac Turn to Junk." *Bloomberg*, May 30, 2007.

Fadil, M. W. "Problems with Weighted-Average Risk Ratings: A Portfolio Management View." *Commercial Lending Review*, Spring 1997, 23–27.

Falkenheim, M., and A. Powell. "The Use of Credit Bureau Information in the Estimation of Appropriate Capital and Provisioning Requirements." Working Paper, Central Bank of Argentina, 2001.

Fan, H. and S. M. Sundaresan. "Debt Valuation, Renegotiation and Optimal Dividend Policy," *Review of Financial Studies*, (2000), 13, no. 4, 1,057–1,099.

"Fears over Banks Prompt Surge in Credit Derivatives." *Financial Times*, October 7, 1998, 1.

Federal Housing Finance Agency News Release, May 27, 2009.

Federal Reserve Bank of New York. Domestic Open Market Operations During 2008, Markets Group. January 2009.

Federal Reserve System Task Force Report. "Credit Risk Models at Major U.S. Banking Institutions: Current State of the Art and Implications for Assessments of Capital Adequacy." Washington, D.C., May 1998.

Federal Reserve System Press Release, "Reporting and Disclosure Requirements," August 29, 1995.

Fehle, F. "Market Structure and Swap Spreads: International Evidence." Working Paper, University of South Carolina, September 1998.

Ferri, G., L. G. Liu, and G. Majnoni. "The Role of Rating Agency Assessments in Less Developed Countries: Impact of the Proposed Basel Guidelines." *Journal of Banking and Finance*, January 2001, 115–148.

Finger, C. C. "Conditional Approaches for CreditMetrics Portfolio Distributions." *Riskmetrics Monitor*, April 1999.

Finger, C. C. "Toward a Better Estimation of Wrong-Way Credit Exposure." *RiskMetrics Journal*, Spring 2000a 25–40.

Finger, C. C. "A Comparison of Stochastic Default Rate Models." *RiskMetrics Journal*, November 2000b, 49–75.

Finnerty, J. D. "Credit Derivatives, Infrastructure Finance and Emerging Market Risk." *The Financier*, February 1996, 64–78.

Flannery, M. J., and S. Sorescu. "Evidence of Bank Market Discipline in Subordinated Debenture Yields: 1983–1991." Journal of Finance, September 1996, 1,347–1,377.

Flood, M. "Basel Buckets and Loan Losses: Absolute and Relative Loan Underperformance at Banks and Thrifts." Working Paper, Office of Thrift Supervision, March 9, 2001.

Fons, J. "Using Default Rates to Model the Term Structure of Credit Risk." *Financial Analysts Journal*, September–October 1994, 25–32.

Fraser, R. "Stress Testing Credit Risk Using CreditManager 2.5." *RiskMetrics Journal* 1 (May 2000): 13–23.

Freixas, X., B. Parigi, and J. C. Rochet. "Systemic Risk, Interbank Relations, and Liquidity Provision by the Central Bank." *Journal of Money, Credit and Banking* 32, no. 3, Part II (August 2000).

Froot, K. A., D. S. Scharfstein, and J. C. Stein. "Risk Management: Coordinating Corporate Investment and Financing Policies." *Journal of Finance* XLVIII, no. 5 (December 1993): 1,629–1,658.

Froot, K. A., and J. C. Stein. "Risk Management, Capital Budgeting, and Capital Structure Policy for Financial Institutions: An Integrated Approach." *Journal of Financial Economics*, January 1998, 55–82.

Frye, J."The Effects of Systematic Credit Risk: A False Sense of Security." In *Recovery Risk*, E. Altman, A. Resti, and A. Sironi (eds.), 187–200. London: Riskbooks, 2005.

Frye, J. "A False Sense of Security." *Risk*, 16, no. 8(2003): 63–68.

Frye, J. "Collateral Damage." *Risk*, April 2000a, 91–94.

Frye, J. "Depressing Recoveries." *Risk*, November 2000b 108–111.

Garmaise, M. J., and T. J. Moskowitz. "Catastrophic Risk and Credit Markets." *Journal of Finance* LXIV, no. 2 (April 2009): 657–707.

Galai, D. A. Raviv, and Z. Wiener. "Liquidation Triggers and the Valuation of Equity and Debt." *Journal of Banking and Finance* 31(2007): 3,604–3,620.

General Accounting Office. "Risk-Based Capital: Regulatory and Industry Approaches to Capital and Risk." Report No. 98–153, July 1998.

Geske, R. "The Valuation of Corporate Liabilities as Compound Options." *Journal of Financial and Quantitative Analysis*, November 1977, 541–552.

Gilbert, R. Alton. "Keep the Leverage Ratio for Large Banks to Limit the Competitive Effects of Implementing Basel II Capital Requirements," Indiana State University Networks Financial Institute 2006-PB-01, January 2006.

Ginzberg, A., K. Maloney, and R. Wilner. "Risk Rating Migration and Valuation of Floating Rate Debt." Working Paper, Citicorp, March 1994.

Goldstein, M., E. Hotchkiss, and E. Sirri. "Transparency and Liquidity: A Controlled Experiment on Corporate Bonds." Working Paper, March 20, 2006.

Goldstein, M., and E. Hotchkiss. "Dealer Behavior and the Trading of Newly Issued Corporate Bonds," Working Paper, October 2, 2007.

Gordy, M. B. "A Comparative Anatomy of Credit Risk Models." *Journal of Banking and Finance*, January 2000, 119–149.

Gordy, M. B. "A Risk-Factor Model Foundation for Ratings-Based Bank Capital Rules." Working Paper, Board of Governors of the Federal Reserve System, February 5, 2001.

Gorton, G., and A. Santomero. "Market Discipline and Bank Subordinated Debt." *Journal of Money, Credit and Banking*, February 1990, 117–128.

Gorton, G. "The Panic of 2007." Working Paper, Yale University, August 25, 2008.

Granger, C. W. J., and L. L. Huang. "Evaluation of Panel Data Models: Some Suggestions from Time-Series." Discussion Paper 97-10, Department of Economics, University of California, San Diego, 1997.

Griep, C., and M. De Stefano. "Standard & Poor's Official Response to the Basel Committee's Proposal." *Journal of Banking and Finance*, January 2001, 149–170.

Griffin, J. M., and M. L. Lemmon. "Book-to-Market Equity, Distress Risk and Equity Returns," *Journal of Finance* 57, no. 2 (October 2002): 2,317–2,336.

Gron, A., and A. Winton. "Risk Overhang and Market Behavior." *Journal of Business* 74, no. 4(2001): 591–612.

Gross, J., and N. Saperia. "Credit Event Auction Primer." www.theice.com/public-docs/ice_trust/credit_event_auction_primer.pdf (2008).

Gully, B., W. Perraudin, and V. Saporta. "Risk and Economic Capital for Combined Banking and Insurance Activities." Paper presented at the Bank of England Conference on Banks and Systemic Risk, London, May 23–25, 2001.

Gunduz, Y., T. Ludecke, and M. Uhrig-Homberg. "Trading Credit Default Swaps via Interdealer Brokers," *Journal of Financial Services Research* (2007)32, no. 3, 141–159.

Guo, X., R. A. Jarrow, and H. Lin. "Distressed Debt Prices and Recovery Rate In Estimation." *Kamakura Research Paper*, January 26, 2009.

Gupton, G. M. "Bank Loan Loss Given Default." *Moody's Investors Service, Special Comment, November 2000.*

Gupton, G. M., D. Gates, and L. V. Carty. "Bank-Loan Loss Given Default," In *Moody's Investors Service*, Global Credit Research, November 2000.

Gupton, G. M., C. C. Finger, and M. Bhatia. "CreditMetrics—Technical Document, RiskMetrics—Technical Document."www.defaultrisk.com, April 1997.

Hakkio, C. S., and W. R. Keeton. "Financial Stress: What Is It, How Can It Be Measured, and Why Does It Matter?" Federal Reserve Bank of Kansas City, *Economic Review* 94, no. 2 (Second Quarter 2009), 5–50.

Hamilton, D. T., R. Cantor, and S. Ou. "Default and Recovery Rates of Corporate Bond Issuers." *Moody's Special Comment*, February 2002.

Hammes, W., and M. Shapiro. "The Implications of the New Capital Adequacy Rules for Portfolio Management of Credit Assets." *Journal of Banking and Finance*, January 2001, 97–114.

Hancock, D., and M. L. Kwast. "Using Subordinated Debt to Monitor Bank Holding Companies: Is it Feasible?" *Journal of Financial Services Research* (forthcoming), 2001.

Harris, L., and M. Piwowar. "Secondary Trading Costs in the Municipal Bond Market," *Journal of Finance* 61(2006): 1,361–1,397.

Harrison, J. M. *Brownian Motion and Stochastic Flow Systems.* Melbourne, FL: Krieger Publishing, January 1990.

Harrison, J. M., and D. Kreps. "Martingales and Arbitrage in Multi-Period Security Markets." *Journal of Economic Theory*, 1979, 381–408.

Harrison, J. M., and S. R. Pliska. "Martingales and Stochastic Integrals in the Theory of Continuous Trading." *Stochastic Processes and Their Applications*, August 1981, 215–260.

Hawley, D. D., J. D. Johnson, and D. Raina. "Artificial Neural Systems: A New Tool for Financial Decision-Making." *Financial Analysts Journal*, November/December 1990, 63–72.

Heid, F. "The Cyclical Effects of the Basel II Capital Requirements," *Journal of Banking and Finance* 31(2007): 3,885–3,900.

Helwege, J., S. Maurer, A. Sarkar, and Y. Wang. "Credit Default Swap Auctions," *Federal Reserve Bank of New York Staff Report No. 372*, May 2009.

Hendricks, D. "Netting Agreements and the Credit Exposures of OTC Derivatives Portfolios." *Federal Reserve Bank of New York, Quarterly Review*, Spring 1994, 36–69.

Hildebrand, Philipp. "Is Basel II Enough? The Benefits of a Leverage Ratio." Financial Markets Group Lecture, London, December 15, 2008.

Hillegeist, S. A., D. P. Cram, E. K. Keating, and K. G. Lundstedt. "Assessing the Probability of Bankruptcy." Working Paper, April 2002.

Hirtle, B. "Credit Derivatives and Bank Credit Supply." *Journal of Financial Intermediation* 18(2009): 125–150.

Hirtle, B. J., M. Levonian, M. Saidenberg, S. Walter, and D. Wright. "Using Credit Risk Models for Regulatory Capital: Issues and Options." *Economic Policy Review, Federal Reserve Bank of New York Economic Policy Review*, March 2001, 19–36.

Ho, T. S. "Allocate Capital and Measure Performances in a Financial Institution." *Financial Markets, Institutions, and Instruments* 8, no. 5(1999): 1–23.

Hong, G., and A. Warga. "An Empirical Study of Bond Market Transactions," *Financial Analysts Journal* 56(2000): 32–46.

Hoggarth, G., R. Reis, and V. Saporta. "Costs of Banking System Instability: Some Empirical Evidence." Paper presented at the Bank of England Conference on Banks and Systemic Risk, London, May 23–25, 2001.

Hotchkiss, E., and G. Jostova. "Determinants of Corporate Bond Trading: A Comprehensive Analysis." Working Paper, 2007.

Houweling, P., and T. Vorst. "Pricing Default Swaps: Empirical Evidence," *Journal of International Money and Finance* (2005), 24, no. 8, 1,200–1,225.

Houston, J., C. James, and D. Marcus. "Capital Market Frictions and the Role of Internal Capital Markets in Banking." *Journal of Financial Economics* 46 (1997): 135–164.

Hu, Y-T., R. Kiesel, and W. Perraudin. "The Estimation of Transition Matrices for Sovereign Credit Ratings." Working Paper, May 2001.

Huang, J. Z., and M. Huang. "How Much of the Corporate-Treasury Yield Spread is Due to Credit Risk?" Working Paper, Stanford University, May 2003.

Huang, J. Z., and H. Zhou. "Specification Analysis of Structural Credit Risk Models." October 2008.

Huang, J-Z., and M. Huang. "How Much of the Corporate-Treasury Yield Spread is Due to Credit Risk? Results from a New Calibration Approach." Working Paper, Penn State University and Stanford University, August 2000.

Hull, J., and A. White. "Valuing Credit Default Swaps II: Modeling Default Correlations." *Journal of Derivatives*, Spring 2001, 12–21.

IIF/ISDA, Institute of International Finance and International Swaps and Derivatives Association. "Modeling Credit Risk: Joint IIF/ISDA Testing Program." February 2000.

Institute of International Finance, Inc. "Response to the Basel Committee on Banking Supervision Regulatory Capital Reform Proposals." September 2000.

Inter-American Development Bank Research Network Project. "Determinants and Consequences of Financial Constraints Facing Firms in Latin America and the Caribbean." Project: Credit Constraints in Argentina, June 2001.

International Swaps and Derivatives Association (ISDA). *Credit Risk and Regulatory Capital*. New York/London, March 1998.

Ivashina, V., and D. Scharfstein. "Bank Lending During the Financial Crisis of 2008." Working Paper, Harvard Business School and NBER, December 15, 2008.

Ivashina, V., and Sun, Z. "Institutional Stock Trading on Loan Market Information." Working Paper, Harvard Business School, August 2007.

Jackson, P., W. Perraudin, and V. Saporta. "Setting Minimum Capital for Internationally Active Banks." Paper presented at the Bank of England Conference on Banks and Systemic Risk, London, May 23–25, 2001.

James, C. "RAROC-Based Capital Budgeting and Performance Evaluation: A Case Study of Bank Capital Allocation." Working Paper, University of Florida, September 1996.

James, J. "Credit Derivatives: How Much Should They Cost?" *CreditRisk,* Risk Special Report, October 1999, 8–10.

Jarrow, R. A. "Default Parameter Estimation Using Market Prices." *Financial Analysts Journal*, September/October 2001, 75–92.

Jarrow, R. A., and S. M. Turnbull. "Pricing Derivatives on Financial Securities Subject to Credit Risk." *Journal of Finance*, 50, no. 1 (March 1995): 53–85.

Jarrow, R., D. Lando, and S. Turnbull. "A Markov Model for the Term Structure of Credit Spreads." *Review of Financial Studies*, Summer 1997, 481–523.

Jarrow, R. A., and S. M. Turnbull. "The Intersection of Market and Credit Risk." *Journal of Banking and Finance*, 24, no. 1(2000).

Jarrow, R. A., and D. R. van Deventer. "Practical Usage of Credit Risk Models in Loan Portfolio and Counterparty Exposure Management." *Credit Risk Models and Management,* Risk Publications, March 1999.

Jarrow, R. A., and D. van Deventer. "Estimating default correlations Using a Reduced-Form Model." *Risk*, 18, no. 1 (January 2005): 83–88.

Jewell, J., and M. Livingston. "A Comparison of Bond Ratings from Moody's, S&P, and Fitch." *Financial Markets, Institutions, and Instruments* 8, no. 4(1999).

Johnson, R. "An Examination of Ratings Agencies Around the Investment-Grade Boundary." Federal Reserve Bank of Kansas City, RWP 03–01 February 2003.

Jokivuolle, E., and S. Peura. "A Model for Estimating Recovery Rates and Collateral Haircuts for Bank Loans," (February 2000) Bank of Finland Discussion Papers.

Jones, D. "Emerging Problems with the Basel Capital Accord: Regulatory Capital Arbitrage and Related Issues." *Journal of Banking and Finance* 24(2000): 35–58.

Jones, E. P., S. P. Mason, and E. Rosenfeld. "Contingent Claims Analysis of Corporate Capital Structures: An Empirical Investigation." *Journal of Finance*, July 1984 611–625.

Jorion, P., and G. Zhang. "Credit Contagion from Counterparty Risk." *Journal of Finance* LXIV, no. 5 (October 2009): 2,053–2,087.

J.P. Morgan & Co., and RiskMetrics Group. *"The JP Morgan Guide to Credit Derivatives: with Contributions from the RiskMetrics Group.* London: Risk Publications, 1999.

Kamakura Corporation, Default Probability Correlations, Kamakura Public Firm Models, Version 4.1, November 2008.

Kambhu, J., T. Schuermann, and K. Stiroh. "Hedge Funds, Financial Intermediation and Systemic Risk." *Federal Reserve Bank of New York Staff Report*, Staff Report 291, July 2007.

Kaminsky, G., and S. Schmukler. "Emerging Markets Instability: Do Sovereign Ratings Affect Country Risk and Stock Returns?" Working Paper, World Bank, February 28, 2001.

Kao, D-L. "Estimating and Pricing Credit Risk: An Overview." *Financial Analysts Journal*, July/August 2000, 50–60.

Karels, G. V., and A. J. Prakash. "Multivariate Normality and Forecasting of Business Bankruptcy." *Journal of Business, Finance and Accounting*, Winter 1987, 573–593.

Kashyap, A. K., R. G. Rajan, and J. C. Stein. "Rethinking Capital Regulation." Paper presented at the Federal Reserve Bank of Kansas City symposium "Maintaining Stability in a Changing Financial System," Jackson Hole, WY, August 21–23, 2008.

Kashyarp, A. K., and J. C. Stein. "Cyclical Implications of the Basel II Capital Standard," *Federal Reserve Bank of Chicago Economic Perspectives*, 2004.

Kealhofer, S. *"Portfolio Management of Default Risk."* San Francisco: KMV Corporation, November 15, 1993.

Kealhofer, S. "Managing Default Risk in Derivative Portfolios." *In Derivative Credit Risk: Further Advances in Measurement and Management*, 2d ed. London: Risk Books, January 1999.

Kealhofer, S. *"The Quantification of Credit Risk."* San Francisco: KMV Corporation, January 2000 (unpublished).

Kealhofer, S., and M. Kurbat. *"The Default Prediction Power of the Merton Approach Relative to Debt Ratings and Accounting Variables."* San Francisco: KMV Corporation, May 2001.

Kealhofer, S., S. Kwok, and W. Weng. *"Uses and Abuses of Bond Default Rates."* San Francisco: KMV Corporation, March 1998.

Keenan, S. C. "Historical Default Rates of Corporate Bond Issuers, 1920–1999." *Moody's Investors Service*, Special Comment, January 2000.

Keswani, A. "Estimating a Risky Term Structure of Brady Bonds." Working Paper, London School of Economics, November 23, 1999.

Kiesel, R., W. Perraudin, and A. Taylor. "The Structure of Credit Risk: Spread Volatility and Rating Transitions." June 2001 (mimeo).

Kim, J. "Conditioning the Transition Matrix." *Credit Risk*, October 1999, 37–40.

Kim, J. "Hypothesis Test of Default Correlation and Application to Specific Risk." *RiskMetrics Journal* 1 (November 2000): 35–48.

Kim, K. S., and J. R. Scott. "Prediction of Corporate Failure: An Artificial Neural Network Approach." Working Paper, Southwest Missouri State University, September 1991.

Kim, Y., and S. Nabar. "Bankruptcy Probability Changes and the Differential Informativeness of Bond Upgrades and Downgrades." *Journal of Banking and Finance* 31(2007): 3,843–3,861.

KMV. "Credit Monitor Overview." San Francisco: KMV Corporation, 1993 (mimeo).

KMV. "Global Correlation Factor Structure." San Francisco: KMV Corporation, August 1996 (mimeo).

KMV. "KMV and CreditMetrics." San Francisco: KMV Corporation, 1997 (mimeo).

KMV. "The KMV EDF Credit Measure and Probabilities of Default." 2000.

KMV. *"Portfolio Manager Model."* San Francisco: KMV Corporation, undated.

Knight, F. *Risk Uncertainty and Profit.* Boston: Houghton Mifflin, 1921.

Korablev, I., and D. Dwyer. "Power and Level Validation of Moody's KMV EDFTM Credit Measures in North America, Europe and Asia." *Moody's KMV Publication,* September 10, 2007.

Koyluoglu, H. U., A. Bangia, and T. Garside.*"Devil in the Parameters.* New York: Oliver, Wyman & Company, July 26, 1999.

Koyluoglu, H. U., and A. Hickman. "A Generalized Framework for Credit Risk Portfolio Models." *Working Paper.* New York: Oliver, Wyman & Co., July 1999.

KPMG. *VAR: Understanding and Applying Value-At-Risk.* New York: Risk Publications, 1997.

KPMG. *"Loan Analysis System."* New York: KPMG Financial Consulting Services, 1998.

Krahnen, J. P., and M. Weber. "Generally Accepted Rating Principles: A Primer." *Journal of Banking and Finance* 25, no. 1(2001): 3–23.

Kreps, D. "Multiperiod Securities and the Efficient Allocation of Risk: A Comment on the Black-Scholes Option Pricing Model." In J.J. McCall (Ed.), *The Economics of Information and Uncertainty.* Chicago: University of Chicago Press, 1982.

Kupiec, P. H. "Techniques for Verifying the Accuracy of Risk Measurement Models." *The Journal of Derivatives,* Winter 1995, 73–84.

Kupiec, P. H., D. Nickerson, and E. Golding. "Assessing Systemic Risk Exposure Under Alternative Approaches for Capital Adequacy." Paper presented at the Bank of England Conference on Banks and Systemic Risk, London, May 23–25, 2001.

Kuritzkes, A. "Transforming Portfolio Management." *Banking Strategies,* July/ August 1998.

Layish, D. N. "A Monitoring Role for Deviations from Absolute Priority in Bankruptcy Resolution." Working Paper, Baruch College, 2001.

Leland, H. "Agency Costs, Risk Management and Capital Structure." *Journal of Finance,* August 1998, 1,213–1,243.

Leland, H. "Corporate Debt Value, Bond Covenants and Optimal Capital Structure." *Journal of Finance,* September 1994, 1,213–1,252.

Leland, H. "Predictions of Default Probabilities in Structural Models of Debt," UC Berkeley Working Paper, April 22, 2004.

Leland, H., and K. Toft. "Optimal Capital Structure, Endogenous Bankruptcy, and the Term Structure of Credit Spreads." *Journal of Finance,* July 1996 987–1,019.

Leonhardt, D. "More Falling Behind on Mortgage Payments." *New York Times*, June 12, 2001, A1, C5.

Levy, A., and Z. Hu. "Incorporating Systematic Risk in Recovery: Theory and Evidence," Moody's KMV Working Paper, April 20, 2007.

Libby, R. "Ratios and the Prediction of Failure: Some Behavioral Evidence." *Journal of Accounting Research*, Spring 1975, 150–161.

Libby, R., K. T. Trotman, and I. Zimmer. "Member Variation, Recognition of Expertise, and Group Performance." *Journal of Applied Psychology*, February 1987, 81–87.

Lim, F. "Comparative Default Predictive Power of EDFs and Agency Debt Ratings." San Francisco: KMV Corporation, December 1999 (mimeo).

Linnell, I. "A Critical Review of the New Capital Adequacy Framework Paper Issued by the Basel Committee on Banking Supervision and its Implications for the Rating Agency Industry." *Journal of Banking and Finance*, January 2001, 187–196.

Lintner, J. "The Valuation of Risk Assets and the Selection of Risk Investments in Stock Portfolios and Capital Budgets." *Review of Economics and Statistics*, February 1965, 13–37.

Litterman, R., and T. Iben. "Corporate Bond Valuation and the Term Structure of Credit Spreads." *Journal of Portfolio Management*, 52–64, Spring 1991.

Loeffler, G. "Caught in the Housing Crash: Model Failure or Management Failure?" Working Paper, University of Ulm, December 2008.

Longstaff, F. A., and A. Rajan. "An Empirical Analysis of the Pricing of Collateralized Debt Obligations." *Journal of Finance* LXIII, no. 2 (April 2008): 529–563.

Longstaff, F. A., S. Mithal, and E. Neis. "Corporate Yield Spreads: Default Risk or Liquidity? New Evidence from Credit-Default Swap Markets." *Journal of Finance* 66(2005): 1,200–1,225.

Longstaff, F., S. Mithal, and E. Neis. "Corporate Yield Spreads: Default Risk or Liquidity? New Evidence from the Credit-Default Swap Market." *Journal of Finance* 60(2005): 2,213–2,253.

Longstaff, F., and E. Schwartz. "Valuing Risky Debt: A New Approach." *Journal of Finance* 50(1995a): 789–820.

Longstaff, F. A., and E. F. Schwartz. "A Simple Approach to Valuing Risky Fixed and Floating Rate Debt." *Journal of Finance*, July 1995b, 789–819.

Longin, F., and B. Solnik. "Extreme Correlation of International Equity Markets." *Journal of Finance* 56, no. 2 (April 2001): 649–676, April 2001.

Lopez, J. A., and M. R. Saidenberg. "Evaluating Credit Risk Models." *Journal of Banking and Finance* 24, no. 1/2 (January 2000): 151–165.

Lown, C., and D. P. Morgan. "The Credit Cycle and the Business Cycle: New Findings Using the Survey of Senior Loan Officers." Working Paper, Federal Reserve Bank of New York, June 25, 2001.

Maclachlan, I. "Recent Advances in Credit Risk Management." Ninth Melbourne Money and Finance Conference, June 19, 1999.

Madan, D. B., and H. Unal. "Pricing the Risks of Default." *Review of Derivative Research* 2(1998): 121–160.

Madan, D. B., and H. Unal. "A Two-Factor Hazard-Rate Model for Pricing Risky Debt and the Term Structure of Credit Spreads." *Journal of Financial and Quantitative Analysis*, March 2000, 43–65.

Mason, J. "Capital Regulations Helped Mask Looming Crisis." *Wall Street Journal Europe*, November 11, 2008.

McAllister, P. M., and J. J. Mingo. "Commercial Loan Risk Management, Credit Scoring, and Pricing: The Need for a New Shared Database." *Journal of Commercial Lending*, May 1994 6–22.

McKinsey and Co. *Credit Portfolio View*. New York: McKinsey and Co., 1997.

McNeil, A. J. "Extreme Value Theory for Risk Managers." Working Paper, Dept. of Mathematics, Swiss Federal Technical University, Zurich, May 1999.

McQuown, J. A. "A Comment on Market vs. Accounting-Based Measures of Default Risk." San Francisco: KMV Corporation, September 1993.

McQuown, J. A. "The Illuminated Guide to Portfolio Management." *Journal of Lending and Credit Risk Management*, August 1997, 29–41.

McQuown, J. A., and S. Kealhofer. "A Comment on the Formation of Bank Stock Prices." San Francisco: KMV Corporation, April 1997.

Mengle, D. "Credit Derivatives: An Overview." *Federal Reserve Bank of Atlanta Economic Review*, Fourth Quarter, 2007, 1–24.

Messier, W. F., and J. V. Hansen. "Inducing Rules for Expert System Development: An Example Using Default and Bankruptcy Data." *Management Science* 34, no. 12 (December 1988): 1,403–1,415.

Mella-Barral, P., and W. Perraudin. "Strategic Debt Service." *Journal of Finance*, June 1997 531–556.

Merrill Lynch. "Credit Default Swaps." New York: Global Fixed Income Research, October 1998.

Merton, R. C. "On the Pricing of Corporate Debt: The Risk Structure of Interest Rates." *Journal of Finance*, June 1974, 449–470.

Mester, L. "What's the Point of Credit Scoring?" *Federal Reserve Bank of Philadelphia Business Review*, September/October 1997, 3–16.

Miller, R. "Refining Ratings." *Risk Magazine*, August 1998.

Mingo, J. J. "Policy Implications of the Federal Reserve Study of Credit Risk Models at Major U.S. Banking Institutions." *Journal of Banking and Finance*, January 2000, 15–33.

Monfort, B., and C. Mulder. "Using Credit Ratings for Capital Requirements on Lending to Emerging Market Economies—Possible Impact of a New Basel Accord." Working Paper WP/00/69, International Monetary Fund, 2000.

Moody, J., and J. Utans. "Architecture Selection Strategies for Neural Networks: Application to Corporate Bond Rating Prediction." In *Neural Networks in Capital Markets,* A. P. Refenes (ed.), (New York: John Wiley & Sons, 1994), 277–300.

Morgenson, G. "A Paper Trail That Often Leads Nowhere," *New York Times*, December 28, 2008, C1, C2.

Morgenson, G. "Guess What Got Lost in the Pool?" *New York Times*, March 1, 2009, C1, C2.

Morrison, A. D., and L. White. "Level Playing Fields in International Financial Regulation." *Journal of Finance*, LXIV, no. 3 (June 2009): 1,099–1,142.

Mossin, J. "Equilibrium in a Capital Asset Market," *Econometrica*, October 1966, 768–783.

Mueller, C. "A Simple Multi-Factor Model of Corporate Bond Prices." Doctoral Dissertation, University of Wisconsin-Madison, October 29, 2000.

Nagpal, K. M., and Bahar, R. "An Analytical Approach for Credit Risk Analysis Under Correlated Defaults." *CreditMetrics Monitor*, April 1999, 51–74.

Nakada, P., H. Shah, H. U. Koyluoglu, and O. Collignon. "P&C RAROC: A Catalyst for Improved Capital Management in the Property and Casualty Insurance Industry. " *Journal of Risk Finance*, Fall 1999, 52–69.

Nandi, S. "Valuation Models for Default-Risky Securities: An Overview." *Federal Reserve Bank of Atlanta, Economic Review*, Fourth Quarter, 1998, 22–35.

Neftci, S. N. "Value at Risk Calculations, Extreme Events, and Tail Estimation." *Journal of Derivatives* 7, no. 3 (Spring 2000): 23–38.

Nickell, P., W. Perraudin, and S. Varotto. "Stability of Rating Transitions." *Journal of Banking and Finance* 24, no. 1/2(2001a): 203–228.

Nickell, P., W. Perraudin, and S. Varotto. "Ratings versus Equity-Based Credit Risk Modeling: An Empirical Analysis." Working Paper 132, Bank of England, May 2001b.

Obama-Geithner Plan, Department of the Treasury. "Financial Regulatory Reform: A New Foundation." June 17, 2009.

OCC and OTS Press Release NR 2009-77, "OCC and OTS Release Mortgage Metrics Report for First Quarter 2009." June 2009.

Oda, N., and J. Muranaga. "A New Framework for Measuring the Credit Risk of a Portfolio: The 'ExVAR' Model." Monetary and Economic Studies, Bank of Japan, December 1997.

Ohlson, J. "Financial Ratios and the Probabilistic Prediction of Bankruptcy." *Journal of Accounting Research* 18(1980): 109–131.

Pan, J., and K. J. Singleton. "Default and Recovery Implicity in the Term Structure of Sovereign CDS Spreads." *Journal of Finance* LXIII, no. 5 (October 2008): 2345–2384.

Parlour, C., and G. Plantin. "Loan Sales and Relationship Banking." *Journal of Finance* LXIII, no. 3 (June 2008): 1291–1314.

Paul-Choudhury, S. "Taming the Wild Frontier." *CreditRisk*, Risk Special Report, October 1999, 14–15.

Paulson, H. M. Jr., R. K. Steel, and D. G. Nason. "The Department of the Treasury Blueprint for a Modernized Financial Regulatory System." March 2008.

Phelan, K., and C. Alexander. "Different Strokes." *CreditRisk*, Risk Special Report, October 1999, 32–35.

Philippon, T., and P. Schnabl. "Efficient Recapitalization." NBER Working Paper No. 14929, April 2009.

Poddig, T. "Bankruptcy Prediction: A Comparison with Discriminant Analysis." In *Neural Networks in Capital Markets*, A. P. Refenes (ed.), (New York: John Wiley & Sons, 1994), 311–323.

Powell, A. "A Capital Accord for Emerging Economies?" Working Paper, World Bank, July 11, 2001.

Powell, D. "Testimony of the Development of the New Basel Accords" Committee on Banking, Housing and Urban Affairs, November 10, 2005. www.fdic.gov/news/news/speeches/archives/2005/chairman/spnov1005b.html.

Press Release. "Banking Agencies Reach Agreement on Basel II Implementation," July 20, 2007. www.federalreserve.gov/newsevents/press/bcreg/20070720a.htm.

Rajan, R. "Insiders and Outsiders: The Choice between Informed and Arm's Length Debt." *Journal of Finance*, September 1992, 1,367–1,400.

Reinhart, C. "Sovereign Credit Ratings Before and After Financial Crises." Department of Economics, University of Maryland. February 21, 2001, presented at the Conference on Rating Agencies in the Global Financial System, Stern School of Business NYU, June 1, 2001.

Reisen, H. "Revisions to the Basel Accord and Sovereign Ratings. In *Global Finance From a Latin American Viewpoint*, R. Hausmann and U. Hiemenz (eds.), IDB/OECD Development Centre 2000.

Reisen, H., and J. von Maltzan. "Boom and Bust and Sovereign Ratings." *International Finance* 2.2 (July 1999): 273–293.

Resti, A., and A. Sironi. "The Risk-Weights in the New Basel Capital Accord: Lessons from Bond Spreads Based on a Simple Structural Model," *Journal of Financial Intermediation* 16(2007): 64–90.

Ronn, E., and A. Verma. "Pricing Risk-Adjusted Deposit Insurance: An Option-Based Model." *Journal of Finance*, September 1986, 871–895.

Ryan, S. G. "Accounting in and for the Subprime Crisis," *Accounting Review*, June 2008.

Rule, D. "The Credit Derivatives Market: Its Development and Possible Implications for Financial Stability." *Financial Stability Review*, June 2001, 117–140.

Sanvicente, A. S., and F. L. C. Bader. "'Filing for Financial Reorganization in Brazil: Event Prediction with Accounting and Financial Variables and the Information Content of the Filing Announcement." Working Paper, São Paulo University, São Paulo, Brazil, October 1998.

Saunders, A. *Financial Institutions Management: A Modern Perspective*, 4th Ed. Burr Ridge, IL: Irwin/McGraw-Hill, August 2002.

Saunders, A., A. Srinivasan, and I. Walter. "Price Formation in the OTC Corporate Bond Markets: A Field Study of the Inter-Dealer Market." *Journal of Economics and Business* 54, no. 1(2002): 95–113.

Schermann, T. "What Do We Know About Loss Given Default? in D. Shimko ed., *Credit Risk Models and Management*(2004), Chapter 9.

Sellers, M., and N. Arora. "Financial EDF Measures: A New Model of Dual Business Lines." *Moody's KMV publication*, August 2004.

Senior Supervisors Group (SSG). "Observations on Risk Management Practices During the Recent Market Turbulence." March 6, 2008.

Schultz, P. "Corporate Bond Trading Costs: A Peek Behind the Curtain." *Journal of Finance*, April 2001, 677–698.

Schwartz, T. "Estimating the Term Structures of Corporate Debt." *The Review of Derivatives Research* 2, No. 2/3(1998): 193–230.

Sharpe, W. A. "Capital Asset Prices: A Theory of Market Equilibrium." *Journal of Finance*, September 1964, 425–442.

Shearer, A. "Pricing for Risk Is the Key in Commercial Lending." *American Banker*, March 21, 1997, 1.

Shepheard-Walwyn, T., and R. Litterman. "Building a Coherent Risk Measurement and Capital Optimization Model for Financial Firms." *Federal Reserve Bank of New York Economic Policy Review*, October 1998.

Shumway, T. "Forecasting Bankruptcy More Accurately: A Simple Hazard Model," *Journal of Business* (2001): 74, 101–124.

Shimko, D., N. Tejima, and D. R. van Deventer. "The Pricing of Risky Debt when Interest Rates Are Stochastic." *Journal of Fixed Income*, September 1993, 58–65.

Singleton, J. C., and A. J. Surkan."Bond Rating with Neural Networks." In *Neural Networks in Capital Markets*, A. P. Refenes (ed.), (New York: John Wiley & Sons, 1994), 301–307.

Smith, C. W., W. Smithson, and D. S. Wilford. *Managing Financial Risk*. Cambridge, MA: Ballinger, 1990.

Smithson, C. *Credit Portfolio Management*. Hoboken, NJ: John Wiley & Sons, Ltd. 2003.

Sobehart, J. R., R. M. Stein, V. Mikityanskaya, and L. Li. "Moody's Public Firm Risk Model: A Hybrid Approach to Modeling Short Term Default Risk." *Moody's Investors Service*, Rating Methodology, April 2000.

Sobehart, J. R., S. Keenan, and R. M. Stein. "Benchmarking Quantitative Default Risk Models: A Validation Methodology." *Moody's Investors Service*, Rating Methodology, March 2000.

Society of Actuaries. "1986–1992 Credit Loss Experience Study: Private Placement Bonds." Schaumburg, IL, 1996.

Stahl, G. "Confidence Intervals for Different Capital Definitions in a Credit Risk Model." Paper presented at Center for Economic Policy Research (CEPR) Conference, London, September 20, 1998.

Standard & Poor's "S&P/Case-Shiller Metro Area Home Price Indices." May 2006.

Standard and Poor's. "Rating Performance 1997—Stability and Transition." New York: Standard and Poor's Research Report, 1998 (mimeo).

Stein, R. M. "The Relationship between Default Prediction and Lending Profits: Integrating ROC Analysis and Loan Pricing." *Journal of Banking and Finance* 29 (2005): 1,213–1,236.

Stein, R. M. "Evidence on the Incompleteness of Merton-type Structural Models for Default Prediction." Moody's, Technical Paper, December 6, 2000.

Stiglitz, J., and A. Weiss. "Credit Rationing in Markets with Imperfect Information." *American Economic Review*, June 1981, 393–410.

Sundaram, R. K. "Equivalent Martingale Measures and Risk-Neutral Pricing: An Expository Note." *Journal of Derivatives*, Fall 1997, 85–98.

Sundaram, R. K. "The Merton/KMV Approach to Pricing Credit Risk." *Extra Credit, Merrill Lynch*, January/February 2001, 59–67.

Swidler, S., and J. A. Wilcox. "Information about Bank Risk from Options Prices." Paper presented at the Bank of England Conference on Banks and Systemic Risk, London, May 23–25, 2001.

Tang, D. Y., and H. Yan. "Liquidity and Credit Default Swap Spreads," presented at the AFA 2007, September 4, 2007.

Taylor, J. D. "Cross-Industry Differences in Business Failure Rates: Implications for Portfolio Management." *Commercial Lending Review*, Winter 1998, 36–46.

Theodore, S. S. "Rating Methodology: Bank Credit Risk (An Analytical Framework for Banks in Developed Markets.)" *Moody's Investors Service*, Rating Methodology, April 1999.

Tomlinson, R., and D. Evans. "CDO Boom Masks Subprime Losses, Abetted by S&P, Moody's, Fitch," *Bloomberg News*, May 31, 2007.

Treacy, W., and M. Carey. "Internal Credit Risk Rating Systems at Large U.S. Banks." *Federal Reserve Bulletin*, November 1998.

Treacy, W. F., and M. Carey. "Credit Risk Rating Systems at Large US Banks." *Journal of Banking and Finance*, January 2000, 167–201.

Turnbull, S. M. "Capital Allocation and Risk Performance Measurement in a Financial Institution," *Financial Markets, Institutions & Instruments* 9, no. 5(2000): 325–357.

Uhrig-Homburg, L. "Valuation of Defaultable Claims—A Survey," *Schmalenbach Business Review* 54 (January 2002): 24–57.

Unal, H., D. Madan, and L. Guntay. "Pricing the Risk of Recovery in Default with Absolute Priority Rule Violation," *Journal of Banking and Finance*,(2003), 27, no. 6, 1,001–1,025.

VanHoose, D. "Theories of Bank Behavior Under Capital Regulation." *Journal of Banking and Finance* 31(2007): 3,680–3,697.

Vasicek, O. *"Probability of Loss on a Loan Portfolio.* San Francisco: KMV Corporation, February 1987.

Vassalou, M., and Y. Xing. "Default Risk in Equity Returns," *Journal of Finance* 59 (2004): 831–868.

Wall, L. D., and T. W. Koch. "Bank Loan-Loss Accounting: A Review of the Theoretical and Empirical Evidence." *Federal Reserve Bank of Atlanta Economic Review*, Second Quarter, 2000, 1–19.

Wall, L., and M. M. Shrikhande. "Credit Derivatives." Paper presented at the FMA Conference, Chicago, October 1998.

Warga, A. *Fixed Income Securities Database.* University of Houston, College of Business Administration, 1999.

White, A. M. "Rewriting Contracts, Wholesale: Data on Voluntary Mortgage Modifications from 2007 and 2008 Remittance Reports," August 2008.

White, L. "The Credit Rating Industry: An Industrial Organization Analysis," Presented at the Conference on Rating Agencies in the Global Financial System, Stern School of Business NYU, June 1, 2001.

Wilson, T. "Credit Risk Modeling: A New Approach." New York: McKinsey Inc., 1997a (mimeo).

Wilson, T. "Portfolio Credit Risk (Parts I and II)." *Risk Magazine*, September and October 1997b.

Wilson, T. "Portfolio Credit Risk." Federal Reserve Bank of New York, *Economic Policy Review*, October 1998, 71–82.

Yang, Z. R., M. B. Platt, and H. D. Platt. "Probabilistic Neural Networks in Bankruptcy Prediction." *Journal of Business Research* 44, no. 2 (February 1999): 67–74.

Zaik, E., J. Walter, and J. G. Kelling. "RAROC at Bank of America: From Theory to Practice." *Journal of Applied Corporate Finance*, Summer 1996, 83–93.

Zhang, J., F. Zhu, and J. Lee. "Asset Correlation, Realized Default Correlation and Portfolio Credit Risk," March 3, 2008, Moody's KMV publication.

Zhou, C. "A Jump Diffusion Approach to Modeling Credit Risk and Valuing Defaultable Securities." Working Paper, Federal Reserve Board of Governors, March 1997.

Zhou, C. "An Analysis of Default Correlations and Multiple Defaults." *Review of Financial Studies*, Summer 2001, 555–576.

Zmijewski, M. E. "Methodological Issues Related to the Estimation of Financial Distress Prediction Models." *Journal of Accounting Research* 22, 1984, 59–82.

Printed and bound by CPI Group (UK) Ltd, Croydon, CR0 4YY

23/04/2025